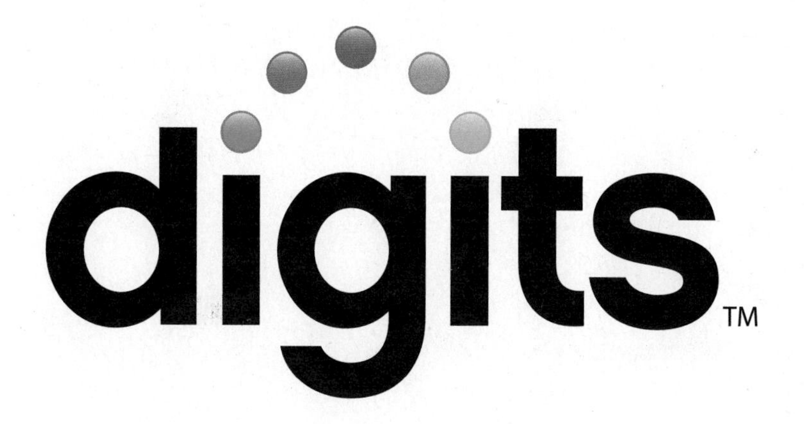

Homework Helper
Grade 6 Volume 2

PEARSON

Boston, Massachusetts • Chandler, Arizona • Glenview, Illinois • Upper Saddle River, New Jersey

Acknowledgments for Illustrations:
Rory Hensley, David Jackson, Jim Mariano, Rich McMahon, Lorie Park, and Ted Smykal

---

ISBN-13: 978-0-13-327630-5
ISBN-10: 0-13-327630-9
6 7 8 9 10 V011 17 16 15

Contents

Unit E: Geometry

Topic 13: Area

Topic 14: Surface Area and Volume

Unit F: Statistics

Topic 15: Data Displays

Topic 16: Measures of Center and Variation

Authors and Advisors

Francis (Skip) Fennell
***digits* Author**
Approaches to mathematics content and curriculum, educational policy, and support for intervention

Dr. Francis (Skip) Fennell is Professor of Education at McDaniel College, and a senior author with Pearson. He is a past president of the National Council of Teachers of Mathematics (NCTM) and a member of the writing team for the Curriculum Focal Points from the NCTM, which influenced the work of the Common Core Standards Initiative. Skip was also one of the writers of the Principles and Standards for School Mathematics.

Art Johnson
***digits* Author**
Approaches to mathematical content and support for English Language Learners

Art Johnson is a Professor of Mathematics at Boston University who taught in public school for over 30 years. He is part of the author team for Pearson's high school mathematics series. Art is the author of numerous books, including Teaching Mathematics to Culturally and Linguistically Diverse Students published by Allyn & Bacon, Teaching Today's Mathematics in the Middle Grades published by Allyn & Bacon, and Guiding Children's Learning of Mathematics, K–6 published by Wadsworth.

Helene Sherman
***digits* Author**
Teacher education and support for struggling students

Helene Sherman is Associate Dean for Undergraduate Education and Professor of Education in the College of Education at the University of Missouri in St. Louis, MO. Helene is the author of Teaching Learners Who Struggle with Mathematics, published by Merrill.

Stuart J. Murphy
***digits* Author**
Visual learning and student engagement

Stuart J. Murphy is a visual learning specialist and the author of the MathStart series. He contributed to the development of the Visual Learning Bridge in enVisionMATH™ as well as many visual elements of the Prentice Hall Algebra 1, Geometry, and Algebra 2 high school program.

Janie Schielack
***digits* Author**
Approaches to mathematical content, building problem solvers,and support for intervention

Janie Schielack is Professor of Mathematics and Associate Dean for Assessment and PreK–12 Education at Texas A&M University. She chaired the writing committee for the NCTM Curriculum Focal Points and was part of the nine-member NCTM feedback and advisory team that responded to and met with CCSSCO and NGA representatives during the development of various drafts of the Common Core State Standards.

Eric Milou
***digits* Author**
Approaches to mathematical content and the use of technology in middle grades classrooms

Eric Milou is Professor in the Department of Mathematics at Rowan University in Glassboro, NJ. Eric teaches pre-service teachers and works with in-service teachers, and is primarily interested in balancing concept development with skill proficiency. He was part of the nine-member NCTM feedback/advisory team that responded to and met with Council of Chief State School Officers (CCSSCO) and National Governors Association (NGA) representatives during the development of various drafts of the Common Core State Standards. Eric is the author of Teaching Mathematics to Middle School Students, published by Allyn & Bacon.

William F. Tate
***digits* Author**
Approaches to intervention, and use of efficacy and research

William Tate is the Edward Mallinckrodt Distinguished University Professor in Arts & Sciences at Washington University in St. Louis, MO. He is a past president of the American Educational Research Association. His research focuses on the social and psychological determinants of mathematics achievement and attainment as well as the political economy of schooling.

Randall I. Charles
***digits* Advisor**

Dr. Randall I. Charles is Professor Emeritus in the Department of Mathematics at San Jose State University in San Jose, CA, and a senior author with Pearson. Randall served on the writing team for the Curriculum Focal Points from NCTM. The NCTM Curriculum Focal Points served as a key inspiration to the writers of the Common Core Standards in bringing focus, depth, and coherence to the curriculum.

> “*Pearson tapped leaders in mathematics education to develop **digits**. This esteemed author team—from diverse areas of expertise including mathematical content, Understanding by Design, and Technology Engagement—came together to construct a highly interactive and personalized learning experience.*”

Jim Cummins
***digits* Advisor**
Supporting English Language Learners

Dr. Jim Cummins is Professor and Canada Research Chair in the Centre for Educational Research on Languages and Literacies at the University of Toronto. His research focuses on literacy development in multilingual school contexts as well as on the potential roles of technology in promoting language and literacy development.

Grant Wiggins
***digits* Consulting Author**
Understanding by Design

Grant Wiggins is a cross-curricular Pearson consulting author specializing in curricular change. He is the author of Understanding by Design published by ASCD, and the President of Authentic Education in Hopewell, NJ. Over the past 20 years, he has worked on some of the most influential reform initiatives in the country, including Vermont's portfolio system and Ted Sizer's Coalition of Essential Schools.

Jacquie Moen
***digits* Advisor**
Digital Technology

Jacquie Moen is a consultant specializing in how consumers interact with and use digital technologies. Jacquie worked for AOL for 10 years, and most recently was VP & General Manager for AOL's kids and teen online services, reaching over seven million kids every month. Jacquie has worked with a wide range of organizations to develop interactive content and strategies to reach families and children, including National Geographic, PBS, Pearson Education, National Wildlife Foundation, and the National Children's Museum.

Welcome to digits™

Using the Homework Helper

digits is designed to help you master mathematics skills and concepts in a way that's relevant to you. As the title ***digits*** suggests, this program takes a digital approach. ***digits*** is digital, but sometimes you may not be able to access digital resources. When that happens, you can use the Homework Helper because you can refer back to the daily lesson and see all your homework questions right in the book.

Your Homework Helper supports your work on ***digits*** in so many ways!

The lesson pages capture important elements of the digital lesson that you need to know in order to do your homework.

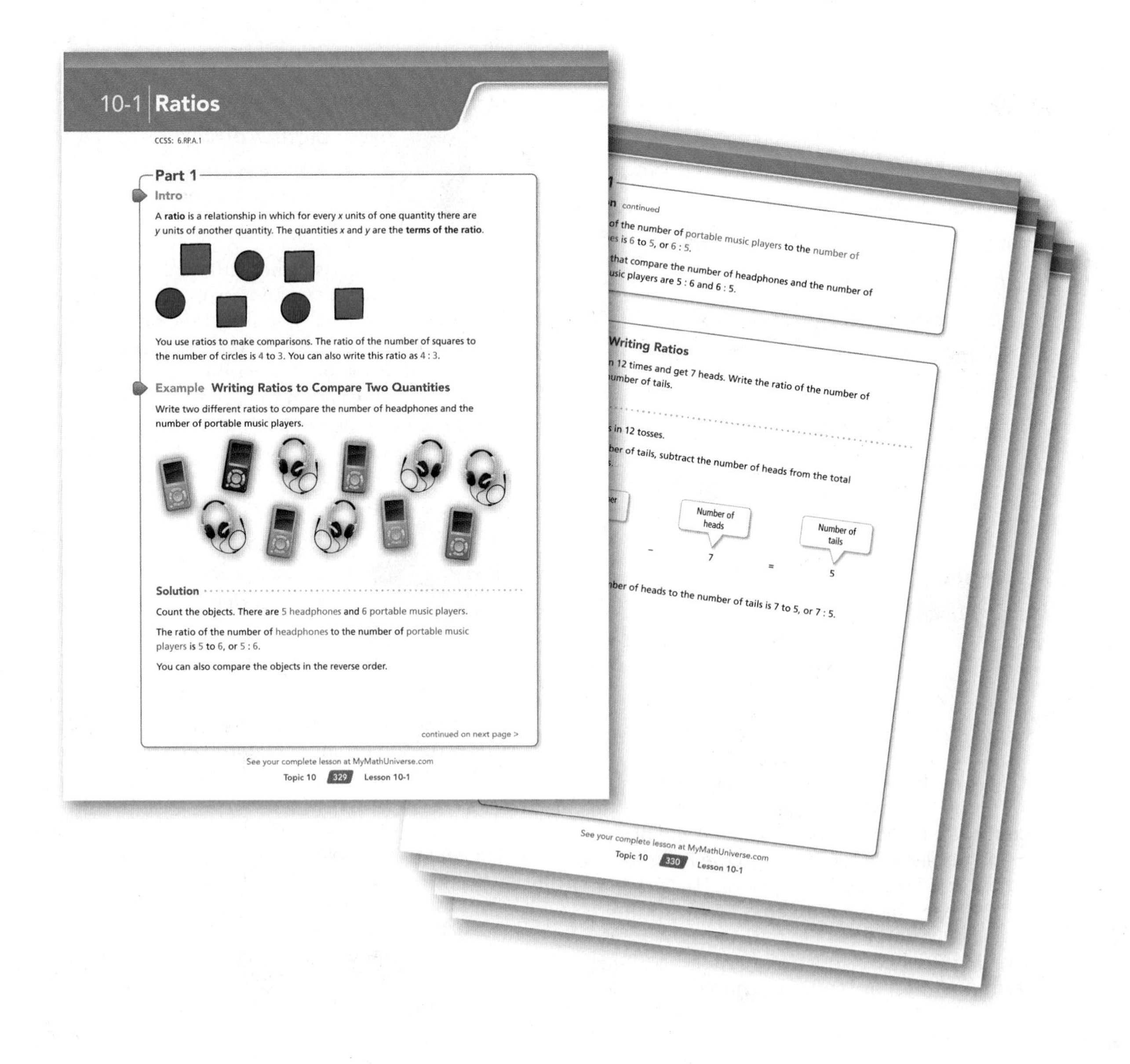

10-1 Ratios

CCSS: 6.RP.A.1

Part 1

Intro

A **ratio** is a relationship in which for every x units of one quantity there are y units of another quantity. The quantities x and y are the **terms of the ratio**.

You use ratios to make comparisons. The ratio of the number of squares to the number of circles is 4 to 3. You can also write this ratio as 4 : 3.

Example **Writing Ratios to Compare Two Quantities**

Write two different ratios to compare the number of headphones and the number of portable music players.

Solution

Count the objects. There are 5 headphones and 6 portable music players.

The ratio of the number of headphones to the number of portable music players is 5 to 6, or 5 : 6.

You can also compare the objects in the reverse order.

continued on next page >

See your complete lesson at MyMathUniverse.com

Topic 10 329 Lesson 10-1

continued

of the number of portable music players to the number of

that compare the number of headphones and the number of

Writing Ratios

12 times and get 7 heads. Write the ratio of the number of

in 12 tosses.

ber of tails, subtract the number of heads from the total

See your complete lesson at MyMathUniverse.com

Topic 10 330 Lesson 10-1

Every lesson in your Homework Helper also includes two pages of homework. The combination of homework exercises includes problems that focus on reasoning, multiple representations, mental math, writing, and error analysis. They vary in difficulty level from thinking about a plan to challenging. The problems come in different formats, like multiple choice, short answer, and open response, to help you prepare for tests.

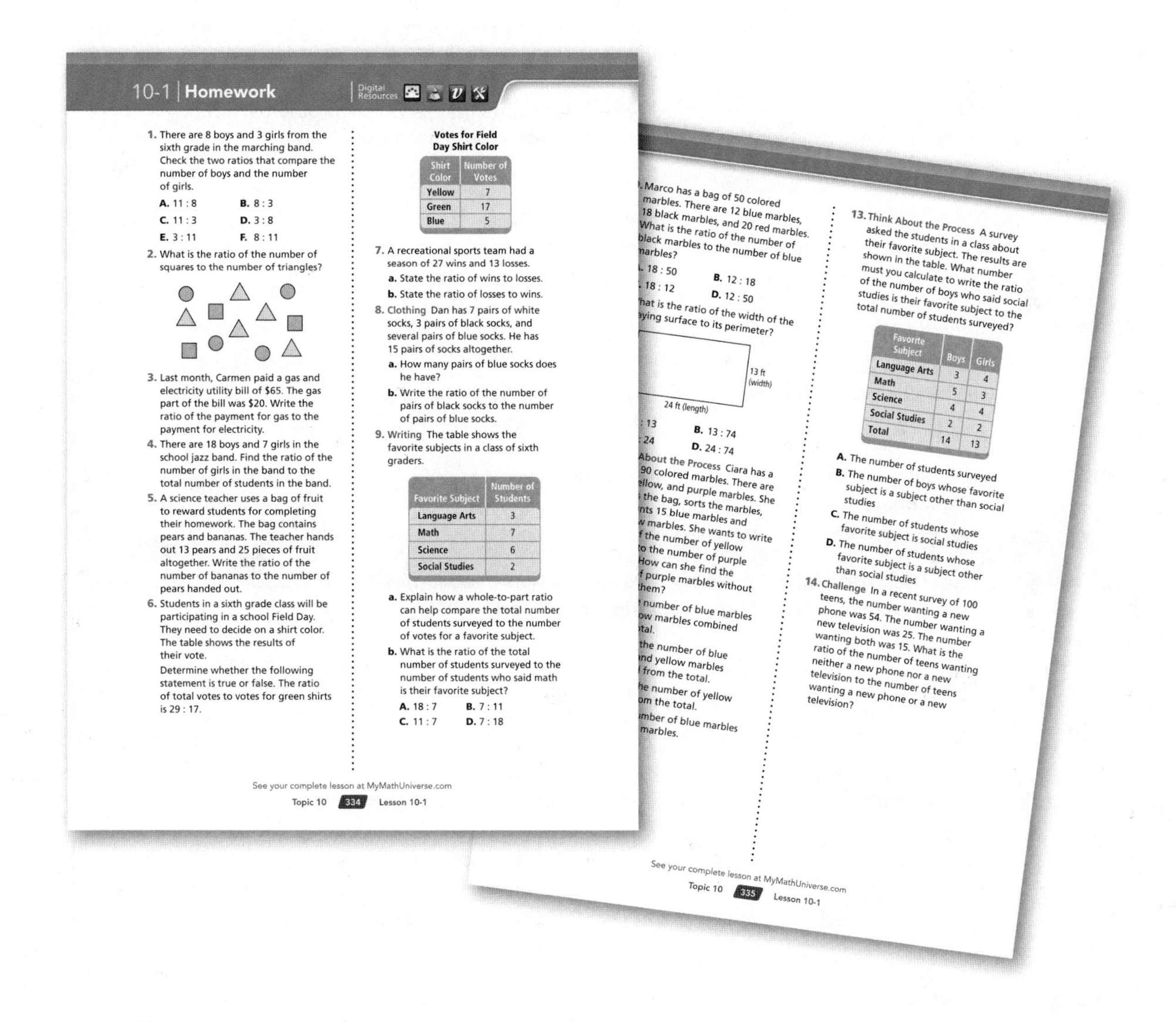

10-1 | Homework

Digital Resources

1. There are 8 boys and 3 girls from the sixth grade in the marching band. Check the two ratios that compare the number of boys and the number of girls.

   A. 11 : 8 B. 8 : 3
   C. 11 : 3 D. 3 : 8
   E. 3 : 11 F. 8 : 11

2. What is the ratio of the number of squares to the number of triangles?

3. Last month, Carmen paid a gas and electricity utility bill of $65. The gas part of the bill was $20. Write the ratio of the payment for gas to the payment for electricity.

4. There are 18 boys and 7 girls in the school jazz band. Find the ratio of the number of girls in the band to the total number of students in the band.

5. A science teacher uses a bag of fruit to reward students for completing their homework. The bag contains pears and bananas. The teacher hands out 13 pears and 25 pieces of fruit altogether. Write the ratio of the number of bananas to the number of pears handed out.

6. Students in a sixth grade class will be participating in a school Field Day. They need to decide on a shirt color. The table shows the results of their vote.
   Determine whether the following statement is true or false. The ratio of total votes to votes for green shirts is 29 : 17.

Votes for Field Day Shirt Color

Shirt Color	Number of Votes
Yellow	7
Green	17
Blue	5

7. A recreational sports team had a season of 27 wins and 13 losses.
   a. State the ratio of wins to losses.
   b. State the ratio of losses to wins.

8. Clothing Dan has 7 pairs of white socks, 3 pairs of black socks, and several pairs of blue socks. He has 15 pairs of socks altogether.
   a. How many pairs of blue socks does he have?
   b. Write the ratio of the number of pairs of black socks to the number of pairs of blue socks.

9. Writing The table shows the favorite subjects in a class of sixth graders.

Favorite Subject	Number of Students
Language Arts	3
Math	7
Science	6
Social Studies	2

   a. Explain how a whole-to-part ratio can help compare the total number of students surveyed to the number of votes for a favorite subject.
   b. What is the ratio of the total number of students surveyed to the number of students who said math is their favorite subject?
   A. 18 : 7 B. 7 : 11
   C. 11 : 7 D. 7 : 18

See your complete lesson at MyMathUniverse.com

Topic 10 334 Lesson 10-1

Marco has a bag of 50 colored marbles. There are 12 blue marbles, 18 black marbles, and 20 red marbles. What is the ratio of the number of black marbles to the number of blue marbles?

18 : 50 B. 12 : 18
18 : 12 D. 12 : 50

hat is the ratio of the width of the ying surface to its perimeter?

13 ft (width)
24 ft (length)

13 B. 13 : 74
24 D. 24 : 74

About the Process Ciara has a 90 colored marbles. There are ellow, and purple marbles. She the bag, sorts the marbles, nts 15 blue marbles and marbles. She wants to write the number of yellow to the number of purple How can she find the f purple marbles without them?

number of blue marbles ow marbles combined tal.

the number of blue nd yellow marbles from the total.

he number of yellow om the total.

mber of blue marbles marbles.

13. Think About the Process A survey asked the students in a class about their favorite subject. The results are shown in the table. What number must you calculate to write the ratio of the number of boys who said social studies is their favorite subject to the total number of students surveyed?

Favorite Subject	Boys	Girls
Language Arts	3	4
Math	5	3
Science	4	4
Social Studies	2	2
Total	14	13

A. The number of students surveyed
B. The number of boys whose favorite subject is a subject other than social studies
C. The number of students whose favorite subject is social studies
D. The number of students whose favorite subject is a subject other than social studies

14. Challenge In a recent survey of 100 teens, the number wanting a new phone was 54. The number wanting a new television was 25. The number wanting both was 15. What is the ratio of the number of teens wanting neither a new phone nor a new television to the number of teens wanting a new phone or a new television?

See your complete lesson at MyMathUniverse.com

Topic 10 335 Lesson 10-1

Number	Standard for Mathematical Content
6.RP Ratios and Proportional Relationships	
Understand ratio concepts and use ratio reasoning to solve problems.	
6.RP.A.1	Understand the concept of a ratio and use ratio language to describe a ratio relationship between two quantities.
6.RP.A.2	Understand the concept of a unit rate $\frac{a}{b}$ associated with a ratio $a : b$ with $b \neq 0$, and use rate language in the context of a ratio relationship.
6.RP.A.3	Use ratio and rate reasoning to solve real-world and mathematical problems, e.g., by reasoning about tables of equivalent ratios, tape diagrams, double number line diagrams, or equations.
6.RP.A.3a	Make tables of equivalent ratios relating quantities with whole number measurements, find missing values in the tables, and plot the pairs of values on the coordinate plane. Use tables to compare ratios.
6.RP.A.3b	Solve unit rate problems including those involving unit pricing and constant speed.
6.RP.A.3c	Find a percent of a quantity as a rate per 100 (e.g., 30% of a quantity means $\frac{30}{100}$ times the quantity); solve problems involving finding the whole, given a part and the percent.
6.RP.A.3d	Use ratio reasoning to convert measurement units; manipulate and transform units appropriately when multiplying or dividing quantities.
6.NS The Number System	
Apply and extend previous understandings of multiplication and division to divide fractions by fractions.	
6.NS.A.1	Interpret and compute quotients of fractions, and solve word problems involving division of fractions by fractions, e.g., by using visual fraction models and equations to represent the problem.
Compute fluently with multi-digit numbers and find common factors and multiples.	
6.NS.B.2	Fluently divide multi-digit numbers using the standard algorithm.
6.NS.B.3	Fluently add, subtract, multiply, and divide multi-digit decimals using the standard algorithm for each operation.
6.NS.B.4	Find the greatest common factor of two whole numbers less than or equal to 100 and the least common multiple of two whole numbers less than or equal to 12. Use the distributive property to express a sum of two whole numbers 1–100 with a common factor as a multiple of a sum of two whole numbers with no common factor.

Number	Standard for Mathematical Content
6.NS The Number System *(continued)*	
Apply and extend previous understandings of numbers to the system of rational numbers.	
6.NS.C.5	Understand that positive and negative numbers are used together to describe quantities having opposite directions or values; use positive and negative numbers to represent quantities in real-world contexts, explaining the meaning of 0 in each situation.
6.NS.C.6	Understand a rational number as a point on the number line. Extend number line diagrams and coordinate axes familiar from previous grades to represent points on the line and in the plane with negative number coordinates.
6.NS.C.6a	Recognize opposite signs of numbers as indicating locations on opposite sides of 0 on the number line; recognize that the opposite of the opposite of a number is the number itself.
6.NS.C.6b	Understand signs of numbers in ordered pairs as indicating locations in quadrants of the coordinate plane; recognize that when two ordered pairs differ only by signs, the locations of the points are related by reflections across one or both axes.
6.NS.C.6c	Find and position integers and other rational numbers on a horizontal or vertical number line diagram; find and position pairs of integers and other rational numbers on a coordinate plane.
6.NS.C.7	Understand ordering and absolute value of rational numbers.
6.NS.C.7a	Interpret statements of inequality as statements about the relative position of two numbers on a number line diagram.
6.NS.C.7b	Write, interpret, and explain statements of order for rational numbers in real-world contexts.
6.NS.C.7c	Understand the absolute value of a rational number as its distance from 0 on the number line; interpret absolute value as magnitude for a positive or negative quantity in a real-world situation.
6.NS.C.7d	Distinguish comparisons of absolute value from statements about order.
6.NS.C.8	Solve real-world and mathematical problems by graphing points in all four quadrants of the coordinate plane. Include use of coordinates and absolute value to find distances between points with the same first coordinate or the same second coordinate.
6.EE Expressions and Equations	
Apply and extend previous understandings of arithmetic to algebraic expressions.	
6.EE.A.1	Write and evaluate numerical expressions involving whole-number exponents.
6.EE.A.2	Write, read, and evaluate expressions in which letters stand for numbers.
6.EE.A.2a	Write expressions that record operations with numbers and with letters standing for numbers.

Number	Standard for Mathematical Content
6.EE Expressions and Equations *(continued)*	
Apply and extend previous understandings of arithmetic to algebraic expressions.	
6.EE.A.2b	Identify parts of an expression using mathematical terms (sum, term, product, factor, quotient, coefficient); view one or more parts of an expression as a single entity.
6.EE.A.2c	Evaluate expressions at specific values of their variables. Include expressions that arise from formulas used in real-world problems. Perform arithmetic operations, including those involving whole number exponents, in the conventional order when there are no parentheses to specify a particular order (Order of Operations).
6.EE.A.3	Apply the properties of operations to generate equivalent expressions.
6.EE.A.4	Identify when two expressions are equivalent (i.e., when the two expressions name the same number regardless of which value is substituted into them).
Reason about and solve one-variable equations and inequalities.	
6.EE.B.5	Understand solving an equation or inequality as a process of answering a question: which values from a specified set, if any, make the equation or inequality true? Use substitution to determine whether a given number in a specified set makes an equation or inequality true.
6.EE.B.6	Use variables to represent numbers and write expressions when solving a real-world or mathematical problem; understand that a variable can represent an unknown number, or, depending on the purpose at hand, any number in a specified set.
6.EE.B.7	Solve real-world and mathematical problems by writing and solving equations of the form $x + p = q$ and $px = q$ for cases in which p, q, and x are all nonnegative rational numbers.
6.EE.B.8	Write an inequality of the form $x > c$ or $x < c$ to represent a constraint or condition in a real-world or mathematical problem. Recognize that inequalities of the form $x > c$ or $x < c$ have infinitely many solutions; represent solutions of such inequalities on number line diagrams.
Represent and analyze quantitative relationships between dependent and independent variables.	
6.EE.C.9	Use variables to represent two quantities in a real-world problem that change in relationship to one another; write an equation to express one quantity, thought of as the dependent variable, in terms of the other quantity, thought of as the independent variable. Analyze the relationship between the dependent and independent variables using graphs and tables, and relate these to the equation.
6.G Geometry	
Solve real-world and mathematical problems involving area, surface area, and volume.	
6.G.A.1	Find the area of right triangles, other triangles, special quadrilaterals, and polygons by composing into rectangles or decomposing into triangles and other shapes; apply these techniques in the context of solving real-world and mathematical problems.
6.G.A.2	Find the volume of a right rectangular prism with fractional edge lengths by packing it with unit cubes of the appropriate unit fraction edge lengths, and show that the volume is the same as would be found by multiplying the edge lengths of the prism. Apply the formulas $V = lwh$ and $V = bh$ to find volumes of right rectangular prisms with fractional edge lengths in the context of solving real-world and mathematical problems.

Number	Standard for Mathematical Content
6.G Geometry *(continued)*	
Solve real-world and mathematical problems involving area, surface area, and volume.	
6.G.A.3	Draw polygons in the coordinate plane given coordinates for the vertices; use coordinates to find the length of a side joining points with the same first coordinate or the same second coordinate. Apply these techniques in the context of solving real-world and mathematical problems.
6.G.A.4	Represent three-dimensional figures using nets made up of rectangles and triangles, and use the nets to find the surface area of these figures. Apply these techniques in the context of solving real-world and mathematical problems.
6.SP Statistics and Probability	
Develop understanding of statistical variability.	
6.SP.A.1	Recognize a statistical question as one that anticipates variability in the data related to the question and accounts for it in the answers.
6.SP.A.2	Understand that a set of data collected to answer a statistical question has a distribution which can be described by its center, spread, and overall shape.
6.SP.A.3	Recognize that a measure of center for a numerical data set summarizes all of its values with a single number, while a measure of variation describes how its values vary with a single number.
Summarize and describe distributions.	
6.SP.B.4	Display numerical data in plots on a number line, including dot plots, histograms, and box plots.
6.SP.B.5	Summarize numerical data sets in relation to their context, such as by:
6.SP.B.5a	Reporting the number of observations.
6.SP.B.5b	Describing the nature of the attribute under investigation, including how it was measured and its units of measurement.
6.SP.B.5c	Giving quantitative measures of center (median and/or mean) and variability (interquartile range and/or mean absolute deviation), as well as describing any overall pattern and any striking deviations from the overall pattern with reference to the context in which the data were gathered.
6.SP.B.5d	Summarize numerical data sets in relation to their context, such as by: Relating the choice of measures of center and variability to the shape of the data distribution and the context in which the data were gathered.

10-1 Ratios

CCSS: 6.RP.A.1

Part 1

Intro

A **ratio** is a relationship in which for every *x* units of one quantity there are *y* units of another quantity. The quantities *x* and *y* are the **terms of the ratio**.

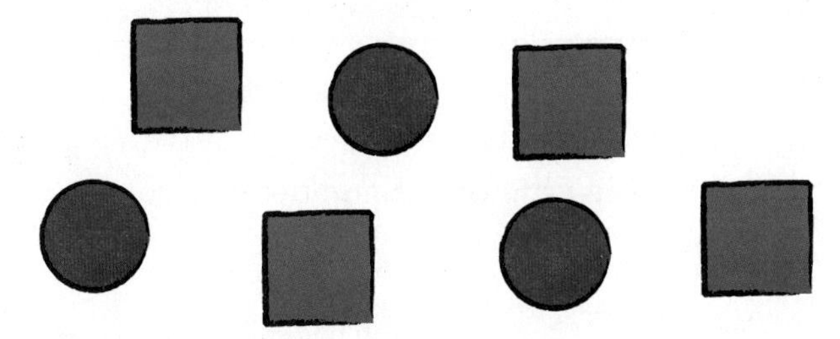

You use ratios to make comparisons. The ratio of the number of squares to the number of circles is 4 to 3. You can also write this ratio as 4 : 3.

Example Writing Ratios to Compare Two Quantities

Write two different ratios to compare the number of headphones and the number of portable music players.

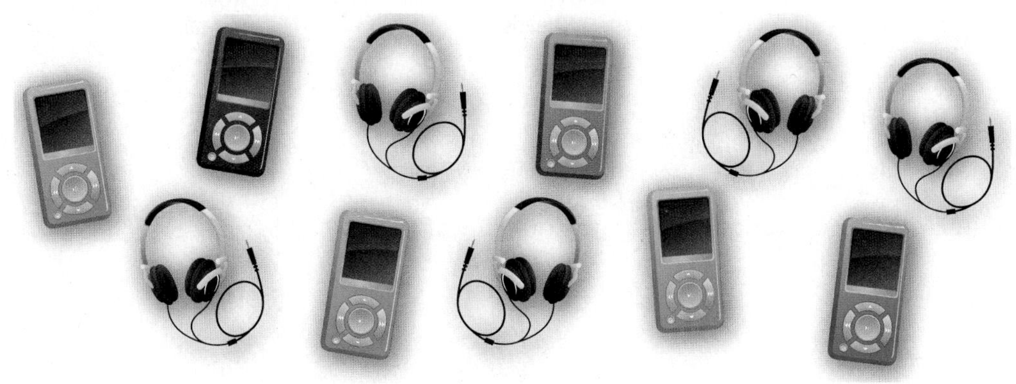

Solution

Count the objects. There are 5 headphones and 6 portable music players.

The ratio of the number of headphones to the number of portable music players is 5 to 6, or 5 : 6.

You can also compare the objects in the reverse order.

continued on next page >

Part 1

Solution continued

The ratio of the number of portable music players to the number of headphones is 6 to 5, or 6 : 5.

Two ratios that compare the number of headphones and the number of portable music players are 5 : 6 and 6 : 5.

Part 2

Example Writing Ratios

You toss a coin 12 times and get 7 heads. Write the ratio of the number of heads to the number of tails.

Solution

You got 7 heads in 12 tosses.

To find the number of tails, subtract the number of heads from the total number of tosses.

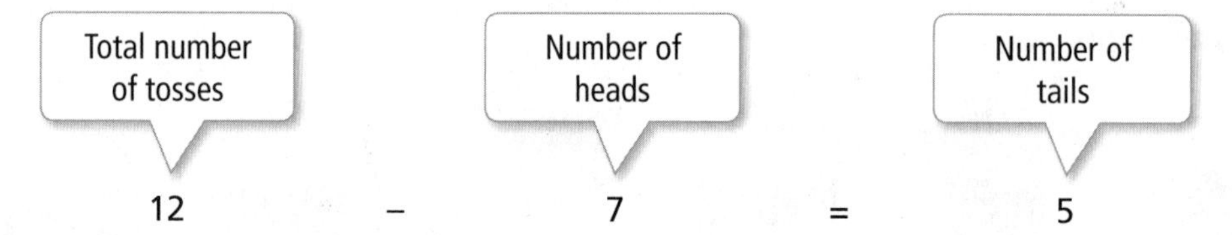

You got 5 tails.

The ratio of the number of heads to the number of tails is 7 to 5, or 7 : 5.

Key Concept

You can use ratios to compare one part to another part or to compare a part to the whole.

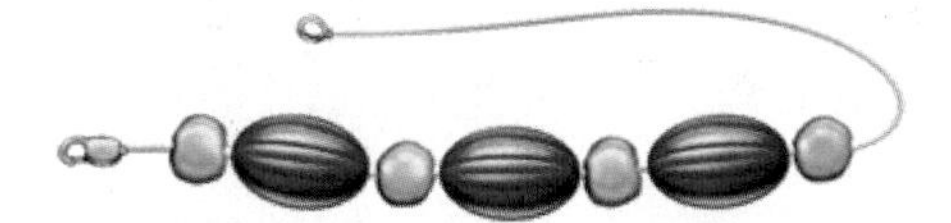

Part-to-part ratios The ratio of the number of round blue beads to the number of oval red beads is 4 : 3. The ratio of the number of oval red beads to the number of round blue beads is 3 : 4.

Part-to-whole ratios The ratio of the number of round blue beads to the total number of beads is 4 : **7**. The ratio of the number of oval red beads to the total number of beads is 3 : **7**.

Whole-to-part ratios The ratio of the total number of beads to the number of round blue beads is **7** : 4. The ratio of the total number of beads to the number of oval red beads is **7** : 3.

Part 3

Example Writing Ratios From a Table

The table shows the results from the sixth-grade election for class president. Determine whether each statement is *true* or *false*.

a. The ratio of votes for Jordyn to total votes is 10 : 35.

b. The ratio of votes for Devin to votes for Jordyn is 10 to 20.

c. The ratio of votes for Micah to total votes is 5 : 30.

d. The ratio of votes for Devin to votes for Micah is 20 : 5.

e. The ratio of total votes to votes for Devin is 35 to 20.

Votes for Class President

Student	Number of Votes
Devin	20
Jordyn	10
Micah	5

continued on next page >

Part 3

Example continued

Solution

a. The ratio of votes for Jordyn to total votes is 10 : 35.
To see if the statement is true, find the part-to-whole ratio.

Votes for Class President

Student	Number of Votes
Devin	20
Jordyn	10
Micah	5

Jordyn received **10** votes.

Add to find the total number of votes.
20 + 10 + 5 = 35

The ratio of votes for Jordyn to total votes is 10 : 35. The statement is true.

b. The ratio of votes for Devin to votes for Jordyn to is 10 to 20.
Find the part-to-part ratio.

Votes for Class President

Student	Number of Votes
Devin	20
Jordyn	10
Micah	5

Jordyn received **10** votes.

Devin received **20** votes.

The ratio of votes for Devin to votes for Jordyn is 20 to 10, not 10 to 20. The statement is false.

c. The ratio of votes for Micah to total votes is 5 : 30.
Find the part-to-whole ratio.

Votes for Class President

Student	Number of Votes
Devin	20
Jordyn	10
Micah	5

Micah received **5** votes.

Add to find the total number of votes.
20 + 10 + 5 = 35

The ratio of votes for Micah to total votes is 5 : 35. The statement is false.

continued on next page >

Part 3

Solution continued

d. The ratio of votes for Devin to votes for Micah is 20 : 5.
Find the part-to-part ratio.

Votes for Class President

Student	Number of Votes
Devin	20
Jordyn	10
Micah	5

Devin received **20** votes.

Micah received **5** votes.

The ratio of votes for Devin to votes for Micah is 20 : 5. The statement is true.

e. The ratio of total votes to votes for Devin is 35 to 20.
Find the whole-to-part ratio.

Votes for Class President

Student	Number of Votes
Devin	20
Jordyn	10
Micah	5

Devin received **20** votes.

Add to find the total number of votes.
20 + 10 + 5 = 35

The ratio of total votes to votes for Devin is 35 to 20. The statement is true.

1. There are 8 boys and 3 girls from the sixth grade in the marching band. Check the two ratios that compare the number of boys and the number of girls.

   A. 11 : 8 **B.** 8 : 3
   C. 11 : 3 **D.** 3 : 8
   E. 3 : 11 **F.** 8 : 11

2. What is the ratio of the number of squares to the number of triangles?

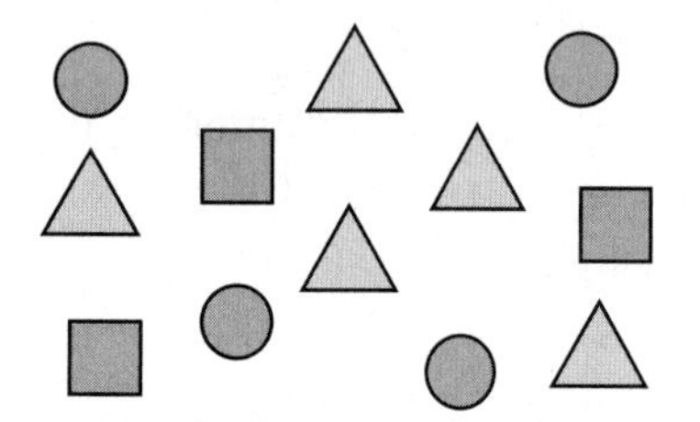

3. Last month, Carmen paid a gas and electricity utility bill of $65. The gas part of the bill was $20. Write the ratio of the payment for gas to the payment for electricity.

4. There are 18 boys and 7 girls in the school jazz band. Find the ratio of the number of girls in the band to the total number of students in the band.

5. A science teacher uses a bag of fruit to reward students for completing their homework. The bag contains pears and bananas. The teacher hands out 13 pears and 25 pieces of fruit altogether. Write the ratio of the number of bananas to the number of pears handed out.

6. Students in a sixth grade class will be participating in a school Field Day. They need to decide on a shirt color. The table shows the results of their vote.

   Determine whether the following statement is true or false. The ratio of total votes to votes for green shirts is 29 : 17.

Votes for Field Day Shirt Color

Shirt Color	Number of Votes
Yellow	7
Green	17
Blue	5

7. A recreational sports team had a season of 27 wins and 13 losses.

   a. State the ratio of wins to losses.

   b. State the ratio of losses to wins.

8. **Clothing** Dan has 7 pairs of white socks, 3 pairs of black socks, and several pairs of blue socks. He has 15 pairs of socks altogether.

   a. How many pairs of blue socks does he have?

   b. Write the ratio of the number of pairs of black socks to the number of pairs of blue socks.

9. **Writing** The table shows the favorite subjects in a class of sixth graders.

Favorite Subject	Number of Students
Language Arts	3
Math	7
Science	6
Social Studies	2

   a. Explain how a whole-to-part ratio can help compare the total number of students surveyed to the number of votes for a favorite subject.

   b. What is the ratio of the total number of students surveyed to the number of students who said math is their favorite subject?

   A. 18 : 7 **B.** 7 : 11
   C. 11 : 7 **D.** 7 : 18

10. Marco has a bag of 50 colored marbles. There are 12 blue marbles, 18 black marbles, and 20 red marbles. What is the ratio of the number of black marbles to the number of blue marbles?

A. 18 : 50 **B.** 12 : 18

C. 18 : 12 **D.** 12 : 50

11. What is the ratio of the width of the playing surface to its perimeter?

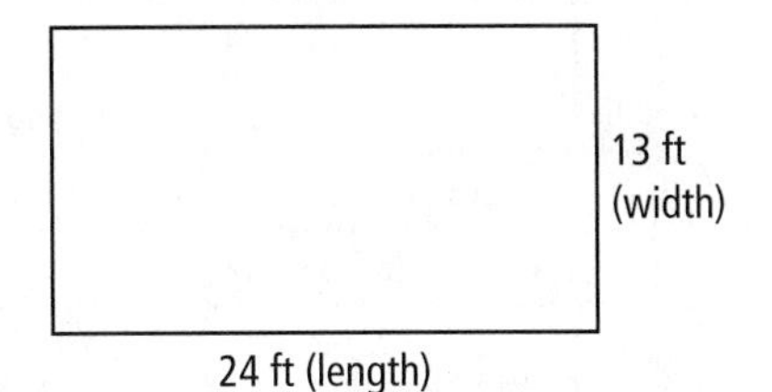

A. 74 : 13 **B.** 13 : 74

C. 13 : 24 **D.** 24 : 74

12. Think About the Process Ciara has a bag of 90 colored marbles. There are blue, yellow, and purple marbles. She empties the bag, sorts the marbles, and counts 15 blue marbles and 27 yellow marbles. She wants to write a ratio of the number of yellow marbles to the number of purple marbles. How can she find the number of purple marbles without counting them?

A. Add the number of blue marbles and yellow marbles combined to the total.

B. Subtract the number of blue marbles and yellow marbles combined from the total.

C. Subtract the number of yellow marbles from the total.

D. Add the number of blue marbles and yellow marbles.

13. Think About the Process A survey asked the students in a class about their favorite subject. The results are shown in the table. What number must you calculate to write the ratio of the number of boys who said social studies is their favorite subject to the total number of students surveyed?

Favorite Subject	Boys	Girls
Language Arts	3	4
Math	5	3
Science	4	4
Social Studies	2	2
Total	14	13

A. The number of students surveyed

B. The number of boys whose favorite subject is a subject other than social studies

C. The number of students whose favorite subject is social studies

D. The number of students whose favorite subject is a subject other than social studies

14. Challenge In a recent survey of 100 teens, the number wanting a new phone was 54. The number wanting a new television was 25. The number wanting both was 15. What is the ratio of the number of teens wanting neither a new phone nor a new television to the number of teens wanting a new phone or a new television?

10-2 Exploring Equivalent Ratios

Vocabulary
equivalent ratios

CCSS: 6.RP.A.3

Key Concept

Equivalent ratios are ratios that express the same relationship.

10 : 15 You can use rows and columns in a multiplication table to find equivalent ratios. The terms of the ratio 10 : 15 are in the 5s column in this multiplication table.

×	1	2	3	4	5	6	7	8	9
1	1	2	3	4	5	6	7	8	9
2	2	4	6	8	10	12	14	16	18
3	3	6	9	12	15	18	21	24	27
4	4	8	12	16	20	24	28	32	36
5	5	10	15	20	25	30	35	40	45
6	6	12	18	24	30	36	42	48	54
7	7	14	21	28	35	42	49	56	63
8	8	16	24	32	40	48	56	64	72
9	9	18	27	36	45	54	63	72	81

Lesser Terms Pairs of numbers to the left of the terms of the original ratio form equivalent ratios with lesser terms. The ratios 8 : 12, 6 : 9, 4 : 6, and 2 : 3 are equivalent to 10 : 15.

×	1	2	3	4	5	6	7	8	9
1	1	2	3	4	5	6	7	8	9
2	2	4	6	8	10	12	14	16	18
3	3	6	9	12	15	18	21	24	27
4	4	8	12	16	20	24	28	32	36
5	5	10	15	20	25	30	35	40	45
6	6	12	18	24	30	36	42	48	54
7	7	14	21	28	35	42	49	56	63
8	8	16	24	32	40	48	56	64	72
9	9	18	27	36	45	54	63	72	81

Greater Terms Pairs of numbers to the right of the terms of the original ratio form equivalent ratios with greater terms. The ratios 12 : 18, 14 : 21, 16 : 24, and 18 : 27 are equivalent to 10 : 15.

×	1	2	3	4	5	6	7	8	9
1	1	2	3	4	5	6	7	8	9
2	2	4	6	8	10	12	14	16	18
3	3	6	9	12	15	18	21	24	27
4	4	8	12	16	20	24	28	32	36
5	5	10	15	20	25	30	35	40	45
6	6	12	18	24	30	36	42	48	54
7	7	14	21	28	35	42	49	56	63
8	8	16	24	32	40	48	56	64	72
9	9	18	27	36	45	54	63	72	81

continued on next page >

Key Concept

continued

Multiples All of the corresponding multiples in two rows or columns form equivalent ratios. Multiplying 2 and 3 by 5 gives the original ratio, 10 : 15.

×	1	2	3	4	5	6	7	8	9
1	1	2	3	4	5	6	7	8	9
2	2	4	6	8	10	12	14	16	18
3	3	6	9	12	15	18	21	24	27
4	4	8	12	16	20	24	28	32	36
5	5	10	15	20	25	30	35	40	45
6	6	12	18	24	30	36	42	48	54
7	7	14	21	28	35	42	49	56	63
8	8	16	24	32	40	48	56	64	72
9	9	18	27	36	45	54	63	72	81

×5

×5

Part 1

Example Using Multiplication Tables to Find Equivalent Ratios

Use a multiplication table to find ratios equivalent to 12 : 16.
Find three ratios with lesser terms and three ratios with greater terms.

Solution

First find the terms of 12 : 16 in the multiplication table.

Move left across the rows to find 3 equivalent ratios with lesser terms.
3 : 4 6 : 8 9 : 12 → 12 : 16

Move right across the rows to find 3 equivalent ratios with greater terms.
12 : 16 → 15 : 20 18 : 24 21 : 28

×	1	2	3	4	5	6	7	8
1	1	2	3	4	5	6	7	8
2	2	4	6	8	10	12	14	16
3	3	6	9	12	15	18	21	24
4	4	8	12	16	20	24	28	32
5	5	10	15	20	25	30	35	40
6	6	12	18	24	30	36	42	48
7	7	14	21	28	35	42	49	56
8	8	16	24	32	40	48	56	64

The ratios 3 : 4, 6 : 8, 9 : 12, 15 : 20, 18 : 24, and 21 : 28 are equivalent to 12 : 16.

Part 2

Example Finding Missing Values in Equivalent Ratios

Complete the equivalent ratios.

a. 21 : 24 = 49 : ■

b. 15 : 21 = ■ : 49

c. 15 : ■ = 25 : 35

×	3	4	5	6	7
5	15		25		
6					
7			35		49
8	24				

Solution

Use the patterns in the multiplication table to find the missing terms.

a. 21 : 24 = 49 : 56

×	3	4	5	6	7
5	15	20	25	30	35
6	18	24	30	36	42
7	21	28	35	42	49
8	24	32	40	48	56

b. 15 : 21 = 35 : 49

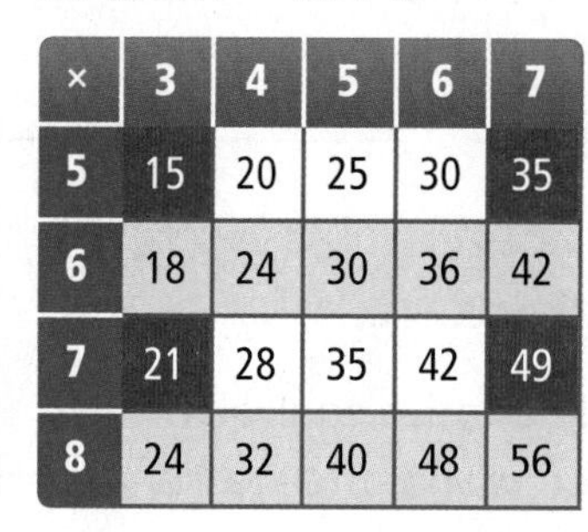

×	3	4	5	6	7
5	15	20	25	30	35
6	18	24	30	36	42
7	21	28	35	42	49
8	24	32	40	48	56

c. 15 : 21 = 25 : 35

×	3	4	5	6	7
5	15	20	25	30	35
6	18	24	30	36	42
7	21	28	35	42	49
8	24	32	40	48	56

Part 3

Example Using Equivalent Ratios to Find Missing Values

In one class, 3 out of every 8 students have braces. There are 32 students in the class. How many of the students have braces?

Solution

Use a multiplication table to find equivalent ratios.

The given ratio of the number of students with braces to the number of students is 3 : 8.

Look for an equivalent ratio that has 32 as its second term.

×	1	2	3	4
3	3	6	9	12
4	4	8	12	16
5	5	10	15	20
6	6	12	18	24
7	7	14	21	28
8	8	16	24	32

The ratio 12 : 32 is equivalent to 3 : 8.

So 12 of the students in the class wear braces.

Digital Resources   

Use the multiplication table to answer some of the following questions.

x	1	2	3	4	5	6	7	8
1	1	2	3	4	5	6	7	8
2	2	4	6	8	10	12	14	16
3	3	6	9	12	15	18	21	24
4	4	8	12	16	20	24	28	32
5	5	10	15	20	25	30	35	40
6	6	12	18	24	30	36	42	48
7	7	14	21	28	35	42	49	56
8	8	16	24	32	40	48	56	64

1. Which ratio is not equivalent to 36 : 42? Use the multiplication table above.

A. 18 : 21 **B.** 12 : 14

C. 18 : 24 **D.** 30 : 35

2. Find the equivalent ratio with lower terms.

a. 18 : 21 = 6 : ■

b. 16 : 24 = ■ : 6

3. Find the equivalent ratio with greater terms.

a. 6 : 15 = 10 : ■

b. 12 : 20 = ■ : 35

4. In Ms. Harrington's sixth grade class, 25 out of 30 students bought their lunch. How many students out of every 6 bought their lunch? Use the table at the top of the page.

5. In Mr. Harrington's sixth grade classes, 6 out of every 7 students turned in their field trip slips. If there is a total of 35 students in his classes, how many turned in their field trip slips? Use the table at the top of the page.

6. Use the multiplication table to find ratios that are equivalent to 70 : 80.

x	5	6	7	8	9	10	11	12
5	25	30	35	40	45	50	55	60
6	30	36	42	48	54	60	66	72
7	35	42	49	56	63	70	77	84
8	40	48	56	64	72	80	88	96
9	45	54	63	72	81	90	99	108
10	50	60	70	80	90	100	110	120
11	55	66	77	88	99	110	121	132
12	60	72	84	96	108	120	132	144

Which of the following ratios is not equivalent to 70 : 80?

A. 63 : 72 **B.** 49 : 56

C. 42 : 48 **D.** 49 : 63

7. a. Open-Ended Write a ratio word problem using the values in the multiplication table. Make your problem such that the solver must find the missing term of the ratio 21 : 35 = 12 : ■.

b. What statement about your ratio problem is true?

A. The problem compares terms in the same ratio.

B. The problem compares two terms to a third term.

C. The problem compares two terms that increase by the same amount.

D. The problem compares two terms that decrease by the same amount.

8. Temperature The temperature fell 10 degrees Fahrenheit from 45°F to 35°F in 8 hours. How much would the temperature fall over 12 hours if the pattern continued? Use the multiplication table found at the top of the page.

See your complete lesson at MyMathUniverse.com

9. Mental Math Micah and Mia are on the yearbook staff at their middle school. Over the weekend, they sold 12 yearbooks for a total of $21. Use mental math to find a ratio equivalent to 12 : 21. Which ratio is equivalent to 12 : 21?

A. 4 : 7 **B.** 7 : 4

C. 5 : 7 **D.** 4 : 8

10. Complete the statement 160 : 200 = ■ : 400.

x	20	30	40	50
5				250
6			240	
7		210		
8	160			
9				
10	200		400	

11. Corey can do 200 push-ups at a steady pace. The table shows how long it takes Corey to do the number of push-ups shown. How many push-ups can Corey do in 45 seconds?

Push-ups	Seconds
42	63
48	72

12. Use the multiplication table on the previous page to find a ratio that is equivalent to 40 : 88.

A. 25 : 55 **B.** 30 : 50

C. 30 : 55 **D.** 25 : 66

13. Complete each statement below.

a. 48 : 60 = 72 : ■

b. 63 : 84 = ■ : 108

14. Think About the Process You want to complete the equivalent ratios 35 : 60 and 42 : ?. You use a multiplication table. First, you find the terms of the first ratio in the same column. What is your second step?

A. Find 42 in the same column as 60.

B. Find 42 in the same column as 35.

C. Find 42 in the same row as 35.

D. Find 42 in the same row as 60.

15. Think About the Process A player threw 105 pitches in a 7-inning game. How can the player estimate the number of pitches he threw in 5 innings?

A. Write the equivalent ratios 5 : 7 and 105 : y. Then find y using a multiplication table.

B. Write the equivalent ratios 105 : 7 and 5 : y. Then find y using a multiplication table.

C. Write the equivalent ratios 5 : 105 and x : 7. Then find x using a multiplication table.

D. Write the equivalent ratios 105 : 7 and x : 5. Then find x using a multiplication table.

16. Challenge For the ratio 28 : 36, find an equivalent ratio with both terms greater than 6 and less than 10.

10-3 Equivalent Ratios

CCSS: 6.RP.A.3

Part 1

Intro

You can use double number lines to find equivalent ratios.

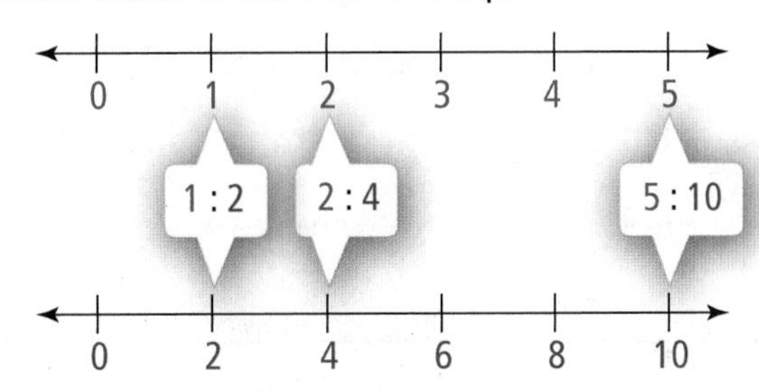

Example Using Number Lines to Find Equivalent Ratios

Use number lines to find ratios equivalent to 9 : 12. Find two ratios with lesser terms and two ratios with greater terms.

Solution

Use a pair of number lines to find equivalent ratios.

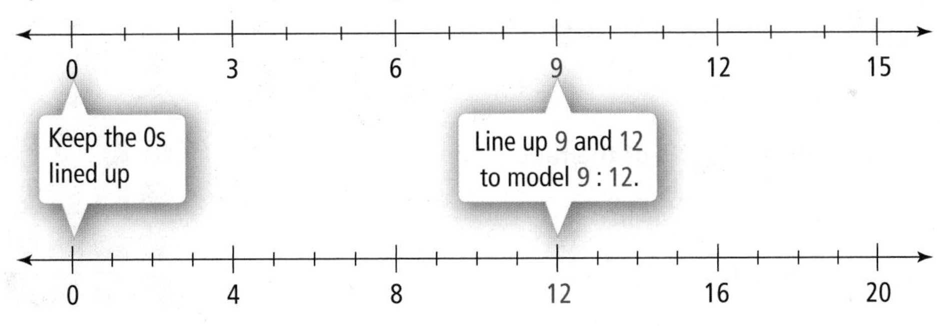

Move left from 9 : 12 to find equivalent ratios with lesser terms.

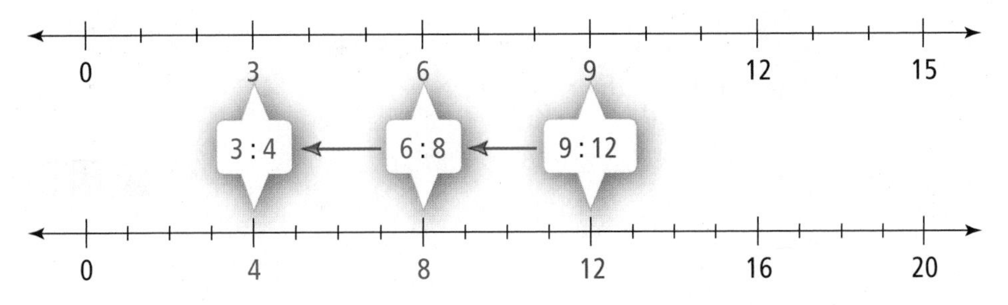

Move right from 9 : 12 to find equivalent ratios with greater terms.

continued on next page >

Part 1

Solution continued

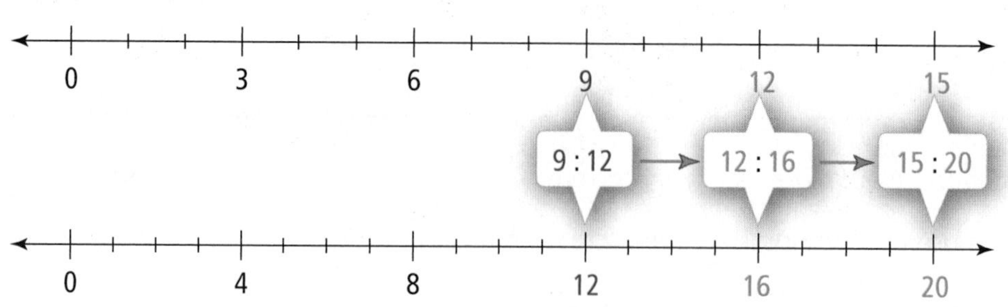

The ratios 3 : 4, 6 : 8, 12 : 16, and 15 : 20 are equivalent to 9 : 12.

Key Concept

You can find equivalent ratios by multiplying or dividing each term of the ratio by the same nonzero number.

This model shows the ratio 2 : 6.

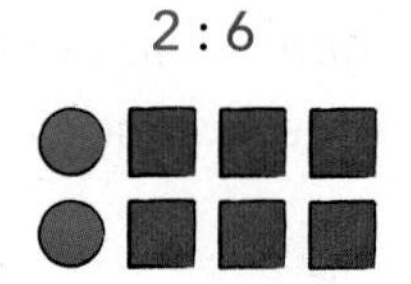

You can multiply each term of the ratio by 2.

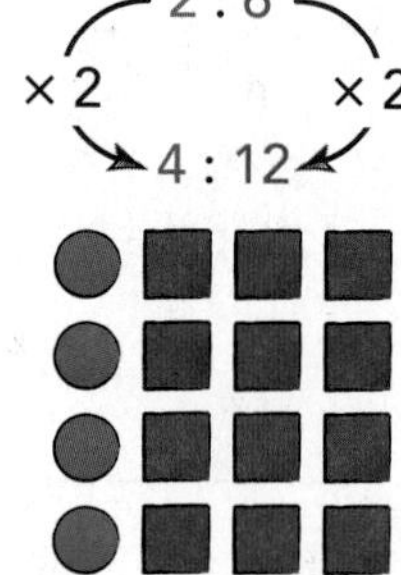

You can also divide each term of the ratio by 2.

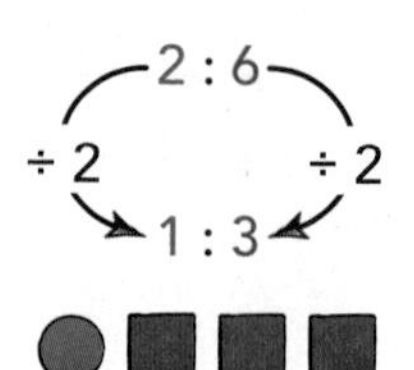

The ratios 2 : 6, 4 : 12, and 1 : 3 are all equivalent ratios.

Part 2

Example Completing Charts of Equivalent Ratios

A volunteer at an animal shelter recorded the ratio of the number of dogs adopted to the number to cats adopted each month. She finds all the ratios are equivalent. Use the information to complete the table.

Number of Animals Adopted

Month	Dogs	Cats
January	4	5
February	8	■
March	12	■

Solution

The ratio of the number of dogs adopted in January to the number of cats adopted in January is 4 : 5.

Number of Animals Adopted

Month	Dogs	Cats
January	4	5
February	8	■
March	12	■

8 dogs were adopted in February. Use the information that all the ratios are equivalent to find the number of cats adopted in February.

Number of Animals Adopted

Month	Dogs	Cats
January	4	5
February	8	10
March	12	■

$\times 2$ $\times 2$

10 cats were adopted in February.

12 dogs were adopted in March. Use the ratio of adopted dogs to adopted cats in January to find the number of cats adopted in March.

Number of Animals Adopted

Month	Dogs	Cats
January	4	5
February	8	10
March	12	15

$\times 3$ $\times 3$

15 cats were adopted in March.

Part 3

Example Finding Equivalent Ratios

You make a playlist with 6 hip hop songs and 9 pop songs for a party. All songs play for the same length of time. Now you want to make a longer playlist and a shorter playlist that each have an equivalent ratio of the number of hip hop songs to the number of pop songs.

a. How many songs of each type can you put on your longer playlist?
b. How many songs of each type can you put on your shorter playlist?

Solution

The ratio of the number of hip hop songs to the number of pop songs on the original playlist is 6 : 9.

To find an equivalent ratio, you can multiply or divide each term of the ratio by any nonzero number.

a.

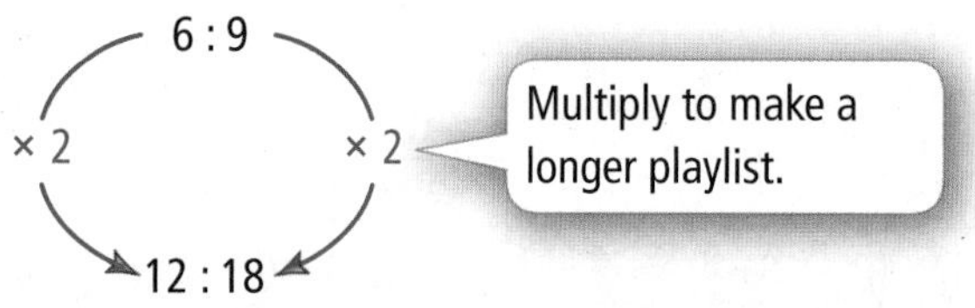

6 : 9
× 2 × 2
12 : 18

Multiply to make a longer playlist.

12 : 18 is equivalent to 6 : 9, so you can put 12 hip hop songs and 18 pop songs on your playlist.

b.

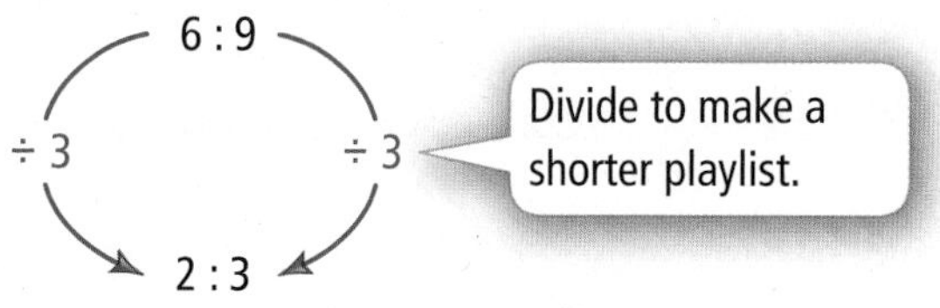

6 : 9
÷ 3 ÷ 3
2 : 3

Divide to make a shorter playlist.

2 : 3 is equivalent to 6 : 9, so you can put 2 hip hop songs and 3 pop songs on your playlist.

1. A teacher kept track of what students consumed at a school picnic. For three grades, the ratios of the amount of water consumed to the amount of fruit juice consumed were equivalent. Use the given information to complete the table.

Grade	Water (gallons)	Juice (gallons)
5th	6	7
6th	24	■
7th	18	■

2. The attendant at a parking lot compared the number of hybrid vehicles to the total number of vehicles in the lot over a weekend. The ratios for the three days were equivalent. Use the given information to complete the table.

Day	Hybrids	Total
Fri.	4	9
Sat.	■	63
Sun.	32	■

3. A baker uses 45 cups of flour and 72 cups of water for a recipe. The flour-to-water ratio is 45 : 72. How much water does the baker need if he uses only 5 cups of flour? Use **Figure 1** to complete the table.

Flour	Water
45 cups	72 cups
5 cups	■ cups

4. The ratio of the weight of zinc to the weight of all raw materials used by a factory is 18 : 42. How many tons of zinc would the factory use if it were to use 7 tons of raw materials? Use **Figure 2** to complete the table.

Zinc	Raw Materials
18 tons	42 tons
■ tons	7 tons

5. A teacher is writing a quiz. He wants the ratio of the number of easy questions to the total number of questions to be 18 : 21. If the teacher wants fewer than 18 easy questions on the quiz, how many easy questions should he write?

6. Reasoning Last season, Kyle had 21 hits and 35 strikeouts. So far this season, Kyle claims to have the same ratio of hits to strikeouts. Yet he has struck out only 5 times. Is it possible to have the same ratio of hits to strikeouts in seasons with different numbers of strikeouts? Explain.

(Figure 1)

(Figure 2)

Double Number Lines

0 ? 18

0 7 42

See your complete lesson at MyMathUniverse.com

7. **Mental Math** The ratio of boys to girls at a movie is 8 : 7. If there are 21 girls, how many boys are at the movie?

8. A small company has a fleet of 4 pickup trucks and 3 delivery vans. A larger company has the same ratio of pickup trucks to delivery vans. If the larger company has 52 pickup trucks, how many delivery vans does it have?

9. In basketball, some baskets are worth two points. Others are worth three points. In one game, a basketball team had 40 two-point tries and 35 three-point tries. Which of the following is a ratio of the number of two-point tries to the number of three-point tries?

   A. 8 : 7 **B.** 7 : 8

   C. 8 : 15 **D.** 7 : 15

10. **Writing** Raul took a test that had 40 questions. The ratio of his correct answers to the number of questions was 3 : 5.

    a. Explain how you would use equivalent ratios to find the number of questions Raul answered correctly.

    b. Find the number of questions he answered correctly.

11. **Think About the Process** A science class went to the seashore. The students surveyed three regions of a large tidal pool. They counted the crabs and snails. The results are in the table.

Animal	Region A	Region B	Region C
Crabs	5	8	3
Snails	25	40	15

The area of the tidal pool is 98 square meters. The class wants to write the ratio of the number of crabs in the regions surveyed to the number of crabs in the entire pool. This ratio is equivalent to the ratio of the area of the regions surveyed to the area of the entire pool. What additional information does the class need to find the number of crabs in the entire pool?

A. The ratio of the area of the three regions surveyed to the area of the coast

B. The area of the three regions surveyed

C. The ratio of the area of the tidal pool to the area of the coast

D. The total number of crabs an snails in the three regions surveyed

12. **Think About the Process** At Field Day, Mr. Arroyo's class earned 3 first-place ribbons, 9 second-place ribbons, and 6 third-place ribbons. A student in Mr. Arroyo's class earned a ratio of first- to second-place ribbons equivalent to the class's ratio. What number do you need to find the number of second-place ribbons earned by this student?

    A. The total number of ribbons earned by the student

    B. The number of first-place ribbons earned by the student

    C. The total number of second-place ribbons earned by the students at the school

    D. The number of third-place ribbons earned by the student

10-4 Ratios as Fractions

CCSS: 6.RP.A.1, 6.RP.A.3

Part 1

Intro

You have compared quantities by writing ratios in the forms *a* to *b* and *a* : *b*.

A fraction also shows a comparison. So you can write a ratio as fraction, $\frac{a}{b}$.

You can write the ratio of the number of squares to the number of circles in three ways.

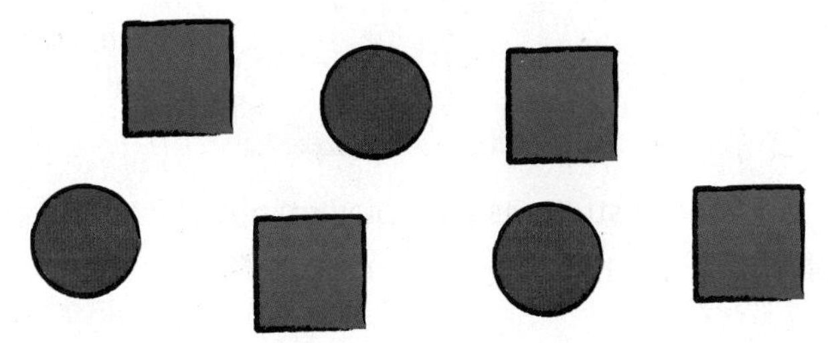

Example Writing Ratios in Different Ways

Instruments in the School Band

Instrument	Number of Students
Flute	27
Saxophone	13
Trumpet	9
Drums	10

The table shows the number of students who play each instrument in a school band. Write each ratio in three ways.

a. the number of students who play saxophone to the number of students who play drums.

b. the number of students who play flute to the total number of students in the band.

continued on next page >

Part 1

Example continued

Solution

a.

Instruments in the School Band

Instrument	Number of Students
Flute	27
Saxophone	13
Trumpet	9
Drums	10

13 students play saxophone.

10 students play drums.

The ratio of the number of students who play saxophone to the number of students who play drums is 13 to 10, 13 : 10, or $\frac{13}{10}$.

b.

Instruments in the School Band

Instrument	Number of Students
Flute	27
Saxophone	13
Trumpet	9
Drums	10

27 students play flute.

Add to find the total number of students. $27 + 13 + 9 + 10 = 59$

The ratio of the number of students who play flute to the total number of students in the band is 27 to 59, 27 : 59, or $\frac{27}{59}$.

Key Concept

When you write equivalent ratios as fractions, they are equivalent fractions. Recall that equivalent fractions are fractions that express the same relationship.

$\frac{1}{2}$ and $\frac{2}{4}$ are equivalent fractions.

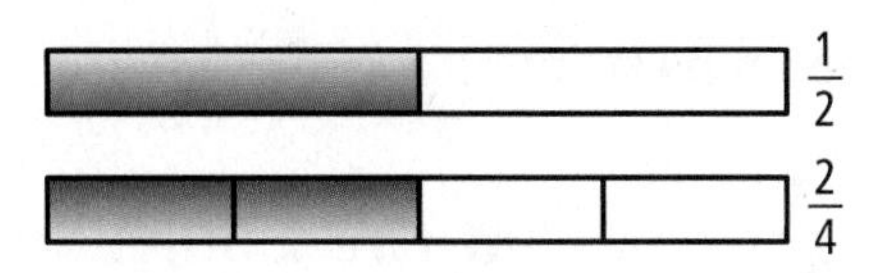

Part 2

Example Writing Fractions That Are Equivalent Ratios

Write two different ratios equivalent to $\frac{10}{25}$.

Solution

To find equivalent ratios, use the process for finding equivalent fractions. Multiply or divide the numerator and the denominator by the same nonzero number.

Answers may vary. Samples are given.

Multiply by 2 so that you can find the products using mental math.

$$\frac{10}{25} \overset{\times 2}{=} \frac{20}{50}$$

Divide by 5 because 5 is a common factor of 10 and 25.

$$\frac{10}{25} \overset{\div 5}{=} \frac{2}{5}$$

Two ratios equivalent to $\frac{10}{25}$ are $\frac{20}{50}$ and $\frac{2}{5}$.

Part 3

Intro

To write a fraction in simplest form, you divide the numerator and denominator by their greatest common factor (GCF).

You can use this same process to write a ratio in simplest form.

Equivalent ratios have the same simplest form.

Example Identifying Fractions That Are Equivalent Ratios

Decide if each of the following ratios is equivalent to $\frac{30}{45}$.

$\frac{14}{21}$ $\frac{100}{150}$ $\frac{3}{2}$ $\frac{6}{9}$ $\frac{35}{50}$

Solution

First, write $\frac{30}{45}$ in simplest form by dividing the numerator and the denominator by the GCF.

The GCF of 30 and 45 is 15.

$$\frac{30}{45} \xrightarrow{\div 15} = \frac{2}{3}$$

Write each of the other ratios in simplest form. Then compare the simplest form of each ratio to $\frac{2}{3}$.

$$\frac{14}{21} \xrightarrow{\div 7} = \frac{2}{3} \qquad \frac{6}{9} \xrightarrow{\div 3} = \frac{2}{3} \qquad \frac{100}{150} \xrightarrow{\div 50} = \frac{2}{3}$$

The simplest form of $\frac{14}{21}$, $\frac{6}{9}$, and $\frac{100}{150}$ is $\frac{2}{3}$, so the three ratios are equivalent to $\frac{30}{45}$.

The GCF of 3 and 2 is 1, so $\frac{3}{2}$ is already in simplest form.

$$\frac{3}{2} \qquad \frac{35}{50} \xrightarrow{\div 5} = \frac{7}{10}$$

The simplest form of $\frac{3}{2}$ and $\frac{35}{50}$ is not $\frac{2}{3}$, so the two ratios are not equivalent to $\frac{30}{45}$.

Digital Resources   

1. In a bouquet of flowers, there are 4 daisies and 19 roses. Write the ratio of daisies to roses in three different ways.
2. A jug of juice has 9 cups of pineapple juice and 8 cups of orange juice. Write the ratio of number of cups of pineapple juice to total number of cups of juice in three different ways.
3. Write a ratio equivalent to $\frac{5}{6}$ that has greater terms.
4. Write a ratio equivalent to $\frac{30}{75}$ that has lower terms.
5. Which ratios are equivalent to $\frac{20}{90}$? Select all that apply.

   A. $\frac{25}{95}$ **B.** $\frac{80}{360}$

   C. $\frac{16}{72}$ **D.** $\frac{9}{2}$

   E. $\frac{8}{36}$

   F. No ratios here are equivalent to $\frac{20}{90}$
6. Are the ratios $\frac{14}{35}$ and $\frac{20}{30}$ equivalent?
7. **Error Analysis** In a wildlife preserve, there are 4 zebras and 13 lions. Fred says you can write the ratios of lions to zebras as 13 to 4, 13 : 4, or $\frac{13}{4}$. Jane says you can write the ratio of lions to zebras as 13 to 4, 13 : 4, or $\frac{4}{13}$. Who is incorrect? What is the error?
8. **a. Reasoning** For any ratio, what process can you use to write an equivalent ratio with greater terms?

   A. Write the ratio as a fraction. Divide the numerator by a whole number greater than 1. Then multiply the denominator by the same number.

   B. Write the ratio as a fraction. Multiply the numerator by a whole number greater than 1. Then divide the denominator by the same number.

   C. Write the ratio as a fraction. Multiply the numerator by a whole number greater than 1. Then multiply the denominator by the same number.

   D. Write the ratio as a fraction. Divide the numerator by a whole number greater than 1. Then divide the denominator by the same number.

   b. Explain your reasoning.
9. **Cooking** In a cooking class, students are measuring ingredients for making a cake. The original recipe calls for 3 teaspoons of vanilla and 6 cups of flour. The students need to make the cake larger. They use 18 teaspoons of vanilla and 24 cups of flour. Is the ratio of teaspoons to cups for the new recipe the same as the original recipe?
10. In basketball, Katrina makes 12 out of every 16 free throws. Her coach claims that if she tries 42 free throws, she should make 18 of them. Is the coach's claim correct?
11. **Multiple Representations** One day, the local hardware store sold 24 buckets of basic house paint and 11 buckets of ultimate house paint. A bucket of basic house paint uses 5 cans of white paint and 6 cans of color paint. For a bucket of basic house paint, which ratio of cans of color paint to cans of white paint, written in 3 different ways, is correct?

    A. 6 to 11, 6 : 11, and $\frac{6}{11}$

    B. 5 to 24, 5 : 24, and $\frac{5}{24}$

    C. 5 to 6, 5 : 6, and $\frac{5}{6}$

    D. 24 to 5, 24 : 5, and $\frac{24}{5}$

    E. 6 to 5, 6 : 5, and $\frac{6}{5}$

    F. 11 to 6, 11 : 6, and $\frac{11}{6}$

12. Personal Communication Fees An Internet, telephone, and cable TV package plan costs $85 each month. The Internet part of the bill is $26. The telephone part of the bill is $16. Which ratio of the Internet bill to the cable TV bill, written in 3 different ways, is correct?

A. 26 to 43, 26 : 43, or $\frac{26}{43}$

B. 26 to 59, 26 : 59, or $\frac{26}{59}$

C. 43 to 16, 43 : 16, or $\frac{43}{16}$

D. 59 to 26, 59 : 26, or $\frac{59}{26}$

E. 16 to 43, 16 : 43, or $\frac{16}{43}$

F. 43 to 26, 43 : 26, or $\frac{43}{26}$

13. Lisa, a professional basketball player, scored 3 points in the first quarter of a game. The two teams scored a total of 43 points in the first quarter. At the end of two quarters, Lisa had scored 20 points. However, her team was trailing by a score of 49 to 47.

a. What are three correct ways to write the ratio of Lisa's first-quarter points to the total points scored in the first quarter?

A. 3 to 43, 3 : 43, or $\frac{3}{43}$

B. 43 to 3, 3 : 43, or $\frac{3}{43}$

C. 43 to 3, 43 : 3, or $\frac{43}{3}$

D. 3 to 43, 43 : 3,or $\frac{43}{3}$

E. 3 to 43, 3 : 43, or $\frac{43}{3}$

F. 43 to 3, 43 : 3, or $\frac{3}{43}$

b. What are three correct ways to write the ratio of Lisa's points for the two quarters to her team's total points for the two quarters?

14. The food stand at the fair sells small, medium, and large fruit drinks. The medium drink is made with 9 parts juice, 5 parts fruit, and 7 parts crushed ice.

a. For a medium drink, what is the ratio of juice to fruit and crushed ice combined in simplified form?

b. Which ratios are equivalent to the ratio of juice to fruit and crushed ice combined? Select all that apply.

A. $\frac{30}{48}$ **B.** $\frac{27}{36}$

C. $\frac{24}{32}$ **D.** $\frac{36}{48}$

E. $\frac{50}{80}$

F. No ratios here are equivalent to the ratio of juice to fruit and crushed ice combined.

15. Think About the Process In the after-school program, 17 students play basketball and 20 students play soccer. You can write the ratio of students who play soccer to students who play basketball as 20 to 17 or 20 : 17. You can also write the ratio of students who play soccer to students who play basketball as a fraction. To do this, which step would you do first?

A. Add 20 and 17 to find the denominator of the fraction.

B. Select 20 as the denominator of the fraction.

C. Select 20 as the numerator of the fraction.

D. Select 17 as the numerator of the fraction.

16. Think About the Process You want to write the ratio $\frac{30}{40}$ in lower terms. You decide to first find a common factor of 30 and 40. What is the next step?

A. Multiply the numerator and the denominator by the common factor.

B. Divide only the denominator by the common factor.

C. Divide the numerator and the denominator by the common factor.

D. Multiply only the numerator by the common factor.

10-5 Ratios as Decimals

CCSS: 6.RP.A.1, 6.RP.A.3

Key Concept

To write a ratio as a decimal, first write the ratio as a fraction. Then write the fraction as a decimal.

$$1 : 2 \rightarrow \frac{1}{2} \rightarrow 0.5$$

A ratio written as a decimal is a comparison of the decimal to 1.

0.5 means 0.5 to 1.

Part 1

Example Writing Ratios as Decimals and Fractions

The aspect ratio of an image is the ratio of the width of the image to the height of the image. The table shows the aspect ratios for three computer monitor settings. Find the missing values in the table.

Computer Monitor Aspect Ratios

Width (pixels)	Height (pixels)	Aspect Ratio	Fraction	Decimal
1,024	768	4 : 3	■	■
1,344	756	16 : 9	■	■
1,280	1,024	5 : 4	■	■

Solution

To write a ratio as a fraction, use the first term as the numerator and the second term as the denominator.

Computer Monitor Aspect Ratios

Width (pixels)	Height (pixels)	Aspect Ratio	Fraction	Decimal
1,024	768	4 : 3	$\frac{4}{3}$	1.33
1,344	756	16 : 9	$\frac{16}{9}$	1.78
1,280	1,024	5 : 4	$\frac{5}{4}$	1.25

continued on next page >

Part 1

Solution continued

To write the fraction as a decimal, divide the numerator by the denominator.

$$\begin{array}{r} 1.333 \\ 3\overline{)4.000} \\ -3 \\ \hline 10 \\ -9 \\ \hline 10 \\ -9 \\ \hline 10 \\ -9 \\ \hline 1 \end{array} \qquad \begin{array}{r} 1.777 \\ 9\overline{)16.000} \\ -9 \\ \hline 70 \\ -63 \\ \hline 70 \\ -63 \\ \hline 70 \\ -63 \\ \hline 7 \end{array} \qquad \begin{array}{r} 1.25 \\ 4\overline{)5.00} \\ -4 \\ \hline 10 \\ -8 \\ \hline 20 \\ -20 \\ \hline 0 \end{array}$$

Round each decimal to the nearest hundredth. Round 1.333 to 1.33 and 1.777 to 1.78.

Part 2

Example Writing Ratios as Fractions in Simplest Form

The gears on a bicycle control how the wheels rotate as the rider rotates the pedals. A rider chooses a gear so that the ratio of the number of wheel rotations to the number of pedal rotations is 0.8. Write the ratio as a fraction in simplest form.

Solution

The ratio of the number of wheel rotations to the number of pedal rotations is 0.8.

Step 1 Write 0.8 as a fraction.

$$0.8 = \frac{8}{10}$$

Step 2 Simplify the fraction.

The GCF of 8 and 10 is 2.

$$\frac{8}{10} \overset{\div 2}{=} \frac{4}{5}$$

The ratio of the number of wheel rotations to the number of pedal rotations is $\frac{4}{5}$. For every 4 wheel rotations, there are 5 pedal rotations.

Part 3

Example Using Equivalent Fractions to Find Unknown Quantities

In baseball, a player's batting average is the ratio of the number of hits to the number of at bats. To find a batting average, divide the number of hits by the number of at bats.

$$\text{batting average} = \frac{\text{number of hits}}{\text{number of at bats}}$$

A new player's batting average is .350. The player has 60 at bats. How many hits does the player have?

Solution

Step 1 Write .350 as a fraction.

$$.350 = \frac{350}{1{,}000}$$

Step 2 Simplify the fraction.

The GCF of 350 and 1,000 is 50.

$$\frac{350}{1{,}000} \overset{\div 50}{=} \frac{7}{20}$$

Step 3 Since the player had 60 at bats, write an equivalent fraction with 60 as the denominator.

Since 20 × 3 = 60, multiply the numerator and denominator by 3.

$$\frac{7}{20} \overset{\times 3}{=} \frac{21}{60}$$

The player has 21 hits.

Check

$$\text{batting average} = \frac{\text{hits}}{\text{at bats}}$$

$$= \frac{21}{60}$$

$$= 0.35$$

The player has 21 hits and 60 at bats.

The player's batting average is .350, which is the given information. The answer is correct.

1. The book store employs 4 people. The ratio of women working in the store to the total number of workers is 3 to 4. The ratio of men working in the store to the total number of workers is 1 to 4.

a. Write the ratio of women workers to all workers in three different ways.

b. Write the ratio of men workers to all workers in three different ways.

2. The ratio of games lost to games played for the school basketball team is 3 : 10. Write the ratio as a fraction and as a decimal.

3. In the workbench drawer, the ratio of hex bolts to all bolts is 0.14. Write the ratio as a fraction in simplest form.

4. Last winter, the ratio of days with snow to days with no snow was 1.12. Write this ratio as a fraction in simplest form.

5. In a recent student government election, the ratio of students who voted for the winner to all the students who voted was 0.64. The number of students who voted was 125. How many votes did the winner get?

6. A salesperson's ratio of successful signups to the number of people called is 0.125. This month, the salesperson has 25 signups. How many people did the salesperson call this month?

7. **Libraries** In the school library, there are 110 fiction books, 125 nonfiction books, and 260 magazines. The ratio of fiction books to nonfiction books is 110 : 125. Write the ratio of fiction books to nonfiction books as a fraction and as a decimal.

8. **Error Analysis** Mr. Bright's math class is working on a puzzle. To solve the puzzle, the students must change a ratio from decimal form to a fraction in simplest form. The ratio is 2.33. Katie says that the ratio 2.33 is equal to $\frac{33}{100}$. Jon says the ratio 2.33 is equal to $\frac{233}{100}$.

a. Which student is correct?

A. Jon **B.** Katie

b. What error was made?

A. The decimal part was not added.

B. The fraction is not in the simplest form.

C. The whole number part was not added.

9. Your friend says that the ratio 0.94 as a fraction in simplest form is $\frac{94}{100}$, but your friend has made an error. What is the ratio as a fraction in simplest form?

10. **Writing** The ratio of free throws made to free throws tried is 0.55 for a professional basketball player. Last year, the player tried 80 free throws.

a. Explain how you can find the number of free throws the player made.

b. How many free throws did the player make last year?

11. **Reasoning** You write a ratio as 7 : 10. You can also write the ratio as a fraction and as a decimal.

a. In how many ways can you write the ratio as a fraction?

A. exactly one way

B. exactly two ways

C. more than three ways

D. exactly three ways

b. In how many ways can you write the ratio as a decimal (without attaching zeros at the end)?

A. exactly two ways

B. exactly three ways

C. more than three ways

D. exactly one way

c. Explain your reasoning.

12. Write the ratio 0.88 as a fraction in simplest form.

13. Multiple Representations A survey asked students in the 6th grade for their preference, water or fruit juice. The table shows the ratio of students who prefer juice to the total number of students.

	Ratio	Fraction	Decimal
All students	33 : 100	$\frac{33}{100}$	0.33

In Ms. Greene's class, 2 students out of 20 prefer juice. Complete a similar table for the ratio of students who prefer juice in Ms. Greene's class to the total number of students in Ms. Greene's class.

Fill in the table below.

	Ratio	Fraction	Decimal
Ms. Greene's Class	■:■	■	■

14. Multiple Representations The first column of the table suggests two ratios. Complete the table by writing each ratio using a colon and then in fraction and decimal forms.

Description	Ratio	Fraction	Decimal
53 total students to 20 girls	■:■	■	■
boys to girls	■:■	■	■

15. In a group of students, the ratio of students wearing red shirts to students wearing blue shirts is 5.64. The ratio of students wearing yellow shirts to blue shirts is 2.94. Write the ratio of students wearing red shirts to students wearing blue shirts as a fraction in simplest form.

16. Think About the Process You know that the ratio of two quantities is 7 : 12. You can also write the ratio as the fraction $\frac{7}{12}$ or as a decimal. To write the ratio as a decimal, what operation do you perform?

A. Divide 7 by 12.

B. Multiply 12 times 7.

C. Divide 12 by 7.

D. Subtract 7 from 12.

17. Think About the Process The ratio of carrots to celery in a bag of mixed vegetables is 0.65. There are 13 carrots. Celery is your favorite, so you want to figure out how much celery is in the bag. You can write 0.65 as the fraction $\frac{65}{100}$. To write an equivalent fraction with 13 in the numerator, what should you do for your next step?

A. Divide the numerator and denominator of the fraction by 13.

B. Multiply the numerator and denominator of the fraction by 13.

C. Divide the numerator and denominator of the fraction by 5.

D. Multiply the numerator and denominator of the fraction by 5.

18. Challenge A company blends fruit juices in whole-gallon batches. In one batch, the ratio of the gallons of Juice A to the gallons of Juice B is 0.125. Find the least number of gallons possible for this batch.

19. Challenge One day in the town of Chattyville, the ratio of calls made on cell phones to calls made on home phones was 0.625. For cell phones, the ratio of calls completed to calls dropped was 0.875. The number of cell phone calls completed that day was 35.

a. Find the total number of cell phone calls.

b. Find the total number of all calls made that day.

10-6 Problem Solving

CCSS: 6.RP.A.1, 6.RP.A.3

Part 1

Example Writing and Comparing Ratios

A teacher buys 10 spotted fish and 10 striped fish for the fish tanks in two classrooms. Class A wants twice as many spotted fish as striped fish. Class B wants three times as many striped fish as spotted fish. How many spotted fish and striped fish should each class get?

Solution

Class A wants a ratio of 2 spotted fish to 1 striped fish, or 2 : 1.

Class B wants a ratio of 1 spotted fish to 3 stripped fish, or 1 : 3.

Class A should get 8 spotted fish and 4 striped fish.

Class B should get 2 spotted fish and 6 striped fish.

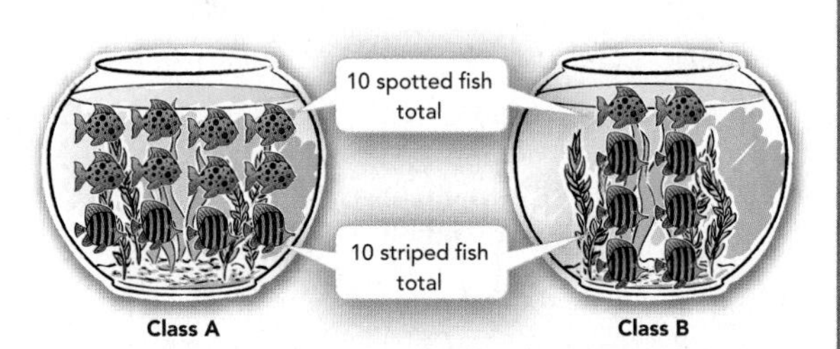

Part 2

Example Finding Unknown Quantities Using Equivalent Ratios

The table shows the amount of each ingredient needed for a pancake recipe. Find the amount of each ingredient needed to make 2 and 3 batches of pancakes.

Pancake Ingredients

Ingredients	Number of Batches		
	1	2	3
Flour (cups)	$1\frac{1}{2}$	3	■
Baking Powder (teaspoons)	$3\frac{1}{2}$	■	■
Sugar (tablespoons)	1	■	■
Milk (cups)	$1\frac{1}{4}$	■	$3\frac{3}{4}$
Eggs	1	■	■
Butter (tablespoons)	3	■	■

continued on next page >

Part 2

Example continued

Solution

In 1 batch there are $1\frac{1}{2}$ cups of flour. Write this as a ratio.

1 batch : $1\frac{1}{2}$ cups of flour

Then find the equivalent ratios for 2 and 3 batches.

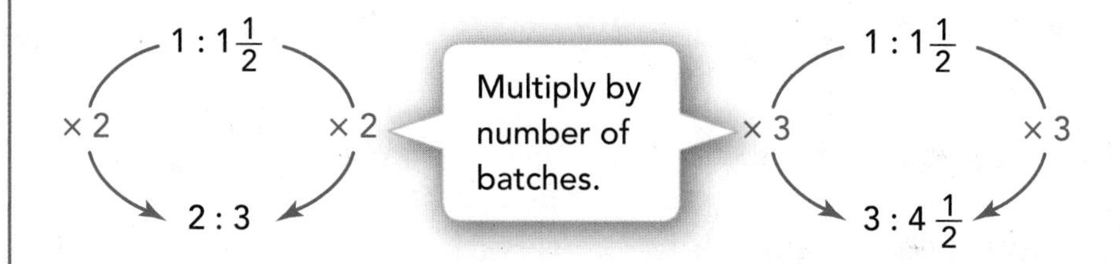

Multiply the amount of each ingredient by 2.

Multiply the amount of each ingredient by 3.

Ingredients	Number of Batches		
	1	2	3
Flour (cups)	$1\frac{1}{2}$	3	$4\frac{1}{2}$
Baking Powder (teaspoons)	$3\frac{1}{2}$	7	$10\frac{1}{2}$
Sugar (tablespoons)	1	2	3
Milk (cups)	$1\frac{1}{4}$	$2\frac{1}{2}$	$3\frac{3}{4}$
Eggs	1	2	3
Butter (tablespoons)	3	6	9

Part 3

Example Finding Unknown Quantities Using Guess and Check

A famous chef has a secret salad dressing recipe. He gives clues about the recipe. How many tablespoons of oil and how many tablespoons of vinegar should you use to make the salad dressing?

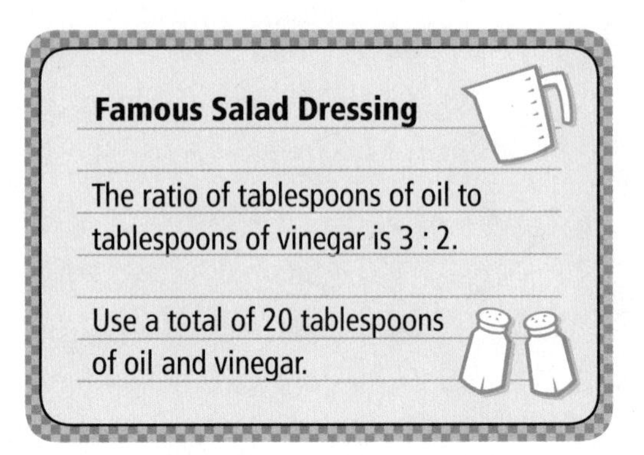

Solution

Use *systematic guess and check*. Use a table to organize your work.

The recipe shows that the ratio of tablespoons of oil to tablespoons of vinegar is 3 : 2. Use this as your first guess.

Now add 3 and 2 to get the total tablespoons. 5 does not equal 20, so this guess is not correct.

Oil (tablespoons)	Vinegar (tablespoons)	Total Tablespoons	
3	2	5	✗
6	4	10	✗
12	8	20	✓

Guess again. Find a ratio equivalent to 3 : 2 for a second guess. Try multiplying by 2. Multiply both the number of tablespoons of oil and the number of tablespoons of vinegar by 2.

Now, add 6 and 4 to get the total tablespoons. 10 does not equal 20, so this guess is also not correct.

If you multiply 10 by 2, however, you get a total of 20 tablespoons. So, double the amount of oil and vinegar for your third guess. Again, multiply by 2. This will keep the ratio of oil to vinegar equivalent to 3 : 2.

Add 12 and 8 to get the total tablespoons, 20.

You should use 12 tablespoons of oil and 8 tablespoons of vinegar to make the salad dressing.

1. The school store opened on the first day of school with 30 notebooks and 18 pencils. Within two days it sold all of these items. On the first day, twice as many notebooks were sold as pencils. On the second day, for every 3 notebooks sold, 2 pencils were sold.
   a. How many notebooks and how many pencils were sold on the first day?
   b. How many notebooks and how many pencils were sold on the second day?

2. The table shows the amounts of some ingredients needed for a waffle recipe. Find the amounts of the ingredients needed to make 3 and 4 batches of waffles.

Waffle Ingredients	
Batches of Waffles	1
Shortening (tablespoons)	2
Baking powder (teaspoons)	5
Flour (cups)	4

3. The ratio of lime juice to soy sauce in a salad dressing is 6 : 7. The total of both ingredients is 39 tablespoons. How many tablespoons of each ingredient are used?

4. The school drama club sponsored a guessing game at a fair. They put some blue marbles and some green marbles in a box. People had to guess how many of each were in the box given two clues.
   1. There were 52 marbles total in the box.
   2. The ratio of blue marbles to green marbles was 8 : 5.

   How many of each color marble were in the box?

5. At Quincy Middle School, there are 45 girls and 27 boys in the sixth grade. There are two sixth-grade classrooms. Ms. Alvarado's class has twice as many girls as boys. The ratio of girls to boys in Mr. Lowry's class is 3 : 2.
   a. Show how to find the number of boys and girls in each class using systematic guess and check.
   b. How many girls and boys are in Ms. Alvarado's class?
   A. 4 girls and 2 boys
   B. 2 girls and 4 boys
   C. 18 girls and 9 boys
   D. 9 girls and 18 boys

6. There are 66 calories in 1 serving of cereal. If a bowl holds 2 servings, how many calories are in the bowl?

7. Two business partners, Ellen and Bob, invested money in their business at a ratio of 3 to 7. Bob invested the greater amount. The total amount invested was $200. How much did each partner invest?

8. Tyrone is making 52 cookies for a party. Some will be pecan cookies. Some will be honey ginger cookies. The ratio of pecan to honey ginger cookies will be 7 : 6. Suppose you use systematic guess and check to find the number of each type of cookie.
   a. If the total for one of your guesses is half of 52, how might you change your guess?
   A. Divide each value by 2.
   B. Subtract 2 from each value.
   C. Add 2 to each value.
   D. Multiply each value by 2.
   b. Explain your reasoning.

9. **Think About the Process** Tara helped with the sixth-grade fundraiser. She sold bags of chocolate chip cookies and oatmeal cookies to her friends and her family. She sold two times as many bags of oatmeal as bags of chocolate chip to her friends. The ratio of bags of chocolate chip to bags of oatmeal sold to her family is 2 : 3.
You want to find how many bags of each type Tara sold to her friends and how many to her family. What additional information do you need?
   A. The total number of bags sold
   B. The total number of bags sold for each type of cookie
   C. The ratio for the number of bags sold to her friends
   D. The total number of bags of chocolate chip cookies sold

10. **Think About the Process** Jorge's two-layer cake recipe includes 7 cups of flour, 3 cups of sugar, and 2 eggs. Jorge wants to make 3 two-layer cakes. What is the correct method to calculate the amount of each ingredient for 3 two-layer cakes?
   A. Add 2 to each quantity in the recipe.
   B. Multiply each quantity in the recipe by 2.
   C. Multiply each quantity in the recipe by 3.
   D. Add 3 to each quantity in the recipe.

11. Bonnie read the nutrition label on the box of her favorite cereal to find out what she was really eating every morning. The table shows some of this information. Estimate how much of each nutrient is in 3 servings and 4 servings.

Cereal Nutrition Information

	Amount per Serving
Potassium	65 mg
Sugars	11 g
Protein	4 g

12. A doctor ordered a patient to exercise. The patient walked for 168 minutes in two weeks. The ratio of the time for the first week to the time for the second week is 8 : 13. How many minutes did the patient walk each week?

13. **Challenge** A new coffee shop sold 468 cups of hot coffee and 351 cups of iced coffee during its first two days. The ratio of cups of hot coffee sold to cups of iced coffee sold on the first day was 17 : 9. On the second day, the shop sold twice as many cups of iced coffee as the first day. The ratio of cups of hot coffee sold to cups of iced coffee sold on the second day was 19 : 18.
   a. How many cups of each type of coffee did the shop sell the first day?
   b. How many cups of each type of coffee did the shop sell the second day?

14. **Challenge** Rachel works a day job and an evening job. She works 78 hours every two weeks. The ratio of the hours she works at her day job to the hours she works at her evening job is 11 : 2. The ratio of the hourly pay for her day job to the hourly pay for her evening job is 5 : 4. Rachel earns $25 an hour at her day job. How much does she earn every two weeks?

11-1 Unit Rates

Vocabulary
rate, unit rate

CCSS: 6.RP.A.2, 6.RP.A.3

Key Concept

A **rate** is a ratio involving two quantities measured in different units. A rate for one unit of a given quantity is called the **unit rate**. When a unit rate is written as a fraction, the denominator is 1 unit. The "1" in a unit rate is read as "per."

$\frac{\text{6 apples}}{\text{3 people}}$

Unit Rate

2 apples per person

Part 1

Example Finding Unit Rates Per Serving

A box of crackers contains 84 crackers and has a total of 7 servings. How many crackers are there per serving?

Solution

Use a model to represent the situation.

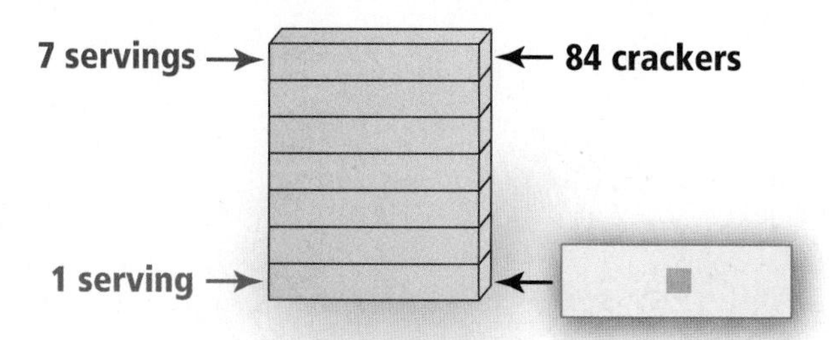

continued on next page >

Part 1

Solution continued

The ratio of crackers to servings is $\frac{84 \text{ crackers}}{7 \text{ servings}}$.

Divide the numerator and denominator by 7 to find the unit rate.

$$\frac{84 \text{ crackers}}{7 \text{ servings}} = \frac{12 \text{ crackers}}{1 \text{ serving}}$$

(÷ 7 applied to numerator and denominator)

The unit rate is $\frac{12 \text{ crackers}}{1 \text{ servings}}$, or 12 crackers per serving.

Part 2

Example Finding Unit Rates Per Year

The trunk of a tree grew approximately 4 inches in width in 16 years. How much did the tree trunk grow per year?

Solution

Write the given ratio: $\frac{4 \text{ inches}}{16 \text{ years}}$.

Divide the numerator and denominator by 16 to find the unit rate.

$$\frac{4 \text{ inches}}{16 \text{ years}} = \frac{(4 \div 16) \text{ inch}}{1 \text{ year}}$$

(÷ 16 applied to numerator and denominator)

Use long division to divide 4 by 16.

```
   0.2 5
16)4.0 0
  -3 2
     8 0
    -8 0
       0
```

The tree grew approximately 0.25 inch, or $\frac{1}{4}$ inch, per year.

Part 3

Example Using a Unit Rate to Complete a Table

A 5-minute shower uses approximately 12 gallons of water. Each minute the shower is running, the rate of water used is the same. Use this rate to complete the table.

Water Usage

Shower Length (minutes)	Water Used (gallons)
1	
2	
3	
5	12
12	
16	

Solution

Find the unit rate.

$$\frac{12 \text{ gallons}}{5 \text{ minutes}} = \frac{2.4 \text{ gallons}}{1 \text{ minute}}$$

(÷ 5 applied to both numerator and denominator)

The unit rate is $\frac{2.4 \text{ gallons}}{1 \text{ minute}}$.

Multiply the unit rate by the length of each shower to find the number of gallons of water used.

$$\frac{2.4 \text{ gallons}}{1 \text{ minute}} \times 1 \text{ minute} = 2.4 \text{ gallons}$$

$$\frac{2.4 \text{ gallons}}{1 \text{ minute}} \times 2 \text{ minutes} = 4.8 \text{ gallons}$$

$$\frac{2.4 \text{ gallons}}{1 \text{ minute}} \times 3 \text{ minutes} = 7.2 \text{ gallons}$$

$$\frac{2.4 \text{ gallons}}{1 \text{ minute}} \times 12 \text{ minutes} = 28.8 \text{ gallons}$$

$$\frac{2.4 \text{ gallons}}{1 \text{ minute}} \times 16 \text{ minutes} = 38.4 \text{ gallons}$$

Water Usage

Shower Length (minutes)	Water Used (gallons)
1	2.4
2	4.8
3	7.2
5	12
12	28.8
16	38.4

Digital Resources    

1. A box of dried fruit has 36 calories in 3 servings. How many calories are there per serving?

2. In a week, 20 hens laid 80 eggs. What is the unit rate for eggs per hen?

3. A 15-pound bag of wildflower seed covers 40 square feet. How many pounds of seed does it take to cover 1 square foot?

4. An animal gained 6 pounds steadily over 12 years. What is the unit rate of pounds per year?

5. A plant grew 19 inches over 5 months. The plant grows the same amount each month. Use this rate to complete the table.

Month	Growth (inches)
1	■
2	■
3	■
4	■
5	19
6	■

6. A migrating bird flies 420 miles in 14 hours. How many miles does it fly in 5 hours?

7. **a. Writing** Exactly 240 years ago, students planted a tree in front of their school. Since then, the tree has grown 30 meters taller, and the distance around the trunk has increased by 3 meters. Describe how you can use this information to find at least two different unit rates.

   b. Find the unit rate for the increase in the tree's trunk.

8. **Reasoning** One 80-pound bag of lawn-care product treats 100 square feet of lawn.

   a. Describe at least three ways to find the number of 80-pound bags needed to treat 1,600 square feet of lawn.

   b. How many 80-pound bags do you need to treat 1,600 square feet of lawn?

9. **Multiple Representations** A vehicle uses 7 gallons of gasoline to travel 252 miles. The vehicle uses gasoline at a steady rate.

   a. Draw a picture that models the situation.

   b. Use the given information to complete the table of equivalent ratios.

Gallons	Miles
1	■
2	■
3	■
7	252
14	■
21	■

   c. Use the table to find the number of gallons of gasoline the vehicle uses to travel 108 miles.

10. **Think About the Process**

    a. Describe how to write the unit rate 0.375 parking space per customer as a ratio.

    b. Then write the unit rate as a ratio of whole numbers in simplest form.

11. **Error Analysis** Adrianne and Burt are in the same keyboarding class. The teacher says they both type at 72 words per minute. Adrianne writes this unit rate as $\frac{1 \text{ minute}}{72 \text{ words}}$. Burt writes it as $\frac{72 \text{ words}}{1 \text{ minute}}$. Which ratio does not correspond to the unit rate 72 words per minute? What is the mistake?

12. **Air Travel** An airplane on autopilot took 7 hours to travel 4,851 kilometers. What is the unit rate for kilometers per hour?

13. **Estimation** A stalactite grows 30 millimeters in 149 years. Estimate the unit rate of growth per year.

14. **Reasoning** The table shows how much fertilizer to use on lawns of different sizes.

Square Feet	Pounds
50	32
100	64
150	96
200	128

a. Describe at least three ways to use the table to find how much fertilizer to use on 500 square feet of lawn.

b. How much fertilizer should be used on 500 square feet of lawn?

15. The 173 workers at a factory together produce 21,452 items per day. What is the daily rate of items per worker?

16. A test found 41 flaws per square meter of an experimental flame-proof cloth. The test counted flaws on 9 square meters of the cloth. What ratio did the testers likely use to find the unit rate for flaws per square meter?

17. **Challenge** A mine produces 37,700 tons of ore during an 8-hour shift. There are 316 miners working during each shift. Each mining cart holds 5 tons of ore. For every 200 tons of ore, there are 3 kilograms of valuable minerals. Assume the valuable minerals are spread evenly in the ore. How many kilograms of valuable minerals are in 1 mining cart full of ore?

18. **Challenge** A breakfast bar comes in two sizes. The 3-ounce bars come in a box of 10. A box of the 7-ounce bars has 6 bars. The 3-ounce bar contains 12 grams of dietary fiber. How many grams of dietary fiber are in one box of the 7-ounce bars?

19. **Think About the Process** The holding pond at a local factory is leaking. A reporter hears that the pond leaks 104.5 gallons of contaminated water every 19 days. The reporter wants to make a table showing how much leaks in 1 day, 1 week, 2 weeks, and 1 month of 30 days.

a. Find the best first step to make this table.

A. Divide the number of days by the unit rate.

B. Multiply the unit rate by the number of days.

C. Convert the number of days to weeks.

D. Use the given ratio to find the unit rate.

b. Complete the table.

Time	Gallons
1 Day	■
1 Week	■
2 Weeks	■
1 Month	■

11-2 Unit Prices

Vocabulary
unit price

CCSS: 6.RP.A.3b

Key Concept

A **unit price** is a unit rate that gives the price of one item.

Rate

$\frac{\$18}{3 \text{ shirts}}$

$\frac{\$6}{1 \text{ shirt}}$ or $6 per shirt

Part 1

Intro

To find a unit price, write the ratio with the total price in the numerator and the total number of items in the denominator. Then find an equivalent ratio with a denominator of 1 item by dividing.

$$\frac{\text{total price}}{\text{total number of items}} = \frac{\text{unit price}}{\text{1 item}}$$

(÷ total number of items in the numerator and ÷ total number of items in the denominator)

Notice that you divide the total price by the total number of items to find the unit price. Since the denominator of the equivalent fraction is 1 item, you can write the unit price as a price per item.

Example $\frac{\$10}{1 \text{ book}} = \$10$ per book

continued on next page >

Part 1

Example Finding Unit Prices with Whole Numbers

What is the unit price of each item?

Shopping Cart

	Item	Price	Quantity	Unit Price
a.	Movie Ticket	$30	5	
b.	Pair of Jeans	$75	3	
c.	Birthday Card	$10	4	

Solution

To find the unit price of each item, divide the total price by the number of items. Then find an equivalent ratio with a denominator of 1.

a. $30 for 5 movie tickets

Total price

Number of tickets

$$\frac{\$30}{5} = \frac{\$6}{1} \quad (\div 5)$$

The unit price is $6 per ticket.

b. $75 for 3 pairs of jeans

Total price

Number of pairs of jeans

$$\frac{\$75}{3} = \frac{\$25}{1} \quad (\div 3)$$

The unit price is $25 per pair of jeans.

c. $10 for 4 birthday cards

Total price

Number of cards

$$\frac{\$10}{4} = \frac{\$2.50}{1} \quad (\div 4)$$

The unit price is $2.50 per card.

Part 2

Example Finding Unit Prices with Decimals

What is the unit price of each item?

Shopping Cart

	Item	Price	Quantity	Unit Price
a.	Pen	$4.50	5	
b.	Pencil	$1.14	6	
c.	Paper clip	40¢	50	

Solution

To find the unit price of each item, divide the total price by the number of items.

a. $4.50 for 5 pens

Total price

Number of pens

$\frac{\$4.50}{5} = \$.90$

$$\begin{array}{r} 0.90 \\ 5\overline{)4.50} \\ -4\,5 \\ \hline 00 \\ -00 \\ \hline 0 \end{array}$$

The unit price is $.90 per pen.

b. $1.14 for 6 pencils

Total price

Number of pencils

$\frac{\$1.14}{6} = \$.19$

$$\begin{array}{r} 0.19 \\ 6\overline{)1.14} \\ -6 \\ \hline 54 \\ -54 \\ \hline 0 \end{array}$$

The unit price is $.19 per pencil.

c. 40¢ for 50 paper clips

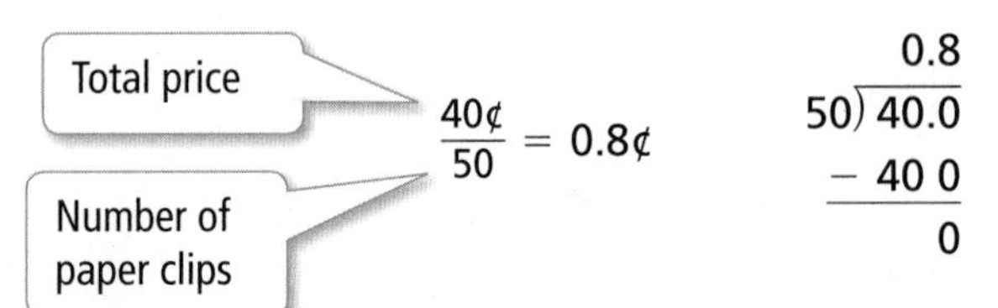

$\frac{40¢}{50} = 0.8¢$

$$\begin{array}{r} 0.8 \\ 50\overline{)40.0} \\ -40\,0 \\ \hline 0 \end{array}$$

The unit price is 0.8¢ per paper clip.

Part 3

Example Comparing Unit Prices

A store sells orange juice in three different-sized containers. Order the containers from the best buy to the worst buy.

32 oz $2.56

64 oz $3.20

96 oz $5.76

Solution

The best buy has the lowest unit price.
Find the unit price for each container of orange juice. Then compare the unit prices. Based on the unit prices, the containers ordered from best to worst buy are:

$\frac{\$3.20}{64 \text{ fluid ounces}} = \$.05$ per fluid ounce

$$\begin{array}{r} 0.05 \\ 64\overline{)3.20} \\ -\ 3\ 20 \\ \hline 0 \end{array}$$

$\frac{\$5.76}{96 \text{ fluid ounces}} = \$.06$ per fluid ounce

$$\begin{array}{r} 0.06 \\ 96\overline{)5.76} \\ -\ 5\ 76 \\ \hline 0 \end{array}$$

$\frac{\$2.56}{32 \text{ fluid ounces}} = \$.08$ per fluid ounce

$$\begin{array}{r} 0.08 \\ 32\overline{)2.56} \\ -\ 2\ 56 \\ \hline 0 \end{array}$$

Digital Resources    

1. If 7 model cars cost $28 what is the unit price of the model cars?

2. A store sells 4 cans of beans for $9. What is the price of 7 cans of beans?

3. If 7 notepads cost $3.15, what is the unit price of the notepads?

4. A package of 4 pairs of insulated gloves costs $29.16. What is the unit price of the pairs of gloves?

5. A box of 200 folders costs $1.40. What is the unit price of the folders?

6. The price of an 8-minute phone call is $1.20. What is the price of a 17-minute phone call?

7. A 25-pound bag of bird food costs $19.50. A 30-pound bag of the same bird food costs $22.80. Which bag of bird food is the better buy?

8. You want to buy some rice. A 6-ounce package costs $2.28. A 14-ounce package costs $5.18. A 26-ounce package costs $10.40. Which package is the best buy?

9. Writing At a home improvement store, you find two ways to buy the kind of roofing nail you need. The 2-pound box sells for $3.72. The 17-pound box sells for $31.96. Find the better buy. Give at least three reasons why a customer might not care which box is the better buy.

10. Think About the Process At a little-known vacation spot, taxi fares are a bargain. A 42-mile taxi ride takes 49 minutes and costs $29.40. You want to find the cost of a 28-mile taxi ride. What unit price do you need?

11. Reasoning A store sells a package of 15 trading cards for $4.20.

a. Explain how you can tell that the unit price per card is less than $1.

b. What is the unit price per card?

12. Think About the Process At a supermarket, an 8-ounce bottle of brand A salad dressing costs $1.76. A 15-ounce bottle costs $3.45. A 28-ounce bottle costs $5.88.

a. What unit prices do you need to know to find the best buy?

A. The unit prices per bottle

B. The unit prices per bottle and per ounce

C. The unit prices per dollar

D. The unit prices per ounce

b. Which bottle is the best buy?

13. Error Analysis A contractor purchases 4 dozen pairs of padded work gloves for $54.24. She incorrectly calculates the unit price as $13.56 per pair for the expense report.

a. What is the correct unit price?

b. Why is the contractor's unit price incorrect?

A. The contractor uses subtraction rather than division to find the unit price.

B. The contractor's unit price is per dozen pairs, not per pair of gloves.

C. The contractor uses multiplication rather than division to find the unit price.

D. The contractor's unit price is per glove, not per pair of gloves.

14. Fundraising The ski team needs new uniforms. The students plan to sell plush toy hawks (the school mascot) for $5 each. The students find three companies online that sell stuffed mascots. Company A sells 15 hawks for $42.72. Company B sells 16 hawks for $45.12. Company C charges $34.56 for 12 hawks. Which company is the best buy?

15. Mental Math A teacher pays $79 for 10 magazines. What is the unit price per magazine?

16. A nursery owner buys 7 panes of glass to fix some damage to his greenhouse. The 7 panes cost $15.05. Unfortunately, he breaks 2 more panes while repairing the damage. What is the cost of another 2 panes of glass?

17. A restaurant owner buys 9 bolts to install an awning. The 9 bolts cost $8.55. The awning looks so nice, she decides to install another one, but needs 2 more bolts. How much do another 2 bolts cost?

18. **Writing** At a home improvement store, you find two ways to buy the kind of roofing nail you need. The 5-pound box sells for $9.35. The 17-pound box sells for $31.96.

   a. Find the better buy.

   b. Give at least three reasons why a customer might not care which box is the better buy.

19. **Think About the Process** At a little-known vacation spot, taxi fares are a bargain. A 27-mile taxi ride takes 36 minutes and costs $10.80. You want to find the cost of a 30-minute taxi ride. What unit price do you need?

20. **Reasoning** A store sells a package of 12 trading cards for $5.88.

   a. Explain how you can tell that the unit price per card is less than $1.

   b. What is the unit price per card?

21. **Think About the Process** At a supermarket, a 6-ounce bottle of brand A salad dressing costs $1.38. A 14-ounce bottle costs $3.36. A 20-ounce bottle costs $4.20.

   a. What unit prices do you need to know to find the best buy?

   A. The unit prices per bottle

   B. The unit prices per bottle and per ounce

   C. The unit prices per ounce

   D. The unit prices per dollar

   b. Which bottle is the best buy?

22. **Error Analysis** A contractor purchases 7 dozen pairs of padded work gloves for $96.60. He incorrectly calculates the unit price as $13.80 per pair for the expense report.

   a. What is the correct unit price?

   b. Why is the contractor's unit price incorrect?

   A. The contractor uses multiplication rather than division to find the unit price.

   B. The contractor uses subtraction rather than division to find the unit price.

   C. The contractor's unit price is per glove, not per pair of gloves.

   D. The contractor's unit price is per dozen pairs, not per pair of gloves.

23. **Challenge** A warehouse store sells 8-ounce cans of soup in cases of 12. A case of the 8-ounce cans costs $27.84. The store also sells 10-ounce cans of the same soup in cases of 16. A case of the 10-ounce cans costs $44.80. Which case is the better buy?

24. **Challenge** A warehouse store sells 6.5-ounce cans of tuna in packages of 6. A package of 6 cans costs $14.04. The store also sells 4.5-ounce cans of the same tuna in packages of 8. A package of 8 cans costs $13.68. The store sells 5.5-ounce cans in packages of 3 cans for $5.61. Which package is the best buy?

11-3 Constant Speed

CCSS: 6.RP.A.3b

Key Concept

The equation $d = rt$ expresses the relationship between distance d, speed r, and time t.

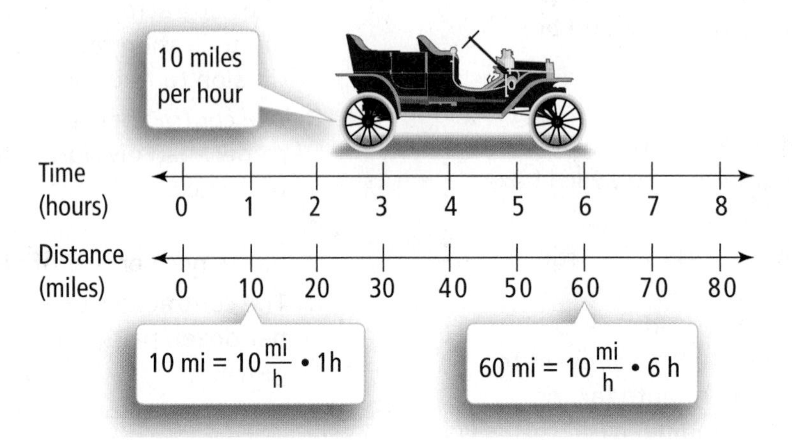

Constant Speed Constant speed is a rate comparing distance to time. If the car travels 10 miles in 1 hour, the car's speed is the rate $10 \frac{\text{miles}}{\text{hour}}$.

Time The total distance the car travels depends on the total amount of time. The speed of the car is given in miles per hour.

Distance For each hour the car travels, the total distance increases by 10 miles.

Using $d = rt$ You can use the equation $d = rt$ to find a distance, rate, or time. The diagram above shows two distances, the first after 1 hour and another after 6 hours.

Part 1

Example Finding Distances Driven For Fixed Time at Constant Speeds

Your aunt drives at a constant speed of 45 miles per hour. How far will your aunt travel in 20 minutes? Use the equation $d = rt$, were d is distance, r is rate, and t is time.

continued on next page >

Part 1

Example continued

Solution

The speed r is 45 miles per hour. The time t is 20 minutes.

Step 1 Rewrite the time in terms of hours.

60 minutes equals 1 hour, so divide 20 by 60.

$$
\begin{aligned}
20 \text{ minutes} &= (20 \div 60) \text{ hour} \\
&= \left(20 \cdot \frac{1}{60}\right) \text{ hour} \\
&= \frac{20}{60} \text{ hour} \\
&= \frac{1}{3} \text{ hour} \\
t &= \frac{1}{3} \text{ hour}
\end{aligned}
$$

So, 20 minutes equals $\frac{1}{3}$ hour.

Step 2 Use the equation $d = rt$ to find the distance traveled.

$$
\begin{aligned}
d &= 45 \, \frac{\text{miles}}{\text{hour}} \cdot \frac{1}{3} \text{ hour} \\
&= 45 \cdot \frac{1}{3} \text{ miles} \\
&= \frac{45}{3} \text{ miles} \\
&= 15 \text{ miles}
\end{aligned}
$$

Your aunt will travel 15 miles in 20 minutes.

Part 2

Example Solving for Constant Speed Given Time and Distance

An airplane is flying from Boston, MA, to San Francisco, CA. What is the speed of the airplane in miles per hour? Use the equation $d = rt$.

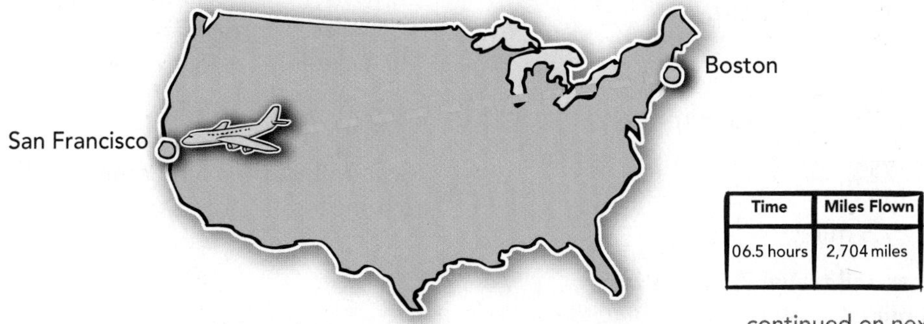

Time	Miles Flown
06.5 hours	2,704 miles

continued on next page >

Part 2

Example continued

Solution

You know the distance and the time.

$d = 2{,}704$ miles $\quad t = 6.5$ hours

Substitute into the equation $d = rt$ and solve for r.

$$d = rt$$

$$2{,}704 \text{ miles} = r \cdot 6.5 \text{ hours}$$

$$\frac{2{,}704 \text{ miles}}{6.5 \text{ hours}} = \frac{r \cdot 6.5 \text{ hours}}{6.5 \text{ hours}}$$

Divide each side by 6.5 hours to get r by itself.

$$\frac{2{,}704 \text{ miles}}{6.5 \text{ hours}} = r$$

$$\frac{416 \text{ miles}}{1 \text{ hour}} = r$$

The airplane's speed is 416 miles per hour.

Part 3

Example Solving Problems Using Constant Speed

On a busy road, cars can travel only 5 miles in 10 minutes.

a. At this speed, how far will a car travel in 15 minutes?

b. At this speed, how long will it take a car to travel 20 miles?

Solution

a. Method 1 Use the equation $d = rt$.

Since both travel times are in minutes, you can write the speed in miles per minute.

Substitute $\frac{5 \text{ miles}}{10 \text{ minutes}}$ for r and 15 minutes for t.

$$d = rt$$

$$= \frac{5 \text{ miles}}{10 \text{ minutes}} \cdot 15 \text{ minutes}$$

$$= \frac{75}{10} \text{ miles}$$

$$= 7.5 \text{ miles}$$

A car will travel 7.5 miles in 15 minutes.

Method 2 Write an equivalent rate.

Multiply each term of the rate by the same number to find an equivalent rate with a denominator of 15 minutes.

$$\frac{5 \text{ miles}}{10 \text{ minutes}} \overset{\times 1.5}{=} \frac{7.5 \text{ miles}}{15 \text{ minutes}}$$

A car will travel 7.5 miles in 15 minutes.

continued on next page >

Part 3

Solution continued

b. **Method 1** Use the equation $d = rt$.

Substitute $\frac{5 \text{ miles}}{10 \text{ minutes}}$ for r and 20 miles for d. Then solve for t.

$$d = rt$$

$$20 \text{ miles} = \frac{5 \text{ miles}}{10 \text{ minutes}} \cdot t$$

$$\frac{10 \text{ minutes}}{5 \text{ miles}} \cdot 20 \text{ miles} = \frac{10 \text{ minutes}}{5 \text{ miles}} \cdot \frac{5 \text{ miles}}{10 \text{ minutes}} \cdot t$$

$$\frac{10 \text{ minutes}}{5 \cancel{\text{miles}}} \cdot 20 \cancel{\text{miles}} = \frac{\cancel{10 \text{ minutes}}}{\cancel{5 \text{ miles}}} \cdot \frac{\cancel{5 \text{ miles}}}{\cancel{10 \text{ minutes}}} \cdot t$$

$$\frac{200}{5} \text{ minutes} = t$$

$$40 \text{ minutes} = t$$

It will take the car 40 minutes to travel 20 miles.

Method 2 Write an equivalent rate.

Multiply each term of the rate by the same number to find an equivalent rate with a numerator of 20 miles.

$$\frac{5 \text{ miles}}{10 \text{ minutes}} \overset{\times 4}{=} \frac{20 \text{ miles}}{40 \text{ minutes}}$$

(× 4 applied to both numerator and denominator)

It will take the car 40 minutes to travel 20 miles.

Digital Resources

1. A delivery truck drove 32 miles per hour. It took 2 hours to travel between two towns. What is the distance between the two towns? Use the equation $d = rt$, where d is distance, r is rate, and t is time.

2. Every morning Jenna runs for 20 minutes. If Jenna runs 6 miles per hour, how far does she travel? Use the equation $d = rt$, where d is distance, r is rate, and t is time.

3. An airplane flies 2,951 miles in 6.5 hours. What is the speed of the airplane in miles per hour? Use the equation $d = rt$, where d is distance, r is rate, and t is time.

4. On a school field trip, the bus travels 23 miles in 30 minutes. Find the speed of the bus in miles per hour. Use the equation $d = rt$, where d is distance, r is rate, and t is time.

5. Ian and his brother are driving from city A to city B. The two cities are 330 miles apart. Ian drives at 55 miles per hour. How long does it take them to make the trip? Use the equation $d = rt$, where d is distance, r is rate, and t is time.

6. A horseback rider travels 2 miles in 12 minutes. At this speed, how long does it take to travel 5 miles? Use the equation $d = rt$, where d is distance, r is rate, and t is time.

7. **Writing** One lap of a high-speed automobile race is 2.60 miles. A driver completes 35 laps traveling at 182 miles per hour.
   - **a.** Explain how you can use the equation $d = rt$ to find the time it takes to complete 35 laps.
   - **b.** How long does it take to complete 35 laps?
     - **A.** 2 hours
     - **B.** 0.5 hour
     - **C.** 1 hour
     - **D.** 0.25 hour

8. **Reasoning** Cheryl biked two days in a row. On the first day, Cheryl biked 7 miles at a steady pace for 15 minutes. On the second day, she biked 14 miles in 30 minutes. Cheryl claims that she rode at the same speed on both days. Is it possible to have the same speed with different distances and times?
   - **A.** It is not possible. There is only one speed that corresponds to each distance and time.
   - **B.** It is not possible. Cheryl was faster on the second day.
   - **C.** It is possible. For both days, Cheryl's speed was 28 miles per hour.
   - **D.** It is possible. For both days, Cheryl's speed was 16 miles per hour.

9. Nancy merges onto the highway at 8 A.M. and drives 110 miles. She takes a 1-hour break and then drives 165 miles. For both drives, the cruise control is set on 55 miles per hour. How long does the trip take? Use the equation $d = rt$.

10. **Error Analysis** At soccer training, the team ran for 30 minutes at 6 miles per hour. Your friend incorrectly says that the team ran a distance of 180 miles.
    - **a.** What is the correct distance?
    - **b.** What error did your friend most likely make?
      - **A.** Your friend divided the rate by the time.
      - **B.** Your friend did not rewrite the rate in terms of miles per hour.
      - **C.** Your friend divided the time by the rate.
      - **D.** Your friend did not rewrite the time in terms of hours.

11. **Snakes** A black racer snake travels 6.9 kilometers in 3 hours. What is the snake's speed in kilometers per hour? Use the equation $d = rt$.

12. a. **Open-Ended** Write a problem using the values 10 meters per second and 50 seconds. Require that the solver use the equation $d = rt$.

b. What is the correct unit for the value the solver will find?

A. meters per second

B. meters

C. seconds

D. hours

13. The table shows distances and travel times of three high-speed trains. Which train is the fastest?

Train	Distance	Time
Train A	800 miles	4 hours
Train B	1,260 miles	7 hours
Train C	1,350 miles	9 hours

A. Train A **B.** Train B

C. Train C

14. Two cyclists start at the same place. The first travels east at 20 miles per hour. The second travels west. They are 22 miles apart after 30 minutes. How fast is the second cyclist traveling? Use the equation $d = rt$.

15. On a Saturday, Peter and Carin agree to leave their homes at the same time, drive toward each other, and have lunch when they meet. They both drive for 2 hours. Carin drives 5 miles per hour faster than Peter. Peter drives a total of 82 miles. How fast does each person drive? Use the equation $d = rt$.

16. **Think About the Process** You are in an airplane traveling 496 miles per hour. What information do you need to find the distance the airplane has traveled so far?

A. The number of hours the airplane has been in the air

B. The speed of the airplane in miles per minute

C. The height of the airplane in miles

D. The distance from takeoff to landing

17. **Think About the Process** You are in the car on your way to a friend's house 24 miles away. You know that the trip takes 30 minutes. How would you find how fast you are traveling, in miles per hour?

A. Multiply 24 miles by $\frac{1}{2}$ hour.

B. Divide $\frac{1}{2}$ hour by 24 miles.

C. Divide 24 miles by $\frac{1}{2}$ hour.

D. Divide 30 minutes by 24 miles.

18. **Challenge** A circus performer is riding a unicycle in a circle. He is riding 2.5 meters per second. He can go 10 times around the circle in 2 minutes. What is the distance around the circle? Use the equation $d = rt$.

19. **Challenge** You and a friend begin hiking a 20-mile trail at noon. You hike 6 miles in 3 hours.

a. Continuing at this rate, how long will it take to hike the entire trail?

b. Will you reach the end of the trail before 8 P.M.?

A. Yes

B. No

11-4 Measurements and Ratios

Vocabulary
conversion factor

CCSS: 6.RP.A.3d

Key Concept

You can often write measurements in more than one way. For example, 1 hour = 60 minutes.

You can express the relationship between the two equivalent measurements as a rate. The rate equals 1 and is called a **conversion factor**.

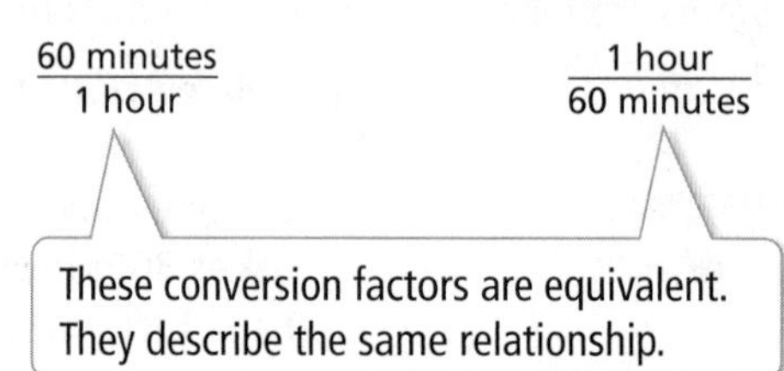

You can use a conversion factor to convert between two units of measure.

Part 1

Example Using Ratio Reasoning to Convert Within Customary Measurement Units

Complete each conversion statement using the values provided.

$\frac{2 \text{ cups}}{1 \text{ pint}}$ 2 $\frac{1}{2}$ $\frac{2 \text{ pints}}{1 \text{ quart}}$

$\frac{1 \text{ pint}}{2 \text{ cups}}$ 8 $\frac{1 \text{ quart}}{2 \text{ pints}}$

a. 4 pints · ■ = (4 · ■) cups
= ■ cups

b. 4 pints · ■ = (4 · ■) quarts
= ■ quarts

Solution

Use a conversion factor that has the original units in the denominator and new units in the numerator.

a. To convert pints to cups, multiply by $\frac{2 \text{ cups}}{1 \text{ pint}}$.

$$4 \text{ pints} \cdot \frac{2 \text{ cups}}{1 \text{ pint}} = (4 \cdot 2) \text{ cups}$$
$$= 8 \text{ cups}$$

b. To convert pints to quarts, multiply by $\frac{1 \text{ quart}}{2 \text{ pints}}$.

$$4 \text{ pints} \cdot \frac{1 \text{ quart}}{2 \text{ pints}} = (4 \cdot \tfrac{1}{2}) \text{ quarts}$$
$$= 2 \text{ quarts}$$

Part 2

Example Comparing Feet and Inches to Centimeters

Is a rider 3 feet 10 inches tall allowed to ride this roller coaster? Use 1 inch = 2.54 centimeters.

Solution

Method 1 Convert centimeters to inches.

Find the height minimum in inches. Use the conversion factor $\frac{1 \text{ inch}}{2.54 \text{ centimeters}}$.

$$100 \text{ centimeters} \cdot \frac{1 \text{ inch}}{2.54 \text{ centimeters}} = \frac{100}{2.54} \text{ inches}$$
$$\approx 39.37 \text{ inches}$$

The rider needs to be at least 39.37 inches tall.

Then find the rider's height in inches.

$$3 \text{ feet} \cdot \frac{12 \text{ inches}}{1 \text{ foot}} + 10 \text{ inches} = 36 \text{ inches} + 10 \text{ inches}$$
$$= 46 \text{ inches}$$

The rider is taller than 39.37 inches, so the rider is allowed to ride the roller coaster.

Method 2 Convert inches to centimeters.

First, convert 3 feet 10 inches to inches.

$$3 \text{ feet} \cdot \frac{12 \text{ inches}}{1 \text{ foot}} + 10 \text{ inches} = 36 \text{ inches} + 10 \text{ inches}$$
$$= 46 \text{ inches}$$

Then convert inches to centimeters. Use the conversion factor $\frac{1 \text{ inch}}{2.54 \text{ centimeters}}$.

$$46 \text{ inches} \cdot \frac{2.54 \text{ centimeters}}{1 \text{ inch}} = 116.84 \text{ centimeters}$$

The rider is taller than 100 centimeters, so the rider is allowed to ride the roller coaster.

Part 3

Example Converting Grams to Pounds

A bread recipe calls for 500 grams of flour. About how many pounds of flour do you need? Use 1 ounce $\approx$ 28.4 grams.

Solution

First, convert grams to ounces. Then convert ounces to pounds.

$$500 \text{ grams} \cdot \frac{1 \text{ ounce}}{28.4 \text{ grams}} \approx 17.6 \text{ ounces}$$

$$17.6 \text{ ounces} \cdot \frac{1 \text{ pound}}{16 \text{ ounces}} = 1.1 \text{ pounds}$$

Use the conversion factors $\frac{1 \text{ ounce}}{28.4 \text{ grams}}$ and $\frac{1 \text{ pound}}{16 \text{ ounces}}$.

You need about 1.1 pounds of flour.

1. Convert 16 yards to feet. Use the rate suggested by the equation 3 feet = 1 yard.

2. Convert 10 pints to quarts. Use the rate suggested by the equation 1 quart = 2 pints.

3. Convert 13 inches to centimeters. Use the rate, or conversion factor, $\frac{2.54 \text{ centimeters}}{1 \text{ inch}}$.

4. Convert 33 centimeters to inches. Use the rate, or conversion factor, $\frac{1 \text{ inch}}{2.54 \text{ centimeters}}$.

5. A chef at a restaurant uses 12 pounds of butter each day. About how many grams of butter does the chef use each day? Use the conversion factors $\frac{16 \text{ ounces}}{1 \text{ pound}}$ and $\frac{28.4 \text{ grams}}{1 \text{ ounce}}$.

6. A cake recipe calls for 550 grams of flour. About how many pounds of flour do you need? Use the conversion factors $\frac{1 \text{ ounce}}{28.4 \text{ grams}}$ and $\frac{1 \text{ pound}}{16 \text{ ounces}}$.

7. **Writing** Paul's car holds at most 19 gallons of gas. Now it has 9 gallons.

   a. Explain how to find the amount of gas he needs, in liters, to fill the gas tank. Use the conversion factors $\frac{4 \text{ quarts}}{1 \text{ gallon}}$ and $\frac{0.94 \text{ liters}}{1 \text{ quart}}$.

   b. How many liters of gas does Paul need to fill his gas tank?

8. **Reasoning** Simone wants to know if a new chest of drawers will fit next to her bed. The chest she would like to buy is 73 centimeters wide. She knows that her room is 86 inches wide. The bed is 76 inches wide.

   Will the chest fit next to her bed? Use the conversion factor $\frac{2.54 \text{ centimers}}{1 \text{ inch}}$.

   A. No, the room needs to be 47.6 centimeters wider in order for the chest to fit.

   B. Yes, the chest fits with 47.6 centimeters of wall space remaining.

   C. No, the room needs to be 69.06 centimeters wider in order for the chest to fit.

   D. Yes, the chest fits with 69.06 centimeters of wall space remaining.

9. Cara and Derek are decorating a wall. They each have a picture that they want to hang on the wall. Cara's picture is 58 centimeters wide. Derek's picture is 26 inches wide. They want to hang the wider picture. Which picture should they use? Use the conversion factor $\frac{1 \text{ inch}}{2.54 \text{ centimeters}}$.

   A. Cara's picture

   B. Derek's picture

   C. Both pictures are the same width. They can use either picture.

10. **Error Analysis** Two students, Stella and Vladimir, complete the conversion statement 12 feet 8 inches = ■ inches.

Stella	12 feet 8 inches = 152 inches
Vladimir	12 feet 8 inches = 9 inches

   a. Which student is correct?

   A. Vladimir **B.** Stella

   b. What is the likely cause of the other student's error? Use the conversion factor $\frac{12 \text{ inches}}{1 \text{ foot}}$.

   A. The student used multiplication instead of division.

   B. The student used the conversion factor $\frac{1 \text{ inch}}{12 \text{ feet}}$.

   C. The student used the conversion factor $\frac{1 \text{ foot}}{12 \text{ inches}}$.

   D. The student used addition instead of multiplication.

11. **Plumbing** A school custodian discovered a leak in a water pipe. The custodian found that 1,920 fluid ounces of water had leaked out. How many gallons of water is this? Use the conversion factor $\frac{1 \text{ gallon}}{128 \text{ fluid ounces}}$.

12. Estimation You need 29 liters of water for a party. You can buy water in containers holding 4, 6, 8, or 10 gallons.

a. Estimate the amount of water you need in gallons. Use the conversion factor $\frac{1 \text{ gallon}}{4 \text{ liters}}$.

b. What size container should you buy to get an amount greater than but closest to 29 liters?

A. 10-gallon **B.** 8-gallon

C. 6-gallon **D.** 4-gallon

13. The hole for a support needs to be 6 feet deep. It is currently 1 foot 8 inches deep. How much deeper must the hole be? Use the conversion factor $\frac{12 \text{ inches}}{1 \text{ foot}}$.

14. Aidan needs 15 liters of cleaning solution. He can buy a 2-gallon jug ($4.28), a 3-gallon jug ($5.92), a 4-gallon jug ($6.56), or a 7-gallon jug ($12.98). Which jug should he purchase to get at least 15 liters of cleaning solution and spend the least amount of money? Use the conversion factors $\frac{1 \text{ quart}}{0.94 \text{ liters}}$ and $\frac{1 \text{ gallon}}{4 \text{ quarts}}$.

15. Tiffany drives 300,960 feet before lunch and 528,000 feet after lunch. About how many kilometers does she drive altogether? Use the conversion factors $\frac{1 \text{ mile}}{5{,}280 \text{ feet}}$ and $\frac{161 \text{ kilometers}}{1 \text{ mile}}$.

16. Think About the Process Two neighbors in a rural area want to know the distance between their homes in miles. They look at a land map that shows the distance between their homes as 4,224 feet. What should the neighbors use as a conversion factor to convert this distance to miles?

A. $\frac{5{,}280 \text{ feet}}{0.8 \text{ mile}}$ **B.** $\frac{5{,}280 \text{ feet}}{1 \text{ mile}}$

C. $\frac{1 \text{ mile}}{4{,}224 \text{ feet}}$ **D.** $\frac{1 \text{ mile}}{5{,}280 \text{ feet}}$

E. $\frac{4{,}224 \text{ feet}}{1 \text{ mile}}$

17. Think About the Process You are making a blanket and need 9 feet of a certain fabric. Online you find a website selling the fabric for $14 per meter. You know the conversion factors $\frac{12 \text{ inches}}{1 \text{ foot}}$, $\frac{2.54 \text{ centimeters}}{1 \text{ inch}}$ and $\frac{1 \text{ meter}}{100 \text{ centimeters}}$. What is the first step in finding the amount of fabric you need in meters?

A. First convert inches to feet.

B. First convert feet to inches.

C. First convert inches to centimeters.

D. First convert centimeters to meters.

E. First convert centimeters to inches.

F. First convert meters to centimeters.

18. Challenge A car is traveling at 25 miles per hour. What is the car's speed in feet per second? Use the conversion factors $\frac{5{,}280 \text{ feet}}{1 \text{ mile}}$ and $\frac{1 \text{ hour}}{3{,}600 \text{ seconds}}$.

19. Challenge Kate is driving to visit a friend. Her gas tank is full with 56 liters at the start. Each time the tank is down to 3 liters, she refills it. She does this two times. After the last refill, Kate uses all of the gas in the tank. Her car gets 8 kilometers per liter. What is the distance that Kate drives in miles? Use the conversion factors $\frac{100{,}000 \text{ centimeters}}{1 \text{ kilometer}}$, $\frac{1 \text{ inch}}{2.54 \text{ centimeters}}$, and $\frac{1 \text{ mile}}{63{,}360 \text{ inches}}$.

11-5 Choosing the Appropriate Rate

CCSS: 6.RP.A.3, 6.RP.A.3b

Part 1

Intro

Given any two measurements, you can write two different rates to compare them.

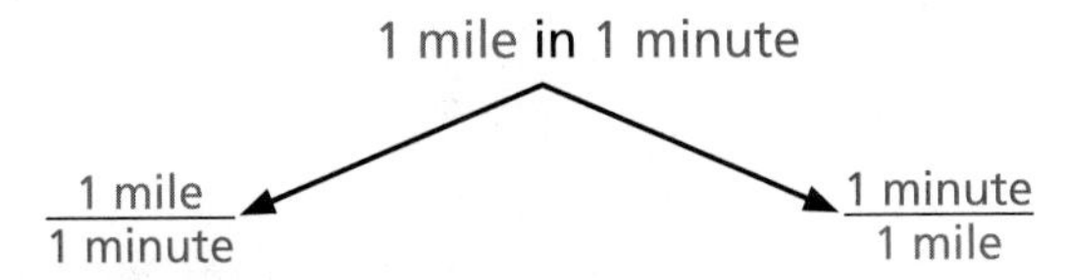

Notice that the two rates are reciprocals.

Example Converting the Units of Rates

The recommended rate for a scuba diver to come to the surface is 30 feet per minute. What is the rate in seconds per foot?

Solution

Write the rate as a fraction. Then convert minutes to seconds.

$$\frac{30 \text{ feet}}{1 \text{ minute}} = \frac{30 \text{ feet}}{60 \text{ seconds}}$$

$$\frac{30 \text{ feet}}{60 \text{ seconds}} \longrightarrow \frac{60 \text{ seconds}}{30 \text{ feet}}$$

Find the reciprocal.

Simplify to find the unit rate in seconds per foot.

$$\frac{60 \text{ seconds}}{30 \text{ feet}} = \frac{2 \text{ seconds}}{1 \text{ foot}}$$

÷ 30 (numerator and denominator)

The recommended rate for a scuba diver to come to the surface is 2 seconds per foot.

Part 2

Example Comparing Rates in Different Units

On your friend's current phone plan, text messages cost 10¢ per message. Which of the following plans offer a better deal than the current plan?

Plan A: $2 for 20 messages

Plan B: 10 messages per dollar

Plan C: $5 for 100 messages

Plan D: 1 message for 5¢

Plan E: 70 messages for $7

Solution

The rate for the current plan is 10¢ per message. Write the rate for each plan as a unit rate in cents per message. For Plans B, D and E, find the reciprocal of the given rate before simplifying.

Plan A: $\frac{\$2}{20 \text{ messages}} = \frac{200¢}{20 \text{ messages}} = 10¢ \text{ per message}$

Plan B: $\frac{10 \text{ messages}}{\$1} = \frac{10 \text{ messages}}{100¢}$

$$\frac{10 \text{ messages}}{100¢} \longrightarrow \frac{100¢}{10 \text{ messages}}$$

$$\frac{100¢}{10 \text{ messages}} = 10¢ \text{ per message}$$

Plan C: $\frac{\$5}{100 \text{ messages}} = \frac{500¢}{100 \text{ messages}} = 5¢ \text{ per message}$

Plan D: $\frac{1 \text{ message}}{5¢} \longrightarrow \frac{5¢}{1 \text{ message}}$

$$\frac{5¢}{1 \text{ message}} = 5¢ \text{ per message}$$

Plan E: $\frac{70 \text{ messages}}{\$7} = \frac{70 \text{ messages}}{700¢}$

$$\frac{70 \text{ messages}}{700¢} \longrightarrow \frac{700¢}{70 \text{ messages}}$$

$$\frac{700¢}{70 \text{ messages}} = 10¢ \text{ per message}$$

Plans A, B, and E have the same cost per message as your friend's current plan. Plans C and D have a cost of 5¢ per message, which is less than 10¢ per message. So Plans C and D offer better deals than the current plan.

Part 3

Example Using Unit Rates to Solve Problems

You get an offer to baby-sit for $6.25 per hour.

a. How much will you earn if you baby-sit for 5 hours?

b. How many hours will you need to baby-sit at this rate to earn $100?

Solution

a. You know the number of hours. You want to find the amount of money.

Use dollars per hour and multiply.

$$\frac{\$6.27}{1 \text{ hour}} \times 5 \text{ hours} = \$31.25$$

You will earn $31.25 in 5 hours.

b. You know the amount of money. You want to find the number of hours.

Use hours per dollar.

$$\frac{1 \text{ hour}}{\$6.25} = \frac{0.16 \text{ hour}}{\$1}$$

(÷ 6.25 numerator and denominator)

$$\frac{0.16 \text{ hour}}{\$1} \times \$100 = 16 \text{ hours}$$

Check

Use the rate of dollars per hour to check your answer.

$$\frac{\$6.25}{1 \text{ hour}} \times 16 \text{ hours} = \$100 \checkmark$$

Digital Resources 

1. A river flows at the rate of 20 feet per minute. What is the rate in seconds per foot?

2. A car travels 250 miles in 5 hours.
   a. What is the rate in miles per hour?
   b. What is the rate in hours per mile?

3. Two stores sell the same item. Which store has the better buy?

Store	Price
A	10 items for $9.00
B	85¢ per item

4. Three stores sell the same item. Which store has the best buy?

Store	Price
A	5 items for $7.00
B	$5.40 for 4 items
C	$1.50 per item

5. A worker earns $12.50 per hour. For how many hours would the worker have to work to earn $300?

6. A factory starts to make a new product. A worker notices that 2 boxes of the new product weigh 7 pounds. The worker moves boxes with a cart that can carry 56 pounds. What is the greatest number of boxes the cart can carry?

7. **Writing** A scientist studies an object that takes 5 minutes to travel one foot. The scientist wants to write this rate in miles per hour.
   a. Explain how the scientist could find the object's rate in miles per hour. Note that 1 mile is 5,280 feet.
   b. What is the rate in miles per hour?

8. **Reasoning** Three shops sell the same type of potting soil. Shop A advertises 17 pounds of the soil for $18.00. Shop B charges $1.15 per pound. At shop C, 0.81 pound of the soil costs $1.00.
   a. Which types of unit rates could you use to find the best buy? Select all that apply.
      A. pounds per bag
      B. dollars per pound
      C. ounces per cent
      D. cents per ounce
      E. ounces per dollar
      F. bags per pound
      G. pounds per cent
      H. pounds per dollar
   b. Explain which unit rate you would use and why.
   c. Find which shop has the best buy.

9. **Error Analysis** A conveyor belt at a recycling center is 280 feet long. The belt moves 5 feet in 4 seconds. A sorter calculates that it takes 350 seconds for an object to travel the length of the belt. He places his plastic water bottle at the start of the belt so he can tie his shoe. He walks to the end of the belt before 350 seconds pass. His bottle is already in the shredder.
   a. How many seconds does it take the water bottle to travel the length of the belt?
   b. What is the sorter's error?

10. **Mining** A team of miners drills a hole 50.6 meters into a rock formation. The miners drill at the steady rate of 4.6 meters per minute. How long does it take to drill the hole?

11. **Mental Math** One store sells 10 pens for $1.00. Another store sells the same pens for 9¢ each. Which is the better buy?

12. a. **Open-Ended** Describe a situation that uses the unit rate 25 miles per year and the reciprocal unit rate is years per mile.
    b. What is the unit rate in years per mile?

13. Open-Ended A company makes a device that shows the speed of an approaching car in hours per mile.

a. Write a letter to the company explaining why showing speed in miles per hour is a better idea. Explain how to change the speed to miles per hour.

b. How would this change a speed of 0.05 hour per mile?

14. A machine makes 13.9 items per minute. How many hours does the machine need to make 3,753 items?

15. An animal moves at the rate of 10 inches per minute. What is the rate in seconds per foot?

16. Think About the Process One auto parts store advertises 9 safety flares for \$2.00. Another store sells the same flares for 21¢ each. A third store has boxes of 8 flares for \$1.92. What rates could you compare to find the best buy? Select all that apply.

A. $\frac{\$2.00}{9\text{ flares}}, \frac{\$0.21}{1\text{ flare}}$, and $\frac{\$1.92}{8\text{ flares}}$

B. $\frac{9\text{ flares}}{\$2.00}, \frac{21¢}{1\text{ flare}}$, and $\frac{8\text{ flares}}{\$1.92}$

C. $\frac{200¢}{9\text{ flares}}, \frac{21¢}{1\text{ flare}}$, and $\frac{192¢}{8\text{ flares}}$

D. $\frac{9\text{ flares}}{\$2.00}, \frac{1\text{ flare}}{\$0.21}$, and $\frac{8\text{ flares}}{\$1.92}$

E. $\frac{9\text{ flares}}{200¢}, \frac{1\text{ flare}}{21¢}$, and $\frac{8\text{ flares}}{192¢}$

F. $\frac{\$2.00}{9\text{ flares}}, \frac{1\text{ flare}}{21¢}$, and $\frac{\$1.92}{8\text{ flares}}$

17. Think About the Process A security system requires 7 sensors for every 2 feet of fence. You want to find the number of sensors for a fence that is 138 feet long. By which rate should you multiply?

18. Writing A scientist studies an object that takes travels 7 miles in one hour. The scientist wants to write this rate in minutes per foot.

a. Explain how the scientist could find the object's rate in minutes per foot. Note that 1 mile is 5,280 feet.

b. What is the rate in minutes per foot?

19. Mental Math One store sells 5 pens for \$1.00. Another store sells the same pens for 22¢ each. Which is the better buy?

20. a. Open-Ended Describe a situation that uses the unit rate 250 grams per month and the reciprocal unit rate is months per gram.

b. What is the unit rate in months per gram?

21. Challenge Marcus finds three new music download sites. Site A offers 5 songs for \$1.00. Site B charges 30¢ per download. For \$6.00 a month, site C has unlimited downloads. Normally, Marcus downloads about 40 songs per month. Which site offers Marcus the best deal?

22. Challenge An elevator rises 2 feet in 5 seconds. How high does the elevator rise in $\frac{1}{2}$ minute?

11-6 Problem Solving

CCSS: 6.RP.A.3

Part 1

Example Making Comparisons Using Rates with Different Units

Do you spend more time each year watching television or in school?

1,680 minutes of TV per week

1,170 hours per year in school

Solution

To compare the rates, write them with the same units.

Method 1 Convert 1,680 minutes per week to hours per year.

$$\frac{1{,}680 \text{ minutes}}{1 \cancel{\text{week}}} \cdot \frac{52 \cancel{\text{weeks}}}{1 \text{ year}} = \frac{(1{,}680 \cdot 52) \text{ minutes}}{1 \text{ year}}$$

$$= 87{,}360 \frac{\text{minutes}}{\text{year}}$$

First convert to minutes per year.

$$\frac{87{,}360 \cancel{\text{minutes}}}{1 \text{ year}} \cdot \frac{1 \text{ hour}}{60 \cancel{\text{minutes}}} = \frac{87{,}360 \text{ hours}}{60 \text{ years}}$$

$$= 1{,}456 \frac{\text{hours}}{\text{year}}$$

Then convert to hours per year.

You spend 1,456 hours per year watching television. You spend only 1,170 hours per year in school. You spend more time watching television than in school.

Method 2 Convert 1,170 hours per year to minutes per week.

$$\frac{1{,}170 \text{ hours}}{1 \cancel{\text{year}}} \cdot \frac{1 \cancel{\text{year}}}{52 \text{ weeks}} = \frac{1{,}170 \text{ hours}}{52 \text{ weeks}}$$

$$= 22.5 \frac{\text{hours}}{\text{week}}$$

First convert to hours per week.

$$\frac{22.5 \cancel{\text{hours}}}{1 \text{ week}} \cdot \frac{60 \text{ minutes}}{1 \cancel{\text{hour}}} = \frac{(22.5 \cdot 60) \text{ minutes}}{1 \text{ week}}$$

$$= 1{,}350 \frac{\text{minutes}}{\text{week}}$$

Then convert to minutes per week.

You spend 1,350 minutes per week in school. You spend 1,680 minutes per week watching television. You spend more time watching television than in school.

Part 2

Example Using Several Unit Rates to Solve a Problem

Mrs. Lott and her husband want to find out how much water they use in their bathroom each day. Her husband takes a 5-minute shower each day, she takes 1 bath each day, and they flush the toilet a total of 6 times each day. How much water do the Lotts use per week in the bathroom?

Water Source	Water Use Rate
Bathtub	35 gallons per bath
Shower	2.2 gallons per minute
Toilet	1.5 gallons per flush

Solution

Find the amount of water used by each water source every week.

Bathtub: $$\frac{35 \text{ gallons}}{1 \text{ }\cancel{\text{bath}}} \cdot \frac{1 \text{ }\cancel{\text{bath}}}{1 \text{ }\cancel{\text{day}}} \cdot \frac{7 \text{ }\cancel{\text{days}}}{1 \text{ week}} = \frac{(35 \cdot 1 \cdot 7) \text{ gallons}}{(1 \cdot 1 \cdot 1) \text{ week}}$$
$$= \frac{245 \text{ gallons}}{1 \text{ week}}$$

Shower: $$\frac{2.2 \text{ gallons}}{1 \text{ }\cancel{\text{minute}}} \cdot \frac{5 \text{ }\cancel{\text{minutes}}}{1 \text{ }\cancel{\text{day}}} \cdot \frac{7 \text{ }\cancel{\text{days}}}{1 \text{ week}} = \frac{(2.2 \cdot 5 \cdot 7) \text{ gallons}}{(1 \cdot 1 \cdot 1) \text{ week}}$$
$$= \frac{77 \text{ gallons}}{1 \text{ week}}$$

Toilet: $$\frac{1.5 \text{ gallons}}{1 \text{ }\cancel{\text{flush}}} \cdot \frac{6 \text{ }\cancel{\text{flushes}}}{1 \text{ }\cancel{\text{day}}} \cdot \frac{7 \text{ }\cancel{\text{days}}}{1 \text{ week}} = \frac{(1.5 \cdot 6 \cdot 7) \text{ gallons}}{(1 \cdot 1 \cdot 1) \text{ week}}$$
$$= \frac{63 \text{ gallons}}{1 \text{ week}}$$

Then add the amounts of water used by each source to find the total amount used.

$$\frac{245 \text{ gallons}}{1 \text{ week}} + \frac{77 \text{ gallons}}{1 \text{ week}} + \frac{63 \text{ gallons}}{1 \text{ week}} = \frac{385 \text{ gallons}}{1 \text{ week}}$$

The Lotts now use 385 gallons of water per week.

Digital Resources    

1. Last June, you spent 40 hours at the beach. You also spent 1,260 minutes each week on summer reading. Did you spend more time at the beach or on summer reading last June?

A. You spent more time at the beach.

B. You spent the same amount of time on each activity.

C. You spent more time on summer reading.

2. Three rivers all flow into the same lake. What is the total amount of water they add to the lake each day?

River	Flow Rate
River A	30 gallons per second
River B	2,400 gallons per minute
River C	1,000,000 gallons per day

3. Whitney wants to estimate how much liquid she drinks each week. Each day, she has 4 glasses of juice. Each day, she has 2 glasses of milk with dinner. Whitney also drinks water throughout the day. How much liquid does Whitney drink in a week?

Drink	Amount
Juice	8 ounces per glass
Milk	6 ounces per glass
Water	63 ounces per day

4. The table shows apple prices.

Apples	Weight and Price
Bushel of Red Delicious	40 pounds for $45
Half-Bushel of Gala	20 pounds for $21
Peck of Granny Smith	10 pounds for $15

a. Explain how a customer could find which type of apple is the best buy.

b. Find the total cost if a customer wants to buy 2 bushels of Red Delicious, 3 half-bushels of Gala, and 2 pecks of Granny Smith.

5. You finish 2 homework problems in 15 minutes. Your friend finishes 4 homework problems in $\frac{1}{2}$ hour. Are you and your friend working at the same rate? Explain.

6. Brandon wants to keep track of his monthly spending. Last month, Brandon shopped, bought 3 meals, and saw 3 movies. He claims his spending totaled $99. Is Brandon's claim correct?

Activity	Cost
Meals	$11 per meal
Movies	$8 per movie
Shopping	$80 per month

A. Brandon's claim is correct.

B. Brandon's claim is incorrect. He did not multiply $11 per meal by 3 meals and $8 per movie by 3 movies.

C. Brandon's claim is incorrect. He did not multiply $8 per meal by 3 meals and $11 per movie by 3 movies.

D. Brandon's claim is incorrect. He did not divide $80 per month by 30 days in a month.

7. **Think About the Process** Suppose your home has 8 rugs and 2 bathrooms. You have to either vacuum the rugs or clean both bathrooms. You can vacuum at a rate of 0.15 hour per rug. You can clean at a rate of 45 minutes per bathroom. You want to do the chore that takes less time.

   a. How would you decide which chore to do?

   A. Compare the number of bathrooms to the number of rugs.

   B. Divide the number of rooms by the time per room and compare the times.

   C. Convert the time it takes to complete each chore to the same unit and compare the times.

   D. Convert the time it takes to complete each chore to the same unit and add the times.

   b. Which chore would you choose?

   A. You would choose to clean the bathrooms.

   B. You would choose to vacuum the rugs.

   C. You could choose either chore.

8. Beach A has 7,100 visitors per day. Beach B has 67,200 visitors every 2 weeks. Which beach has more visitors?

   A. Beach B has more visitors.

   B. Beach A has more visitors.

   C. Both beaches have the same number of visitors.

9. Describe a daily activity that takes you about 30 minutes. Think about other units of time you could use. Then write 30 minutes per day in minutes per week and hours per week.

10. A farmer wants to hire a farmhand for some year-round work. He wants to hire the worker who is able to work the most. Worker A is available for 20 hours per week. Worker B can work 1,300 hours for the year. Worker C can be at the farm 7 hours per day, 5 days a week. Which worker should the farmer choose?

    A. Worker B **B.** Worker C

    C. Worker A

11. **Think About the Process** A movie theater shows 13 movies per day. The theater also holds 7 midnight screenings per month. The manager wants to know the number of movies for the month of September. The first step is to multiply 13 movies per day by 30 days to get 390 movies. What is the second step?

    A. Add 13 to 390.

    B. Multiply 7 by 390.

    C. Multiply 13 by 7.

    D. Add 7 to 390.

12. **Challenge** Jon wants to find out how many calories he burns in a week by exercising. He swims 3 times per week, runs 3 miles per day, and bikes 4 hours per week. How many total calories does he burn per week by exercising?

Activity	Calories Burned
Swimming	180 calories per swim
Running	100 calories per mile
Biking	200 calories per hour

13. **Challenge** On a vacation, Miley spends 2 hours per day at the pool and 180 minutes per week kayaking. Miley gets 8 hours of sleep every night. If Miley is on vacation for 2 weeks, how much time is left over for other activities?

12-1 Plotting Ratios and Rates

CCSS: 6.RP.A.3a, 6.EE.C.9

Part 1

Example Using Tables to Graph Equivalent Ratios

A radio station plays 2 minutes of commercials for every 20 minutes of music. Use this information to complete the table and then graph the ratios.

Radio Station Airtime

Commercials (minutes)	Music (minutes)
2	20
4	
6	
8	
10	

Solution

First, find the ratio of minutes of music to minutes of commercials from the table.

From the first row of the table, you know that there are 20 minutes of music for 2 minutes of commercials.

$$\frac{\text{20 Minutes Music}}{\text{2 Minutes Commercials}}$$

Now find the unit rate. You can simplify this ratio to 10 minutes of music per minute of commercials.

$$\frac{\text{10 Minutes Music}}{\text{1 Minute Commercials}}$$

Use the unit rate to find the number of minutes of music for each row of the table. Using the results from the table, plot each ratio on the graph.

continued on next page >

Part 1

Solution continued

Radio Station Airtime

Commercials (minutes)	Music (minutes)
2	20
4	40
6	60
8	80
10	100

The unit rate is 10 minutes of music per minute of commercials.

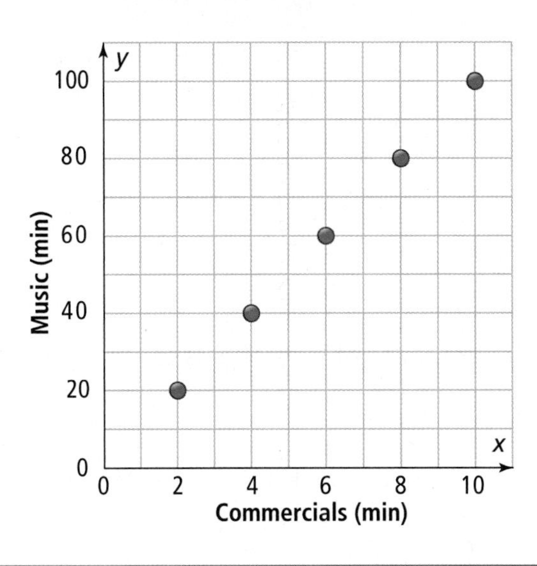

Key Concept

Ratios can be represented as points on a coordinate grid. Graphing all of the ratios equivalent to one ratio forms a straight line that passes through the origin. The line contains all of the ratios that are equivalent.

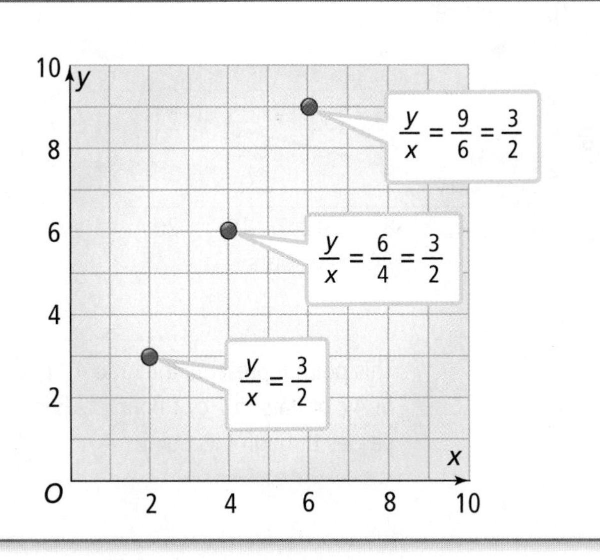

Part 2

Example Understanding Graphs of Rates

The graph shows the relationship between the number of cups of oats and the number of cups of flour in a recipe for oatmeal bars.

Decide if each statement is true or false.

a. One ratio of cups of oats to cups of flour is 8 : 2.

b. The point (16, 4) represents 16 cups of oats and 4 cups of flour.

c. To use 2 cups of oats, you need 8 cups of flour.

d. You need 4 cups of oats for every cup of flour.

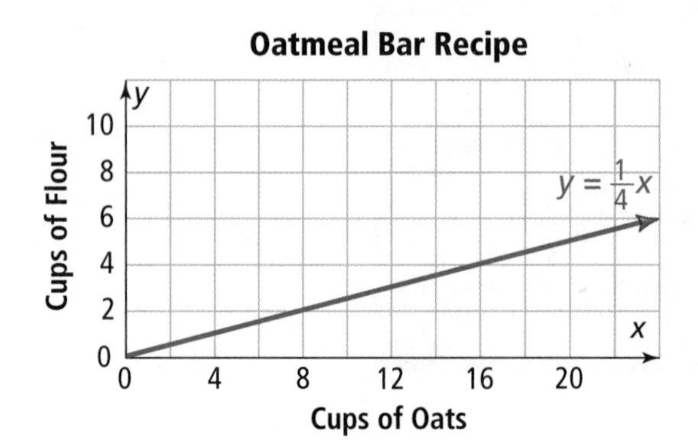

Solution

The true statements are a, b, and d.

The graph below represents all of the equivalent ratios of cups of oats to cups of flours in the oatmeal bars.

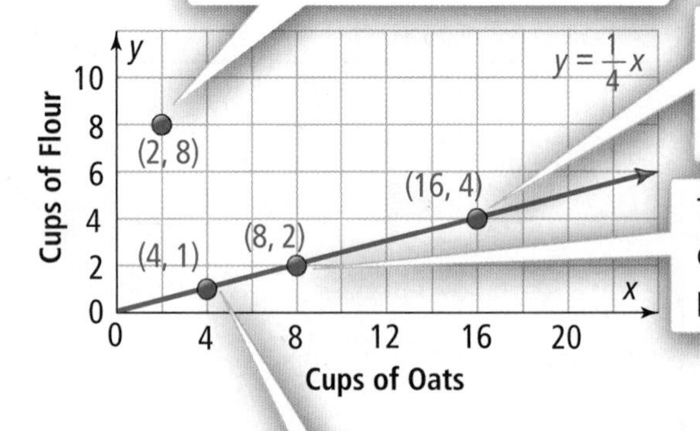

Part 3

Example Analyzing Equations Describing Rates

Your tour bus driver says the equation $y = \frac{1}{2}x$ describes the number of miles y the bus travels in x minutes. What is the constant speed of the bus? How does y change as x changes? Describe what the change means in this situation.

Solution

Start by graphing the equation. Use the table of values to graph.

Bus Travel

Minutes, x	Miles, y
2	1
10	5
20	10
40	20
60	30

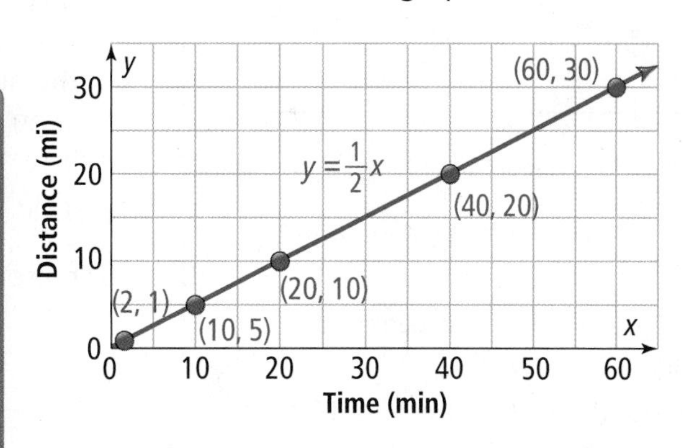

The constant speed of the bus is $\frac{30 \text{ miles}}{60 \text{ minutes}}$ or $\frac{30 \text{ miles}}{1 \text{ hour}}$.

As x increases by 2, y increases by 1. This means that every 2 minutes the bus travels 1 mile.

Digital Resources   

1. The graph shows the relationship between the number of cups of sugar and the number of cups of flour in a recipe. Decide which statements are true. Select all that apply.

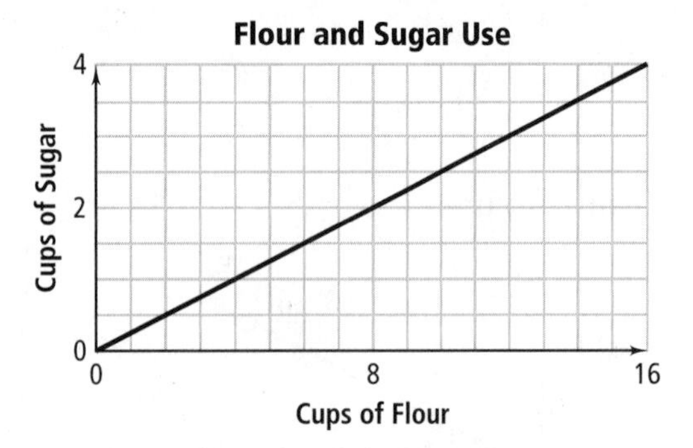

A. To use 2 cups of flour, you need 8 cups of sugar.

B. You need 0.25 cup of sugar for every cup of flour.

C. The point (16, 4) represents 16 cups of flour to 4 cups of sugar.

D. One ratio of cups of flour to cups of sugar is 8 : 2.

2. The equation $y = \frac{1}{5}x$ describes the number of calls y a salesperson makes in x minutes. How does y change as x changes, and which statement describes what the change means?

A. As x increases by 1, y increases by 5. This means that every 1 minute the salesperson makes 5 calls.

B. As x increases, by 5, y increases by 1. This means that every 5 minutes the salesperson makes 1 call.

C. As x increases by 5, y increases by 1. This means that every 1 minute the salesperson makes 5 calls.

D. As x increases by 1, y increases by 5. This means that every 5 minutes the salesperson makes 1 call.

3. Multiple Representations The equation $y = \frac{11}{6}x$ describes the number of miles y that a train travels in x minutes.

a. What is the constant speed of the train in miles per hour?

b. Express the speed in two other ways.

4. Reasoning The graph shows the relationship between the number of points a basketball team scores and the number of minutes the team has been playing. It shows a unit rate of 0.16 minute per point. Based on the graph, could another unit rate be 5.25 points per minute? Explain your reasoning.

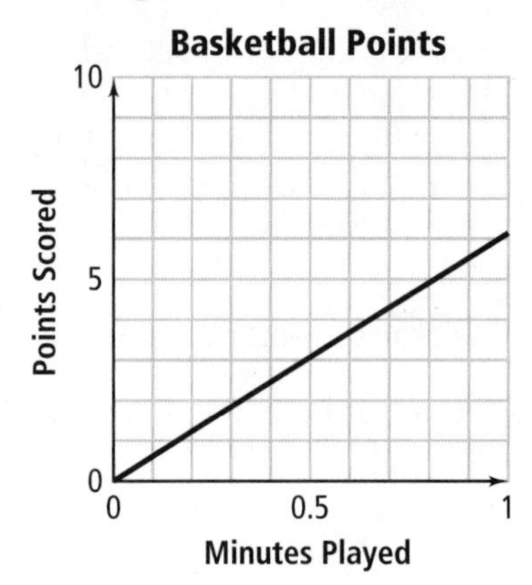

5. The equation $y = \frac{7}{12}x$ describes the number of miles y that a truck travels in x minutes. The constant speed of a car traveling on the same road is 40 miles per hour.

a. What is the constant speed of the truck in miles per hour?

b. Which vehicle is traveling faster?

See your complete lesson at MyMathUniverse.com

6. Think About the Process You spend $12.00 for every 3 pounds of pet food you buy. The first step in completing the table is to find the unit rate per pound.

a. What is the next step in completing the table?

A. Divide the numerator and denominator of the unit rate by 6.

B. Multiply the numerator and denominator of the unit rate by 6.

C. Subtract 6 from the numerator and denominator of the unit rate.

D. Add 6 to the numerator and denominator of the unit rate.

b. Complete the table.

Cost of Pet Food					
Pet Food (pounds)	3	6	9	12	15
Amount (dollars)	12	■	■	■	■

c. Choose the correct graph of the ratios below.

A.

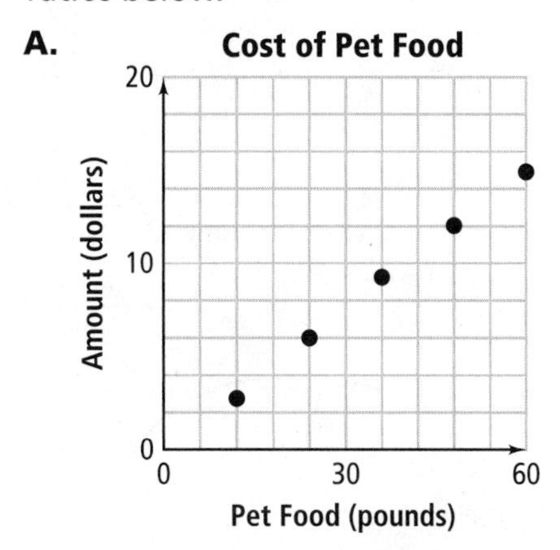

B.

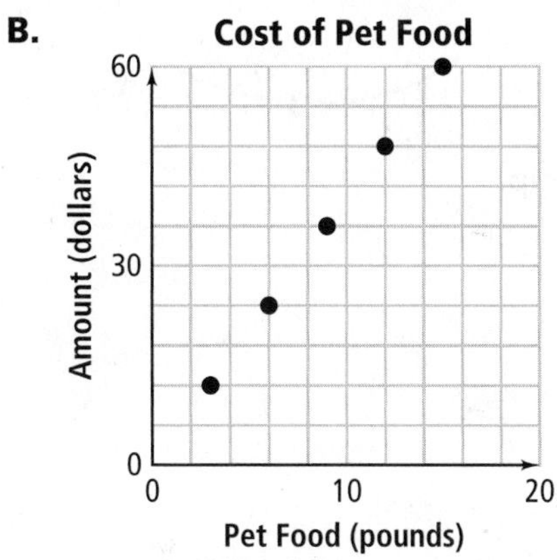

C.

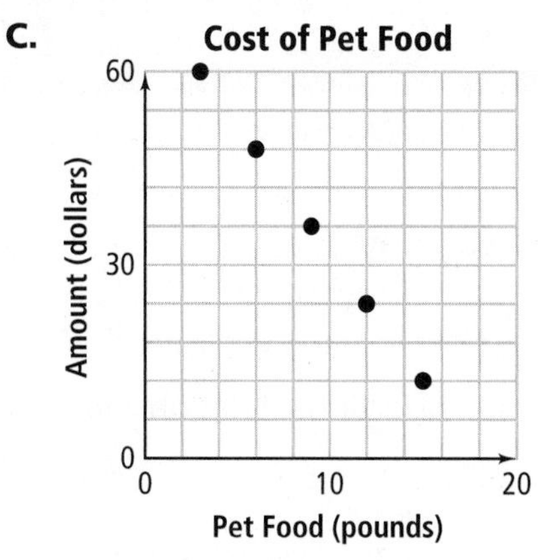

7. Think About the Process You buy 10 juice boxes for $5.20.

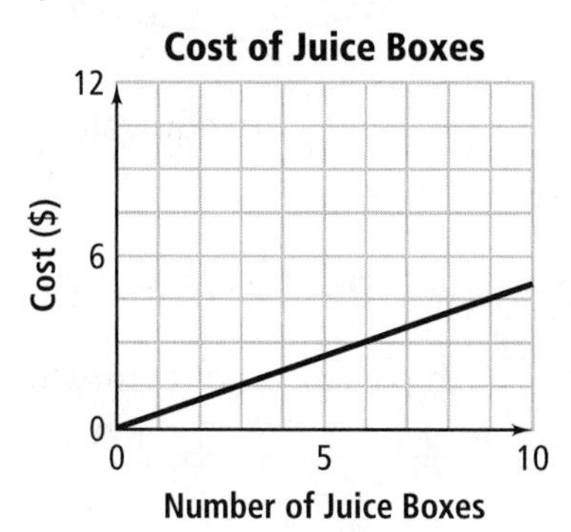

a. What step should you take to find the unit price using the graph?

A. Find the point (5.20, 10) on the graph.

B. Find the point on the graph that represents the ratio of the number of juice boxes to $1.

C. Find the point on the graph that represents the ratio of the number of dollars to one juice box.

D. Find the point (10, 5.20) on the graph.

b. What is the unit price?

A. $0.52 per juice box

B. 10 juice boxes per $1

C. $5.20 per juice box

D. $10 per juice box

E. 5.20 juice boxes per $1

F. 0.52 juice box per $1

12-2 Recognizing Proportionality

CCSS: 6.RP.A.2, 6.RP.A.3, 6.RP.A.3a

Part 1

Intro

A proportional relationship can be represented by equivalent ratios.

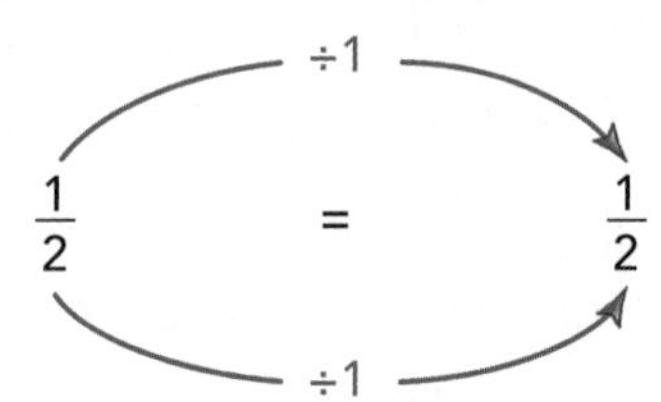

÷ 4

$\frac{4}{8}$ = $\frac{1}{2}$

÷ 4

The ratios $\frac{1}{2}$ and $\frac{4}{8}$ are equivalent. So, the ratios $\frac{1}{2}$ and $\frac{4}{8}$ form a proportional relationship.

Example Recognizing Proportional Relationships from Ratios

Does each pair of ratios form a proportional relationship?

a. $\frac{2}{8}, \frac{3}{12}$ **b.** $\frac{1}{3}, \frac{3}{9}$ **c.** $\frac{6}{15}, \frac{9}{18}$ **d.** $\frac{5}{20}, \frac{6}{24}$

Solution

Compare the simplest forms of each ratio.

a. $\frac{2}{8}, \frac{3}{12}$

Divide the numerator and denominator by 2.

÷ 2

$\frac{2}{8}$ = $\frac{1}{4}$

÷ 2

Divide the numerator and denominator by 3.

÷ 3

$\frac{3}{12}$ = $\frac{1}{4}$

÷ 3

Yes, $\frac{2}{8}$ and $\frac{3}{12}$ form a proportional relationship.

continued on next page >

Part 1

Solution continued

b. $\frac{1}{3}, \frac{3}{9}$

$\frac{1}{3}$ is in simplest form.

Divide the numerator and denominator by 3.

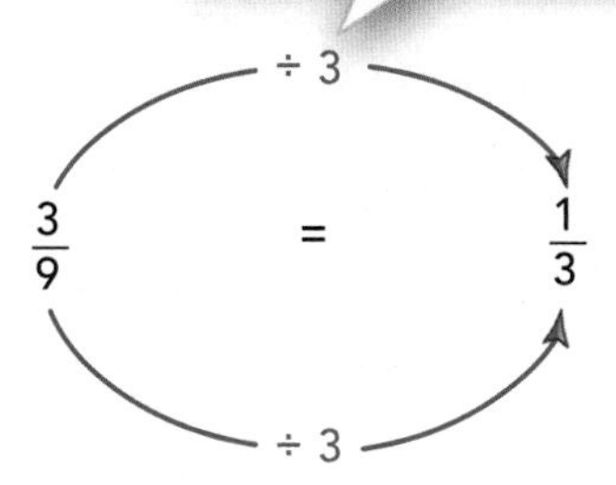

Yes, $\frac{1}{3}$ and $\frac{3}{9}$ form a proportional relationship.

c. $\frac{6}{15}, \frac{9}{18}$

Divide the numerator and denominator by 3.

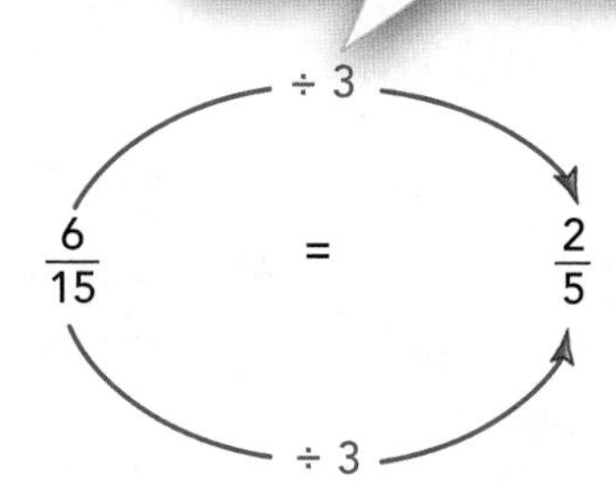

Divide the numerator and denominator by 9.

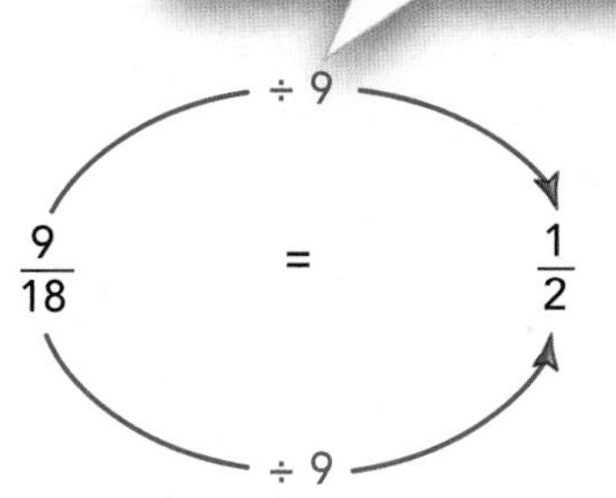

No, $\frac{6}{15}$ and $\frac{9}{18}$ do *not* form a proportional relationship.

d. $\frac{5}{20}, \frac{6}{24}$

Divide the numerator and denominator by 5.

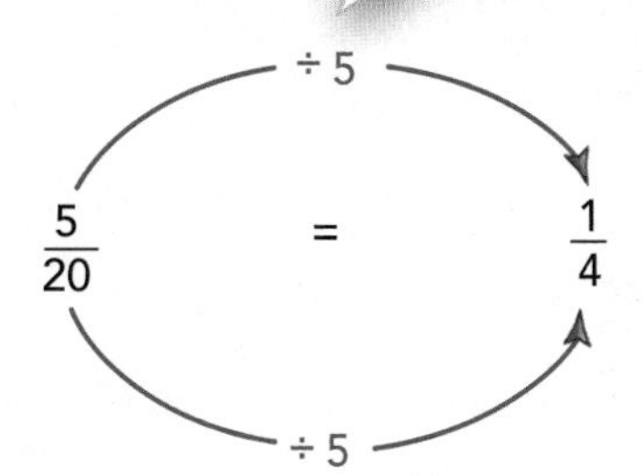

Divide the numerator and denominator by 6.

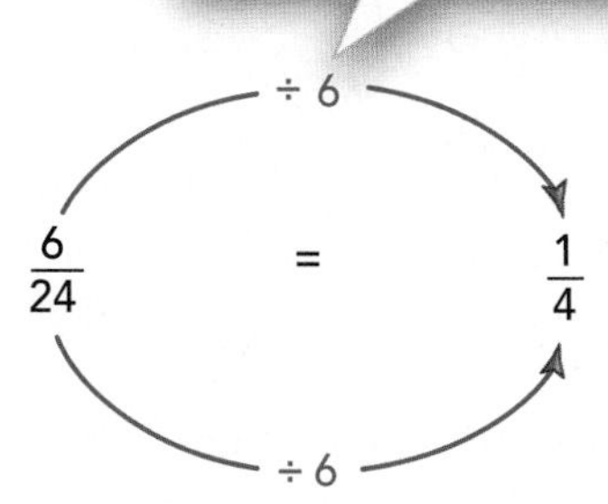

Yes, $\frac{5}{20}$ and $\frac{6}{24}$ form a proportional relationship.

Key Concept

Proportional relationships can be shown using tables, graphs, and equations.

A table shows a proportional relationship when the ratios between the entries in each row are equivalent.

The ratio $\frac{x}{y} = \frac{2}{1}$.

x	y
2	1
4	2
6	3
8	4

A graph shows all the points with a proportional relationship if it is a straight line that passes through the origin (0, 0). All of the points the line passes through are equivalent to the same ratio.

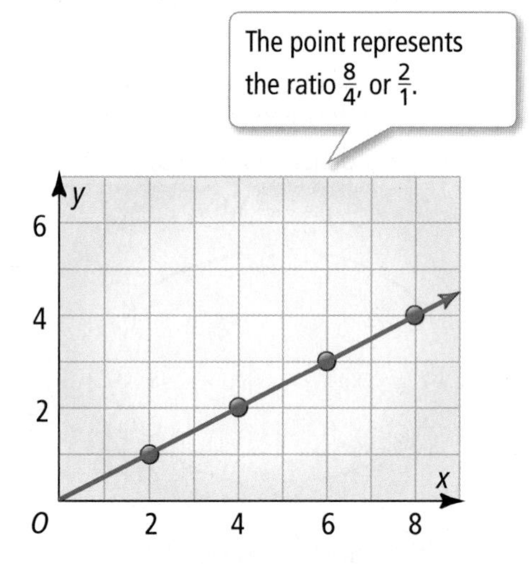

Equations in the form $y = mx$ represent proportional relationships. For example, the equation $y = \frac{1}{2}x$ represents all the x- and y-values related by the ratio $\frac{2}{1}$, or when y is half x.

The equation of the line is $y = \frac{1}{2}x$.

Part 2

Example Recognizing Proportional Relationships from Tables

Does each table show a proportional relationship? Explain.

a.

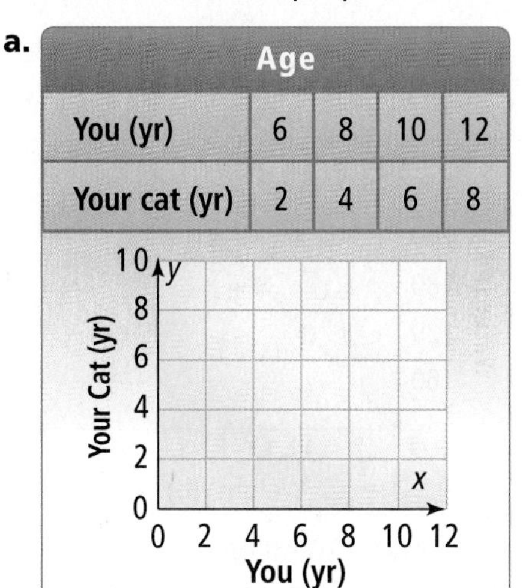

Age				
You (yr)	6	8	10	12
Your cat (yr)	2	4	6	8

b.

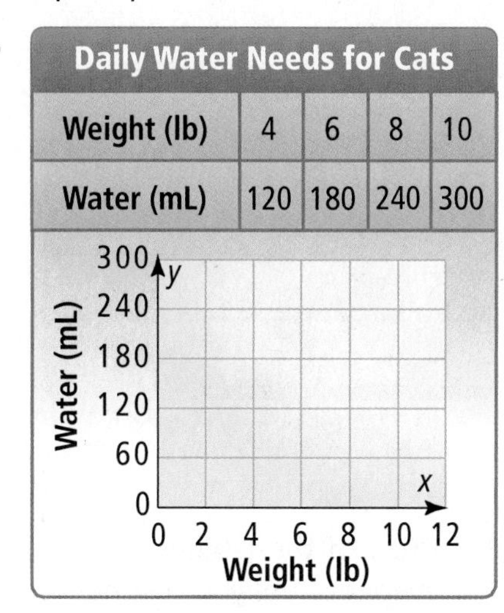

Daily Water Needs for Cats				
Weight (lb)	4	6	8	10
Water (mL)	120	180	240	300

Solution

a. No, there is not a proportional relationship between your age and your cat's age. The table does not show a proportional relationship.

Ages	
You (yr)	Your Cat (yr)
6	2
8	4
10	6
12	8

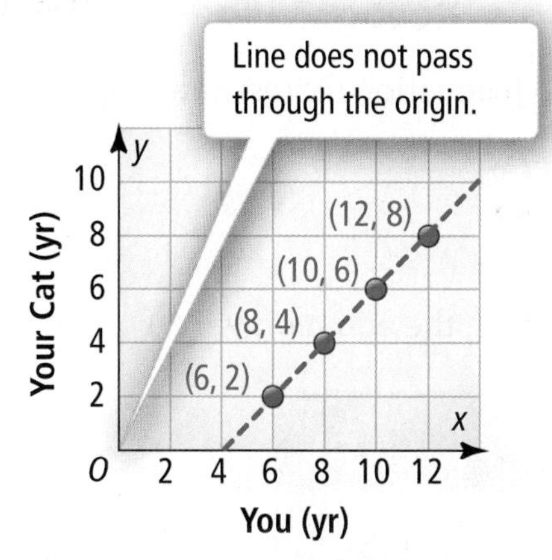

You are always 4 years older than your cat, so the ratio between your ages changes every year. A line drawn through the point is a straight line but does not pass through the origin.

continued on next page >

Part 2

Solution continued

b. Yes, there is a proportional relationship between your cat's daily water needs and your cat's weight. The table shows a proportional relationship.

Daily Water Needs for Cats

Weight (lb)	Water (mL)
4	120
6	180
8	240
10	300

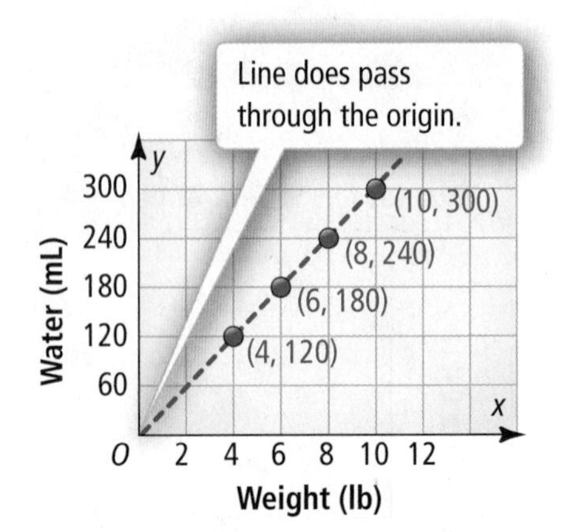

Each row of the table is equivalent to the unit rate 30 mL per pound. For every pound, your cat needs 30 mL of water. A line drawn through the points is a straight line that passes through the origin.

Part 3

Example Recognizing Proportional Relationships from Equations

Does each equation represent a proportional relationship? Explain.

a. $y = \frac{4}{3}x$

b. $y = \frac{4}{3}x + 3$

Solution

a. Graph the equation $y = \frac{4}{3}x$.

x	$y = \frac{4}{3}x$
3	4
6	8
9	12
12	16

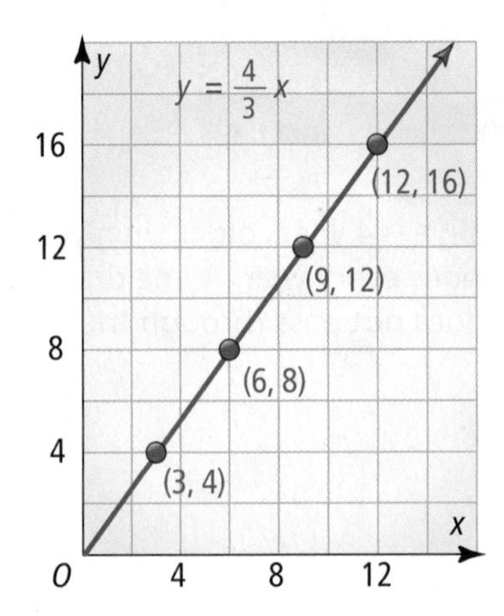

The graph is a straight line that passes through the point (0, 0). The equation is in the form $y = mx$. The equation represents a proportional relationship.

continued on next page >

Part 3

Solution continued

b. Graph the equation $y = \frac{4}{3}x + 3$.

x	$y = \frac{4}{3}x + 3$
3	7
6	11
9	15
12	19

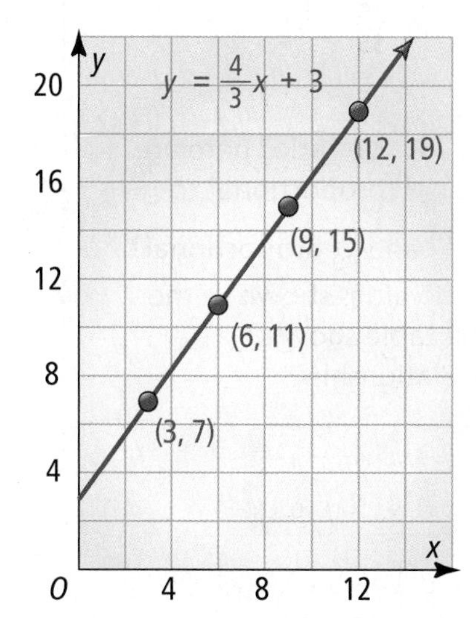

The graph is a straight line that does not pass through the point (0, 0). The equation is not in the form $y = mx$. The equation does not represent a proportional relationship.

Digital Resources   

1. Select all ratios that are proportional to $\frac{20}{50}$.

A. $\frac{16}{40}$ **B.** $\frac{25}{55}$

C. $\frac{5}{2}$ **D.** $\frac{8}{20}$

E. $\frac{100}{250}$ **F.** No ratios here are proportional to $\frac{20}{50}$.

2. Are the ratios $\frac{24}{42}$ and $\frac{40}{90}$ proportional?

3. Plot the pairs of values shown in the table. Does the table show a proportional relationship?

x	2	3	4	5
y	3	4	5	6

4. a. Writing Are the ratios $\frac{12}{9}$ and $\frac{20}{15}$ proportional? Explain your reasoning.

b. Describe a situation in which these ratios might come up. Explain why it would be important to know whether the ratios are proportional.

5. Mental Math

a. Are the ratios $\frac{50}{60}$ and $\frac{200}{240}$ proportional?

b. Explain how you were able to get the answer using mental math.

6. a. Reasoning There are different ways to tell whether an equation represents a proportional relationship. Is there one way that is always best? Explain your reasoning.

b. Which of the equations $y = 2x$ and $y = 2x + 15$, if either, represents a proportional relationship?

A. only $y = 2x + 15$

B. neither equation

C. both equations

D. only $y = 2x$

7. Error Analysis Mr. Greene gave his class a list of ratios. Then he asked which of the ratios, if any, are proportional to $\frac{4}{5}$. One of his students incorrectly said that only $\frac{8}{10}$ is proportional to $\frac{4}{5}$.

a. Which of the given ratios are proportional to $\frac{4}{5}$? Select all that apply.

A. $\frac{9}{10}$ **B.** $\frac{28}{35}$

C. $\frac{40}{50}$ **D.** $\frac{8}{10}$

E. $\frac{5}{4}$ **F.** $\frac{56}{55}$

G. none of these

b. What was the student's error?

A. The ratio $\frac{8}{10}$ is not the only ratio in the list that is proportional to $\frac{4}{5}$.

B. At lease one of the given ratios is proportional to $\frac{4}{5}$, but $\frac{8}{10}$ is not one of them.

C. None of the given ratios is proportional to $\frac{4}{5}$.

8. Fertilizer You can make liquid fertilizer by mixing powdered fertilizer with water. The amount of liquid fertilizer you make depends on the amount of powdered fertilizer you use. This is shown in the table. Plot the pairs of values shown in the table. Does the table show a proportional relationship?

Amounts of Fertilizer			
Powdered Fertilizer (teaspoons)	6	12	18
Liquid Fertilizer (gallons)	7	14	21

9. a. Mental Math Select all ratios that are proportional to $\frac{9}{10}$.

A. $\frac{90}{100}$ **B.** $\frac{20}{18}$

C. $\frac{180}{200}$ **D.** $\frac{45}{50}$

b. Explain how you were able to get the answer using mental math.

10. Plot the pairs of values shown in the tables. Which of the tables, if either, shows a proportional relationship?

Table I

x	1	2	5	6
y	8	10	16	18

Table II

x	2	3	4	5
y	7	10	13	16

A. Both tables

B. Neither table

C. Only table II

D. Only table I

11. a. Which of the equations $y = \frac{3}{4}x + 2$ and $y = \frac{3}{4}x$, if either, represents a proportional relationship?

A. neither equation

B. only $y = \frac{3}{4}x + 2$

C. both equations

D. only $y = \frac{3}{4}x$

b. If either equation represents a proportional relationship, write two proportional ratios represented by the equation.

12. Think About the Process The table shows how your dog's age and your age relate. You want to see if there is a proportional relationship between your age and your dog's age. You make a graph by plotting the pairs of values, using the x-axis for your dog's age. Is there a proportional relationship? Would this result be different if you used the x-axis for your age?

Ages				
Your Dog's Age	2	5	6	8
Your Age	8	11	12	14

A. No, there is not a proportional relationship. This result would not be different if you used the x-axis for your age.

B. Yes, there is a proportional relationship. This result would not be different if you used the x-axis for your age.

C. No, there is not a proportional relationship. This result would be different if you used the x-axis for your age.

D. Yes, there is a proportional relationship. This result would be different if you used the x-axis for your age.

13. Think About the Process

a. If an equation represents a proportional relationship, what must be true? Select all that apply.

A. In a table of values for the equation, the number pairs all suggest the same ratio.

B. The equation can be written in the form $y = mx + b$, where b is not 0.

C. The equation can be written in the form $y = kx$.

D. The graph of the equation is a line that passes through the origin, (0,0).

E. The graph of the equation is a line that passes through the point (1,1).

b. Does the equation $y = 6x$ represent a proportional relationship?

14. Challenge A girl is making bracelets and necklaces to sell at a yard sale. Each bracelet uses 3 red beads, 9 blue beads, and 21 white beads. Each necklace uses 4 red beads, 16 blue beads, and 20 white beads.

a. What is the ratio in simplest fraction form of the number of red beads to the total number of beads for the bracelets?

b. What is the ratio in simplest fraction form of the number of red beads to the total number of beads for the necklaces?

c. Are these ratios proportional? Explain your reasoning.

12-3 Introducing Percents

Vocabulary
percent

CCSS: 6.RP.A.3c

Key Concept

A percent is a ratio that compares a number to 100. The symbol for percent is %. You can write a percent as a fraction with a denominator of 100.

You can represent a percent using a grid.

45% of the squares are shaded.

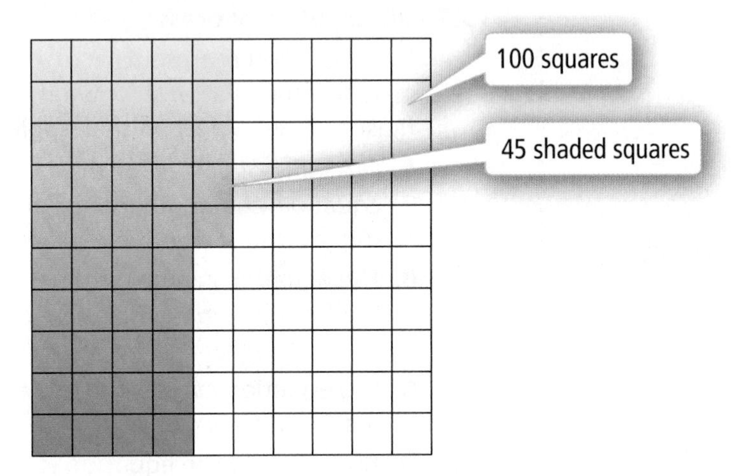

You can represent a percent using a fraction.

$\frac{45}{100} = 45\%$

You can represent a percent using words.

45 out of 100 equals 45%.

Part 1

Example Using Models of Percents

Complete each statement about the types of video games sold.

a. ■% of the games sold were sports games.

b. ■% more sports games than strategy games were sold.

c. ■% of the games sold were *not* racing games.

d. More ■ games were sold than any other type of game.

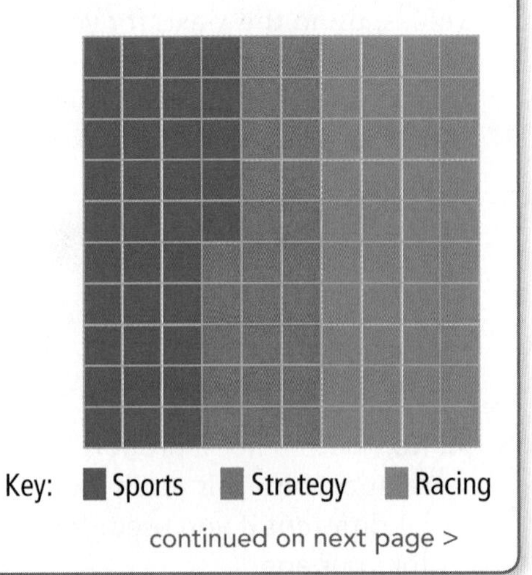

continued on next page >

Part 1

Example continued

Solution

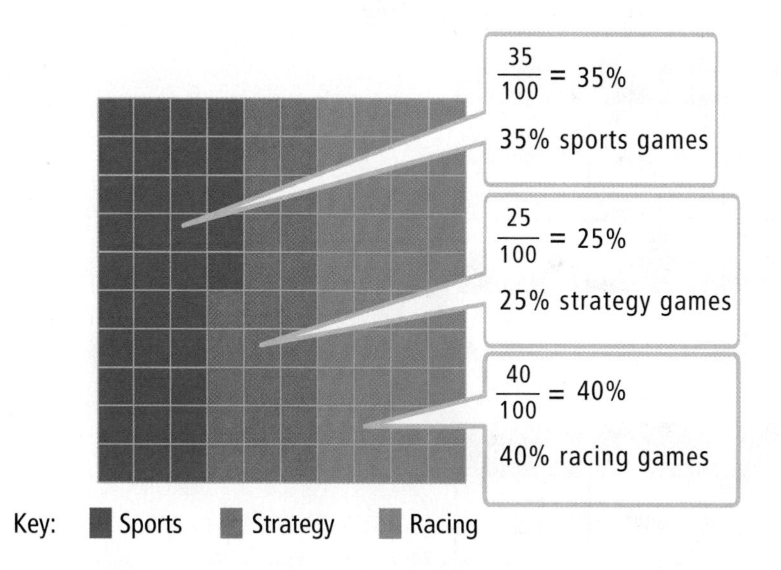

a. 35 of the 100 squares are purple, so 35% of the games sold are sports games.

b. Find the difference between sports games and strategy games. 35% of the games were sports games, 25% of the games were strategy games.

$$35\% - 25\% = \frac{35}{100} - \frac{25}{100} = \frac{10}{100} = 10\%$$

10% more sports games that strategy games were sold.

c. Find the percent of the games sold that were sports or strategy games.

sports games + strategy games

$$35\% + 25\% = \frac{35}{100} + \frac{25}{100} = \frac{60}{100} = 60\%$$

60% of the games sold were not racing games.

d. Order the percents from greatest to least.

$$40\% > 35\% > 25\%$$

The greatest percent is 40%, so more racing games were sold than any other type of game.

Part 2

Example Converting Between Ratios, Fractions, and Percents

Use the information given to complete the table.

	Ratio	Fraction	Percent
a.	1 : 2	$\frac{■}{100}$	■
b.	■ : 10	$\frac{10}{100}$	■
c.	■ : 10	$\frac{■}{100}$	70%

Solution

	Ratio	Fraction	Percent
a.	1 : 2	$\frac{50}{100}$	50%
b.	1 : 10	$\frac{10}{100}$	10%
c.	7 : 10	$\frac{70}{100}$	70%

a. Write the ratio 1 : 2 as a fraction.

$1 : 2 = \frac{1}{2}$

Find the ratio equivalent to $\frac{1}{2}$ with a denominator of 100.

$$\frac{1}{2} \underset{\times 50}{\overset{\times 50}{=}} \frac{50}{100}$$

Multiply the numerator and denominator by 50.

$\frac{50}{100} = 50\%$

b. Write the fraction $\frac{10}{100}$ as a ratio with a second term of 100.

$\frac{10}{100} = 10 : 100$

Find the equivalent ratio with a second term of 10.

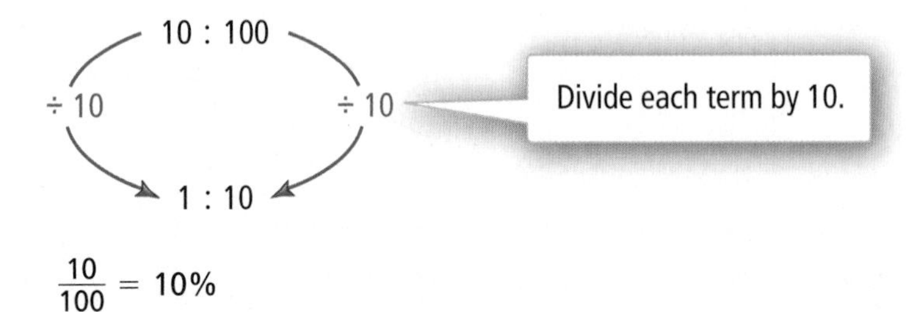

$\frac{10}{100} = 10\%$

continued on next page >

Part 2

Solution continued

c. Write the percent 70% as a fraction.

$70\% = \frac{70}{100}$

Write the fraction as a ratio with a second term of 100.

$\frac{70}{100} = 70 : 100$

Find the equivalent ratio with a second term of 10.

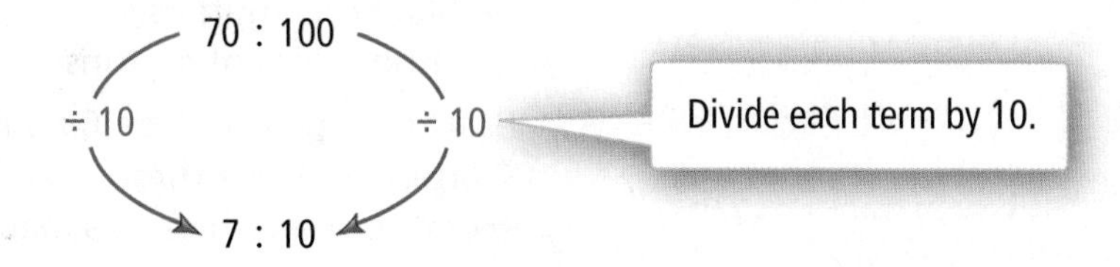

Part 3

Example Expressing Parts of a Whole as Percents

In your class, 2 out of every 5 students wear braces. What percent of the students in your class wear braces?

Solution

Write the ratio 2 out of 5 as a fraction with a denominator of 100.

$$\frac{2}{5} \overset{\times 20}{=} \frac{40}{100}$$

Multiply the numerator and denominator by 20.

$\frac{40}{100} = 40\%$

So, 40% of the students in your class wear braces.

1. A library tracks the percent of each type of book checked out. The grid shows the percents from last week. What percent of the books were fiction?

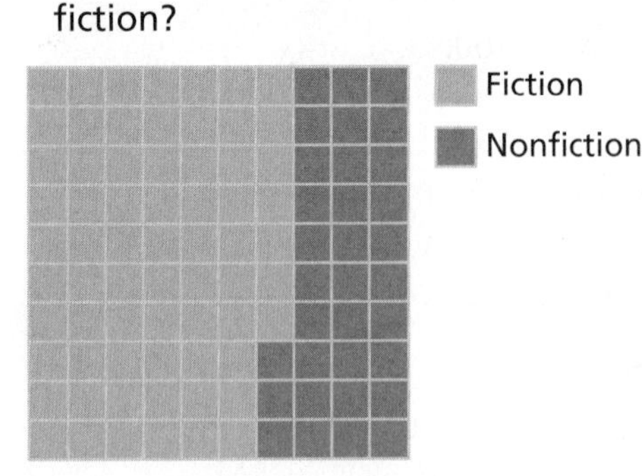

2. The workers at a local bakery track the types of muffins they sell. They find that 44% of the muffins are blueberry. Which 100-square grid models this percent?

A.

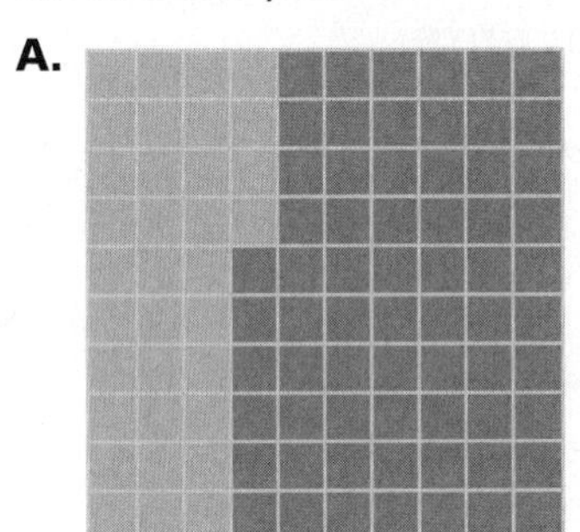

B.

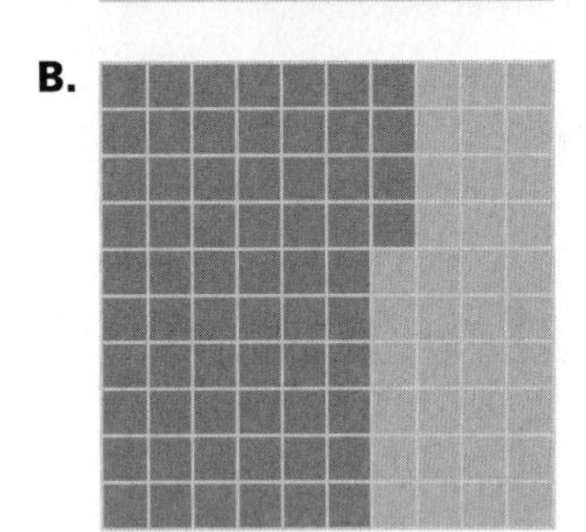

C.

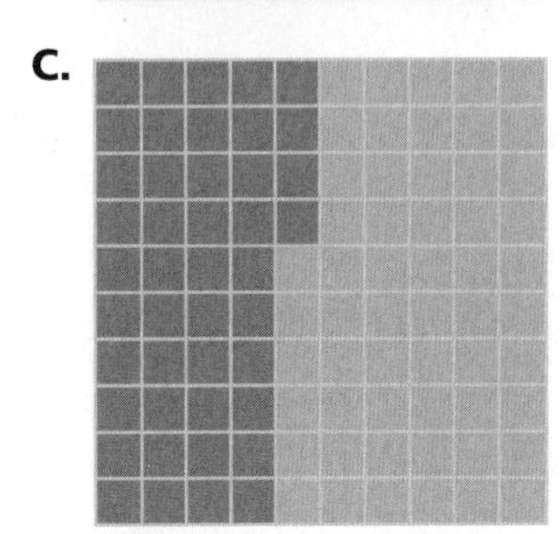

D.

■ Blueberry muffins
■ Other types of muffins

3. A basketball player made 63 out of 100 attempted free throws. What percent of free throws was made?

4. Your friend shows you a coin collection. In it, $\frac{45}{50}$ of the coins are quarters. What percent of the coins are quarters?

5. a. Reasoning Complete the table by writing each ratio as a fraction and as a percent.

Ratio	Fraction	Percent
4 : 20	$\frac{■}{100}$	■ %
25 : 50	$\frac{■}{100}$	■ %

b. Can you say that one of the two ratios is "greater" than the other? Explain your reasoning.

6. a. Error Analysis Ryder writes $\frac{11}{20}$ as the ratio 11 : 20. He incorrectly finds the equivalent percent to be 11%. What percent is equivalent to $\frac{11}{20}$?

b. What is Ryder's error?

A. He did not write $\frac{11}{20}$ as an equivalent fraction with denominator 100.

B. He wrote $\frac{11}{20}$ as an equivalent fraction with denominator 1,000.

C. He did not write $\frac{20}{11}$ as an equivalent fraction with denominator 100.

D. He wrote $\frac{20}{11}$ as an equivalent fraction with denominator 1,000.

7. **Estimation** A movie studio took a poll after showings of a new movie. The studio found that 4 out of every 21 people did not like the movie. About what percentage of the people did not like the movie?

8. According to a survey of workers, $\frac{2}{20}$ of them walk to work, $\frac{1}{20}$ bike, $\frac{4}{20}$ carpool, and $\frac{13}{20}$ drive alone. What percent of workers walk or bike to work?

9. Complete the table by writing the fraction as a ratio and as a percent.

Ratio	Fraction	Percent
■ : 60	$\frac{90}{300}$	■ %

10. **Forestry** In a forest, $\frac{4}{25}$ of the trees are oak trees and $\frac{51}{100}$ are pine trees.
    a. Write these fractions as percents.
    b. Can you tell which type of tree there is more of in the forest? Explain your answer.

11. In a group of bird-watchers, 7 out of every 10 people have seen a bald eagle. What percent of the bird-watchers have not seen a bald eagle?

12. **Think About the Process** You want to write an equivalent ratio and an equivalent percent for $\frac{20}{25}$. How should you write the percent?
    A. Divide the numerator and the denominator of the fraction by 5 to write the fraction in simplest form. Use the new numerator as the percent.
    B. Divide the numerator and the denominator of the fraction by 5 to write the fraction in simplest form. Use the new denominator as the percent.
    C. Multiply the numerator and the denominator of the fraction by 4 to write an equivalent fraction with denominator 100. Use the new numerator as the percent.
    D. Multiply the numerator and the denominator of the fraction by 2 to write an equivalent fraction with denominator 100. Use the new denominator as the percent.

13. **Think About the Process** For every 20 items sold at a farm stand, 12 items are potatoes and 3 items are pumpkins. A worker uses this information to find that 15% of the items sold are pumpkins. What could the worker do next to find the percent of items sold that are not potatoes or pumpkins? Select all that apply.
    A. Find the percent of items sold that are potatoes.
    B. Add 15% to 100% to find the percent of items sold that are not potatoes.
    C. Subtract 3 from 12 to find the number of items that are not potatoes or pumpkins.
    D. Subtract 15% from 100% to find the percent of items sold that are not pumpkins.
    E. Find the percent of items sold that are pumpkins.
    F. Add 12 and 3 to find the number of items that are potatoes or pumpkins.

12-4 Using Percents

Vocabulary
circle graph

CCSS: 6.RP.A.3c

Key Concept

A percent can always be used to compare a part to a whole. In a percent, the whole is always 100.

First, find a part.

What is 85% of 20?

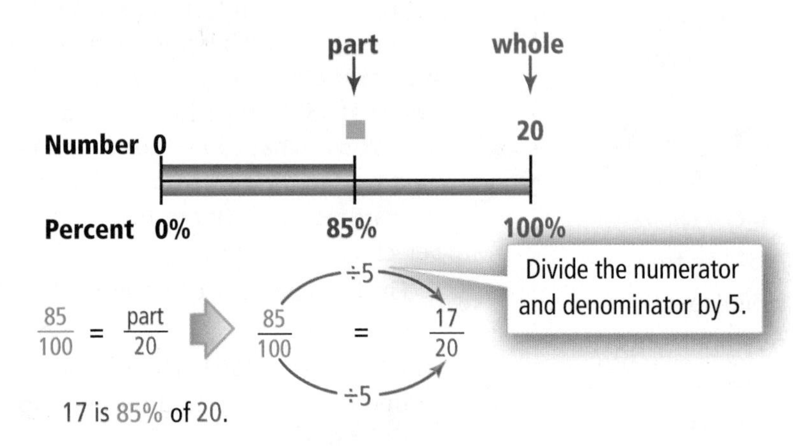

Find a whole.

17 is 85% of what number?

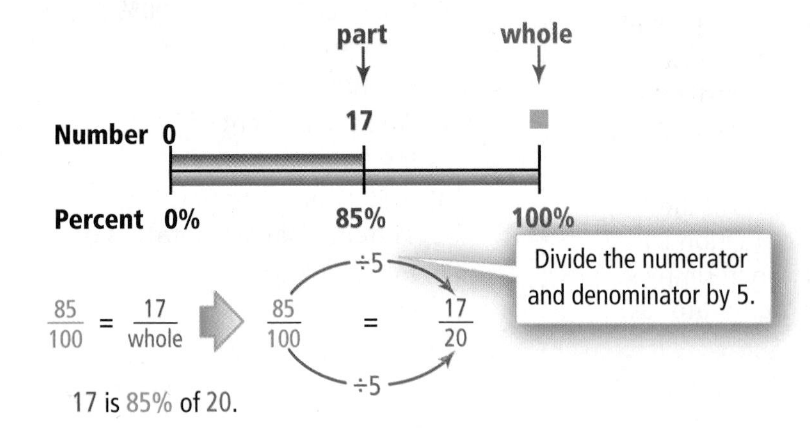

Part 1

Example Finding a Part from Percents

Complete each statement with the value that makes each statement true.

a. ■ is 30% of 50. **b.** ■ is 80% of 25.

c. ■ is 15% of 200. **d.** ■ is 200% of 20.

Solution

a. You can write 30% as $\frac{30}{100}$. This means 30% of 100 is 30. To find 30% of 50, find the ratio equivalent to $\frac{30}{100}$ with a denominator of 50.

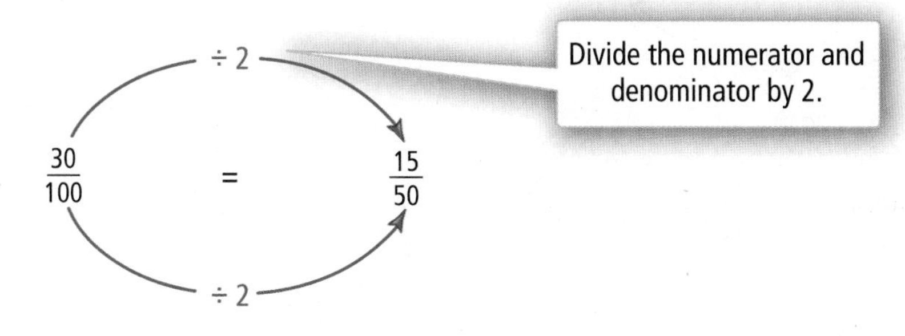

So 15 is 30% of 50.

b. You can write 80% as $\frac{80}{100}$. This means 80% of 100 is 80. To find 80% of 25, find the ratio equivalent to $\frac{80}{100}$ with a denominator of 25.

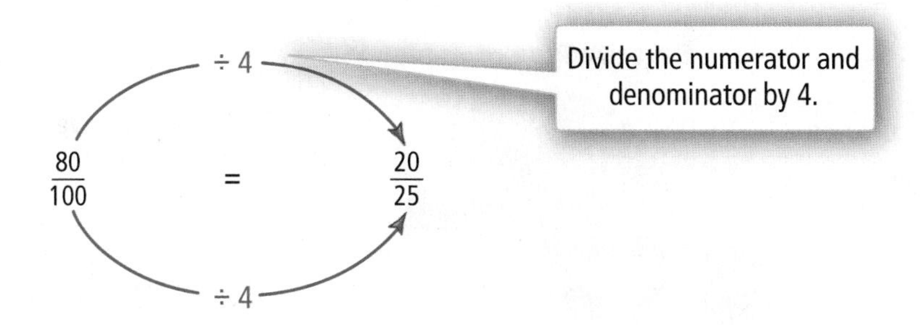

So 20 is 80% of 25.

c. You can write 15% as $\frac{15}{100}$. This means 15% of 100 is 15. To find 15% of 200, find the ratio equivalent to $\frac{15}{100}$ with a denominator of 200.

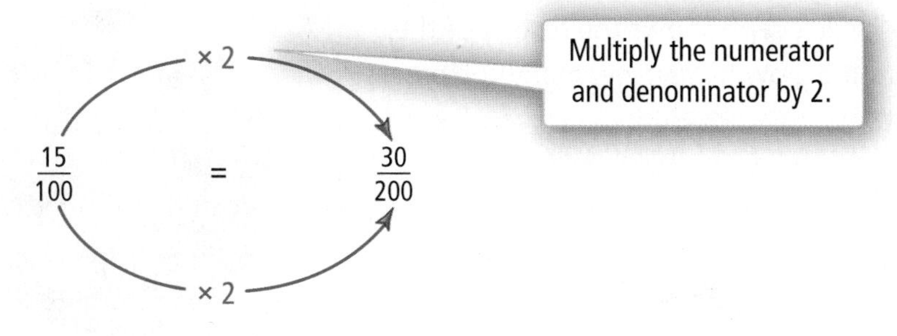

So 30 is 15% of 200.

continued on next page >

Part 1

Solution continued

d. You can write 200% as $\frac{200}{100}$. This means 200% of 100 is 200. To find 200% of 20, find the ratio equivalent to $\frac{200}{100}$ with a denominator of 20.

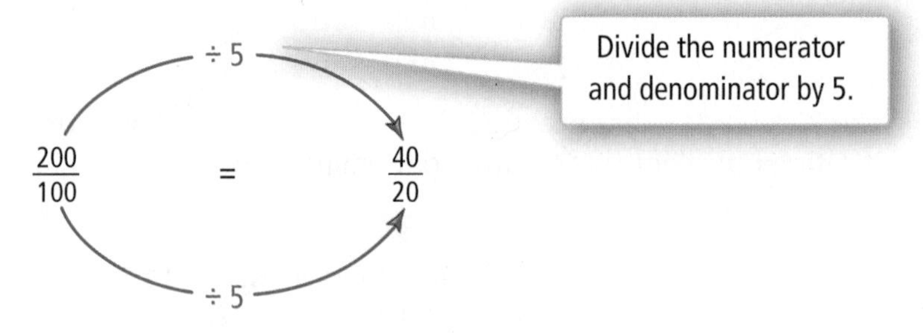

So 40 is 20% of 200.

Part 2

Intro

One way you can display the results of a survey is in a circle graph. A circle graph is a graph that represents a total divided into parts. Each slice of the circle represents part of the whole. In a circle graph, the percents will sum to 100%.

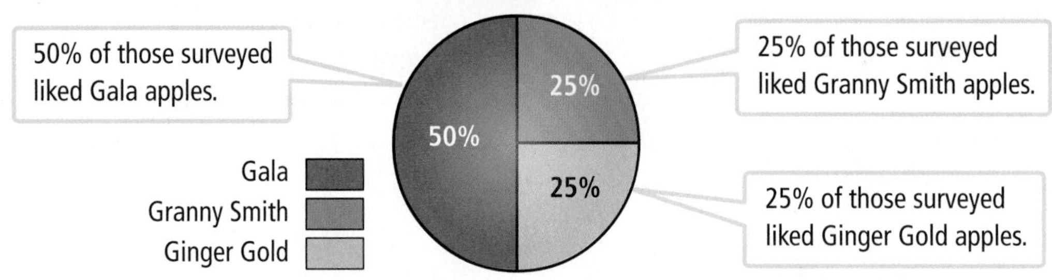

Example Finding the Whole from Circle Graphs

Customers in a pet store were asked what type of pet they own. The circle graph shows the results of the survey. If 8 customers own cats, how many customers were surveyed?

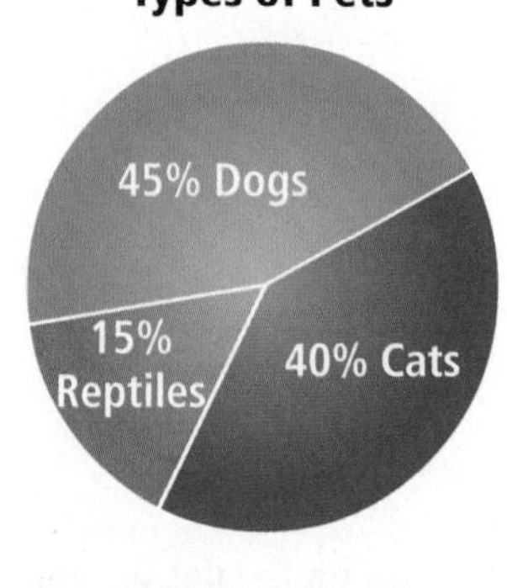

continued on next page >

Part 2

Example continued

Solution

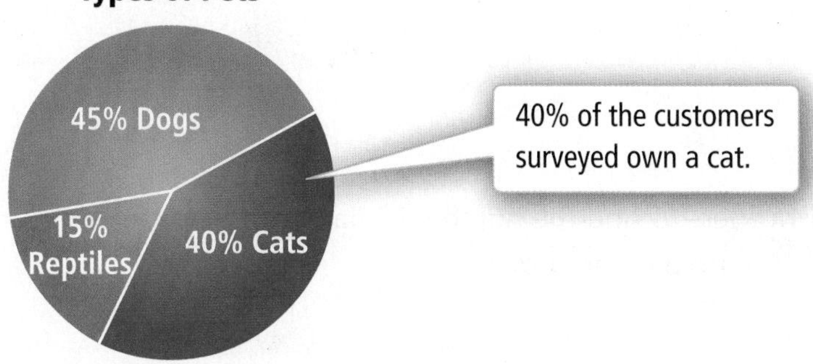

You can write 40% as $\frac{40}{100}$. This means that if 100 customers were surveyed, 40 own a cat.

You know only 8 customers own a cat. Find the ratio equivalent to $\frac{40}{100}$ with a numerator of 8.

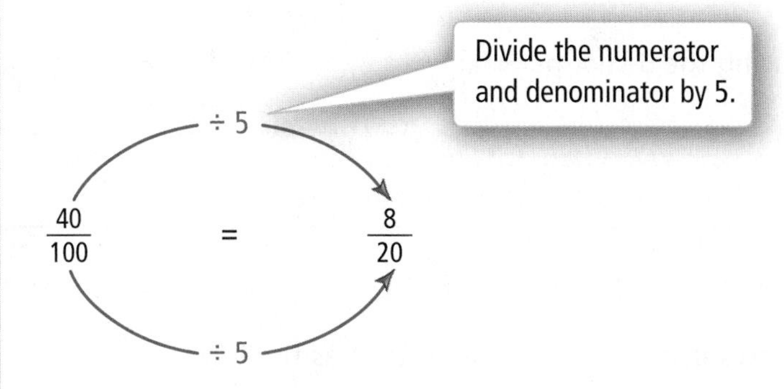

8 out of 20 is equal to 40%. So, 20 customers were surveyed.

Part 3

Example Finding the Whole from Percents

During a 5-year period, 55% of the named storms became hurricanes. If during the 5-year period there were 22 hurricanes, how many named storms were there?

Solution

You can write 55% as $\frac{55}{100}$.

You know there were 22 hurricanes. To find the number of named storms, find the ratio equivalent to $\frac{55}{100}$ with a numerator of 22.

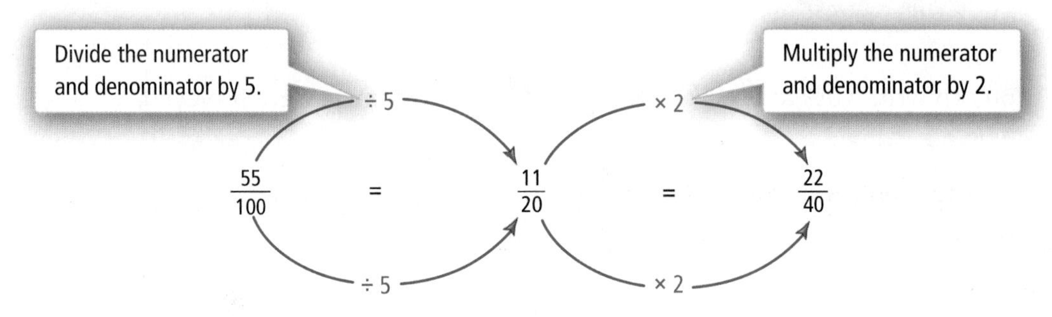

There were 40 named storms during the 5-year period.

Part 4

Intro

You have used equivalent ratios to solve percent problems such as finding what number is 22% of 150.

You can also use an equation to solve this type of problem.

Words Part = Percent of Whole

to

Equation

Let x = the part.

$x = 22\% \cdot 150$

The word "of" tells you to multiply.

$$x = 22\% \cdot 150$$
$$= \frac{22}{100} \cdot 150$$
$$= \frac{3{,}300}{100}$$
$$= 33$$

Part 4

Example Solving Percent Problems with Equations

What number is 24% of 75?

Solution

Words Part = Percent of Whole

to Let x = the part.

Equation $x = 24\% \cdot 75$

Now solve the equation.

Write the equation.	$x = 24\% \cdot 75$
Write 24% as a fraction.	$= \frac{24}{100} \cdot 75$
Simplify.	$= \frac{1{,}800}{100}$
Divide.	$= 18$

So 18 is 24% of 75.

1. What is 20% of 25?
2. On a local sports team, 20% of 50 players are left-handed. How many left-handed players are there?
3. 90% of what number is 45?
4. **Mental Math** Find 15% of 400.
5. 34% of what number is 153?
6. A restaurant wants to study how well its salads sell. The circle graph shows the sales over the past few days. If 5 of the salads sold were Caesar salads, how many total salads did the restaurant sell?

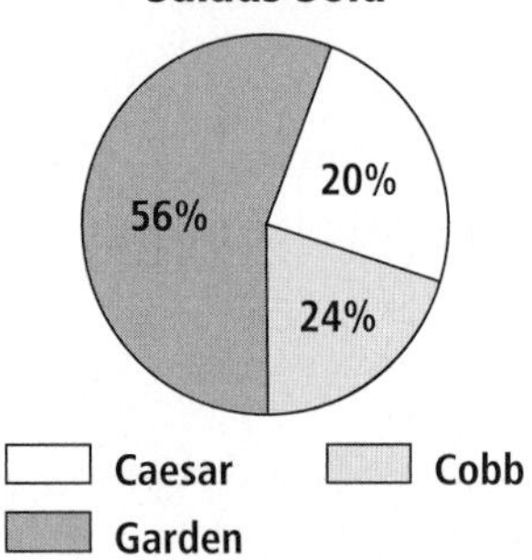

7. 44% of what number is 33?
8. At a school, 122 students play at least one sport. This is 40% of the students at the school. How many students are at the school?
9. **Writing** A school wants to add a new sports team. The school sent out surveys asking for the students' favorite sport. Nineteen students named lacrosse. Others named volleyball or swimming. Explain how to use the circle graph and ratios to find the number of students surveyed. Then find this number.

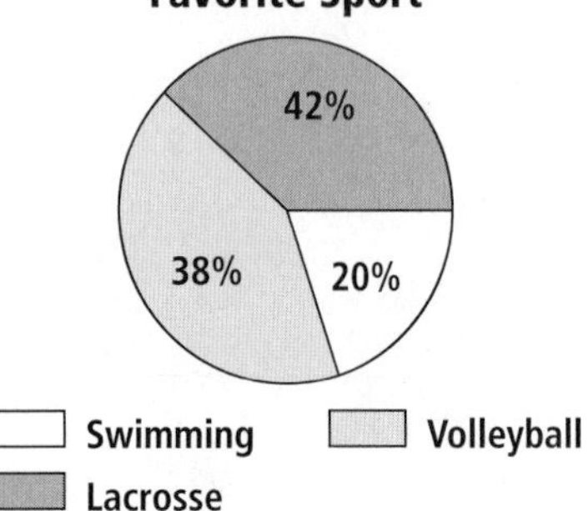

10. **Reasoning** You know that 26% of a number, x, is 39. You also know that 53% of a number, y, is 91.
    a. What are the values of x and y?
    b. Which number is greater?
    c. Explain how you can find whether x or y is greater without finding their values.
11. **Error Analysis** Krysti is ordering T-shirts for 20 classmates. She knows that 75% of the classmates want the small size. In her order, Krysti mistakenly asked for 25 small shirts.
    a. How may small T-shirts should she have ordered?
    b. What was Krysti's error?
       A. Krysti multiplied the numerator of the percent ratio by 3 instead of 5.
       B. Krysti divided the numerator of the percent ratio by 3 instead of 5.
       C. Krysti divided the numerator of the percent ratio by 5 instead of 3.
       D. Krysti multiplied the numerator of the percent ratio by 5 instead of 3.
12. **Think About the Process** You want to find 20% of 25. You know to write 20% as the ratio $\frac{20}{100}$.
    a. How could you find an equivalent ratio with denominator 25?
       A. Divide the numerator and denominator by 4.
       B. Multiply the numerator and denominator by 2.
       C. Divide the numerator and denominator by 2.
       D. Multiply the numerator and denominator by 4.
    b. What is 20% of 25?

See your complete lesson at MyMathUniverse.com

13. Think About the Process Your teacher asks, "45% of what number is 9?" You know to write 45% as the ratio $\frac{45}{100}$.

a. How could you find an equivalent ratio with numerator 9?

A. Multiply the numerator and denominator by 9.

B. Multiply the numerator and denominator by 5.

C. Divide the numerator and denominator by 9.

D. Divide the numerator and denominator by 5.

b. 45% of what number is 9?

14. Snowstorms During a 5-year period, 56% of snowstorms in a certain city caused power outages. Thirty-three of the snowstorms did not cause power outages. Find the total number of snowstorms in this city over the 5-year period.

15. Estimation Connor and Maria are doing yard work for a neighbor. They make a total of $404.88. Since Maria works more hours than Connor, Maria gets 59% of the money. About how much (in whole dollars) does Maria make?

16. Mental Math Zach invests $5 in the stock market at the beginning of the week. He decides to invest an additional $15 at the end of the week. He loses 50% of his total investment. How much money does Zach lose?

17. At one store, Matt saved $20 with a coupon for 80% off his total purchase. At another store, the $28 he spent on books is 56% of his total bill. How much did Matt spend in all at the two stores?

18. Challenge An office is ordering pizza for two groups. Of the 25 workers in Accounting, 72% want pepperoni. The others in Accounting want eggplant. Of the 50 people in Sales, 52% want eggplant. The others in Sales want pepperoni. In all, how many workers want eggplant pizza?

19. Challenge A school is planning a field trip to a theme park. A ticket to the park costs $21. For a group of 50 or more, there is a 12% discount. The school saved $819 with the discount. How many tickets did the school buy?

12-5 Problem Solving

CCSS: 6.RP.A.3, 6.RP.A.3c

Part 1

Example Writing Ratios in Simplest Form

Your teacher's web browser has 50 bookmarks. What is the ratio of school bookmarks to sports bookmarks in simplest form?

Bookmarks

Category	Quantity	Percent
School	■	■
News	■	20
Games	5	■
Sports	■	4
Cooking	3	■

Solution

Complete the table to find the ratio of the number of school bookmarks to the number of sports bookmarks.

The percents need to sum to 100.

Bookmarks

Category	Quantity	Percent
School	30	60
News	10	20
Games	5	10
Sports	2	4
Cooking	3	6

Find the percent of bookmarks that are games:

5 of the 50 bookmarks are games.

$$\frac{5}{50} = \frac{10}{100} = 10\%$$

10% of the bookmarks are game bookmarks.

Find the percent of bookmarks that are cooking:

Of the 50 bookmarks, 3 are cooking.

$$\frac{3}{50} = \frac{6}{100} = 6\%$$

6% of the bookmarks are cooking bookmarks.

continued on next page >

Part 1

Solution continued

School bookmarks make up the rest of the bookmarks.

$$20\% + 10\% + 4\% + 6\% = 40\%$$

$100\% - 40\% = 60\%$ of the 50 bookmarks are school.

$$60\% = \frac{60}{100} = \frac{30}{50}$$

30 of the bookmarks are school bookmarks.

Find the number of news bookmarks:

Of the 50 bookmarks, 20% are news.

$$20\% = \frac{20}{100} = \frac{10}{50}$$

10 of the bookmarks are news bookmarks.

Find the number of bookmarks that are sports:

Of the 50 bookmarks, 4% are sports.

$$4\% = \frac{4}{100} = \frac{2}{50}$$

2 of the bookmarks are sports bookmarks.

Find the ratio of school bookmarks to sports bookmarks.

$$30 : 2 = 15 : 1$$

The ratio of school bookmarks to sports bookmarks is 15 : 1.

Part 2

Example Using Ratios and Percents to Solve Problems

An artist is mixing paint for a mural.

a. The artist mixes 3 gallons of yellow paint and 2 gallons of blue paint to have a certain shade of green paint. How many gallons of yellow paint and blue paint does the artist need to make 20 gallons of the green paint?

b. The artist also wants 40 gallons of a green paint that is 15% blue paint. How many gallons of yellow paint does the artist need?

continued on next page >

Part 2

Example continued

Solution

a. 3 gallons + 2 gallons = 5 gallons

The artist mixed 5 gallons of green paint to start. The artist needs 20 gallons of green paint, or four times as much as she currently has. So, the artist needs four times as much yellow paint and four times as much blue paint.

Find the ratio of yellow paint to blue paint.

$$\frac{\text{yellow paint}}{\text{blue paint}} = \frac{3}{2}$$

Next find an equivalent ratio by multiplying both the numerator and denominator by 4.

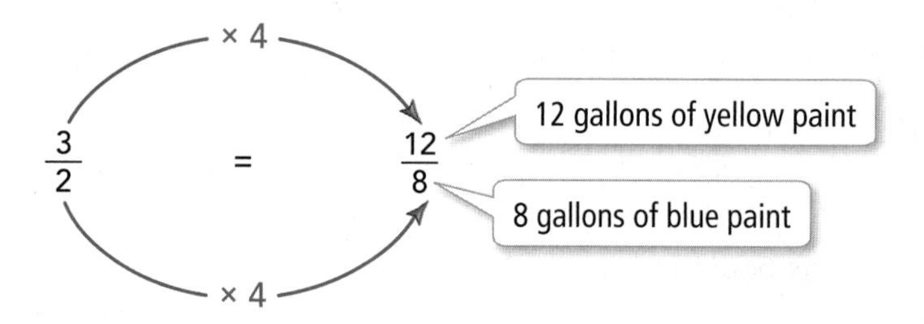

The artist needs 12 gallons of yellow paint and 8 gallons of blue paint to make 20 gallons of green paint.

b. If the green paint is 15% blue paint, then it is 85% yellow paint. Find the ratio equivalent to $\frac{85}{100}$ with a denominator of 40.

First divide the numerator and denominator by 5, then multiply the numerator and denominator by 2.

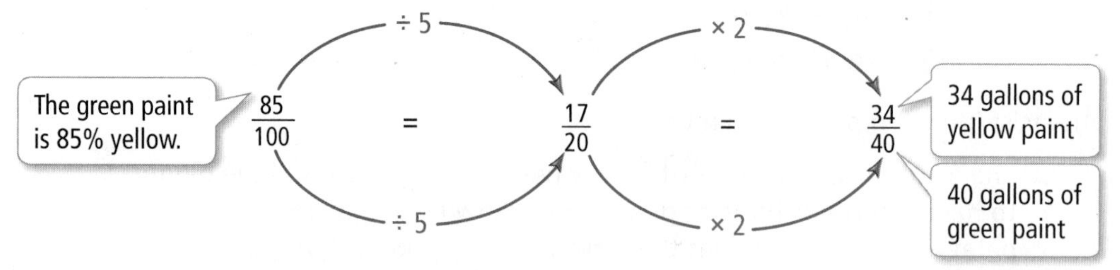

To have 40 gallons of a green paint that is 15% blue, the artist needs 34 gallons of yellow paint.

Digital Resources    

1. Last Monday, a parking lot had 80 cars. Of those 80 cars, 35% were blue, 24 were black, and the rest were tan. What percent of the cars were tan?

2. In a bookcase, there are 6 fiction books for every 7 nonfiction books. There are 39 books in the bookcase. How many fiction books are in the bookcase?

3. **Think About the Process** In a certain part of a city, the ratio of the number of men to the number of women is 11 to 9. A total of 80 men and women live there. You want to find the number of men.

   a. Which of these ratios is likely the best to use?

   A. The ratio of the number of men to the number of women

   B. The ratio of the number of men to the number of men and women

   C. The ratio of the number of women to the number of men and women

   b. How many men are there?

4. A newspaper article said that the paper had 340 stories about three sports last year. The article included this circle graph. A reader incorrectly said that the ratio of baseball stories to soccer stories is 119 : 85.

Sports Stories

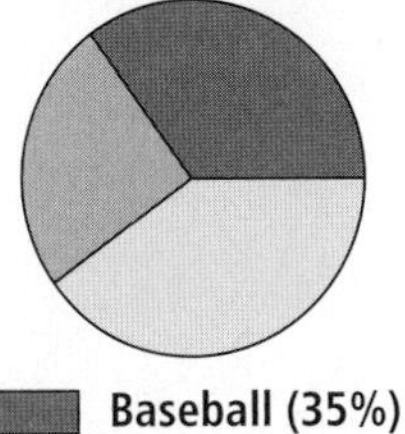

Baseball (35%)
Football (25%)
Soccer

   a. What is the correct ratio?

   A. 136 : 340 **B.** 119 : 340
   C. 85 : 136 **D.** 340 : 136
   E. 119 : 136 **F.** 136 : 119

   b. What was the reader's error?

   A. The reader found the ratio of football stories to soccer stories.

   B. The reader found the ratio of soccer stories to baseball stories.

   C. The reader found the ratio of baseball stories to football stories.

5. **Think About the Process** There are 180 cars in a parking lot. Each car is blue, red, or green. The cars are described by the circle graph. You want to find the number of green cars.

Cars in Parking Lot

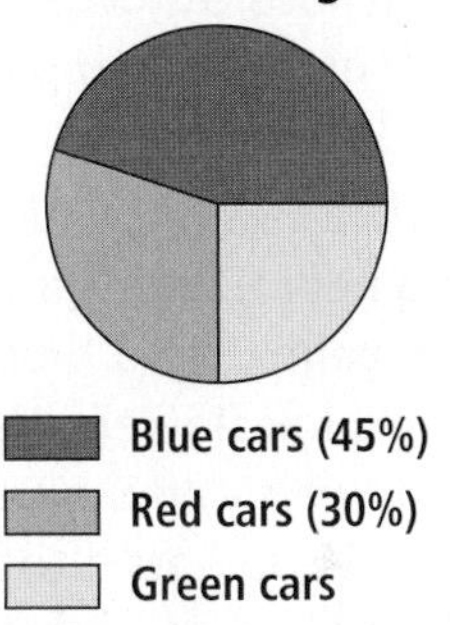

Blue cars (45%)
Red cars (30%)
Green cars

   a. What is a good first step?

   A. Find the ratio of green cars to red cars.

   B. Find the percent of green cars.

   C. Find the percent of green cars and red cars.

   D. Find the percent of green cars and blue cars.

   E. Find the ratio of blue cars to red cars.

   F. Find the ratio of green cars to blue cars.

   b. How many green cars are there?

6. You want to make fruit punch using two kinds of juice. For every 3 cups of grape juice, there should be 2 cups of apple juice. You have 9 cups of apple juice. Do you have enough apple juice to make 15 cups of this fruit punch? Explain your reasoning.

7. A movie complex is showing the same movie in three theaters. In theater A, 64 of the 80 seats are taken. In theater B, 42 seats are taken and 28 seats are empty. In theater C, 21 of the 60 seats are empty. Which theater has the greatest percentage of its seats taken?

   A. Theater C

   B. Theater A

   C. Theater B

8. An artist wants to paint a mural. He mixes red paint and yellow paint to make paint that is a certain shade of orange. The ratio of red paint to yellow paint should be 2 to 3. He needs 20 gallons of the orange paint. How much more yellow paint than red paint does he need?

9. Some landscapers just finished planting a new flower garden. They used pink, yellow, and blue flowers. For every 2 pink flowers, there are 7 yellow flowers and 5 blue flowers. There are 364 flowers altogether. How many of the flowers are pink?

10. In a bookcase, there are 4 fiction books for every 7 nonfiction books. There are 77 books in the bookcase. How many nonfiction books are in the bookcase?

11. You want to make fruit punch using two kinds of juice. For every 6 cups of apple juice, there should be 5 cups of grape juice. You have 17 cups of grape juice. Do you have enough grape juice to make 44 cups of this fruit punch? Explain your reasoning. If you see a second way to solve the problem, describe it also.

12. A web browser has 50 bookmarks. They are described in the table in **Figure 1**. Complete the table. Then give the ratio (in simplest form) of cooking bookmarks to sports bookmarks.

13. A box of cashews, peanuts, and almonds contains 144 nuts. For every 2 cashews, there are 3 peanuts and 7 almonds. How many more peanuts are there than cashews?

14. **Challenge** A bag contains pennies, nickels, dimes, and quarters. There are 50 coins in all. Of the coins, 10% are pennies and 42% are dimes. There are 4 more nickels than pennies. How much money does the bag contain?

15. **Challenge** Debbie is making fruit smoothies to sell at a fair. For every 2 cups of peaches, she uses 3 cups of strawberries and 6 cups of pineapple. Peaches cost $1.04 per cup. Strawberries cost $0.99 per cup. Pineapple costs $1.09 per cup. How much would it cost Debbie to make a batch of 176 cups?

(Figure 1)

Web Browser Bookmarks

Category	Cooking	School	Games	Sports	News
Bookmarks	■	■	6	■	2
Percent of 50	■	20	■	8	■

13-1 Rectangles and Squares

Vocabulary
area, area of a rectangle, area of a square

CCSS: 6.G.A.1

Key Concept

Area of a Rectangle

The **area** of a figure is the number of square units the figure encloses. To find the area of this rectangle, you can count the number of square units inside the rectangle.

Area = 8 square units

2 units

4 units

What if you increase the dimensions of the rectangle? Now there are too many squares to count. Look for another way to count the squares.

12 columns

6 squares in each column

Area $= 12 \cdot 6 = 72$ square units

Area of a rectangle = base · height

$A = bh$

Common units for base and height are feet (ft), inches (in.), and meters (m).

Common units for area are square feet (ft^2), square inches ($in.^2$), and square meters (m^2).

Part 1

Example Using Area Models of Rectangles

Which rectangles have an area of 12 square units?

$2\frac{2}{3}$

$4\frac{1}{2}$

0.75

9

4

2 2

4

continued on next page >

Part 1

Example continued

Solution

To find the areas of the rectangles, you can use the formula $A = bh$. For the rectangles with grid lines, you can also count the unit squares.

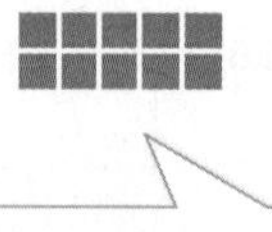

There are 10 unit squares.

$A = bh$
$= 5 \cdot 2$
$= 10$
Area $\neq$ 12 square units

$2\frac{2}{3}$ by $4\frac{1}{2}$

$A = bh$
$= 4\frac{1}{2} \cdot 2\frac{2}{3}$
$= \frac{\overset{3}{\cancel{9}}}{\underset{1}{\cancel{2}}} \cdot \frac{\overset{4}{\cancel{8}}}{\underset{1}{\cancel{3}}}$
$= 3 \cdot 4$
$= 12$
Area $=$ 12 square units

$A = bh$
$= 3 \cdot 4$
$= 12$
Area $=$ 12 square units

0.75 by 9

$A = bh$
$= 9 \cdot 0.75$
$= 6.75$
Area $\neq$ 12 square units

4, 2, 2, 4

$A = bh$
$= 4 \cdot 2$
$= 8$
Area $\neq$ 12 square units

$A = bh$
$= 6 \cdot 2$
$= 12$
Area $=$ 12 square units

Part 2

Intro

A square is a special type of rectangle. Because the base and height of a square are the same, you can find the **area of a square** by using the formula $A = s^2$, where A represents the area and s represents a side length.

$A = bh$
$A = s \cdot s$
$A = s^2$

Square

s

s

Part 2

Example Finding Areas of Squares

The booklet in a CD case is a square with side length 4.72 in. What is the area of the booklet? Round your answer to the nearest hundredth.

Solution

The booklet is a square with a side length of 4.72 in.

Use the formula for the area of a square.	$A = s^2$
Substitute 4.72 for the side length *s*.	$= 4.72^2$
Simplify.	$= 22.2784$
Round to the nearest hundredth.	$= 22.28$

The area of the booklet is about 22.28 in.^2

Part 3

Example Solving for Widths of Rectangles

The area of a rectangular carpet is 54 ft^2. The carpet is 9 ft long. How wide is the carpet?

Solution

The area of the carpet is 54 ft^2.

Use the formula for the area of a rectangle.	$A = bh$
Substitute 54 for the area and 9 for the base.	$54 = 9 \cdot h$
Divide each side by 9.	$\frac{54}{9} = \frac{h}{9}$
Simplify.	$6 = h$

The carpet is 6 ft wide.

1. Find the area of the rectangle.

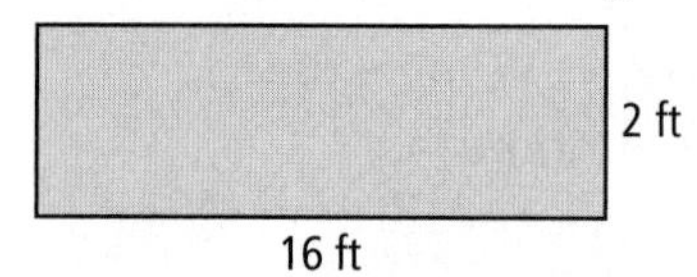

2. The Newmans' living room measures 19 ft by 23 ft. What is its area?

3. Find the area of the square.

4. **Think About the Process** You want new carpeting for your rectangular bedroom. Your bedroom is 7 feet long by 11 feet wide. The carpet store charges by the square foot. How would you find the number of square feet of carpeting that you need?

   A. Multiply 7 and 11.

   B. Add 7 and 11.

   C. Add 7 and 11, then multiply by 2.

   D. Multiply 7 and 4.

5. The school is planning a new playground. The playground will be in the shape of a square that measures 19 m on a side. What will be the area of the new playground?

6. A rectangular poster has an area of 22 square feet. It is $3\frac{2}{3}$ feet wide at its base. What is the height of the poster?

7. **Writing** Explain how the formula for the area of a rectangle gives the formula for the area of a square. Then find the area of the square.

8. A square has a side length of 12 yards. What is its area in square feet? Show two ways to find the answer.

9. **Reasoning** You want to increase the size of a small square image to make a poster. What happens to the area of the image if you multiply the length of each side by 5?

   A. The area of the new image is 5 times the area of the original.

   B. The area of the new image is 25 times the area of the original.

   C. The area of the new image is 20 times the area of the original.

   D. The area of the new image is 10 times the area of the original.

   E. The change in the area cannot be found without the original side length.

10. **Error Analysis** The base of a rectangle is $3\frac{1}{3}$ feet. The area of this rectangle is 40 square feet. Michaela claims the height of the rectangle is $133\frac{1}{3}$ feet.

   a. What is the correct height?

   b. What is Michaela's error?

   A. To solve $3\frac{1}{3} = h = 40$, Michaela used subtraction instead of addition.

   B. To solve $40 \cdot h = 3\frac{1}{3}$, Michaela used division instead of multiplication.

   C. To solve $3\frac{1}{3} + h = 40$, Michaela used addition instead of subtraction.

   D. To solve $3\frac{1}{3} \cdot h = 40$, Michaela used multiplication instead of division.

   E. To solve $3\frac{1}{3} \cdot h = 40$, Michaela used division instead of multiplication.

11. Decorations A banner measures 5 ft by 7 ft. How much material do you need for eight banners?

12. a. Multiple Representations Find the area of the inner rectangle.

b. Draw at least two different rectangles with the same area.

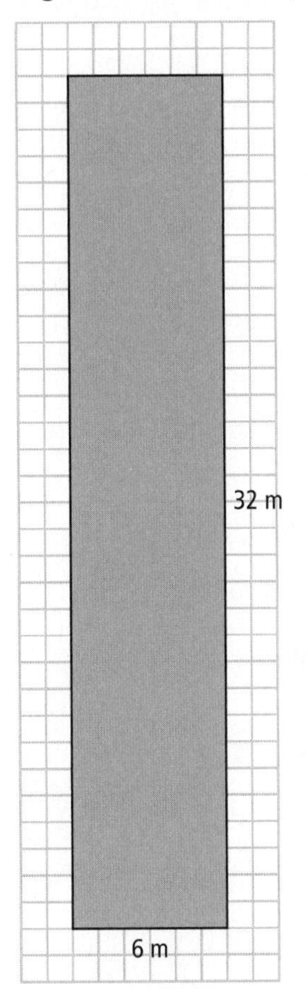

13. Mental Math A square concrete patio is 18 feet long on each side. What is the area of the patio in square yards?

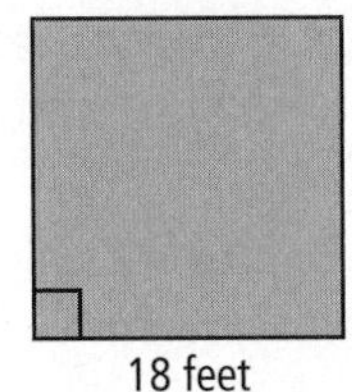

14. Mental Math Peter Planter's square garden has a side length of 10 feet.

a. What is the area of the garden?

b. What is the perimeter?

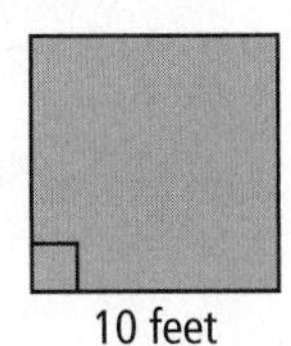

15. Land is often measured in acres. An acre is 4,840 square yards. The Kostas family bought a house built on a rectangular plot that is exactly 2 acres. The plot is $67\frac{2}{9}$ yards long. How wide is the plot?

16. Think About the Process A rectangular stamp measures 3.68 cm at its base, and has an area of 18.40 cm^2.

a. Which equation helps you solve for the height of the stamp?

A. $3.68 \cdot 18.40 = h$

B. $3.68 \cdot h = 18.40$

C. $3.68 \div h = 18.40$

D. $18.40 \cdot h = 3.68$

E. $2 \cdot h + 2 \cdot 3.68 = 18.40$

b. What is the height of the stamp?

17. Challenge A contractor is replacing the ceiling in a rectangular office. The area of the ceiling is 350 ft^2. The width of the ceiling is 25 ft. The contractor uses rectangular ceiling panels that are 2.5 ft by 3.5 ft.

a. What is the length of the ceiling?

b. How many ceiling panels does the contractor need? Show two ways to find the answer.

18. Challenge The yearbook has 6 pages for ads. Each page measures 6 in. by 12 in. Each ad measures 2 in. by 3 in. If all the ad space sells at $15 per ad, how much money will this raise for the yearbook?

13-2 Right Triangles

Vocabulary
area of a right triangle, base of a triangle, compose a shape, height of a triangle

CCSS: 6.G.A.1

Part 1

Example Using Rectangles to Find Areas of Right Triangles

A rectangular sheet of paper has dimensions $8\frac{1}{2}$ in. by 11 in. A diagonal of the paper forms two matching right triangles. What is the area of one of the triangular regions?

Solution

Step 1 Find the area of the rectangle.

Draw a diagram and label what you know.

$8\frac{1}{2}$ in.

11 in.

Use the formula for the area of a rectangle.	$A = bh$
Substitute for the base and height.	$= 11 \cdot 8\frac{1}{2}$
Write $8\frac{1}{2}$ as an improper fraction.	$= 11 \cdot \frac{17}{2}$
Multiply.	$= \frac{187}{2}$

The area of the rectangle is $\frac{187}{2}$ in.^{2}

Step 2 Find the area of one triangular region.

Draw a diagonal on the paper to form two matching right triangles.

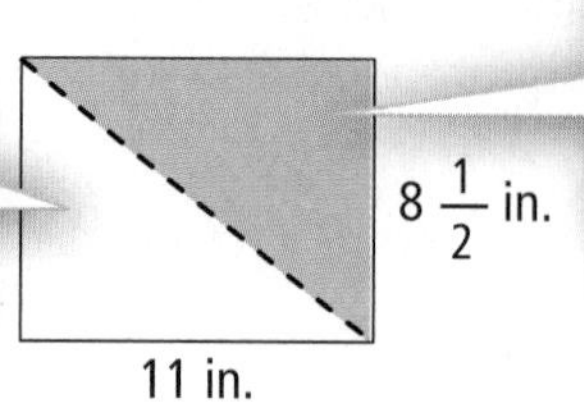

The area of one triangle is half the area of the rectangle.

Multiply the area of the rectangle by $\frac{1}{2}$.	$A = \frac{1}{2} \cdot \frac{187}{2}$
Multiply.	$= \frac{187}{4}$
Write as a mixed number.	$= 46\frac{3}{4}$

The area of one triangular region is $46\frac{3}{4}$ in.^{2}.

Part 2

Intro

To **compose** a shape, join two (or more) shapes so there is no gap or overlap.

You can compose a rectangle from a right triangle. First, make a copy of the triangle.

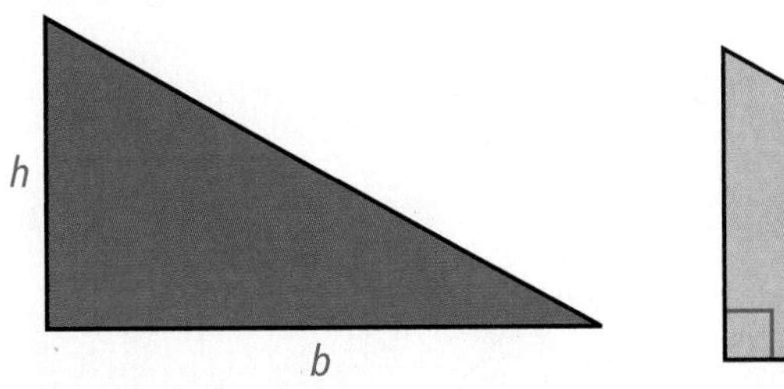

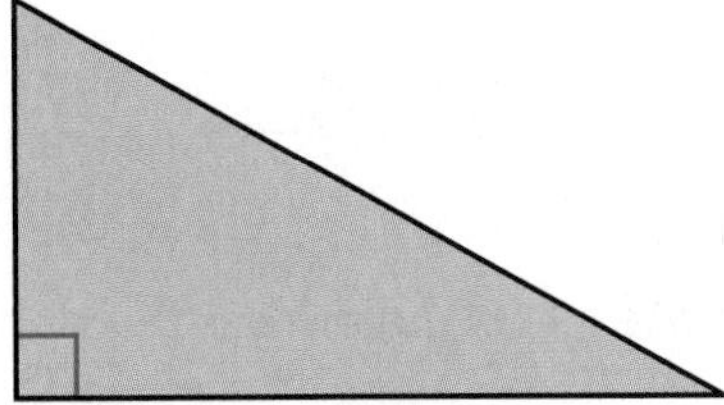

Then, rotate the triangle and push the two triangles together.

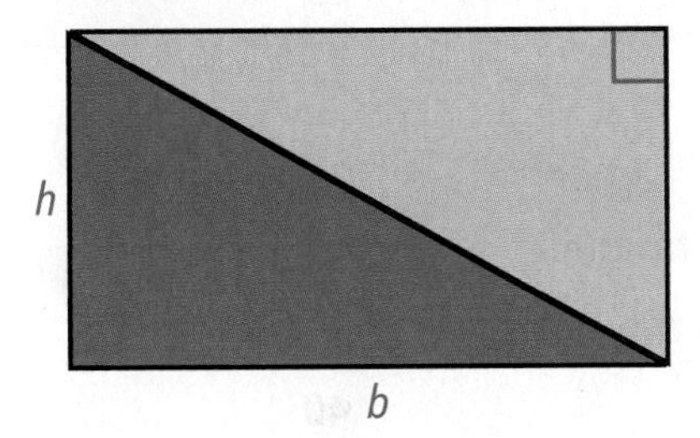

So you can use a right triangle to compose a rectangle with the same base and height as the right triangle.

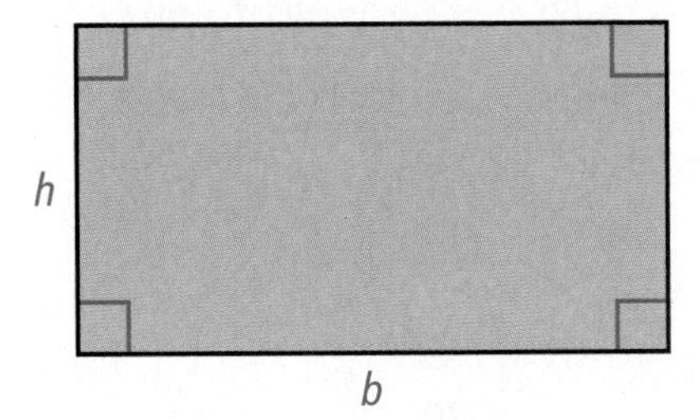

Part 2

Example Composing Rectangles to Find Areas of Right Triangles

What is the area of the right triangle shown?

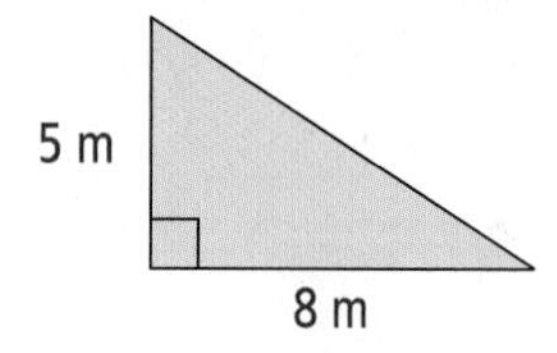

Solution

Step 1 Compose a rectangle from the right triangle.

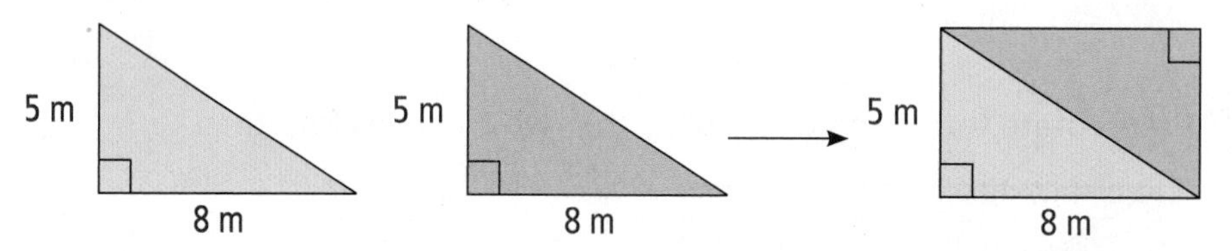

Step 2 Find the area of the rectangle.

Use the formula for the area of a rectangle.	$A = bh$
Substitute 5 for the height and 8 for the base.	$= 8 \cdot 5$
Multiply.	$= 40$

The area of the rectangle is 40 m^2.

Step 3 Find the area of the right triangle.

Multiply the area of the rectangle by $\frac{1}{2}$.	area of triangle $= \frac{1}{2} \cdot$ area of rectangle
Substitute 40 for the area of the rectangle.	$= \frac{1}{2} \cdot 40$
Multiply.	$= 20$

The area of the right triangle is 20 m^2.

Key Concept

The formula for the area of a right triangle is related to the formula for the area of a rectangle.

The **base of a triangle** is any side of the triangle.

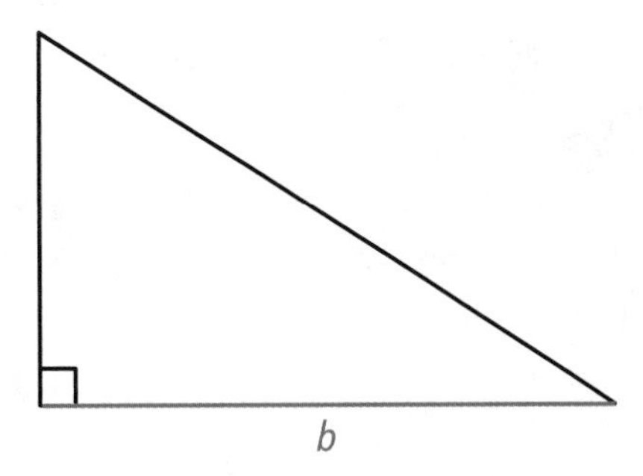

The **height of a triangle** is the length of the perpendicular segment from a vertex to the base opposite that vertex.

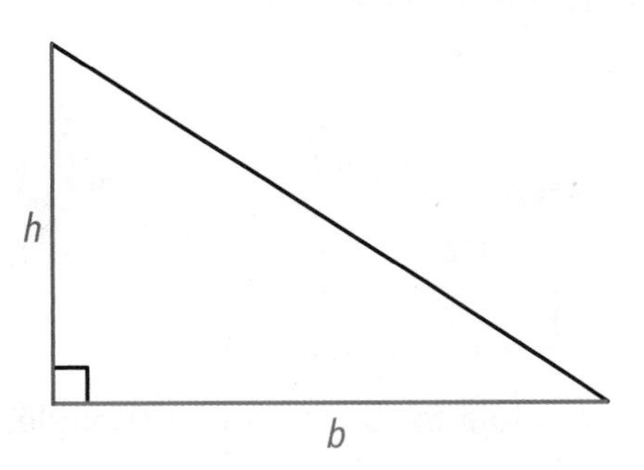

The formula for the area of a rectangle is $A = bh$, where A represents the area, b represents the base, and h represents the height.

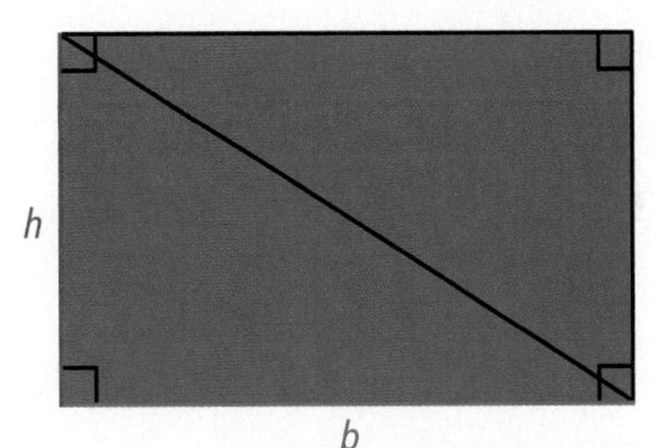

Rectangle: $A = bh$

The formula for the **area of a right triangle** is $A = \frac{1}{2}bh$, where A represents the area, b represents a base, and h represents the corresponding height.

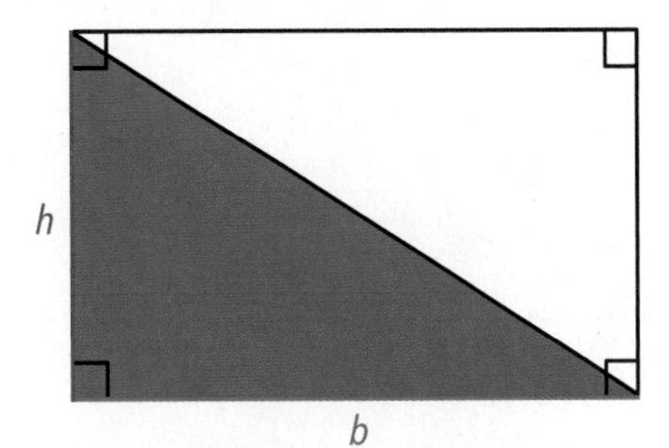

Rectangle: $A = bh$

Right Triangle: $A = \frac{1}{2}bh$

Part 3

Example Using the Formula for the Area of a Right Triangle

What is the area of the right triangle?

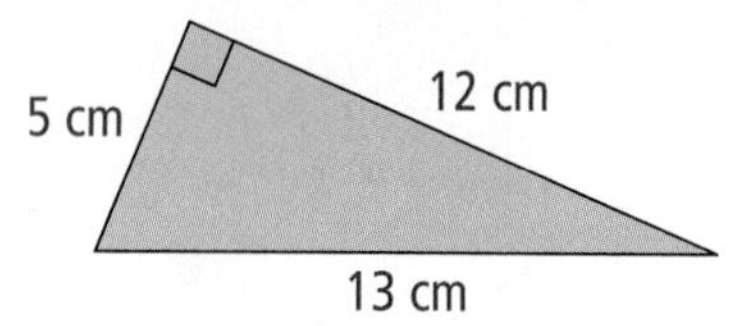

Solution

You can compose the triangle into a rectangle so that you can identify its base and height more easily.

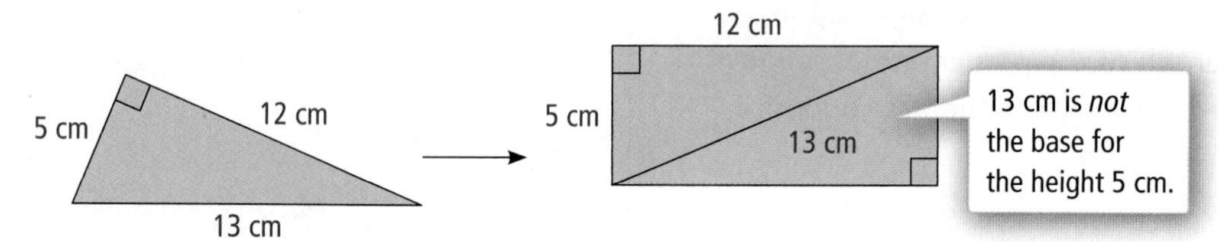

Use the formula for the area of a triangle.	$A = \frac{1}{2}bh$
Substitute 12 for the base and 5 for the height.	$= \frac{1}{2} \cdot 12 \cdot 5$
Multiply.	$= 30$

The area of the right triangle is 30 cm^2.

1. A rectangle has dimensions $6\frac{1}{5}$ in. by 13 in. A diagonal of the rectangle forms two matching right triangles. What is the area of one of the triangles?

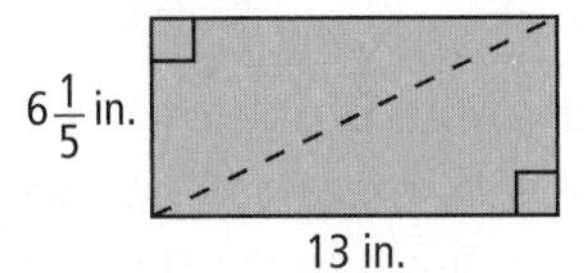

2. Alison and Tyrone each bought a slice of pizza in the shape of a right triangle as shown.

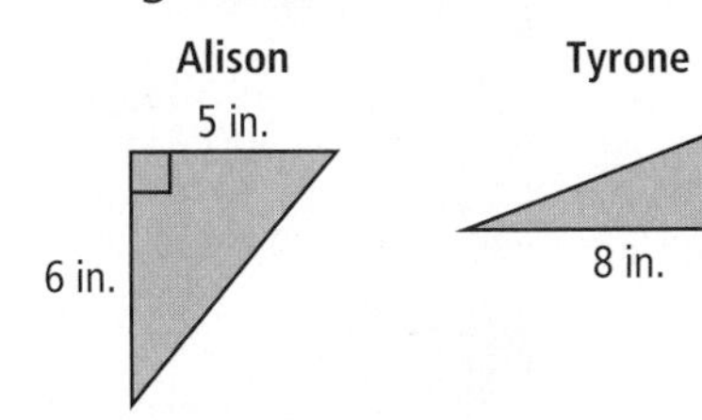

a. What is the area of each slice of pizza?

b. Who has the larger slice of pizza?

A. Tyrone

B. Alison

C. Both slices are the same size.

3. Pedro is building a playground in the shape of a right triangle. He wants to know the area of the playground to help him decide how much sand to buy.

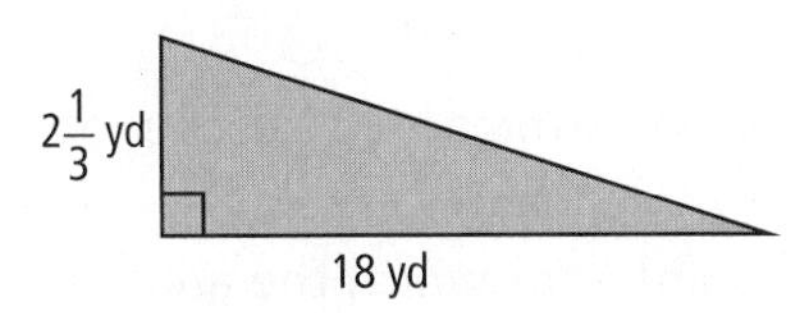

a. Compose the playground and a matching triangle into a rectangle.

b. What are the dimensions of the rectangle?

A. $2\frac{1}{3}$ yd by 18 yd

B. $20\frac{1}{3}$ yd by $40\frac{2}{3}$ yd

C. 18 yd by 18 yd

D. $2\frac{1}{3}$ yd by $2\frac{1}{3}$ yd

c. What is the area of the playground?

4. Find the area of the right triangle.

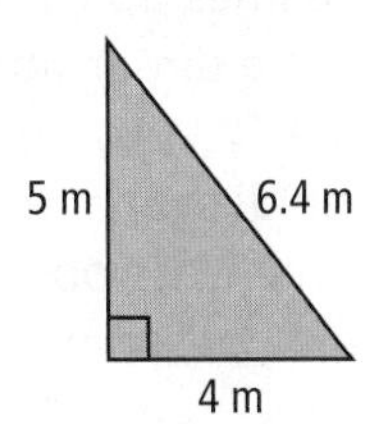

5. Find the area of the right triangle. Round to the nearest tenth as needed.

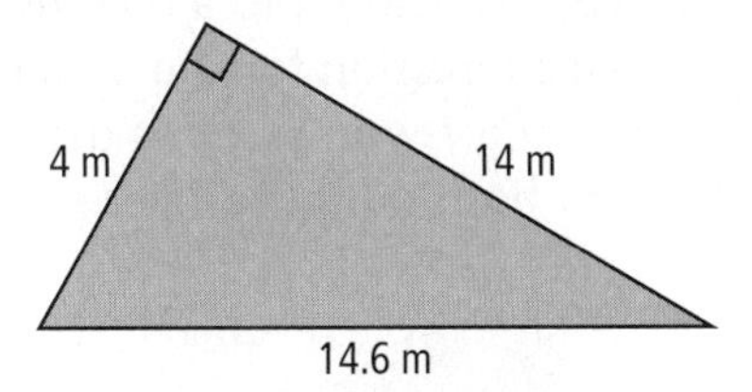

6. Think About the Process

a. What information is not needed to find the area of the right triangle?

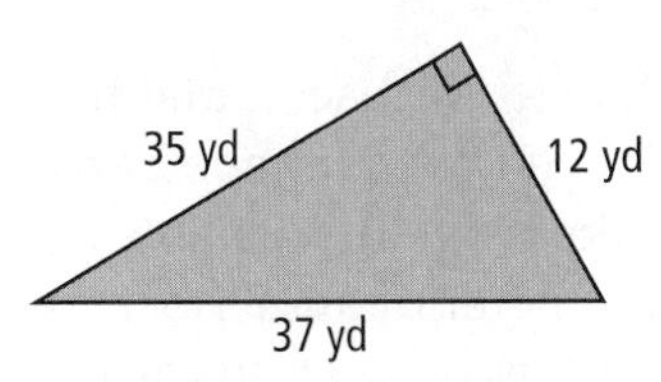

A. The length of the side that is 12 yd

B. The 90° angle

C. The length of the side that is 37 yd

D. The length of the side that is 35 yd

b. What is the area of the right triangle?

7. Reasoning A rectangle has dimensions 19 in. by $29\frac{4}{5}$ in. It is cut along a diagonal.

a. Explain how to find the area of the right triangles formed by cutting the rectangle along a diagonal.

b. What is the area of one of the right triangles?

8. Mr. Parker is dividing his rectangular classroom into two matching right triangles. He lines up the desks along a diagonal. The dimensions of the classroom are 12 ft by 16 ft. The length of the diagonal is 20 ft. Draw a diagram of the classroom. What is the area of one of the triangles?

9. Think About the Process The given triangle is split into two right triangles. Compose each right triangle and a copy of itself into a rectangle. Write an expression for the area of each rectangle, where x ft is the height of both right triangles.

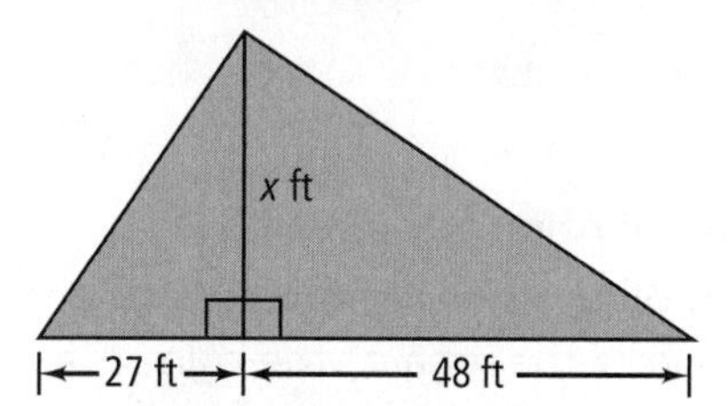

10. Gardening Michael is planting a garden. It has the shape of a right triangle. He wants 4 plants for each square meter of area. How many plants does he want in the garden?

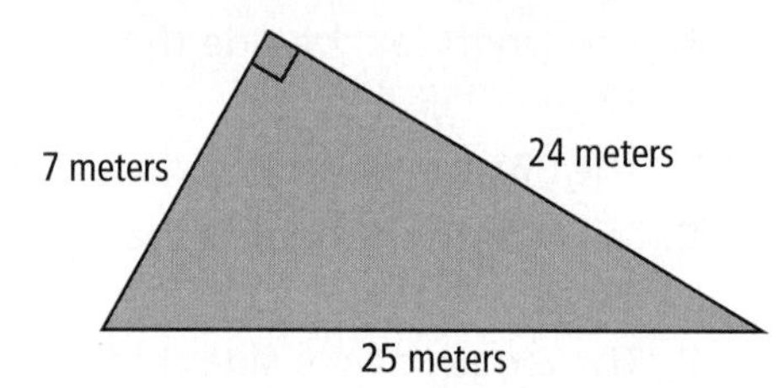

11. Estimation Estimate the area of the triangle.

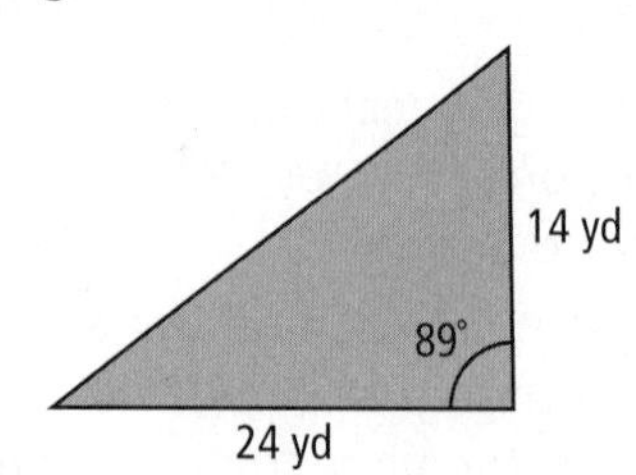

12. Find the area of the right triangle, where the base, x ft, is 4 times the height.

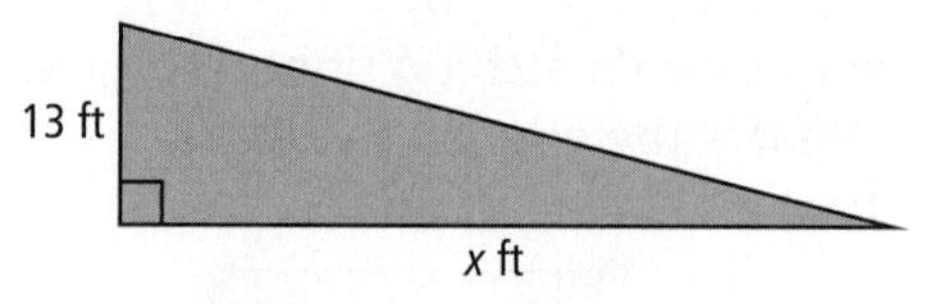

13. Find the area of the right triangle in square centimeters. First convert all measurements to centimeters. Use the conversion factors $\frac{2.54 \text{ centimeters}}{1 \text{ inch}}$ and $\frac{12 \text{ inch}}{1 \text{ foot}}$. Note that the figure is not drawn to scale.

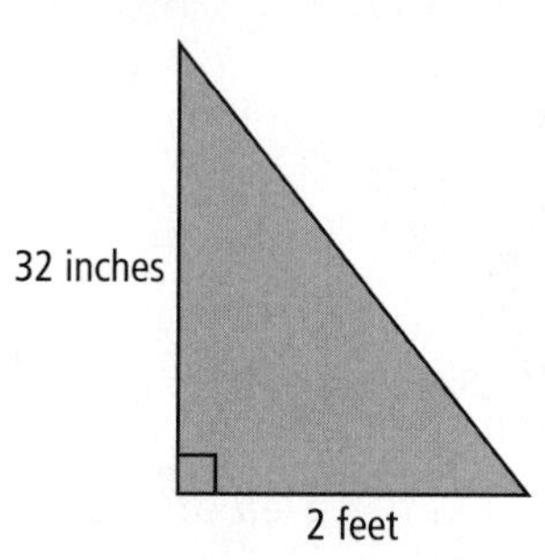

14. Challenge Two plots of land form a right triangle as shown. The plots have equal areas.

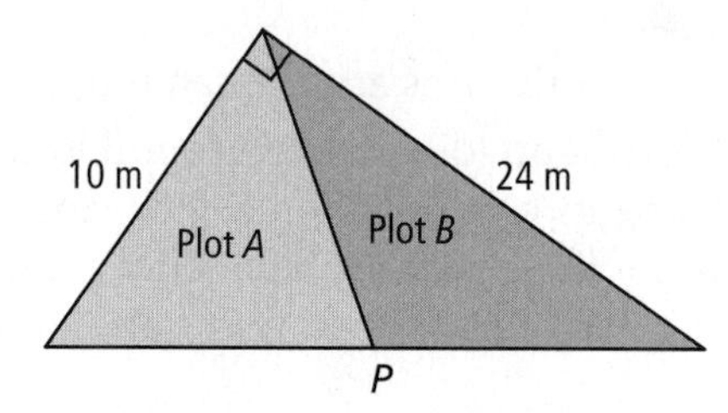

a. What is the area of each plot?

b. Explain why there must be a point P for which the area of plot A equals the area of plot B.

13-3 Parallelograms

CCSS: 6.G.A.1

Vocabulary
area of a parallelogram, base of a parallelogram, decompose a shape, height of a parallelogram

Part 1

Intro

To **decompose** a shape, break it up to form other shapes.

You can decompose a parallelogram to form a rectangle.

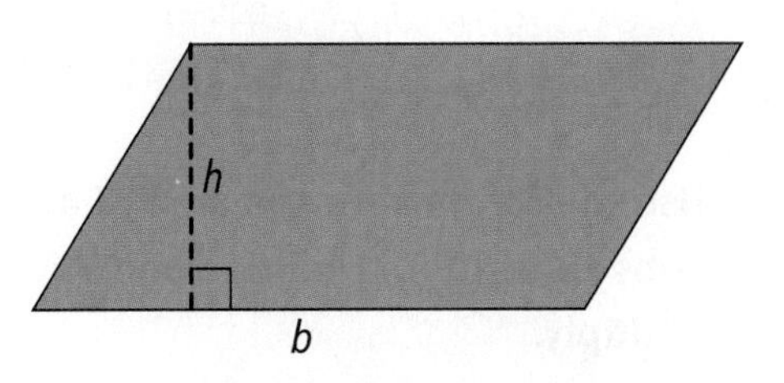

Cut the parallelogram along its height.

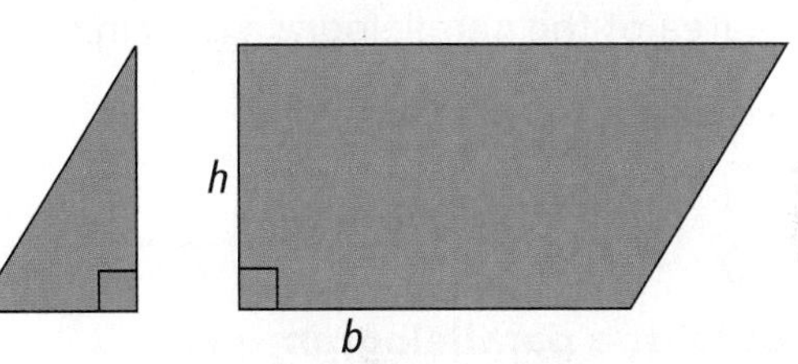

Move the triangle to the other side. Then push the pieces together to form a rectangle.

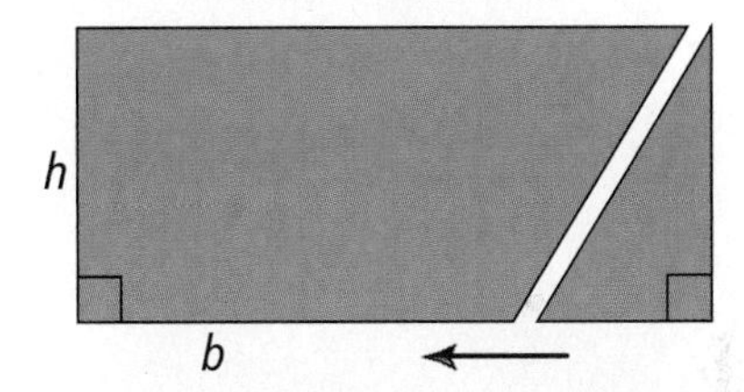

The rectangle has the same base and height as the parallelogram.

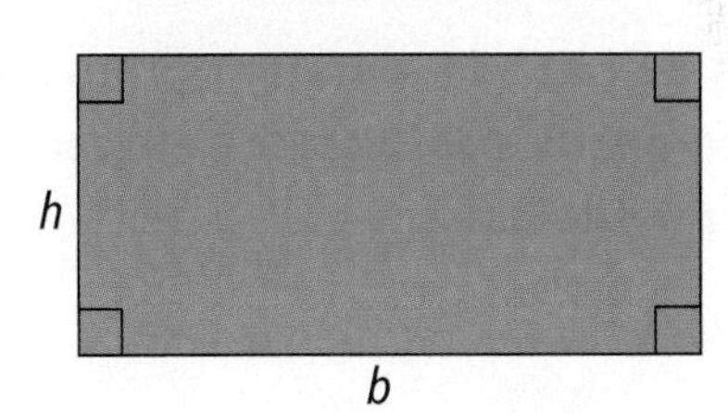

Example Decomposing Parallelograms to Find Their Areas

Find the area of the parallelogram by decomposing the parallelogram into rectangle.

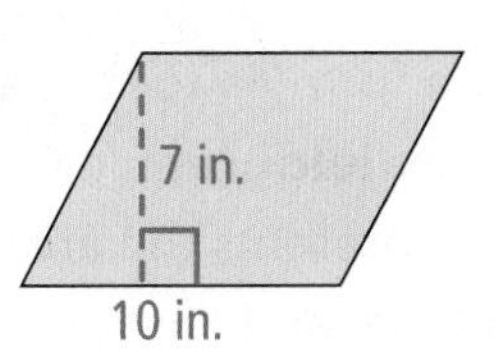

Solution

Decompose the parallelogram to form a rectangle with the same dimensions.

continued on next page >

Part 1

Solution continued

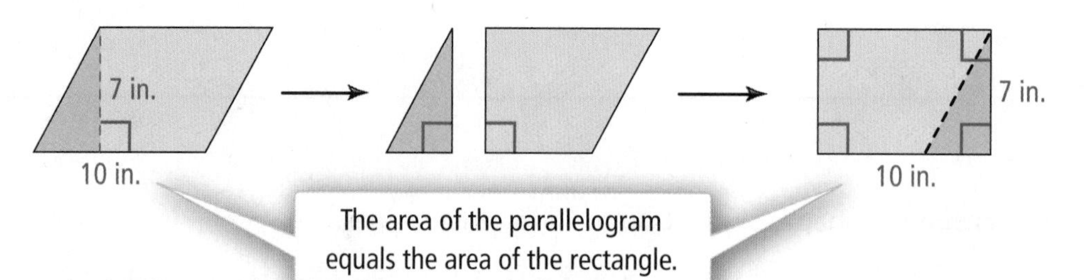

Use the formula for the area of a rectangle.	$A = bh$
Substitute 10 for the base and 7 for the height.	$= 10 \cdot 7$
Multiply.	$= 70$

The area of the parallelogram is 70 in.^{2}.

Key Concept

A **base of a parallelogram** is any side of the parallelogram.

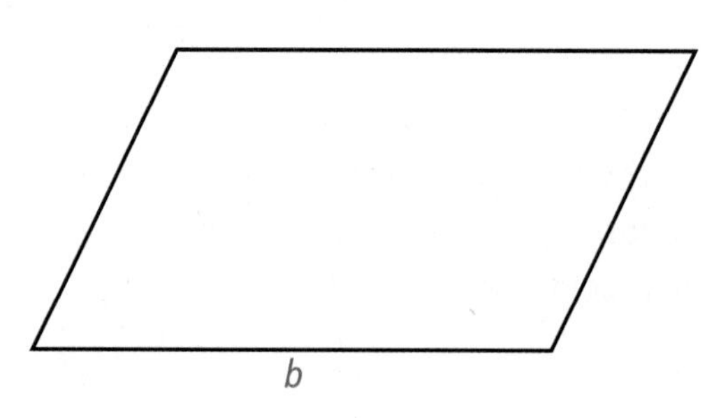

A **height of a parallelogram** is the perpendicular distance between opposite bases.

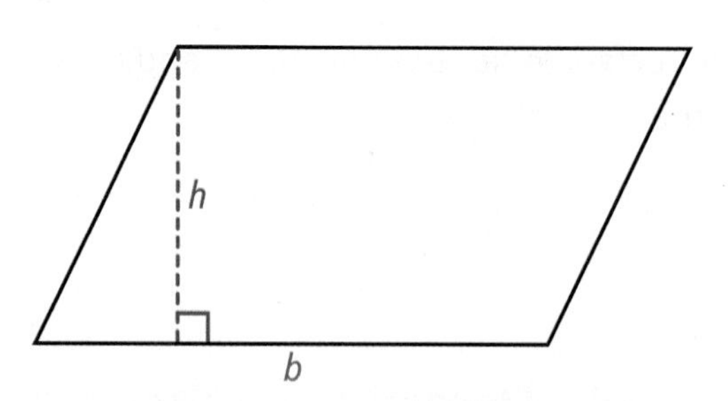

The formula for the **area of a parallelogram** is $A = bh$, where A represents the area, b represents a base, and h is the corresponding height.

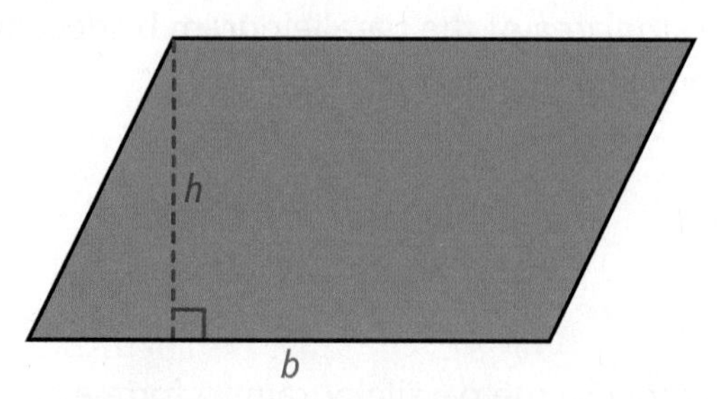

Parallelogram: $A = bh$

Part 2

Example Finding Areas of Parallelograms

Which parallelograms have an area of 16 cm²?

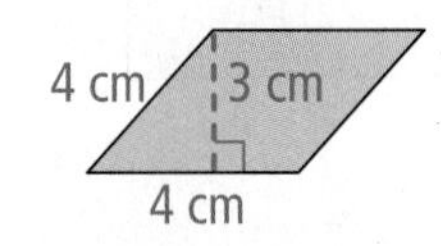

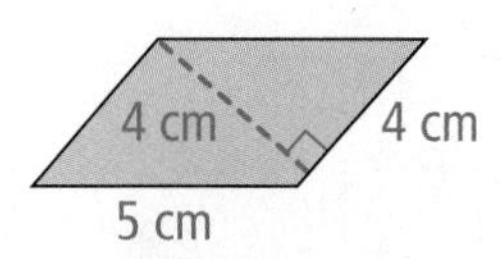

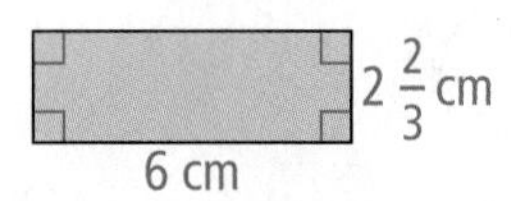

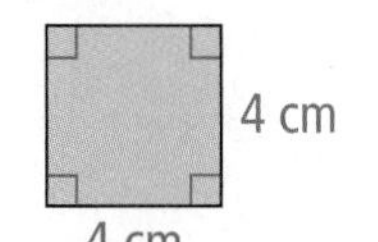

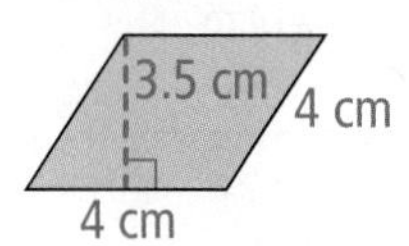

Solution

To find the areas of the parallelograms, you can use the formula $A = bh$.

$A = bh$	$A = bh$	$A = bh$
$= 4 \cdot 3$	$= 8 \cdot 2$	$= 4 \cdot 4$
$= 12$	$= 16$	$= 16$
Area $\neq$ 16 cm²	Area = 16 cm²	Area = 16 cm²

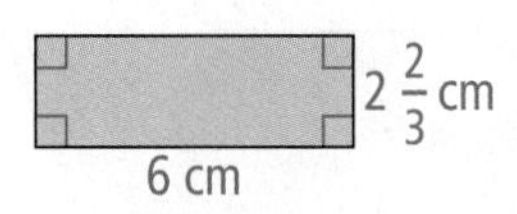

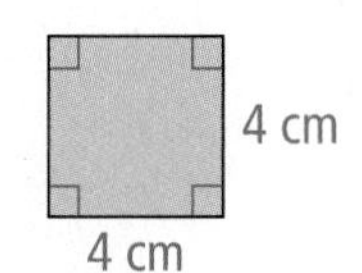

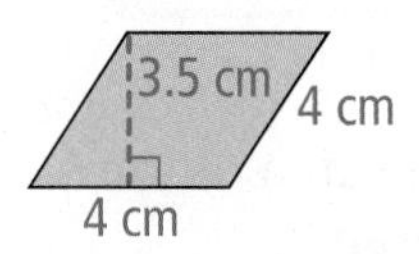

$A = bh$

$= 6 \cdot 2\frac{2}{3}$

$= 6 \cdot \frac{8}{3}$

$= \frac{48}{3}$

$= 16$

Area = 16 cm²

$A = bh$

$= 4 \cdot 4$

$= 16$

Area = 16 cm²

$A = bh$

$= 4 \cdot 3.5$

$= 14$

Area $\neq$ 16 cm²

Digital Resources    

1. **a.** Decompose the parallelogram into a rectangle. Choose the correct rectangle.

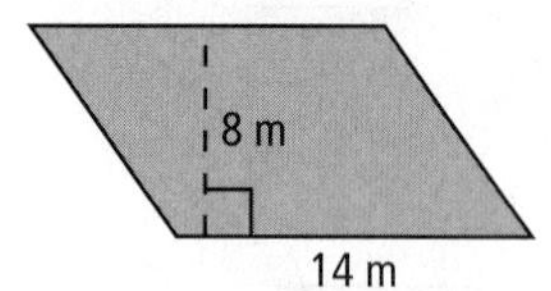

A. 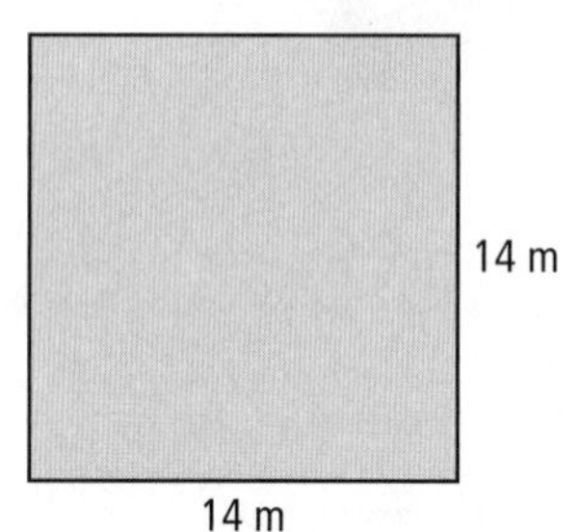

B. 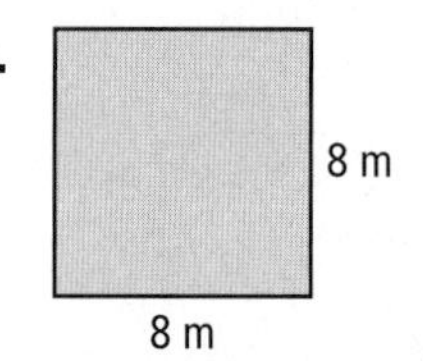

C. 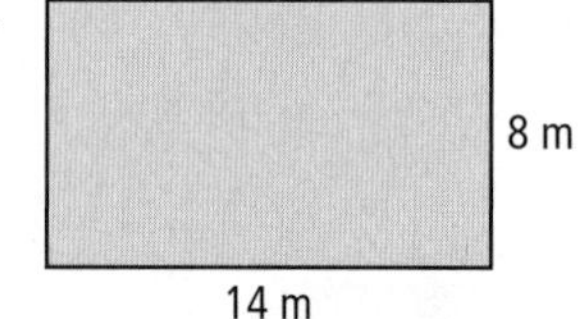

b. What is the area of the parallelogram?

2. Find the area of the parallelogram.

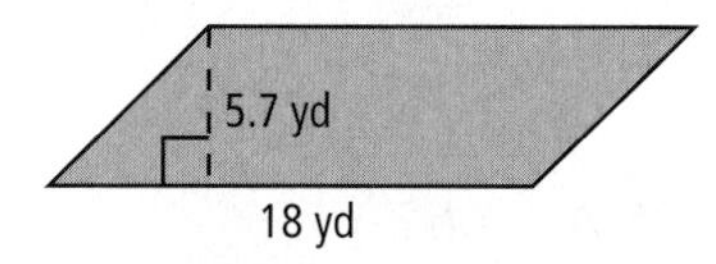

3. Find the area of the parallelogram.

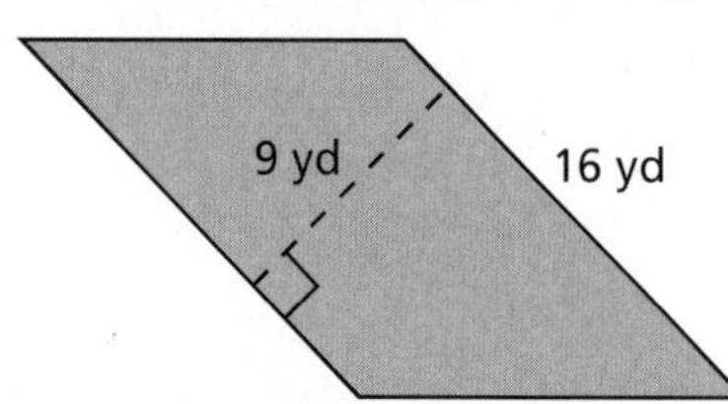

4. **Writing** Does the rectangle have the same area as the parallelogram? How many parallelograms are there that have the same area as the rectangle? Explain.

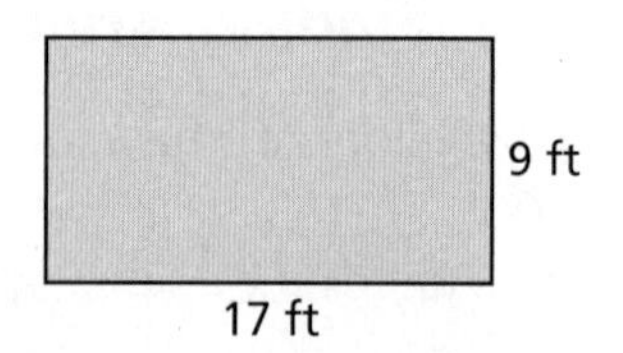

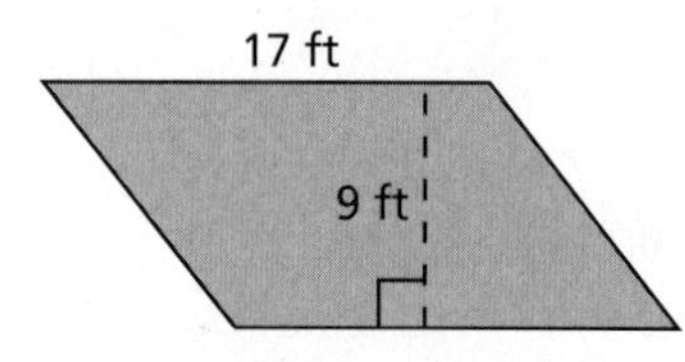

(The diagrams are not to scale.)

5. **Reasoning** Do these parallelograms have the same area? Explain how you can answer this question without making any calculations.

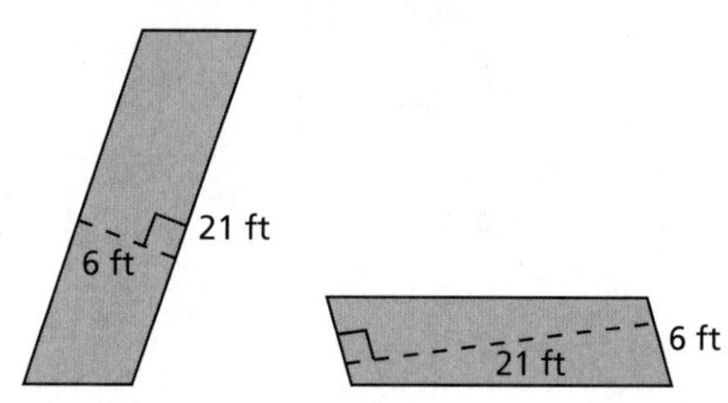

6. **Estimation** What is the easiest way to estimate the area?

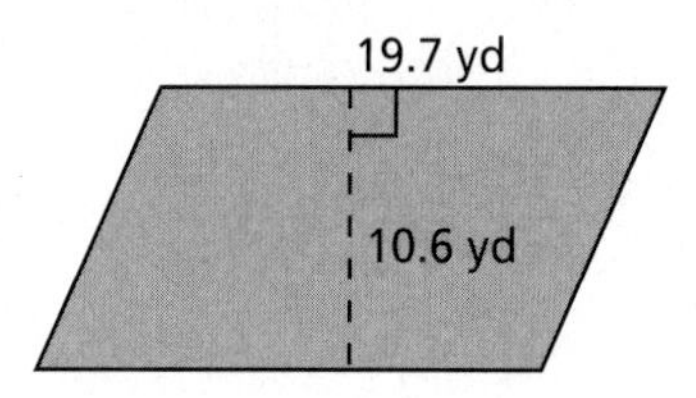

A. Multiply 19.7 by 10 to get 197 yd^2.

B. Multiply 20 by 10 to get 200 yd^2.

C. Multiply 20 by 10.6 to get 212 yd^2.

D. Multiply 19.7 by 10.6 and round the result to get 209 yd^2.

7. **Think About the Process** You want to use the formula $A = bh$ to find the area of this parallelogram. What values should you use for b and h?

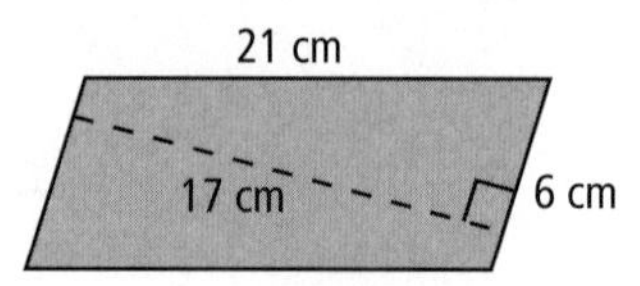

8. Error Analysis Two students must find the area of this parallelogram. (The diagram is not to scale.) Ari says the area is 130 m^2. Shelly says the area is 143 m^2. One of them is correct. Who is incorrect? Explain that student's error.

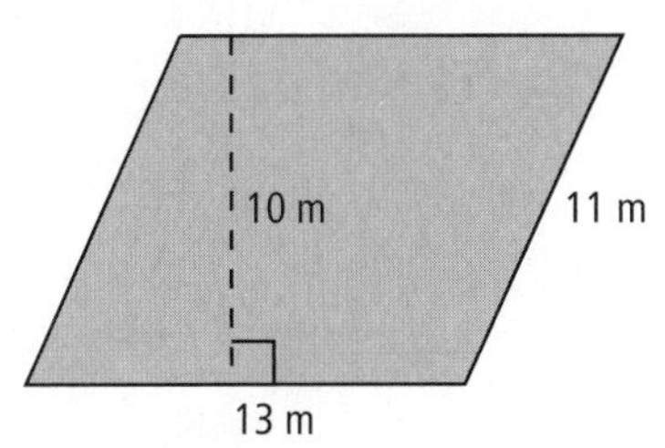

A. Shelly is incorrect. She used the wrong side for the base.

B. Ari is incorrect. He used two sides instead of a base and the corresponding height.

C. Ari is incorrect. He used the wrong side for the base.

D. Shelly is incorrect. She used two sides instead of a base and the corresponding height.

E. Ari is incorrect. He added a base and the corresponding height instead of multiplying.

F. Shelly is incorrect. She added a base and the corresponding height instead of multiplying.

9. a. Decompose the parallelogram into a rectangle.

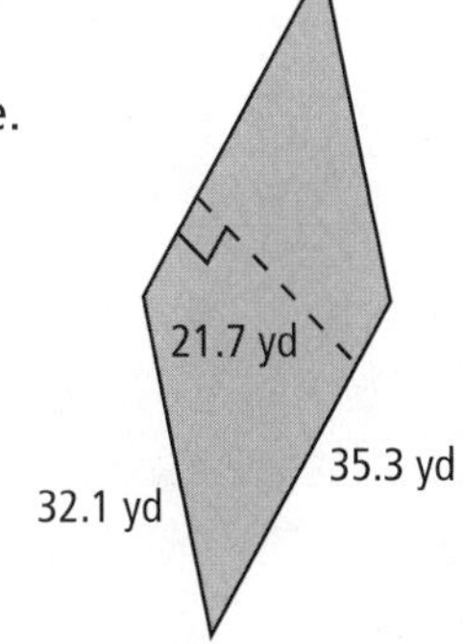

A.

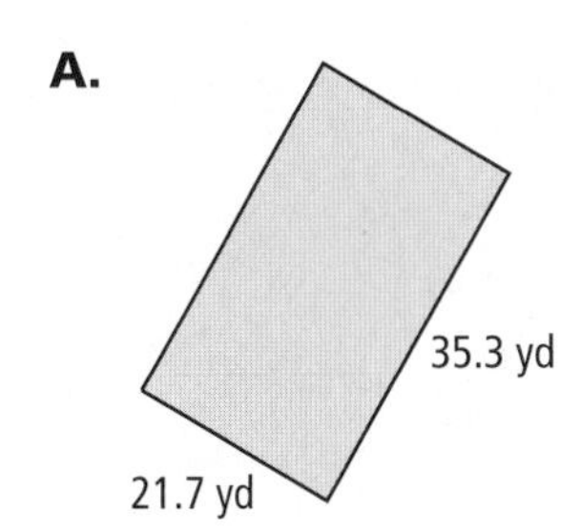

B.

32.1 yd

21.7 yd

C.

35.3 yd

32.1 yd

b. Use the rectangle to find the area of the parallelogram.

10. Think About the Process You want to find the area of this parallelogram. The first step is to decompose the parallelogram into a rectangle. What is the next step? What is the area of the parallelogram?

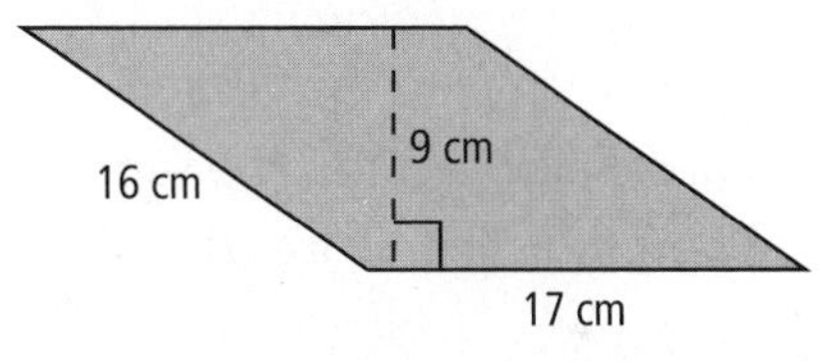

A. Multiply 9 by itself. The area of the parallelogram is 81 cm^2.

B. Multiply 17 by 16. The area of the parallelogram is 272 cm^2.

C. Multiply 16 by itself. The area of the parallelogram is 256 cm^2.

D. Multiply 17 by 9. The area of the parallelogram is 153 cm^2.

E. Multiply 17 by itself. The area of the parallelogram is 289 cm^2.

F. Multiply 16 by 9. The area of the parallelogram is 144 cm^2.

11. Challenge A mosaic is made from 26 pieces. Each piece is a parallelogram, as shown in the figure. What is the total area of the mosaic?

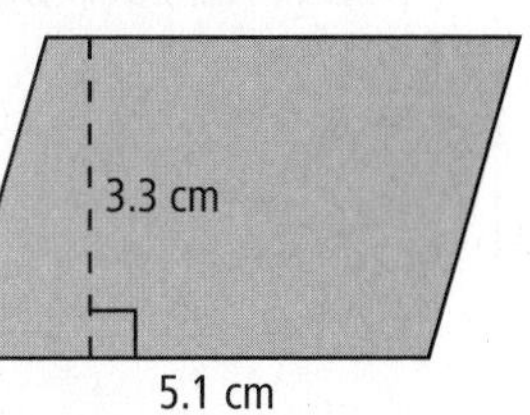

13-4 Other Triangles

CCSS: 6.G.A.1

Part 1

Intro

You can compose a parallelogram from an acute triangle.

First, make a copy of the acute triangle.

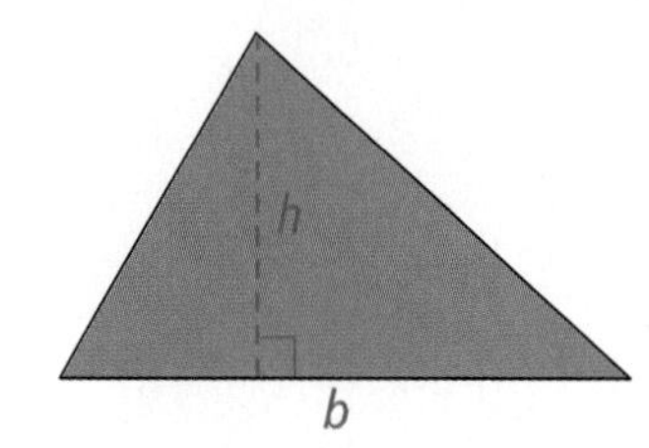

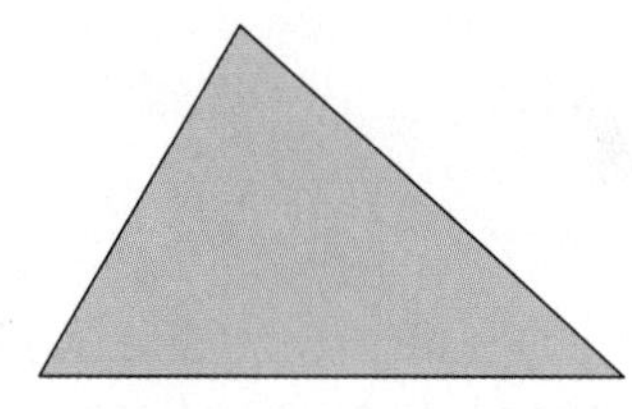

Then, rotate the copy and push the two copies together to make a parallelogram.

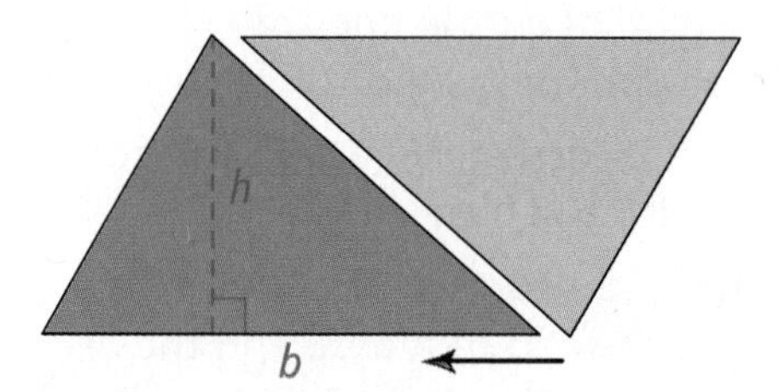

The parallelogram has the same base and height as the acute triangle.

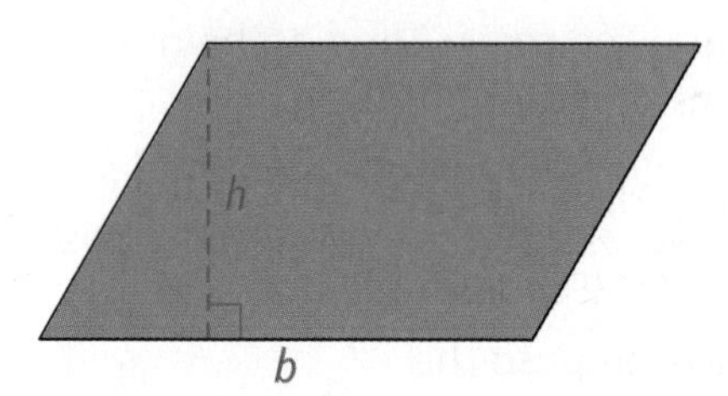

Example Finding Areas of Acute Triangles

A school club plans to sell cheering pennants at football games. Compose the triangle into a parallelogram to find how many square inches of cloth the school needs for each pennant.

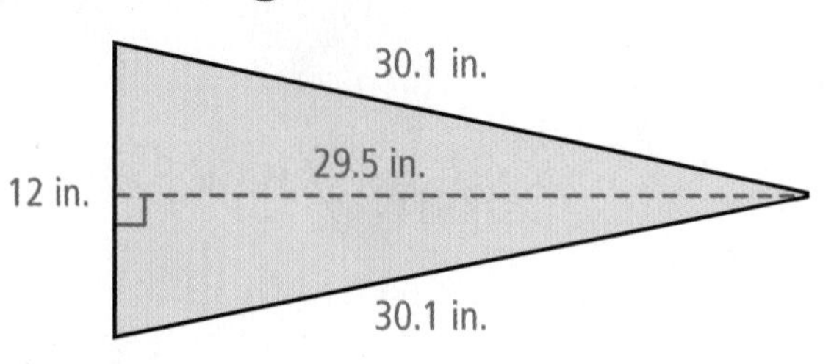

continued on next page >

Part 1

Example continued

Solution

Step 1 Compose a parallelogram from the triangle.

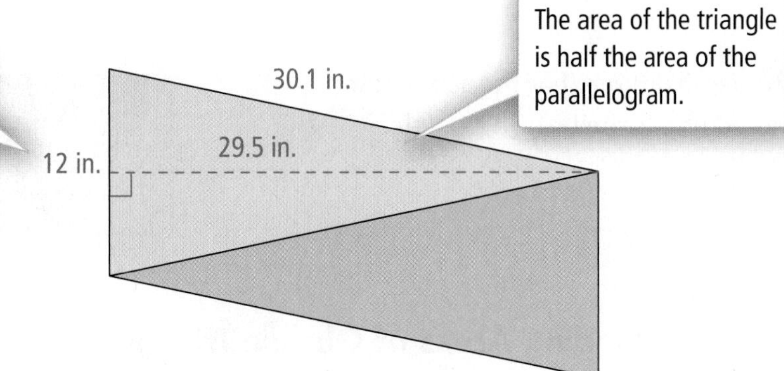

Step 2 Find the area of the pennant.

Use the formula for half the area of a parallelogram.	$A = \frac{1}{2}bh$
Substitute 12 for the base and 29.5 for the height.	$= \frac{1}{2} \cdot 12 \cdot 29.5$
Multiply.	$= 177$

The school club needs 177 in.^{2} of cloth for each pennant.

Part 2

Intro

You can compose a parallelogram from an obtuse triangle.

First, make a copy of the obtuse triangle.

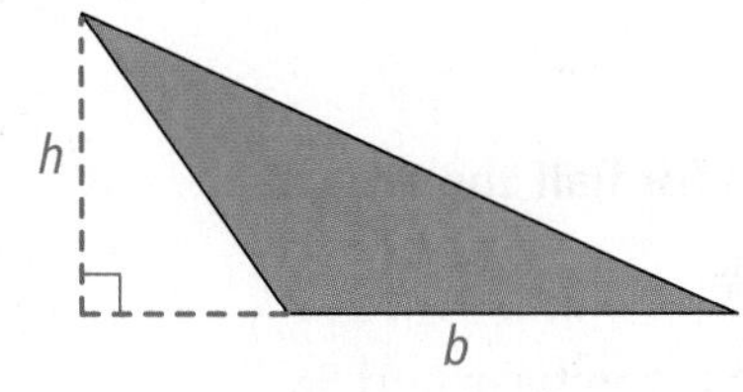

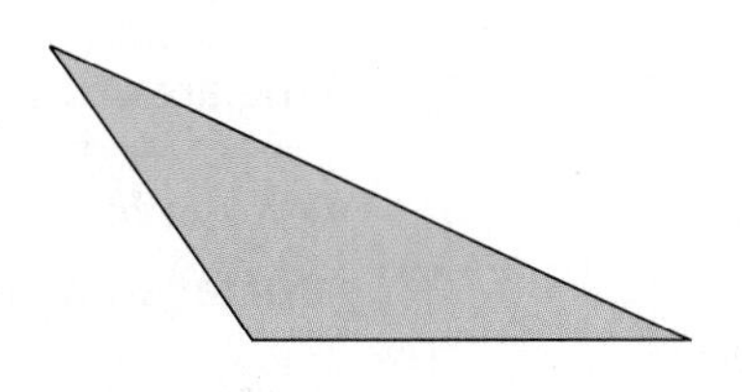

continued on next page >

Part 2

Intro continued

Then, rotate the copy and push the two copies together to make a parallelogram.

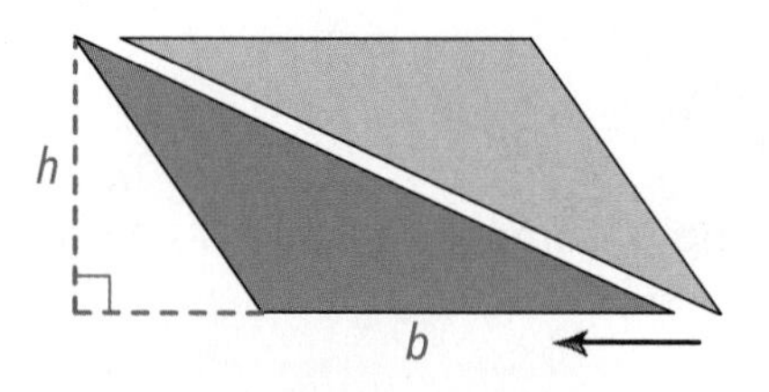

The parallelogram has the same base and height as the obtuse triangle.

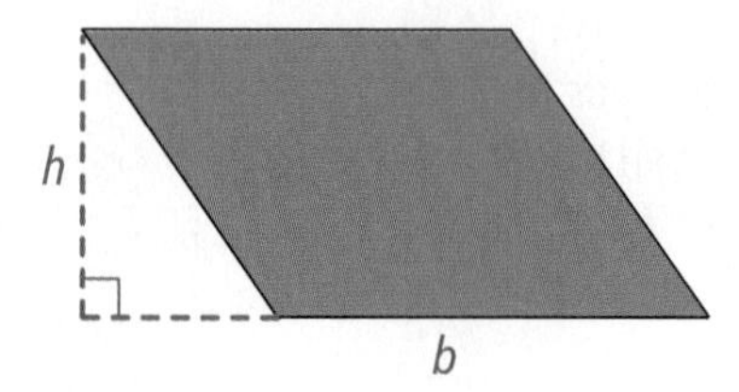

Example Finding Areas of Obtuse Triangles

A nature club plans to buy a piece of land to keep as a nature preserve. The land is in the shape of an obtuse triangle. Compose the obtuse triangle into a parallelogram to find the area of the piece of land.

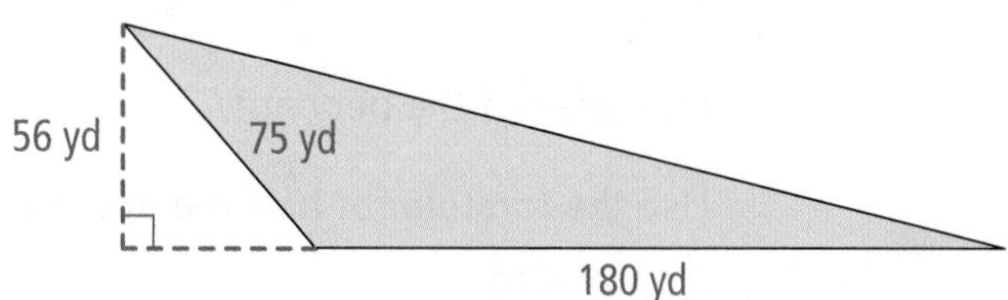

Solution

Step 1 Compose a parallelogram from the triangle.

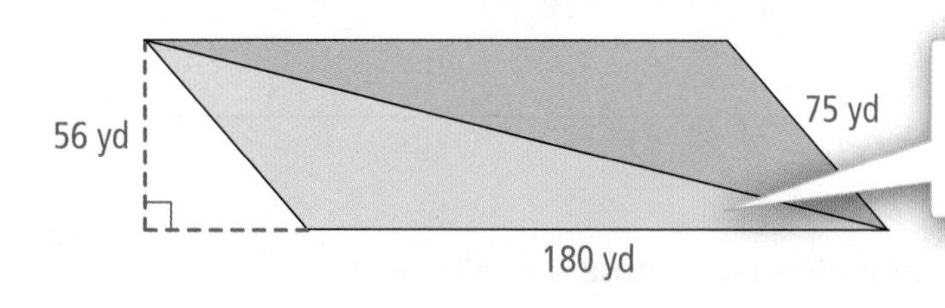

The area of the triangle is half the area of the parallelogram.

Step 2 Find the area of the triangle.

Use the formula for half the area of a parallelogram.	$A = \frac{1}{2}bh$
Substitute 180 for the base and 56 for the height.	$= \frac{1}{2} \cdot 180 \cdot 56$
Multiply.	$= 5{,}040$

The area of the triangle is 5,040 yd^2.

Key Concept

The formula for the area of a parallelogram is $A = bh$, where A represents the area, b represents a base, and h is the corresponding height.

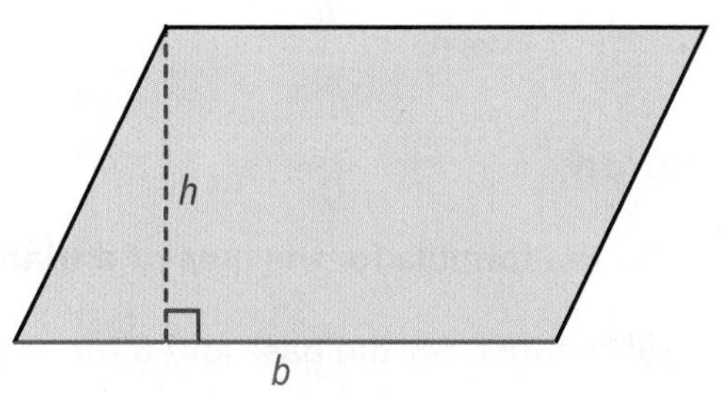

Parallelogram: $A = bh$

The formula for the area of an acute triangle is $A = \frac{1}{2}bh$, where A represents the area, b represents the length of a base, and h represents the corresponding height.

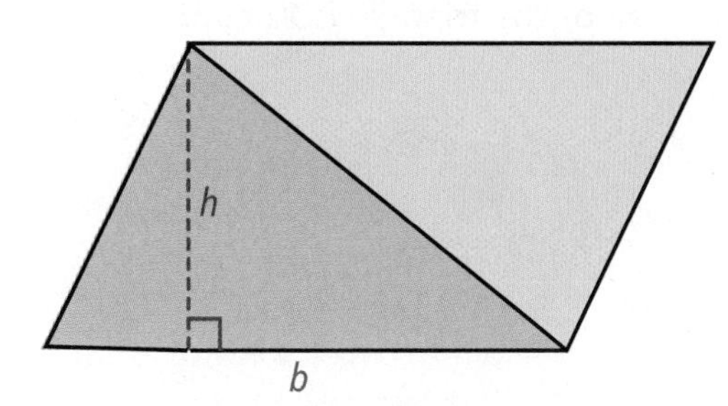

Parallelogram: $A = bh$

Acute Triangle: $A = \frac{1}{2}bh$

The formula for the area of an obtuse triangle is $A = \frac{1}{2}bh$, where A represents the area, b represents the length of a base, and h represents the corresponding height.

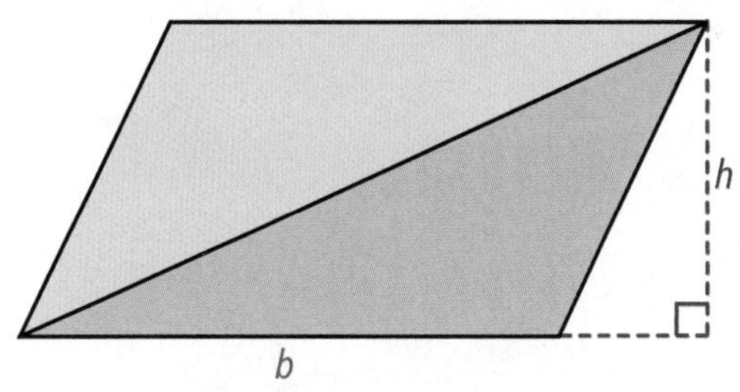

Parallelogram: $A = bh$

Obtuse Triangle: $A = \frac{1}{2}bh$

Part 3

Example Using the Formula for the Area of a Triangle

What is the area of the triangle?

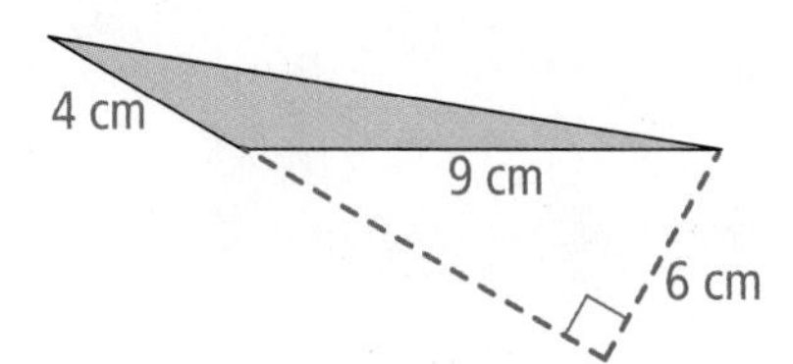

continued on next page >

Part 3

Example continued

Solution

Use the formula for the area of a triangle. $A = \frac{1}{2}bh$

Substitute 4 for the base and 6 for the height. $= \frac{1}{2} \cdot 4 \cdot 6$

Multiply. $= 12$

The area of the triangle is 12 cm^2.

Digital Resources    

1. For a geometry project, the students are cutting triangles like the one shown. All measurements are in inches.

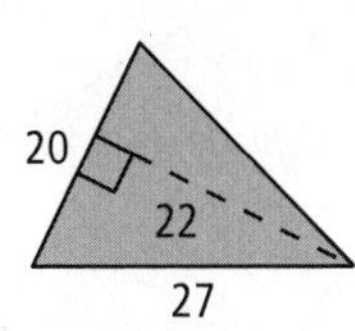

a. Which figure below shows the triangle composed into a parallelogram?

A.

B.

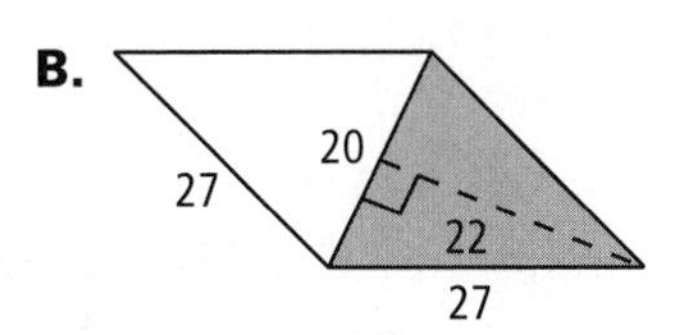

C.

b. What is the area of the triangle?

2. Pieces of fabric for costumes are shaped as obtuse triangles as shown. You cut a parallelogram to make two of the triangles.

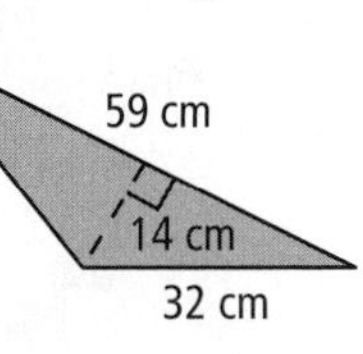

a. Which diagram shows an original parallelogram fabric piece?

A.

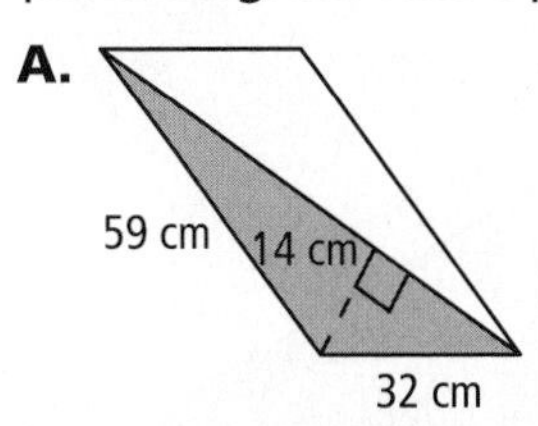

B.

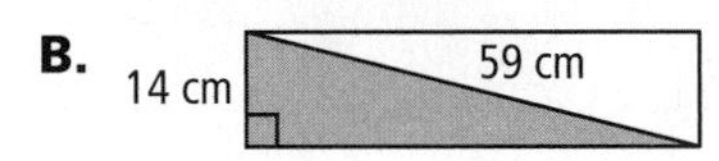

C.

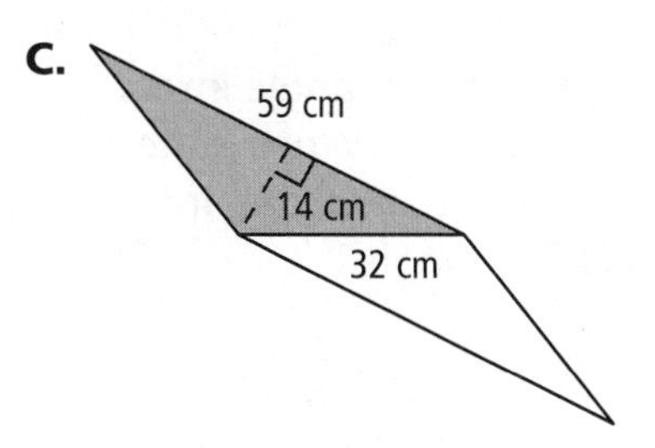

b. What is the area of each triangular piece?

3. Find the area of the triangle.

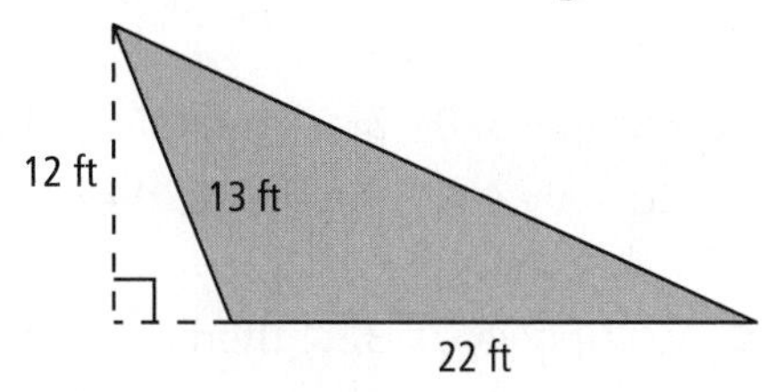

4. Find the area of a triangle that has a base of $6\frac{1}{2}$ yd and a height of $3\frac{1}{6}$ yd.

5. a. Which figure below shows the triangle composed into a parallelogram?

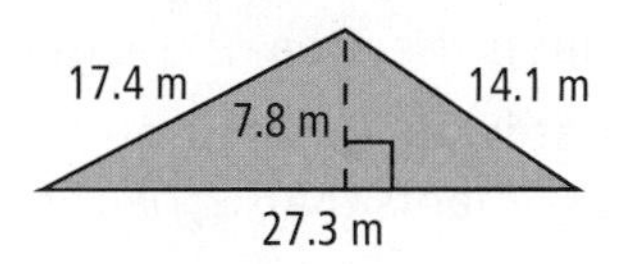

A.

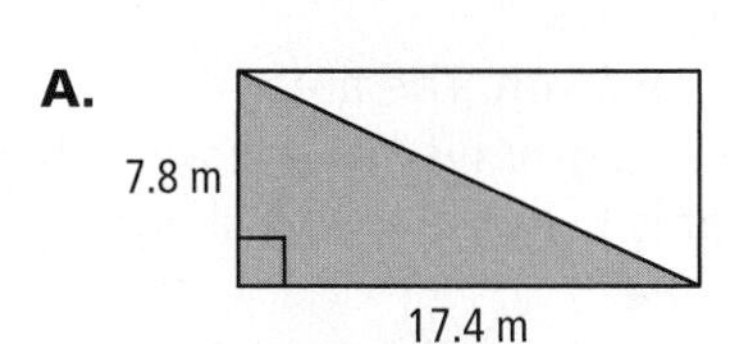

B.

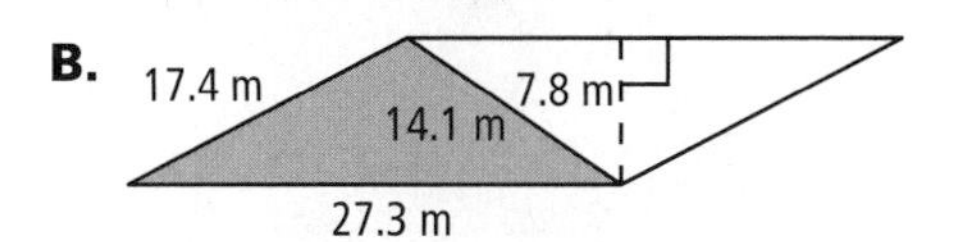

C.

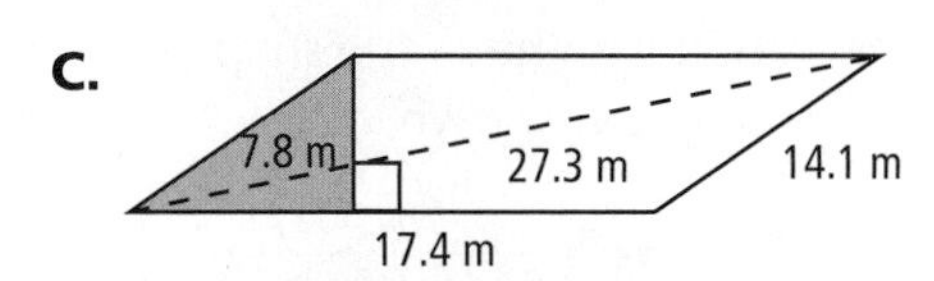

D.

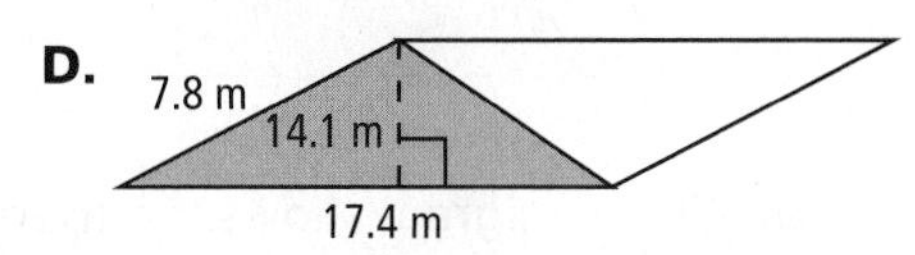

b. What is the area of the triangle?

c. What is the perimeter of the triangle?

See your complete lesson at MyMathUniverse.com

6. **Think About the Process** One way to find the area of a triangle is to compose the triangle into a parallelogram. What is the correct procedure to find the area of the shaded triangle?

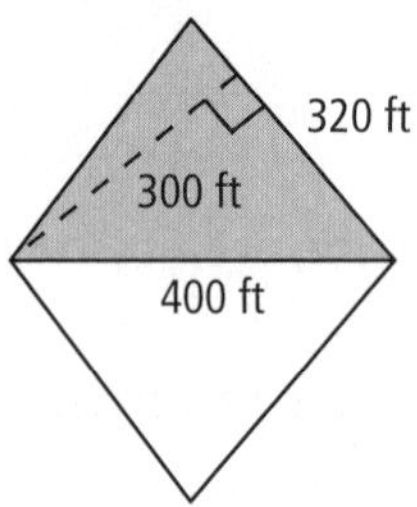

A. Multiply 320 · 300, then divide by 2.

B. Multiply 400 · 300 · 320, then divide by 2.

C. Multiply 400 · 320, then divide by 2.

D. Multiply 400 · 300, then divide by 2.

7. **Gardening** Gabe's garden is in the shape of a triangle with a base of 28 ft and a height of 24 ft. Gabe has plants that require 8 ft^2 each to grow properly.

a. What is the area of the garden?

b. What is the greatest number of these plants that Gabe can fit into the garden?

8. **Mental Math** The area of the parallelogram is 684 square inches. What is the area of the shaded triangle?

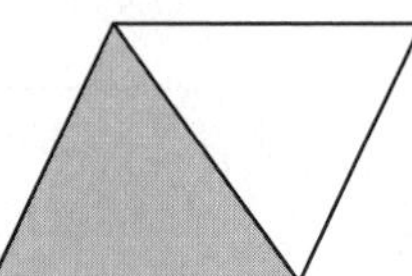

9. A flag is to have the shape of a triangle as shown.

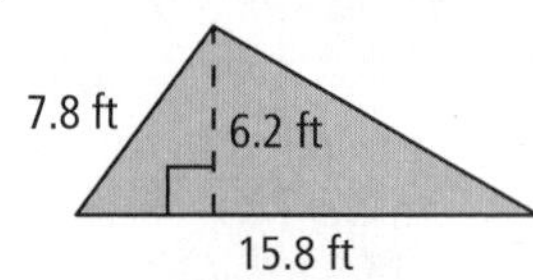

a. Which diagram shows the triangle composed into a parallelogram?

A.

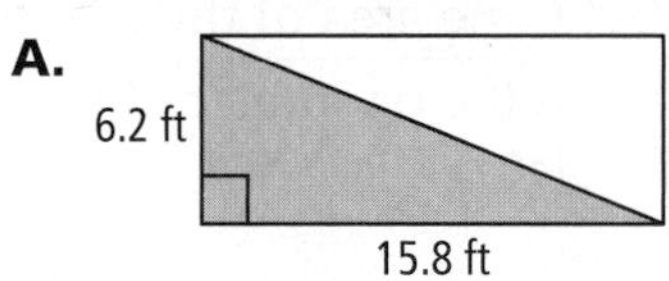

B.

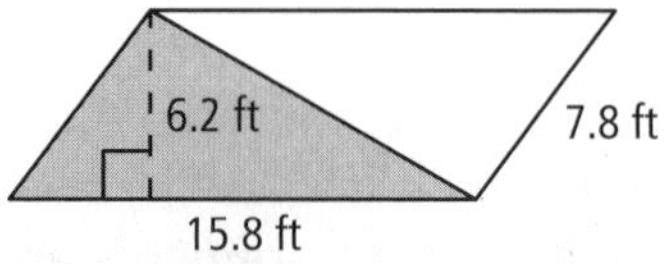

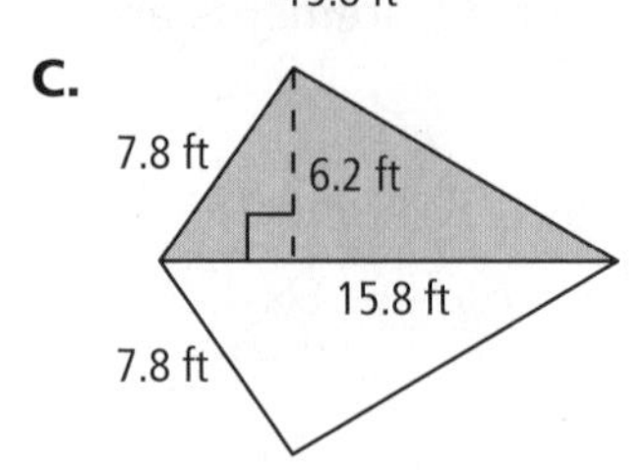

C.

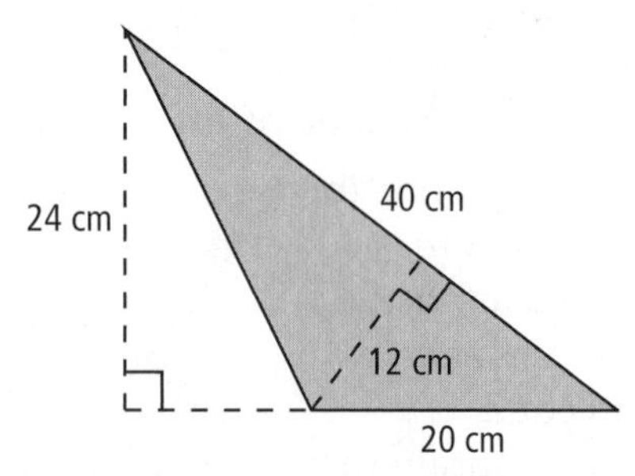

b. The material for the flag costs $6 per ft^2. How much will all the material for the flag cost?

10. The owner of an ice cream shop is making signs to advertise. Each sign will be in the shape of a triangle to represent an ice cream cone. The sides of the triangle measure 34 cm, 34 cm, and 32 cm. The height from the shortest side to the opposite vertex is 30 cm.

a. What is the area of one sign?

b. How much material does the owner need to make 4 dozen signs?

11. **Think About the Process** You want to find the area of this triangle. If you choose 40 cm as the base, what is the corresponding height?

24 cm

40 cm

12 cm

20 cm

12. **Challenge** What is the value of *n*? Explain how you can solve for *n* without finding the area of the triangle.

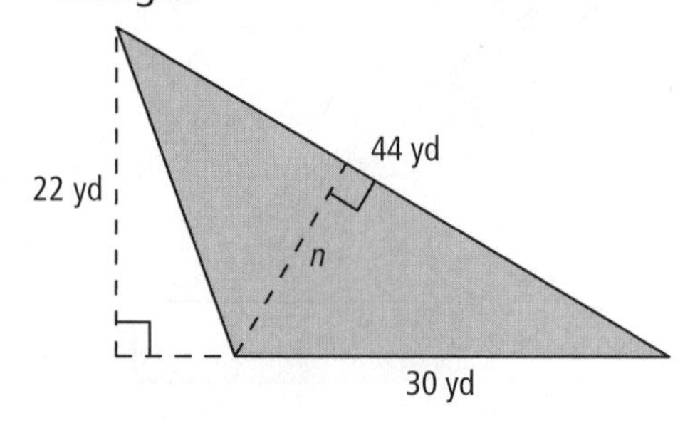

13-5 Polygons

Vocabulary
polygon, regular polygon

CCSS: 6.G.A.1

Key Concept

A **polygon** is a closed figure formed by three or more line segments that do not cross.

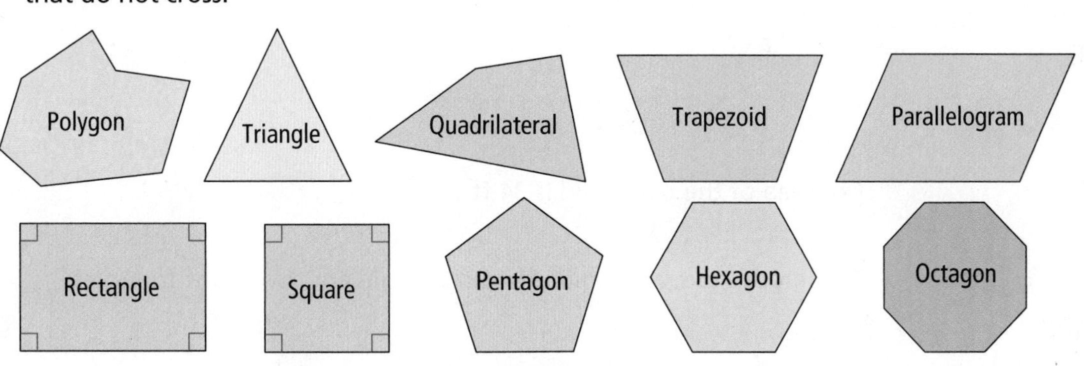

Part 1

Example Finding Areas of Trapezoids

What is the area of the trapezoid?

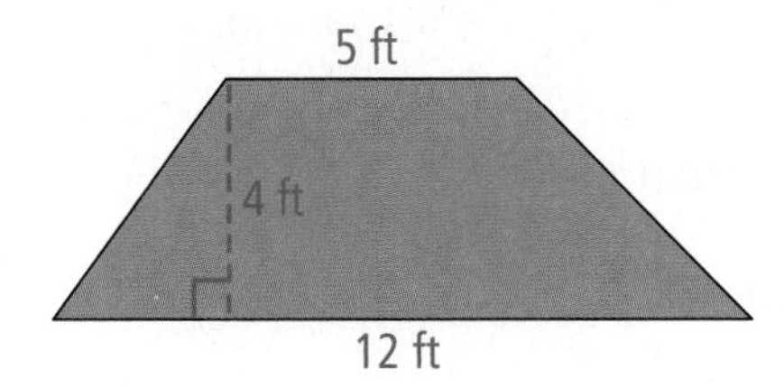

Solution

Method 1 Compose the trapezoid into a parallelogram.

First, make a copy of the trapezoid. Then, rotate the copy. Then push the trapezoids together to form a parallelogram. The parallelogram has the same height as the original trapezoid, and the base of the parallelogram is equal to the sum of the bases of the trapezoid. So the base of the parallelogram is 17 feet. The area of the original trapezoid equals half of the area of the parallelogram.

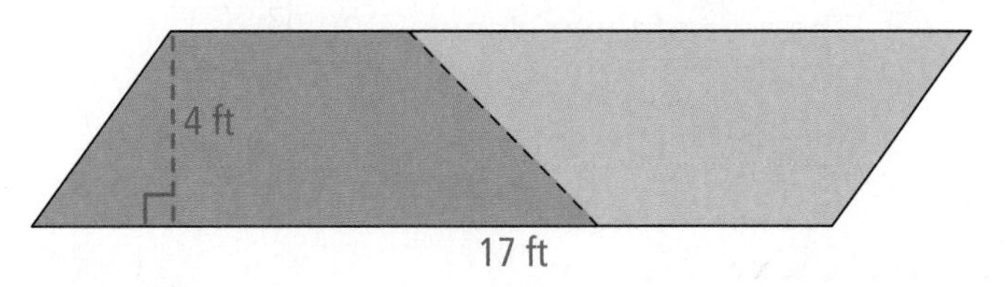

continued on next page >

Part 1

Solution continued

$$\text{area of trapezoid} = \frac{1}{2} \cdot \text{area of parallelogram}$$

$$= \frac{1}{2} \cdot b \cdot h$$

$$= \frac{1}{2} \cdot 17 \cdot 4$$

$$= 34$$

The area of the trapezoid is 34 ft^2.

Method 2 Decompose the trapezoid into a rectangle and two right triangles.

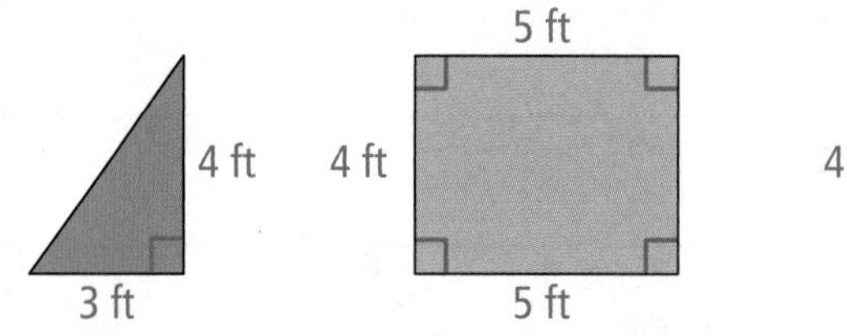

area of trapezoid = area of right triangle + area of rectangle + area of right triangle

Step 1 Find the area of the first right triangle.

$$\text{area of right triangle} = \frac{1}{2}bh$$

$$= \frac{1}{2} \cdot 3 \cdot 4$$

$$= 6$$

The area of the first right triangle is 6 ft^2.

Step 2 Find the area of the rectangle.

$$\text{area of rectangle} = bh$$

$$= 5 \cdot 4$$

$$= 20$$

The area of the rectangle is 20 ft^2.

continued on next page >

Part 1

Solution continued

Step 3 Find the area of the second right triangle.

$$\text{area of right triangle} = \frac{1}{2}bh$$
$$= \frac{1}{2} \cdot 4 \cdot 4$$
$$= 8$$

The area of the second right triangle is 8 ft^2.

$$\text{area of trapezoid} = 6 \text{ ft}^2 + 20 \text{ ft}^2 + 8 \text{ ft}^2$$
$$= 34 \text{ ft}^2$$

The area of trapezoid is 34 ft^2.

Part 2

Intro

A **regular polygon** is a polygon with all sides of equal length and all angles of equal measure. You can decompose a regular polygon to find its area.

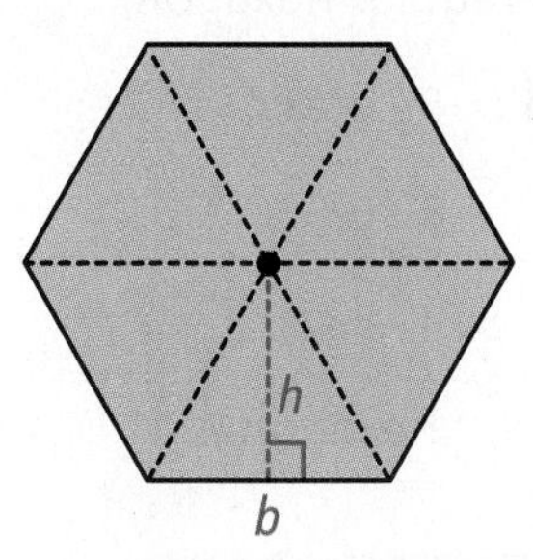

Example Finding Areas of Regular Hexagons

Decompose the regular hexagon into six matching triangles to find the area of the hexagon.

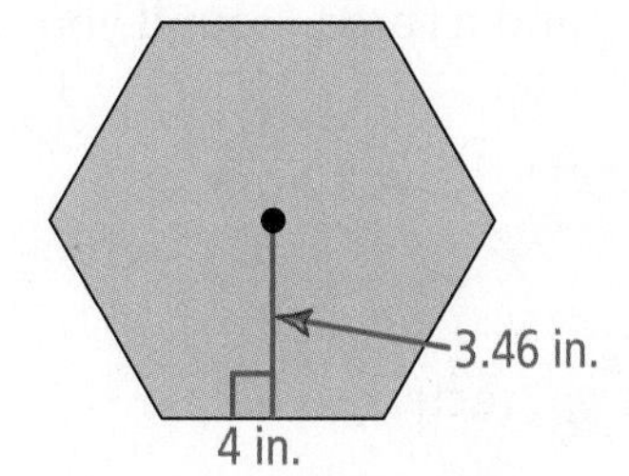

continued on next page >

Part 2

Example continued

Solution

Step 1 Decompose the hexagon into six equilateral triangles.

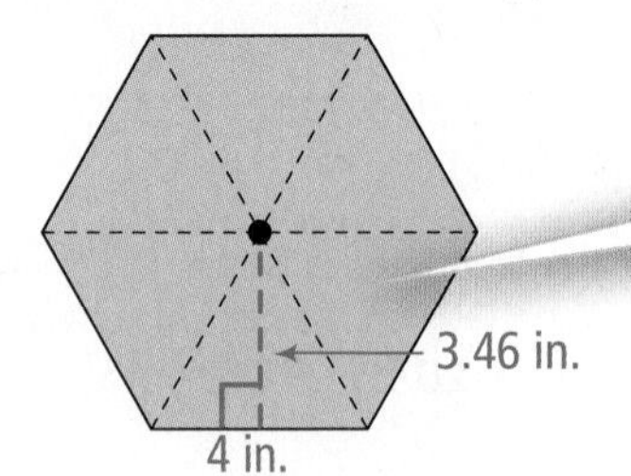

Each triangle has a height of 3.46 in. and a corresponding base of 4 in.

Step 2 Find the area of one triangle.

Use the formula for the area of a triangle.	$A = \frac{1}{2}bh$
Substitute for the height and the base.	$= \frac{1}{2} \cdot 4 \cdot 3.46$
Multiply.	$= 6.92$

The area of one triangle is 6.92 in.^{2}.

Step 3 Find the area of the regular hexagon.

$$\text{area of hexagon} = 6 \cdot \text{area of a triangle}$$
$$= 6 \cdot 6.92$$
$$= 41.52$$

The area of the regular hexagon is 41.52 in.^{2}.

Part 3

Example Finding Areas of Regular Octagons

Decompose the regular octagon to find its area. Round your answer to the nearest whole number.

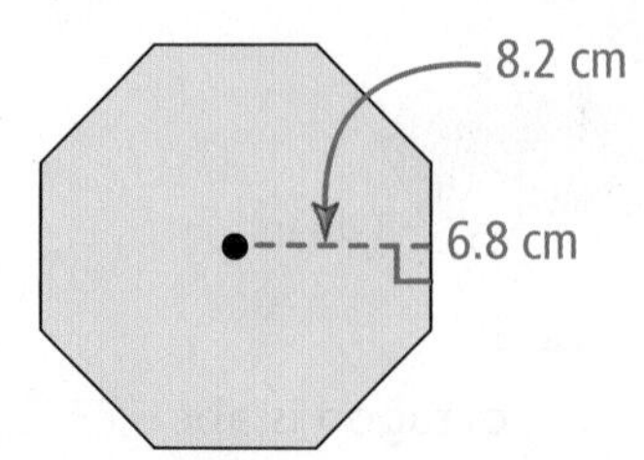

continued on next page >

Part 3

Example continued

Solution

Method 1 Decompose the regular octagon into eight matching triangles.

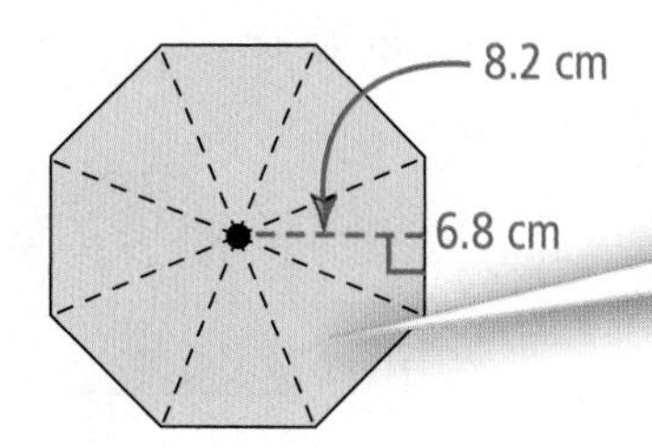

Each triangle has a height of 8.2 cm and a corresponding base of 6.8 cm.

$$\text{area of triangle} = \frac{1}{2} \cdot bh$$
$$= \frac{1}{2} \cdot 6.8 \cdot 8.2$$
$$= 27.88$$

area of the octagon $= 8 \cdot$ area of triangle $= 8 \cdot 27.88 = 223.04$

The area of the regular octagon is about 223 cm^2.

Method 2 Decompose the polygon into a rectangle and two trapezoids.

The rectangle and trapezoids have a base of $2 \cdot 8.2$, or 16.4 cm.

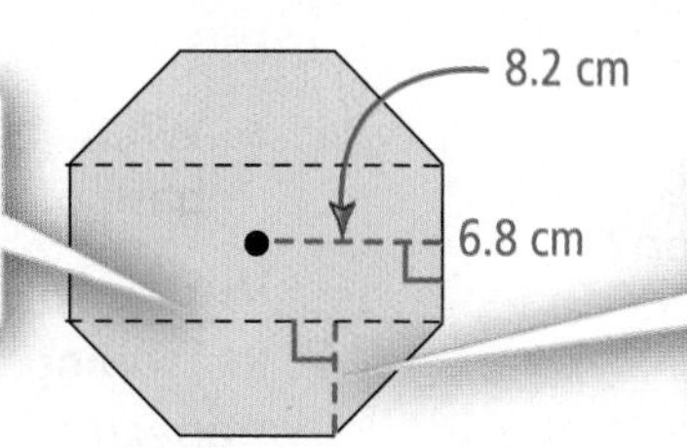

Each of the trapezoids has a height of $(16.4 - 6.8) \div 2$, or 4.8 cm.

area of rectangle $= bh = 16.4 \cdot 6.8 = 111.52$

$$\text{area of trapezoid} = \frac{1}{2} \cdot \text{area of composed parallelogram}$$
$$= \frac{1}{2} \cdot bh$$
$$= \frac{1}{2}(16.4 + 6.8) \cdot 4.8$$
$$= 55.68$$

$$\text{area of polygon} = \text{area of rectangle} + 2 \cdot \text{area of trapezoid}$$
$$= 111.52 + 2 \cdot 55.68$$
$$= 111.52 + 111.36$$
$$= 222.88$$

The area of the regular octagon is about 223 cm^2.

Digital Resources    

1. Compose the trapezoid into a parallelogram. What is the area of this trapezoid? Note that the diagram is not to scale.

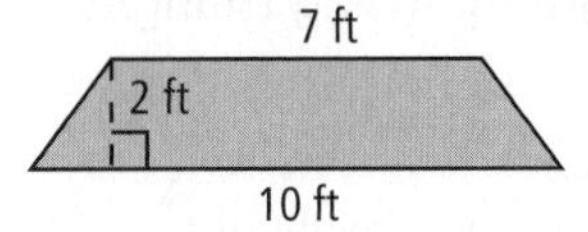

2. Decompose the trapezoid into a rectangle and two right triangles. What is the area of the trapezoid? Note that the diagram is not to scale.

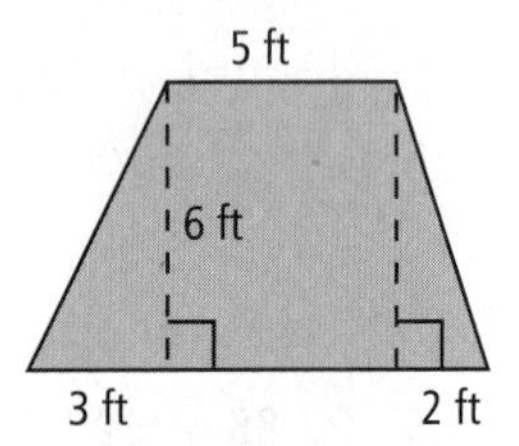

3. Multiple Representations

a. Show three different ways that you can decompose the regular hexagon into other shapes.

b. If you decompose the hexagon shown into six matching triangles, what is the area of the hexagon?

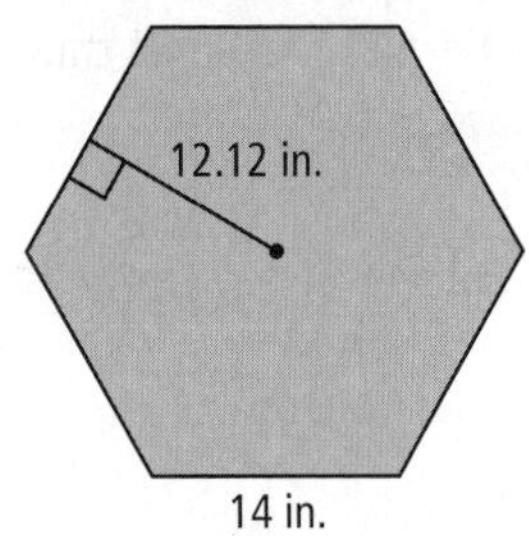

4. You win an award in the shape of a regular hexagon. Decompose the hexagon into six matching triangles. What is the area of the award?

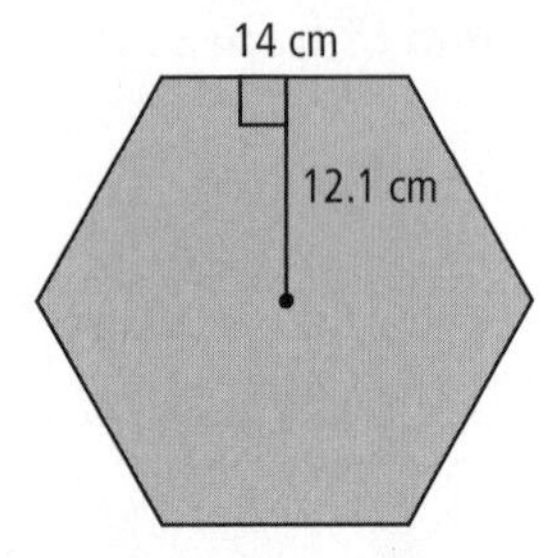

5. a. Writing Compose the trapezoid into a parallelogram to find a formula for the area of a trapezoid. Explain how you got your formula.

b. Draw a picture to support your answer.

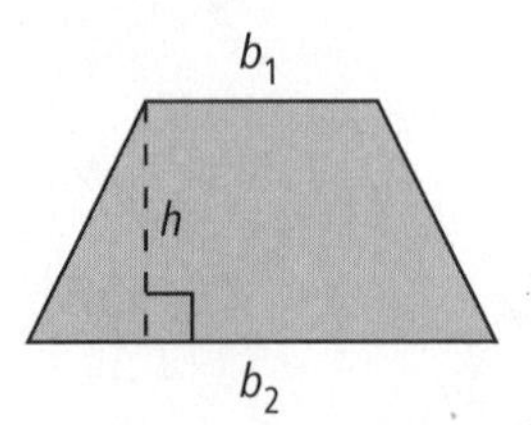

6. Think About the Process To find the area of this trapezoid, compose the trapezoid into a parallelogram. (Note that the diagram is not to scale.)

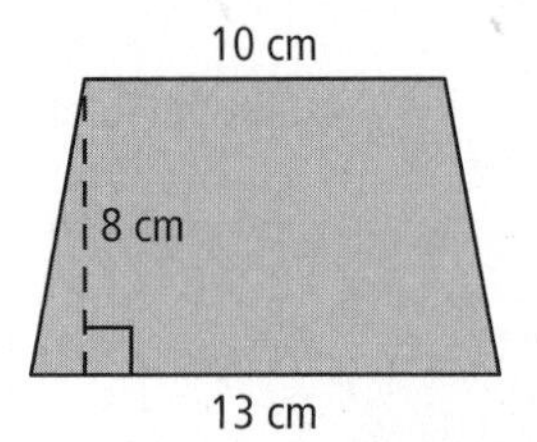

a. What should be the length of the base of the parallelogram?

b. What is the area of this trapezoid?

7. Reasoning You are told that a trapezoid has bases of 11 in. and 18 in., and a height of 10 in. You are asked to find the area of the trapezoid by decomposing it into a rectangle and two right triangles.

a. Show your picture of the trapezoid. Then show a picture that your friend could draw with the trapezoid having a shape different from yours.

b. Explain how each of you would find the area and why your results would be the same. What is the area of the trapezoid?

8. Error Analysis Paul decomposes the regular hexagon into six matching triangles to find the area. He says that the area of the hexagon is 62.34 m^2, but he is incorrect.

a. What is the area of the hexagon?

b. What error did Paul make?

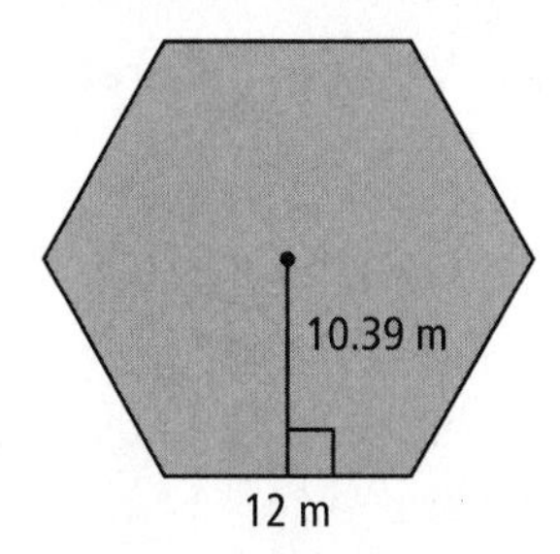

A. He found the area of 6 triangles, not one of them.

B. He multiplied 6 by bh, not $\frac{1}{2}bh$.

C. He multiplied 6 by $\frac{1}{2}b$, not $\frac{1}{2}h$, not $\frac{1}{2}bh$.

D. He found the area of one of the triangles, not 6 of them.

9. Furniture Surface Area A table in an art room has the shape of a regular octagon. You and your friend want to find the area of the top of the table. Decompose the top of the table into eight matching triangles. What is the area of the top of the table?

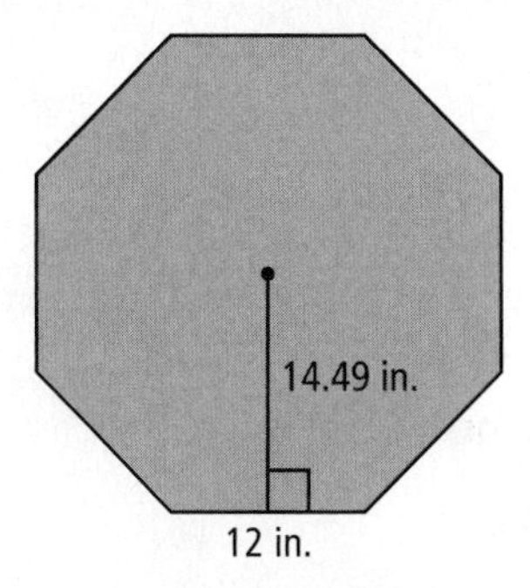

10. Think About the Process

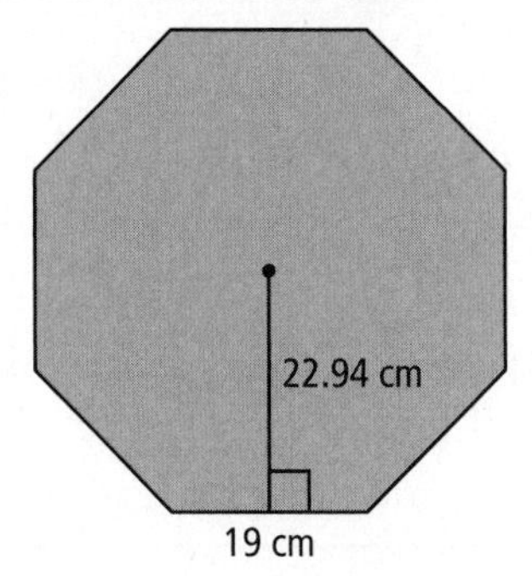

a. Explain how you can use the area of a triangle to find the area of the octagon, and why the octagon must be regular.

b. Find the area of the octagon.

11. a. Open-Ended Draw a regular octagon. Decompose your octagon into other shapes to find the area. Decompose your octagon in at least two different ways.

b. Other than triangles, which shapes can be used to decompose a regular octagon? Select all that apply.

A. a hexagon

B. a trapezoid

C. a rectangle

D. a parallelogram that is not a rectangle

12. The floor of a gazebo is in the shape of a regular octagon. Decompose this regular octagon into a rectangle and two trapezoids. What is the area of the floor?

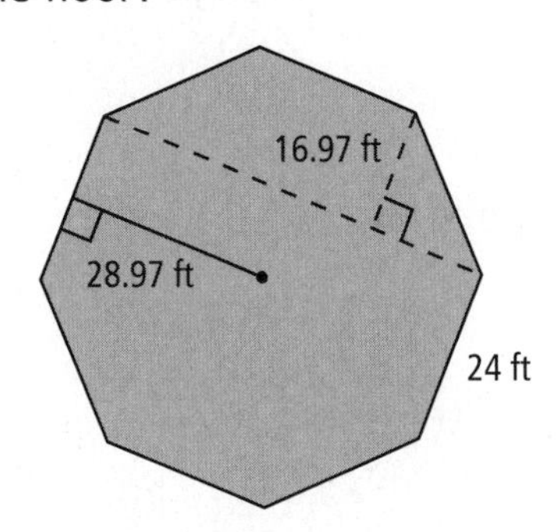

13. Challenge A ceiling is made up of 60 tiles. Each tile is in the shape of a regular hexagon. Decompose one of the hexagonal tiles into matching triangles.

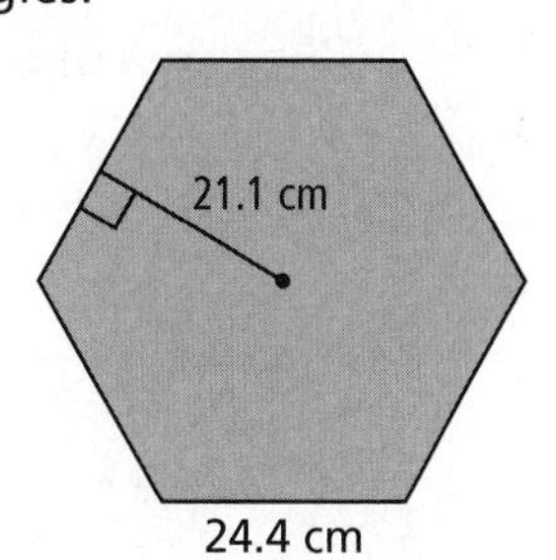

a. What is the area of one tile?

b. What is the area of the ceiling?

13-6 Problem Solving

CCSS: 6.G.A.1

Part 1

Example Finding Areas of Irregular Polygons

The polygon is a floor plan for a new music area in a school. What is the area of the polygon?

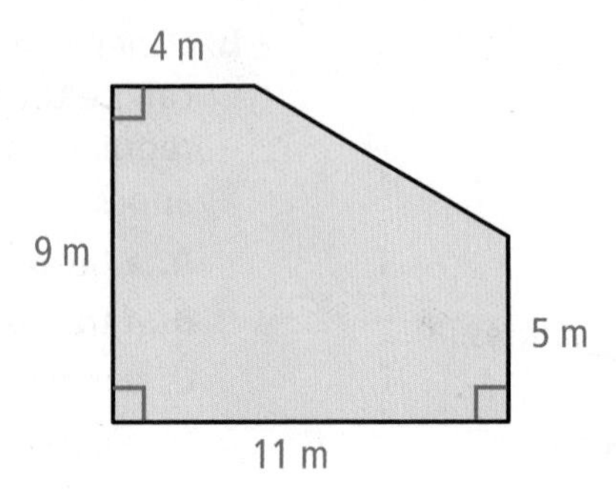

Solution

Method 1 Decompose the polygon into a square, a right triangle, and a rectangle.

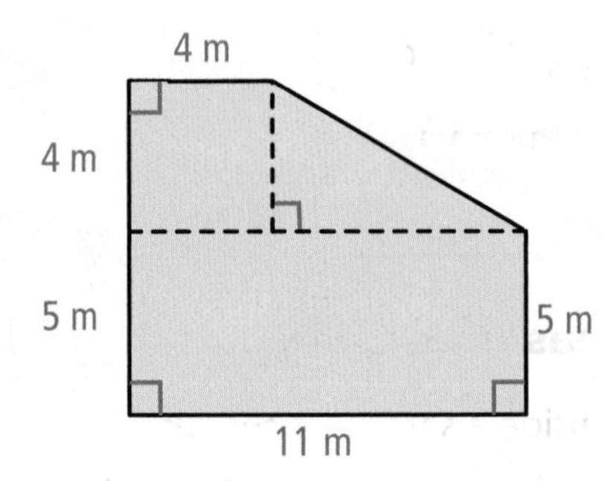

Area of square: $4^2 = 16$, or $16\ m^2$

Area of right triangle: $\frac{1}{2} \cdot 7 \cdot 4 = 14$, or $14\ m^2$

Area of rectangle: $11 \cdot 5 = 55$, or $55\ m^2$

area of polygon = area of square + area of right triangle + area of rectangle

$= 16 + 14 + 55$

$= 85$

The area of the polygon is $85\ m^2$.

continued on next page >

Part 1

Solution continued

Method 2 Decompose the polygon into a rectangle and a trapezoid.

Area of rectangle:
$11 \cdot 5 = 55$, or 55 m^2

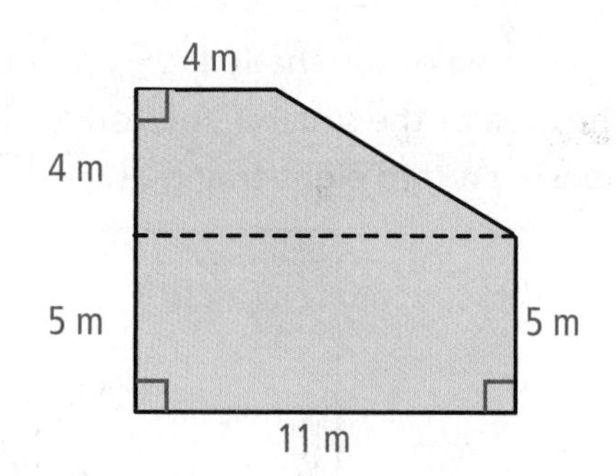

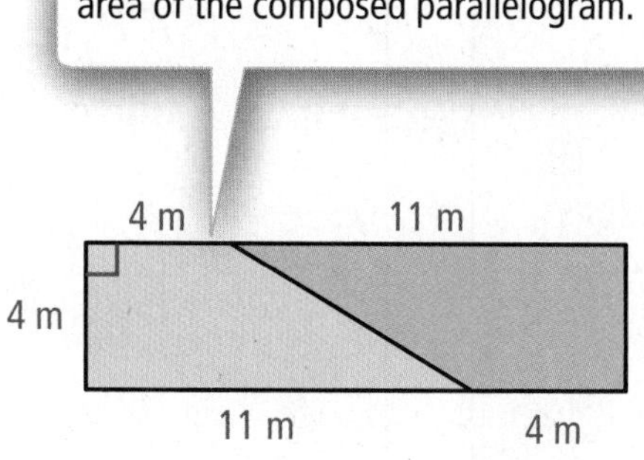

Area of trapezoid: $\frac{1}{2}(11 + 4)(4) = 30$, or 30 m^2.

area of polygon = area of rectangle + area of trapezoid

= 55 + 30

= 85

The area of the polygon is 85 m^2.

Part 2

Example Finding Areas of Shaded Regions of Squares

A regular octagon just fits inside a square as shown. What is the area of the shaded region? Round your answer to the nearest whole number.

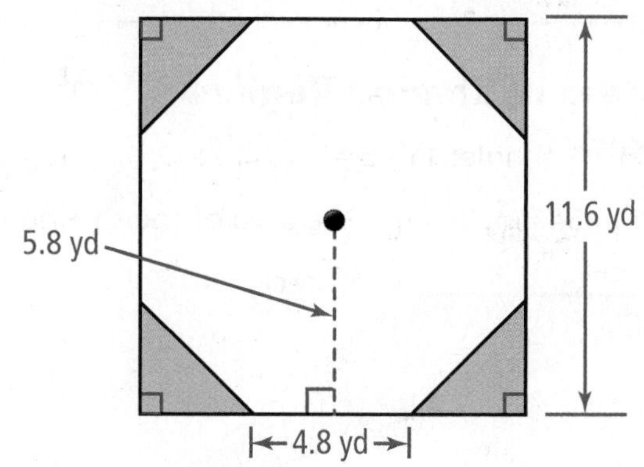

continued on next page >

Part 2

Example continued

Solution

To find the area of the shaded region, subtract the area of the octagon from the area of the square. You can find the area of the octagon by decomposing it into eight triangles.

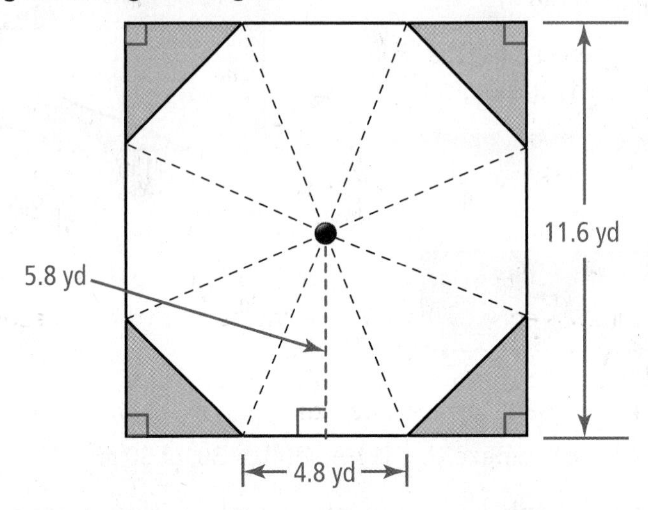

Area of square: $11.6^2 = 134.56$, or $134.56\ \text{yd}^2$

Area of one triangle: $\frac{1}{2} \cdot 4.8 \cdot 5.8 = 13.92$, or $13.92\ \text{yd}^2$

Area of octagon: $8 \cdot 13.92 = 111.36$, or $111.36\ \text{yd}^2$

$$\begin{aligned}\text{Area of shaded region} &= \text{area of square} - \text{area of octagon}\\ &= 134.56 - 111.36\\ &= 23.2\end{aligned}$$

The area of the shaded region is $23.2\ \text{yd}^2$.

Part 3

Example Finding Areas of Shaded Regions of Trapezoids

The trapezoid has an area of $54\ \text{in.}^2$. What is the area of the shaded region?

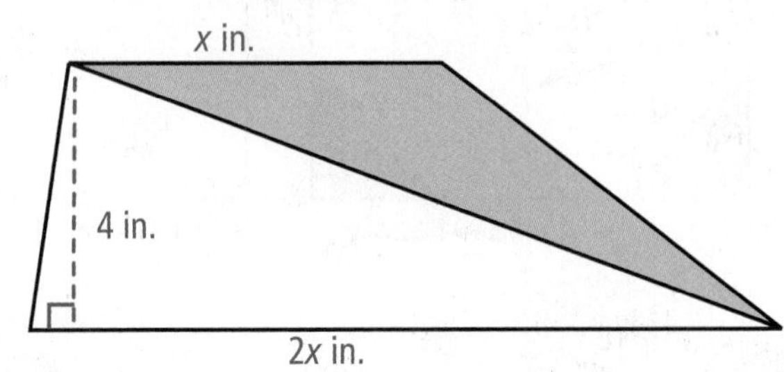

continued on next page >

Part 3

Example continued

Solution

area of shaded region = area of trapezoid − area of triangle

You know the area of the trapezoid. To find the area of the triangle, you first need to find the value of x. Start by composing the trapezoid into a parallelogram.

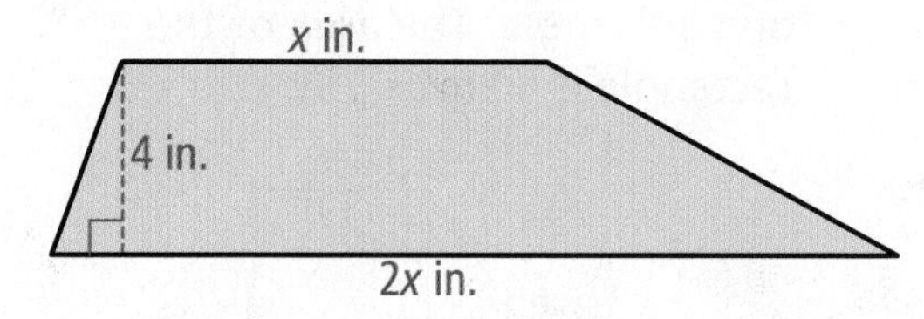

The parallelogram has the same height as the original trapezoid and the base of the parallelogram is equal to the sum of the bases of the trapezoid. So the base of the parallelogram is $3x$ in.

The area of the original trapezoid equals half the area of the parallelogram.

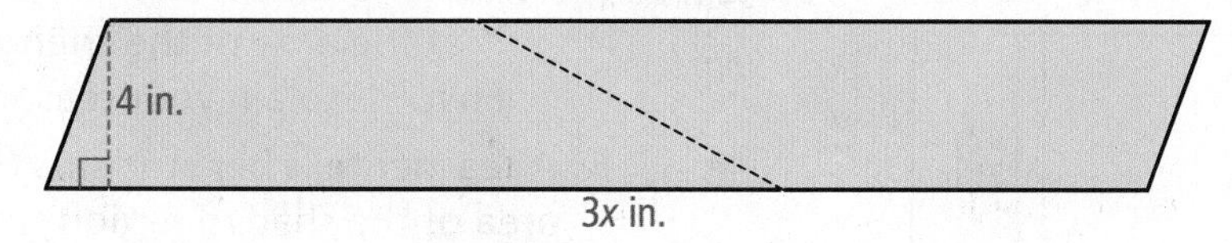

$$\begin{aligned} \text{area of parallelogram} &= bh \\ &= 3x \cdot 4 \\ &= 12x \end{aligned}$$

$$\begin{aligned} \text{area of trapezoid} &= \frac{1}{2} \cdot \text{area of parallelogram} \\ 54 &= \frac{1}{2} \cdot \text{area of parallelogram} \\ 108 &= \text{area of parallelogram} \end{aligned}$$

So the area of the parallelogram is 108 in.^{2}. Now you can solve for x.

$$\begin{aligned} 108 &= 12x \\ \frac{108}{12} &= \frac{12x}{12} \\ 9 &= x \end{aligned}$$

If the value of x is 9, then the value of 2 times x is 18.

$$\begin{aligned} \text{area of triangle} &= \frac{1}{2}bh \\ &= \frac{1}{2} \cdot 18 \cdot 4 \\ &= 36 \end{aligned}$$

$$\begin{aligned} \text{area of shaded region} &= \text{area of trapezoid} - \text{area of triangle} \\ &= 54 - 36 \\ &= 18 \end{aligned}$$

The area of the shaded region is 18 in.^{2}.

Digital Resources

1. The outside wall of a dollhouse has the shape of this polygon. What is the area of the polygon?

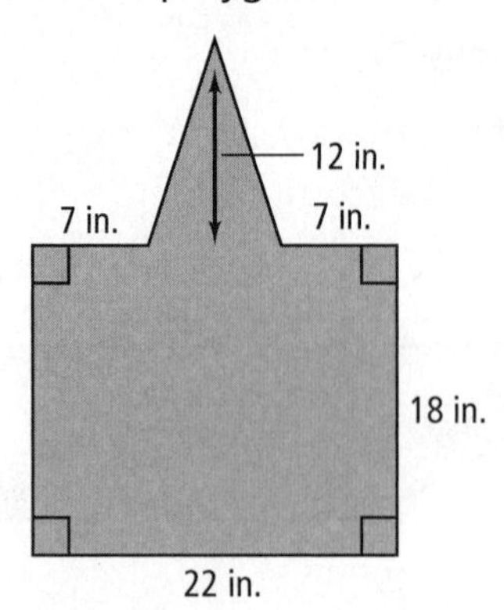

2. A sidewalk is built around two sides of a building. What is the area of the sidewalk? Note that the diagram is not to scale.

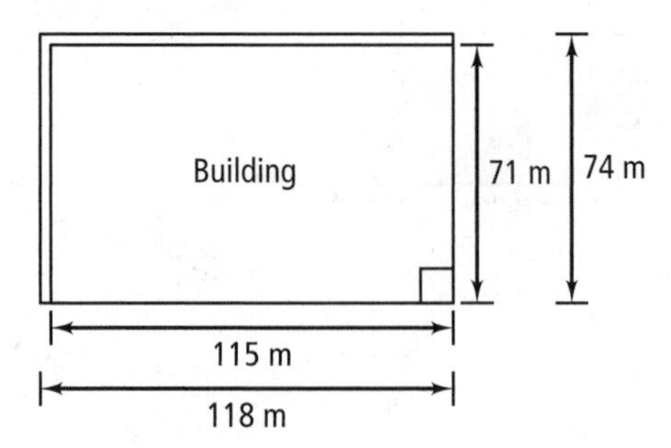

3. Chloe colors a border around a drawing. The height of the drawing is 2 in. greater than the 6-in. base. What is the area of the border?

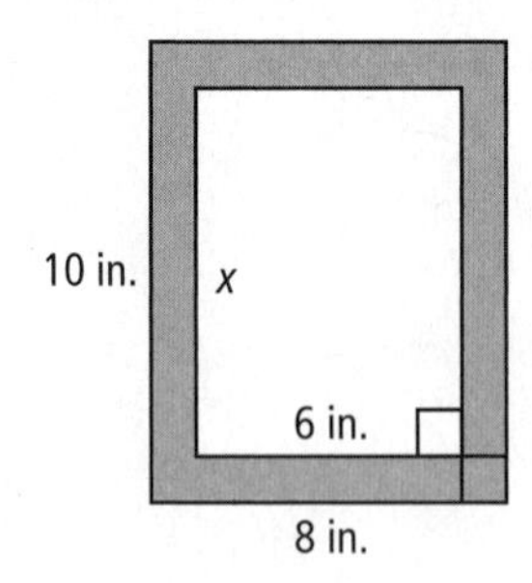

4. How can the polygon be decomposed? Select all that apply.

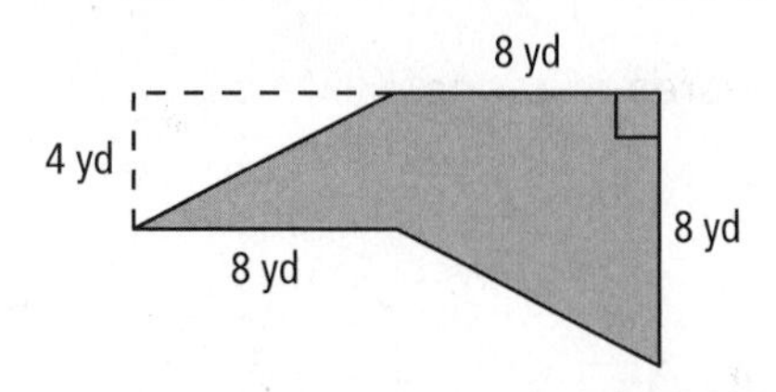

A. one hexagon and two rectangles
B. one rectangle and two triangles
C. one triangle and one trapezoid
D. one triangle and one square
E. one triangle and two rectangles
F. one trapezoid and two squares

5. The polygon is made up of a rectangle and a triangle. The area of the rectangle is 60 m^2.

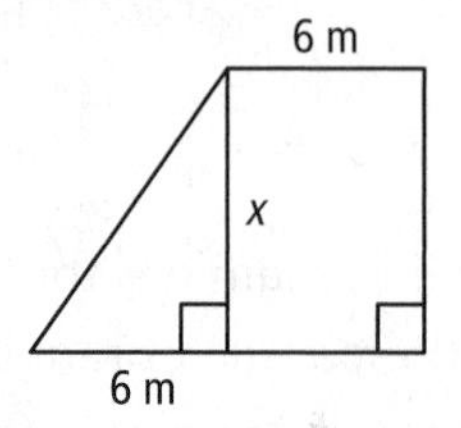

a. Find the area of the polygon.

b. Is the result the same if you know that the area of the triangle is 60 m^2? Explain your reasoning.

6. A teacher tells her students to find the area of the shaded region. The class is to use the area of a triangle and the area of a square. A student incorrectly states that the area is 793 cm^2.

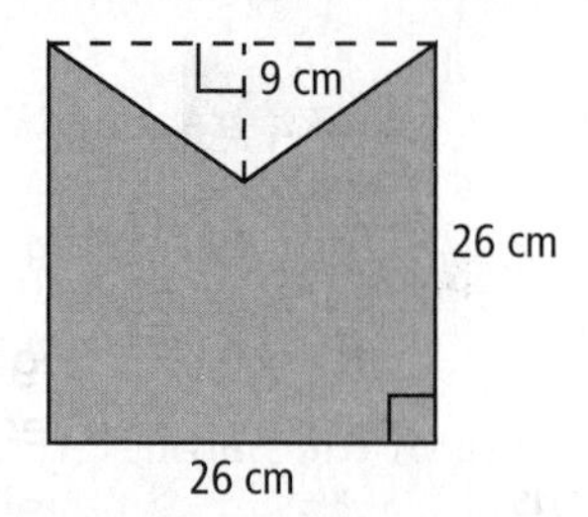

a. What is the correct area of the shaded region?

b. What is the student's error?

A. The student subtracted the area of the triangle from the area of the square.
B. The student multiplied the area of the triangle and the area of the square.
C. The student subtracted the area of the square from the area of the triangle.
D. The student added the area of the triangle and the area of the square.

See your complete lesson at MyMathUniverse.com

7. The polygon is a cross-section view of a building block. What is the area of the polygon?

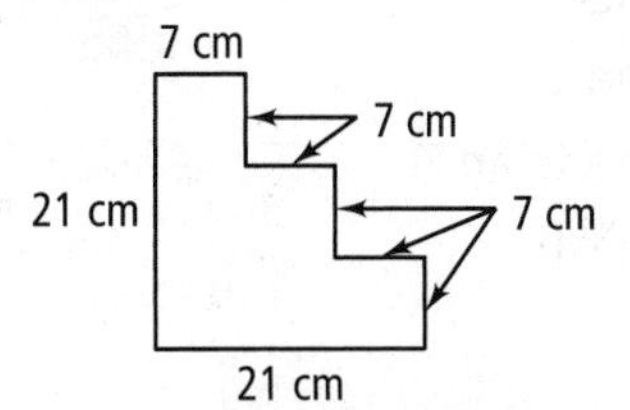

8. **a.** Draw a polygon that is made up of squares, triangles, and parallelograms.

   b. Which of these formulas would you use to find the area of the polygon? Select all that apply.

   A. $A = \frac{h}{b}$ **B.** $A = \frac{1}{2}bh$

   C. $A = s^2$ **D.** $A = bh$

   E. $A = b + h$ **F.** $A = \frac{b}{h}$

9. **Think About the Process** A square fits inside a rectangle. Describe the area of the shaded region.

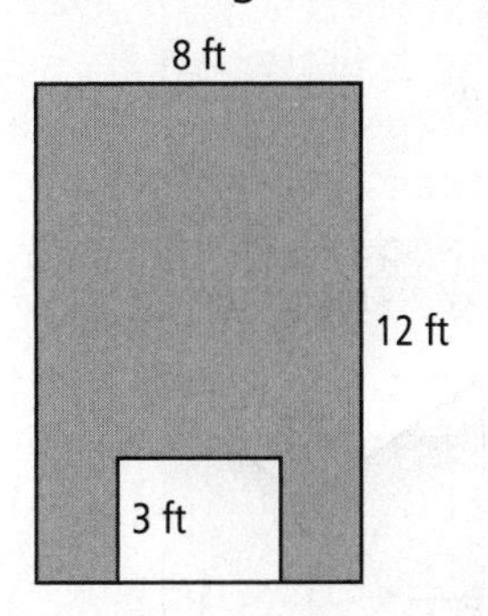

   A. The area of the shaded region is equal to the area of the rectangle minus the area of the square.

   B. The area of the shaded region is equal to the area of the square minus the area of the rectangle.

   C. The area of the shaded region is equal to the area of the square times the area of the rectangle.

   D. The area of the shaded region is equal to the area of the rectangle plus the area of the square.

10. **Think About the Process** A regular octagon is decomposed into two matching trapezoids and a rectangle. The area of the rectangle is 195.48 cm². You want to find the area of the two trapezoids. The first step is to find the value of x. How do you find the value of x?

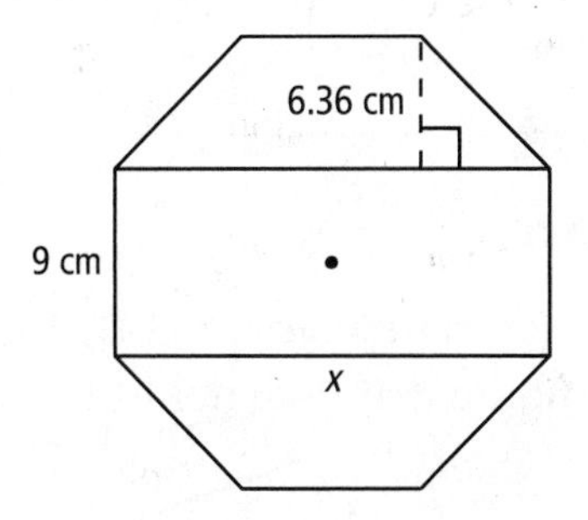

   A. Multiply 195.48 by 3.

   B. Divide 9 by 195.48.

   C. Divide 195.48 by 9.

   D. You need more information to find the value of x.

11. **Challenge** The rectangular lot has a square sandbox surrounded by lawn. Mowing the lawn costs $0.02 per square foot.

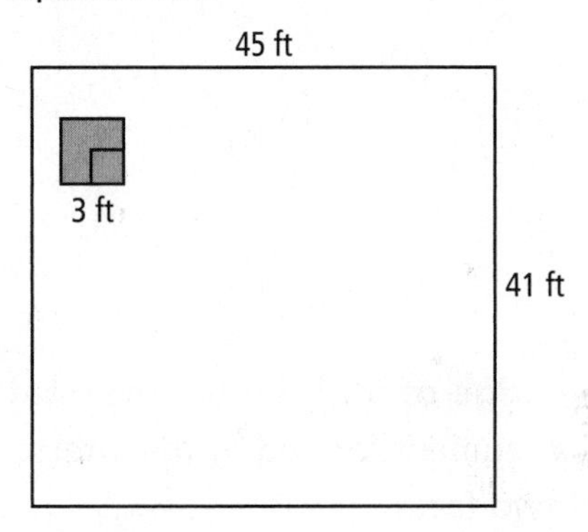

   a. How much does it cost to mow the whole lawn?

   b. How does the location of the sandbox affect the cost of mowing the whole lawn?

12. **Challenge** The area of the regular hexagon is 584.57 cm². What is the height, x, of the hexagon?

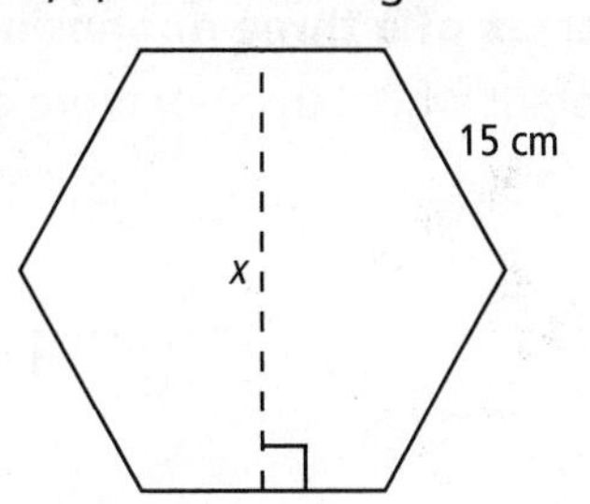

14-1 Analyzing Three-Dimensional Figures

CCSS: 6.G.A.4

Vocabulary
base, edge, face, height, lateral face, prism, pyramid, three-dimensional figure, vertex of a three-dimensional figure

Part 1

Intro

A **three-dimensional (3-D) figure** is a figure that does not lie in a plane.

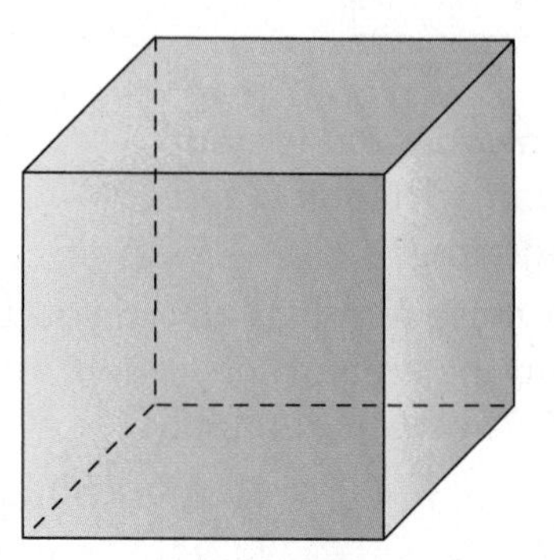

A **face of a three-dimensional figure** is a flat surface shaped like a polygon.

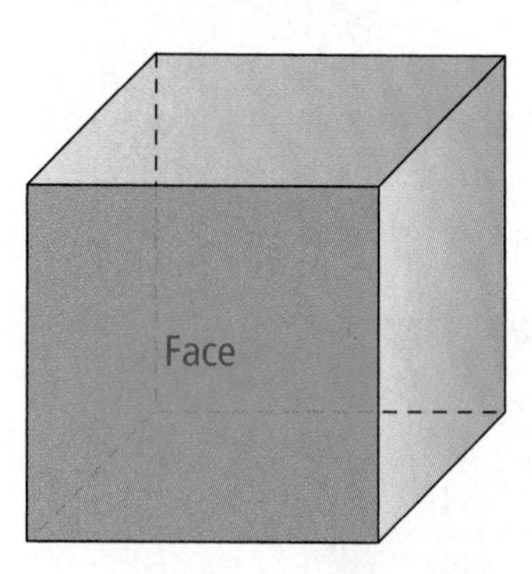

An **edge of a three-dimensional figure** is a segment formed by the intersection of two faces.

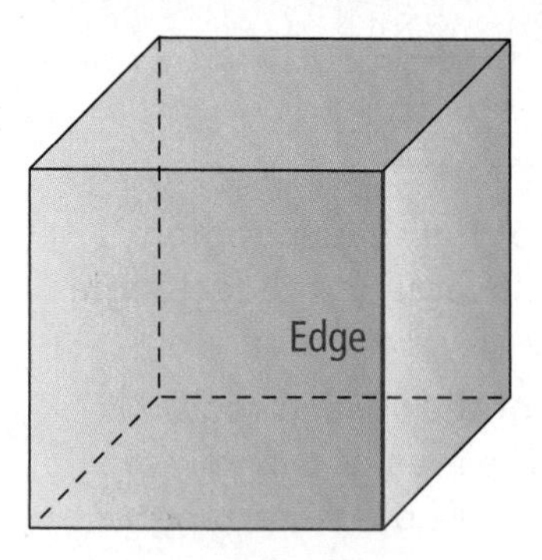

A **vertex of a three-dimensional figure** is a point where three or more edges meet.

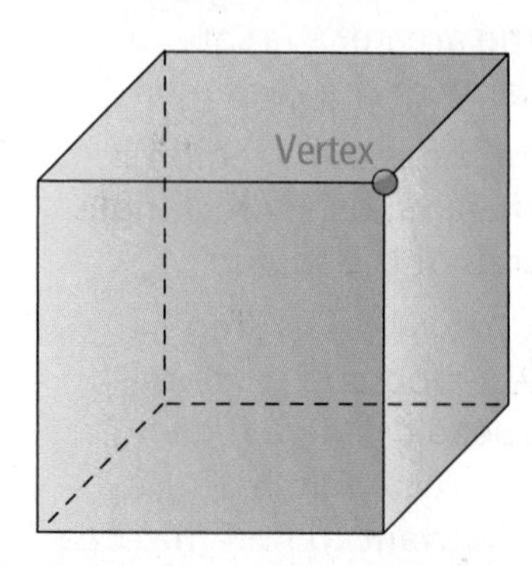

Part 1

Example Identifying Characteristics of 3-D Figures

Decide whether each statement is *true* or *false*.

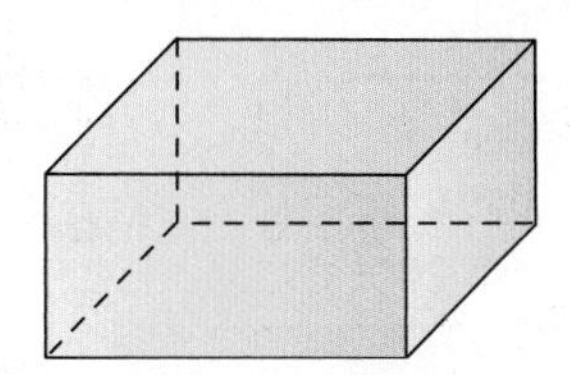

a. The figure is a three-dimensional figure.

b. The figure has three faces.

c. The faces are triangles.

d. The figure has 12 edges.

e. The figure has six vertices.

Solution

a. True; the figure does not lie in a plane, so it is a three-dimensional figure.

b. False, the figure has six faces.

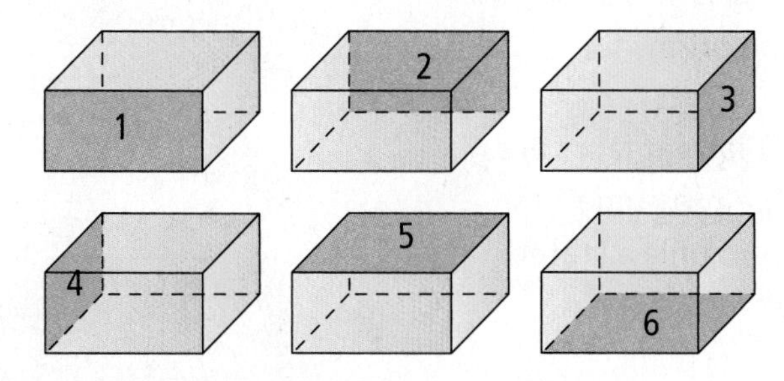

c. False, the faces are rectangles.

d. True, there are 12 segments where two faces intersect, so the figure has 12 edges.

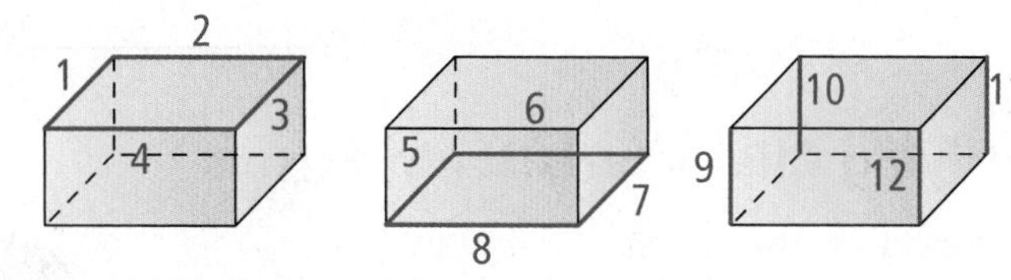

e. False, there are eight vertices.

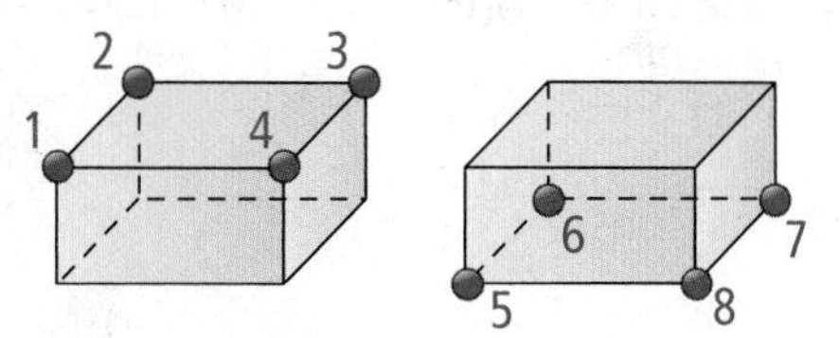

Part 2

Intro

A **prism** is a three-dimensional figure with two parallel polygonal faces that are the same size and shape.

A **base of a prism** is one of a pair of parallel polygonal faces that are the same size and shape. You name a prism for the shape of its bases.

The **height of a prism** is the length of a perpendicular segment that joins the bases.

A **lateral face of a prism** is a face that joins the bases of the prism.

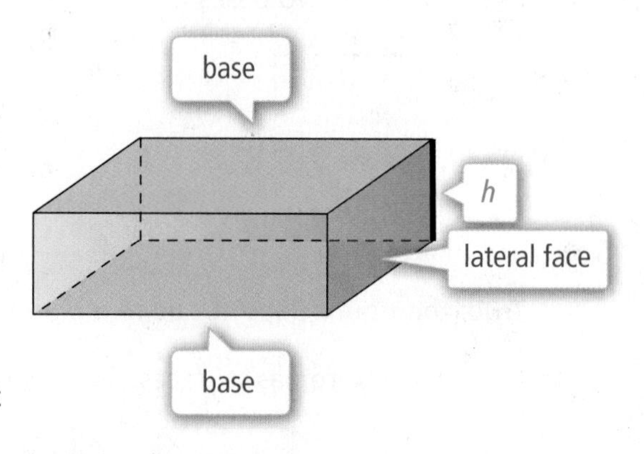

In a **right prism**, all lateral faces are rectangles. In this Topic, assume that a prism is a right prism unless stated otherwise.

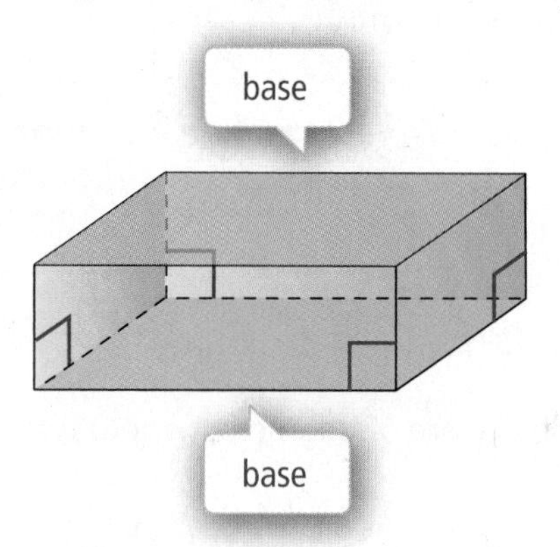

Example Identifying Characteristics of Prisms

a. How many bases does the prism have?

b. What shape does a base of the prism have?

c. Name the prism.

d. How many lateral faces does the prism have?

e. What is the height of the prism?

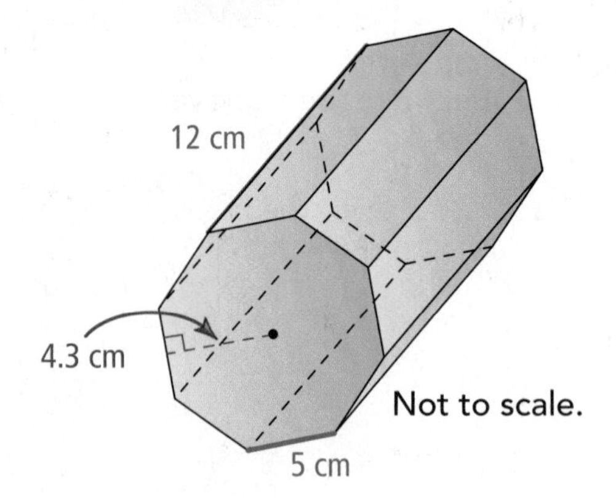

continued on next page >

Part 2

Example continued

Solution

a. The prism has two bases.

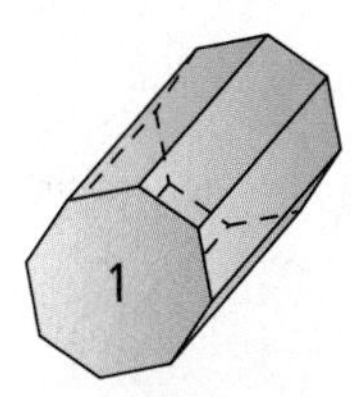

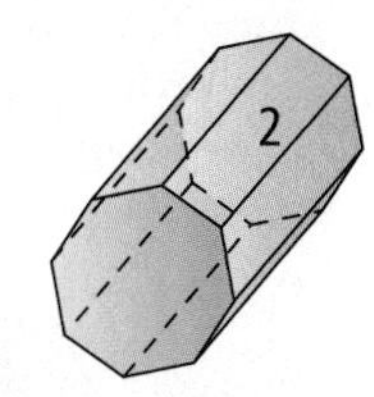

b. The bases are octagons.

The base has 8 sides, so it is an octagon.

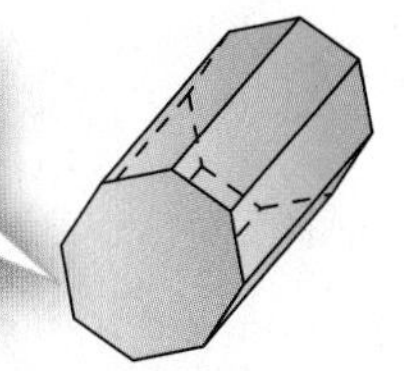

c. You name a prism for the shape of its bases. Since the bases of the prism are octagons, the prism is an octagonal prism.

d. The prism has eight lateral faces.

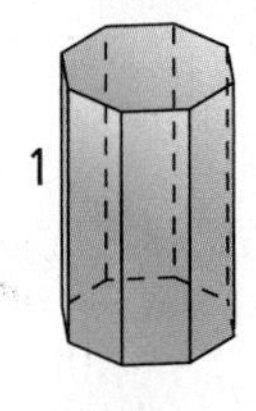

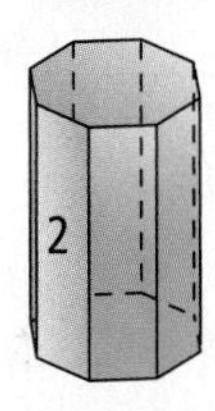

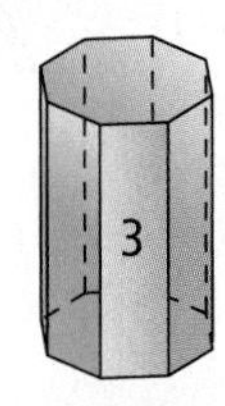

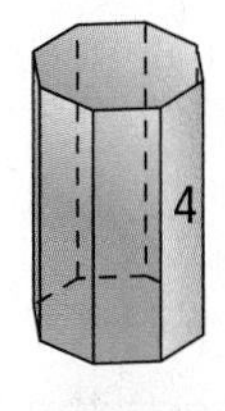

It's easier to count the faces if you rotate the octagonal prism.

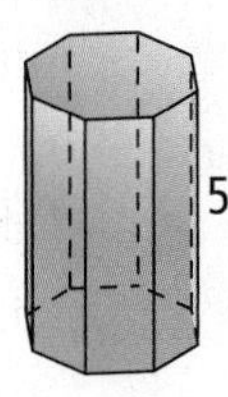

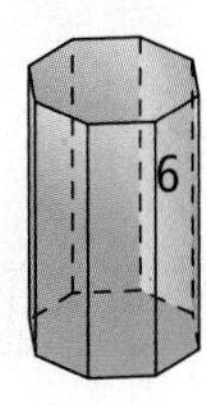

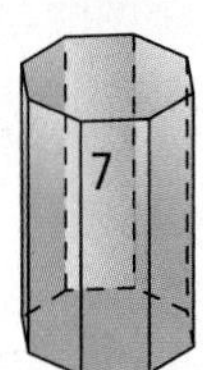

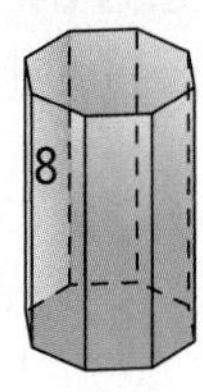

e. The height of the prism is the length of a perpendicular segment that joins the bases, so the height is 12 cm.

Height

12 cm

Base

Base

4.3 cm

5 cm

Part 3

Intro

A **pyramid** is a three-dimensional figure with a base that is a polygon and triangular faces that meet at a vertex.

A **base of a pyramid** is a polygonal face that does not connect to the vertex. You name a pyramid for the shape of its base.

The **height of a pyramid** is the length of the segment perpendicular to the base that joins the vertex and the base.

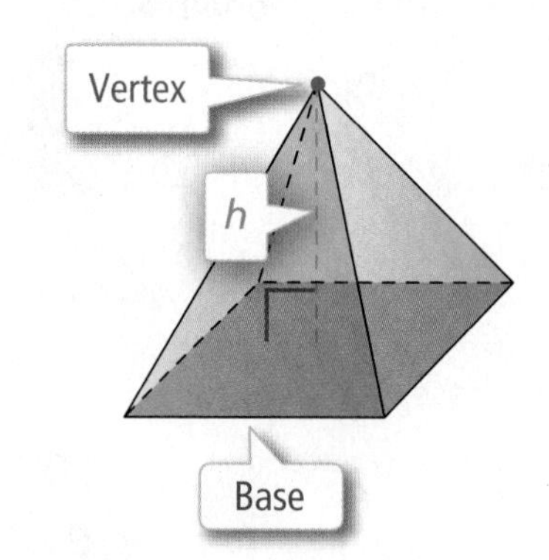

A **lateral face of a pyramid** is a triangular face that joins the base and the vertex.

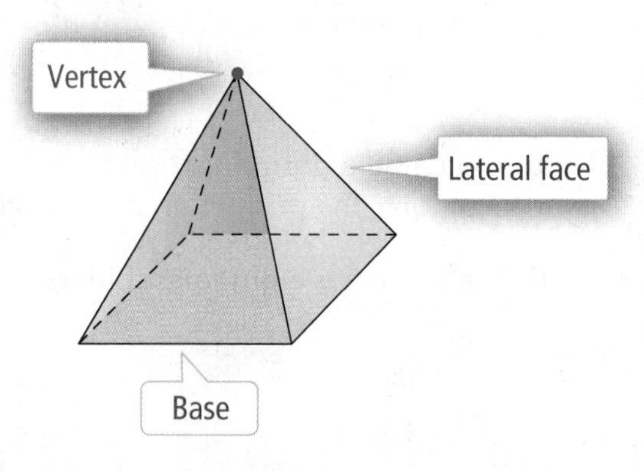

In a **right pyramid,** the segment that represents the height intersects the base at its center. In this Topic, assume that a pyramid is a right pyramid unless stated otherwise.

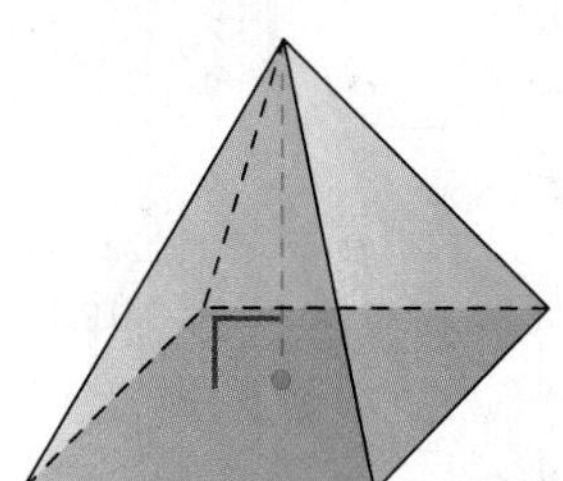

Example Identifying Characteristics of Pyramids

a. How many bases does the pyramid have?

b. What shape are the bases?

c. Name the pyramid.

d. How many lateral faces does the pyramid have?

e. What is the height of the pyramid?

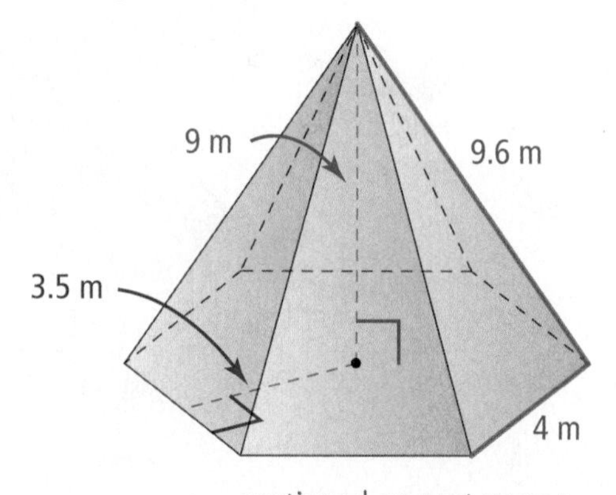

continued on next page >

Part 3

Example continued

Solution

a. The pyramid has one base.

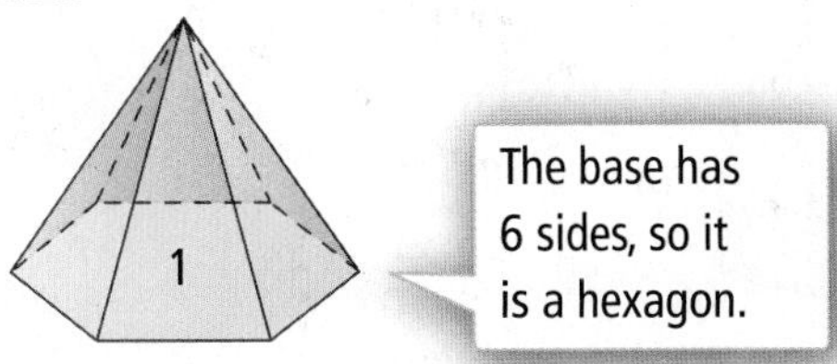

b. The base is a hexagon.

c. You name a pyramid for the shape of its base. Since the base of the pyramid is a hexagon, the pyramid is a hexagonal pyramid.

d. The pyramid has six lateral faces.

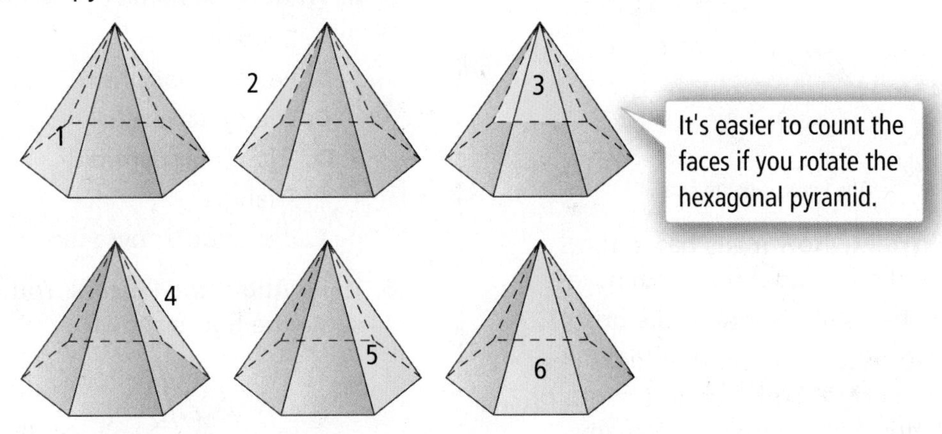

e. The height of the pyramid is the length of the segment perpendicular to the base that joins the vertex and the base. The height is 9 m.

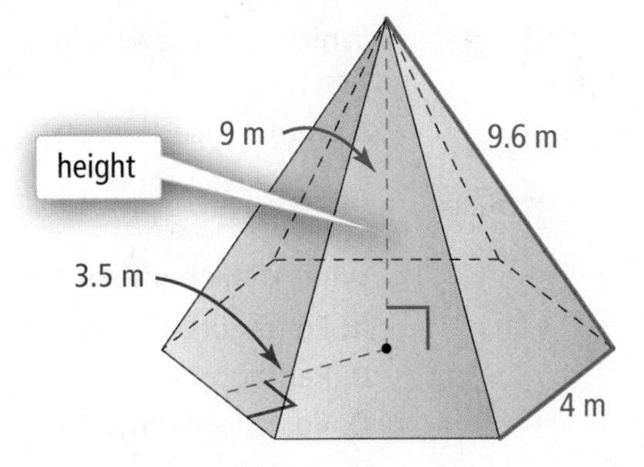

Digital Resources   

1. How many faces, edges, and vertices does the three-dimensional figure have?

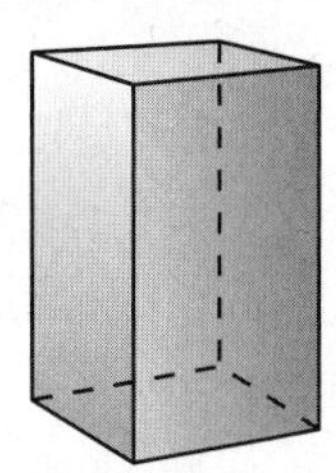

2. a. How many bases and lateral faces does the prism have?

b. What is the height of the prism?

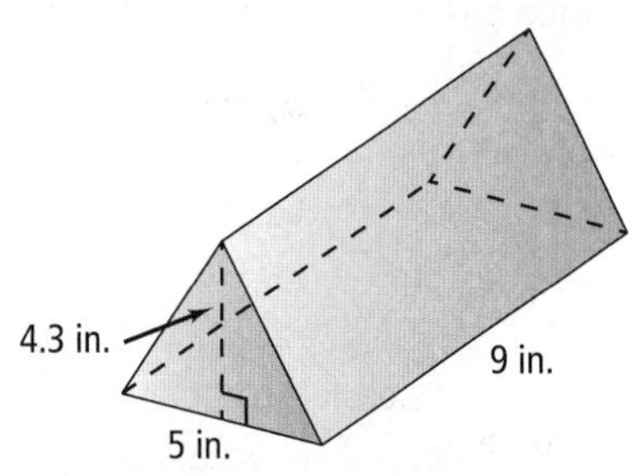

(The figure is not to scale.)

3. a. Writing How many bases, faces, and edges does the prism have?

b. What is the height of the prism?

c. Describe an object that looks like the prism. Explain why it might be important to know how many edges it has.

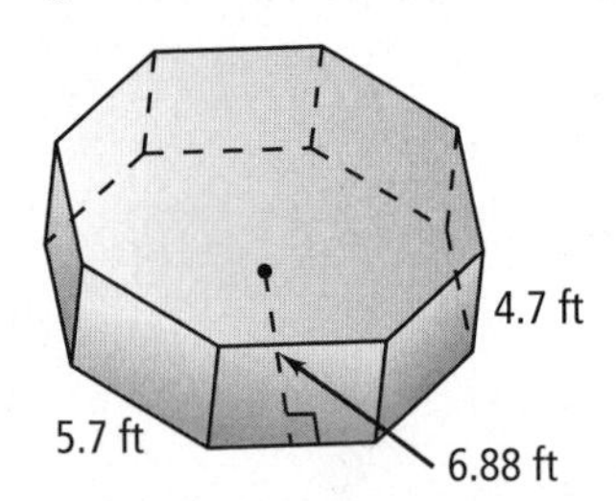

(The figure is not to scale.)

4. a. Reasoning How many faces, edges, and vertices does the three-dimensional figure have?

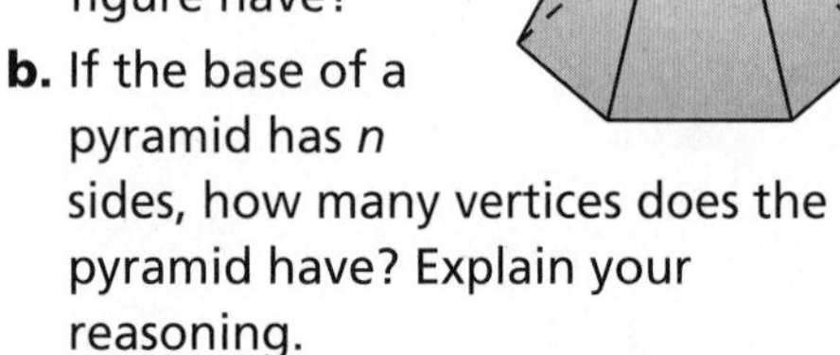

b. If the base of a pyramid has *n* sides, how many vertices does the pyramid have? Explain your reasoning.

5. Think About the Process You need to name the figure shown.

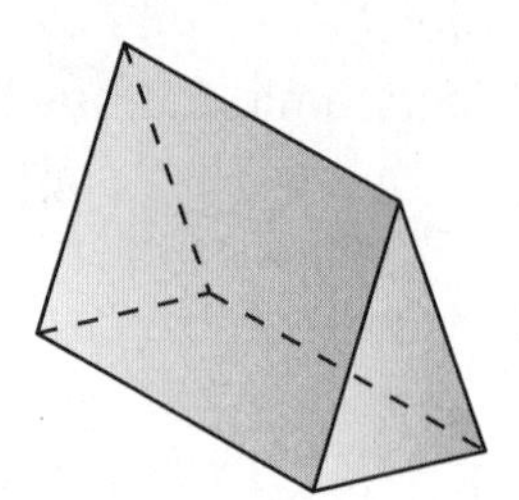

a. Which of these would be the best first step?

A. Find a face.
B. Count the faces.
C. Find a base.

b. What is the name of the figure?

A. Rectangle
B. Rectangular prism
C. Triangular prism
D. Triangular pyramid
E. Triangle
F. Rectangular pyramid

6. Think About the Process You need to name the figure shown.

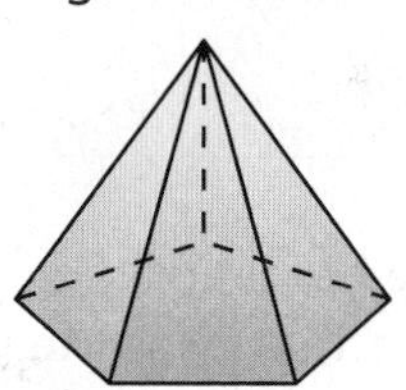

a. Which of these would be the best first step?

A. Find a face.
B. Count the faces.
C. Find a base.

b. What is the name of the figure?

A. Pentagonal prism
B. Pentagon
C. Rectangular pyramid
D. Pentagonal pyramid
E. Rectangular prism
F. Rectangle

7. **Landscaping** A landscaper makes a patio using tiles. Some of the tiles are shaped like this figure.

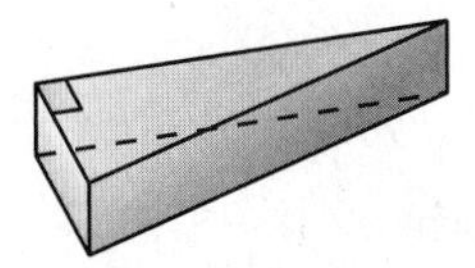

a. Name the figure.

b. Describe what the finished patio might look like. Include a sketch.

8. a. **Open-Ended** Name the figure shown.

b. How are pyramids similar to prisms? How are they different?

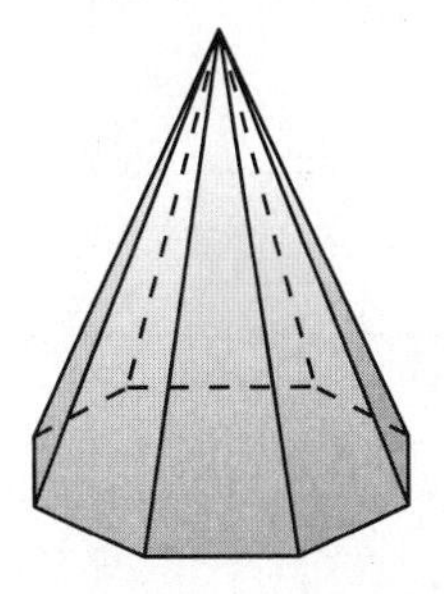

9. How many faces, edges, and vertices does the three-dimensional figure have?

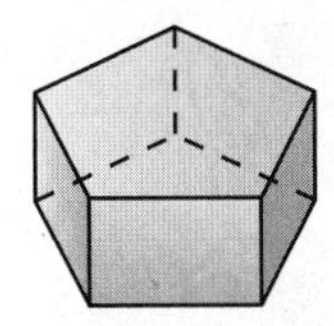

10. a. How many bases, faces, lateral faces, edges, and vertices does the pyramid have?

b. What is the height of the pyramid?

c. In general, how are the numbers of faces and lateral faces of pyramids related? Explain your reasoning.

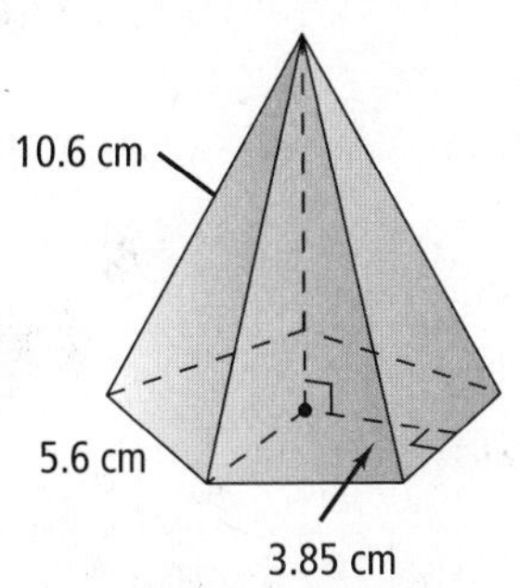

(The figure is not to scale.)

11. a. How many bases, faces, edges, and vertices does the pyramid have?

b. What is the height of the pyramid?

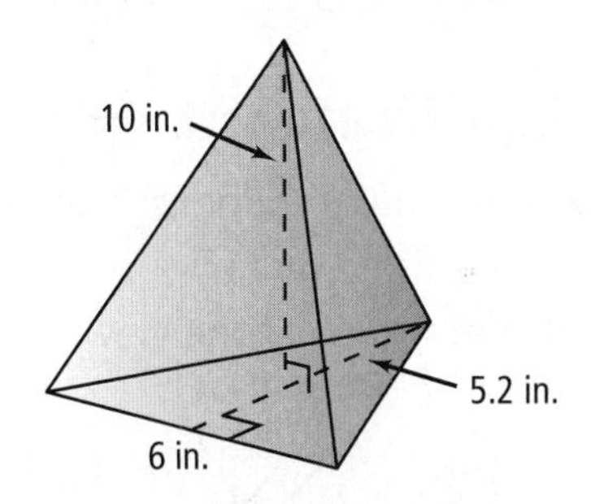

(The figure is not to scale.)

12. a. **Challenge** Name the figure shown.

b. If the figure is a pyramid, draw a figure that has the same base but is not a pyramid. If the figure is a prism, draw a figure that has the same base but is not a prism. Explain your answer.

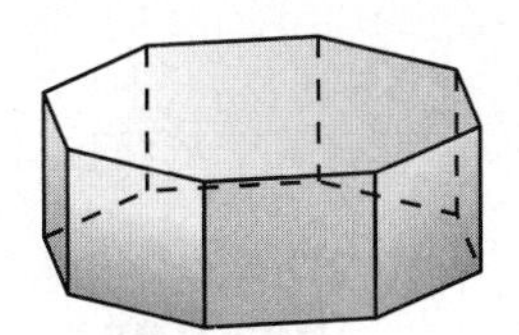

14-2 Nets

Vocabulary
net

CCSS: 6.G.A.4

Key Concept

A **net** is a two-dimensional pattern that you can fold to form a three-dimensional figure. A net of a figure shows all of the surfaces of that figure in one view.

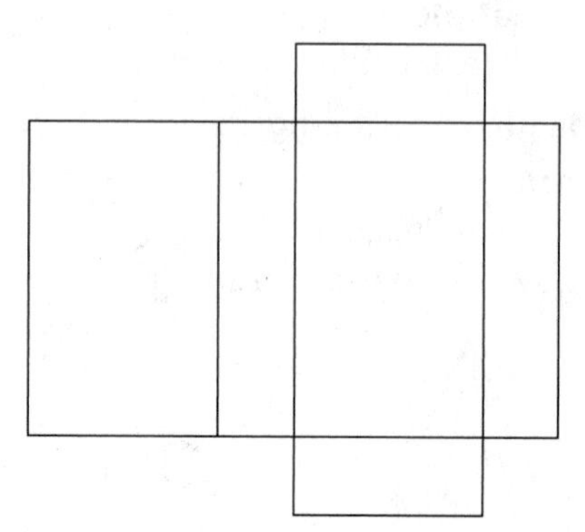

Part 1

Example Matching Nets With Three-Dimensional Figures

Match each package with its net.

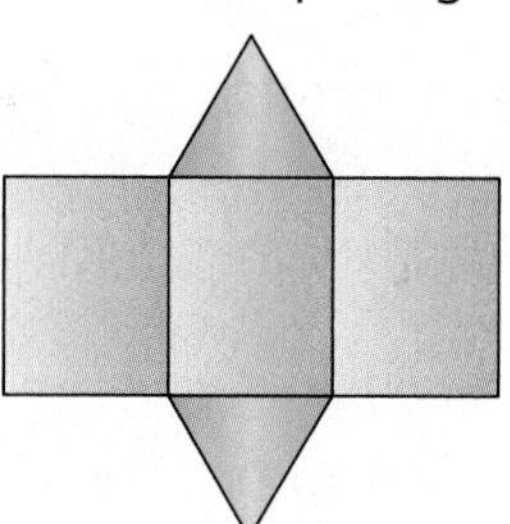

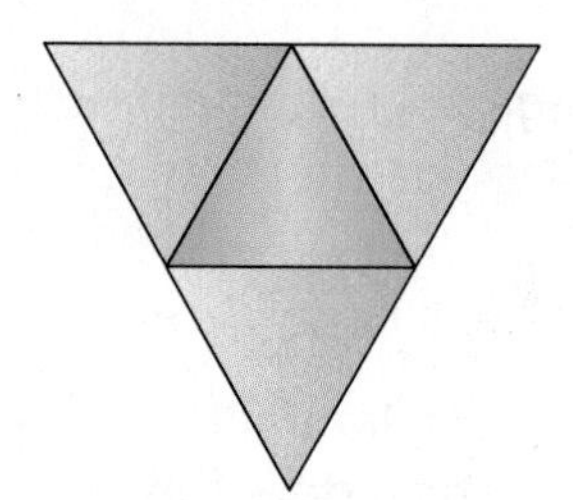

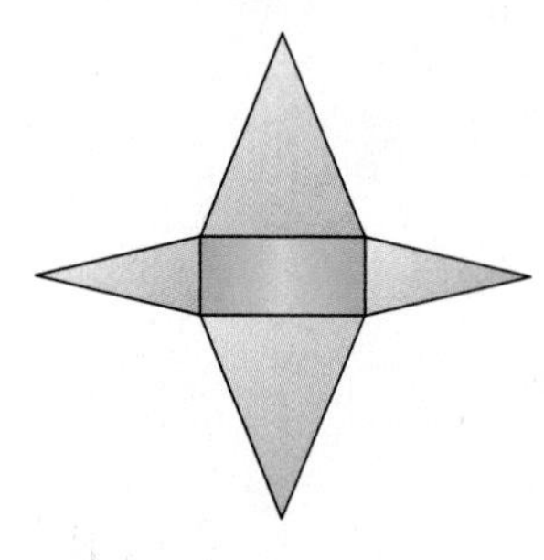

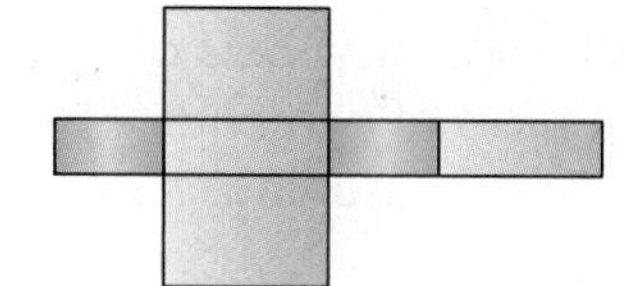

continued on next page >

Part 1

Example continued

a.

b.

c.

d.

Solution

Look at each package individually and visualize its net.

a. The juice box is a rectangular prism. A rectangular prism has two rectangular bases and four rectangular lateral faces. Unfold the rectangular prism into its net. The net of a rectangular prism is made up of six rectangles.

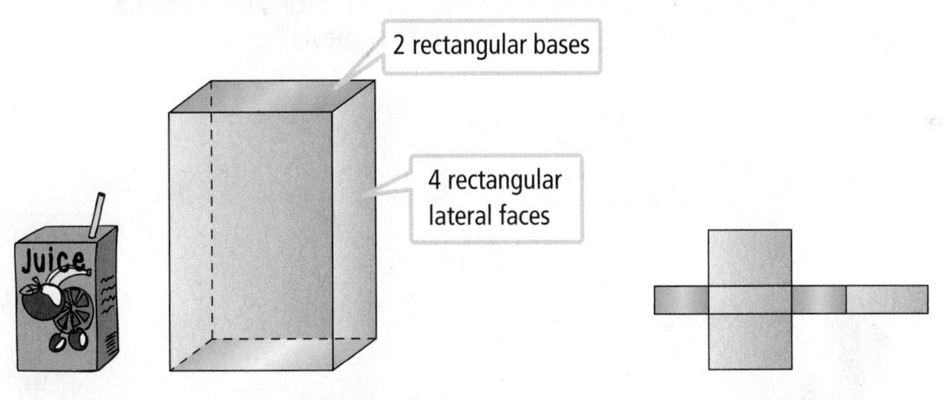

b. The toy package is a rectangular pyramid. A rectangular pyramid has one rectangular base and four triangular lateral faces. The net of a rectangular pyramid is made up of one rectangle and four triangles.

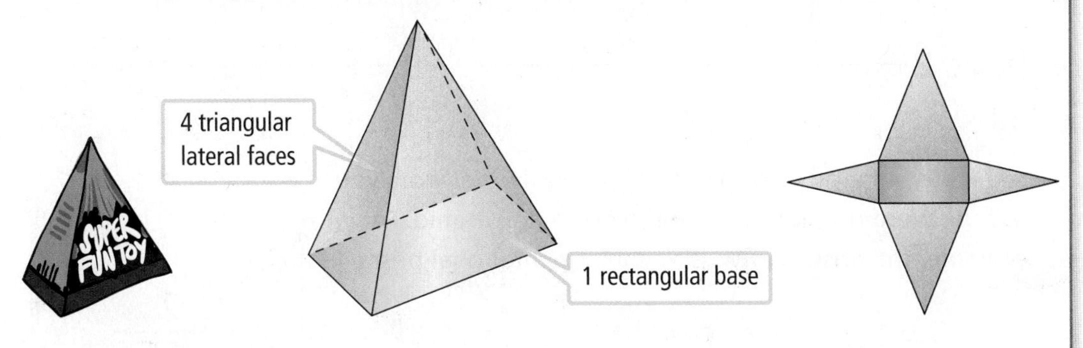

continued on next page >

Part 1

Solution continued

c. The spice package is a triangular prism. A triangular prism has two triangular bases and three rectangular lateral faces. The net of a triangular prism is made up of two triangles and three rectangles.

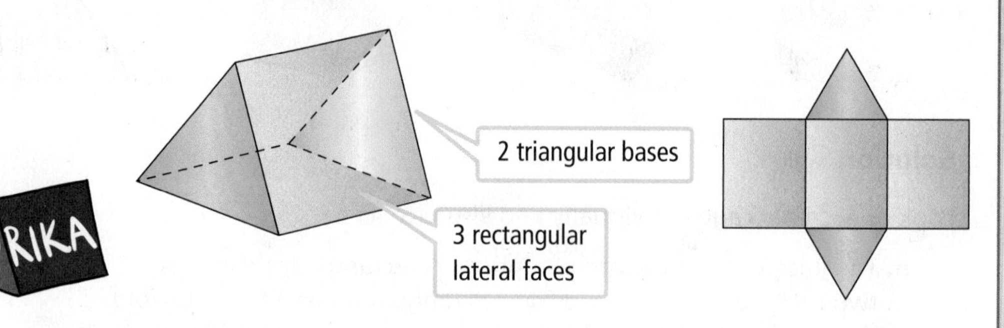

d. The milk package is a triangular pyramid. A triangular pyramid has a triangular base and three triangular lateral faces. The net of a triangular pyramid is made up of four triangles.

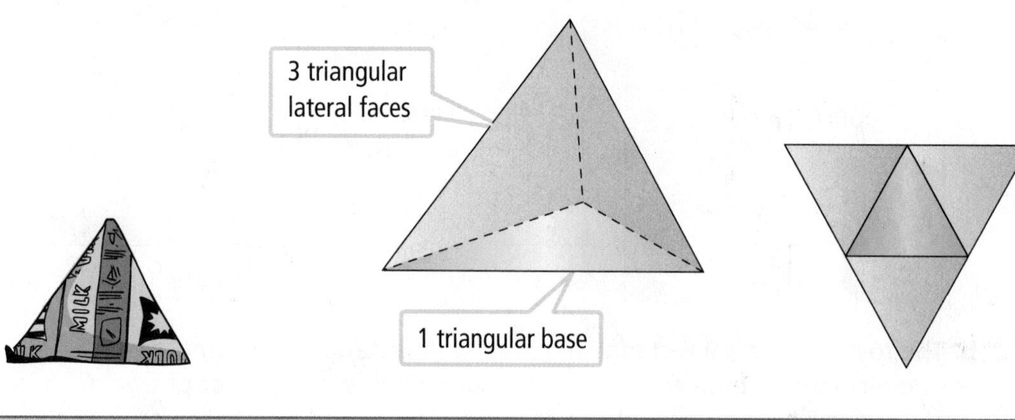

Part 2

Intro

If the base of a prism or pyramid is a regular polygon, you use the word regular to name the prism or pyramid. For example, the prism shown is a regular pentagonal prism.

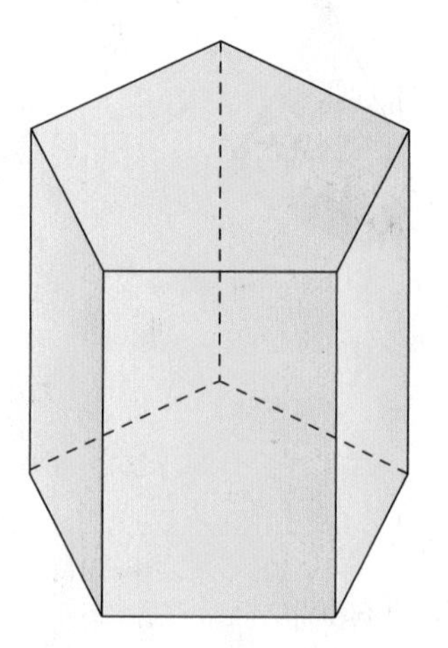

Part 2

Example Identifying Three-Dimensional Figures From Nets

Identify the regular three-dimensional figure that the given net forms.

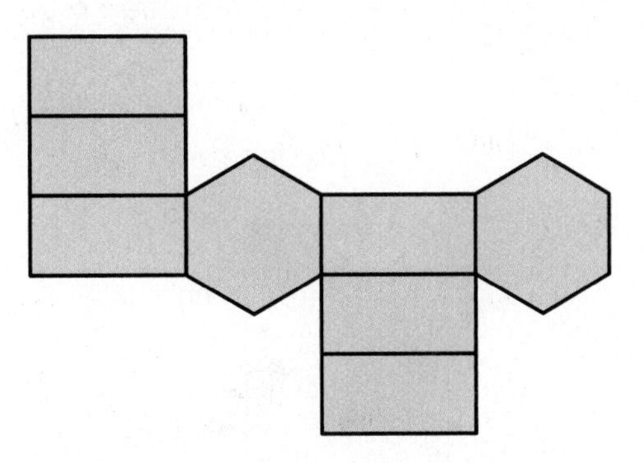

Solution

The net shows two regular hexagonal bases and six rectangular lateral faces that are the same size and shape, so the three-dimensional figure the given net forms is a regular hexagonal prism.

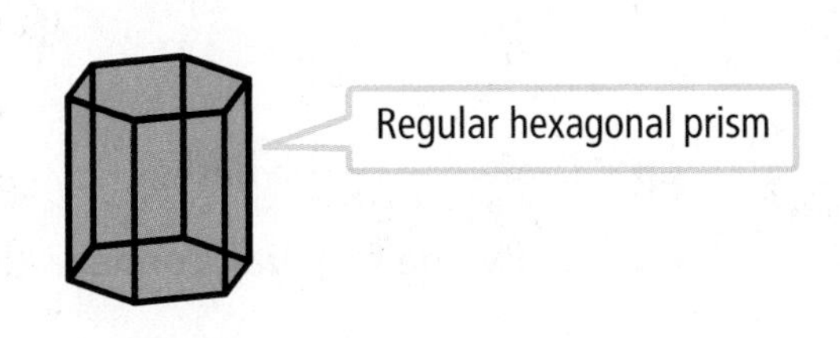

Part 3

Example Drawing Nets of Three-Dimensional Figures

Draw a net for the given triangular prism.

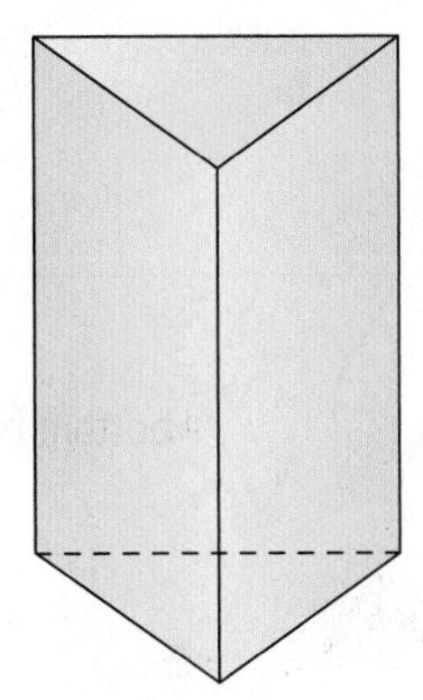

continued on next page >

Part 3

Example continued

Solution

Step 1 The first step of drawing a net for a 3-D figure is to label its bases and lateral faces.

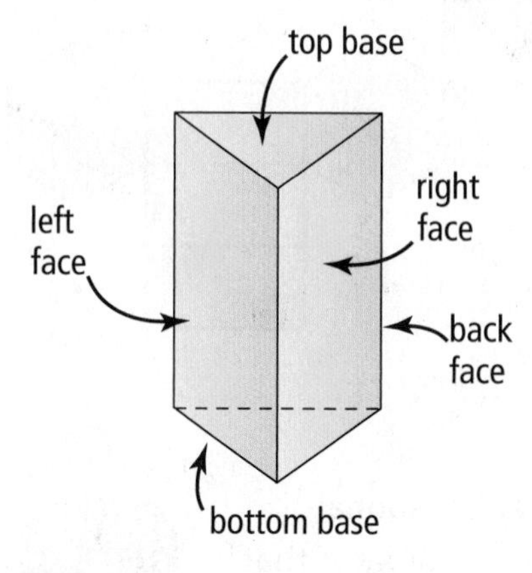

Step 2 Draw one of the bases.

Step 3 Draw one face that connects the two bases.

Step 4 Draw the other base.

Step 5 Draw the remaining faces of the figure.

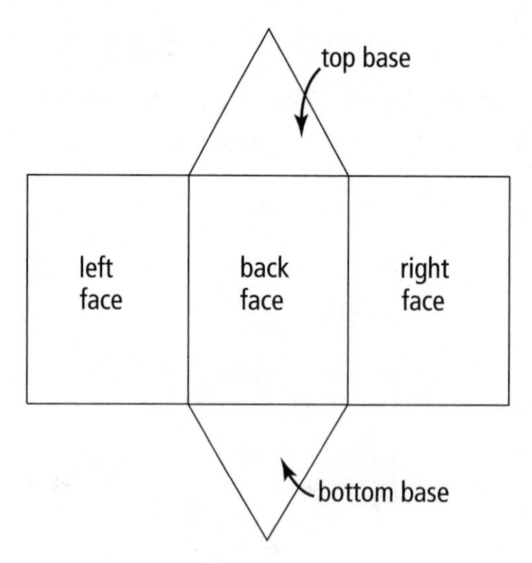

1. Which net matches the given figure?

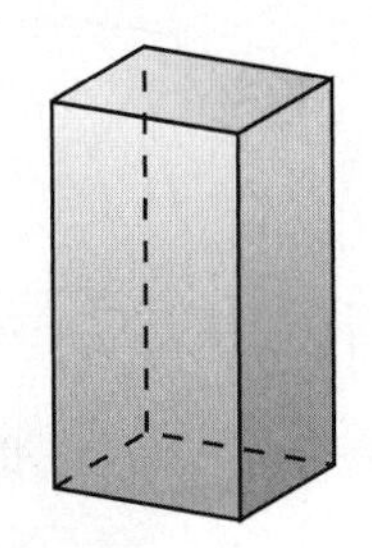

A.

B.

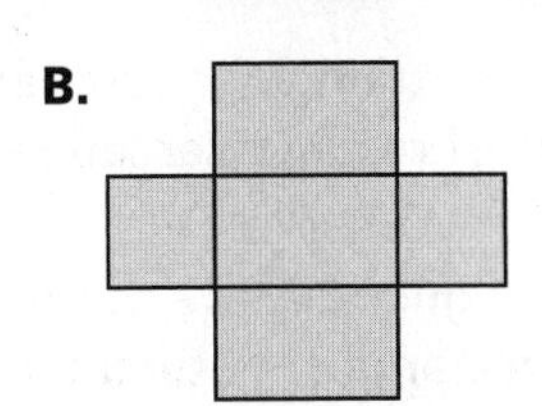

C.

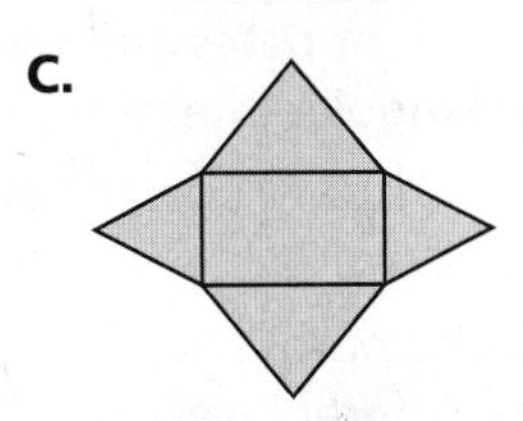

2. Identify the three-dimensional figure the given net forms.

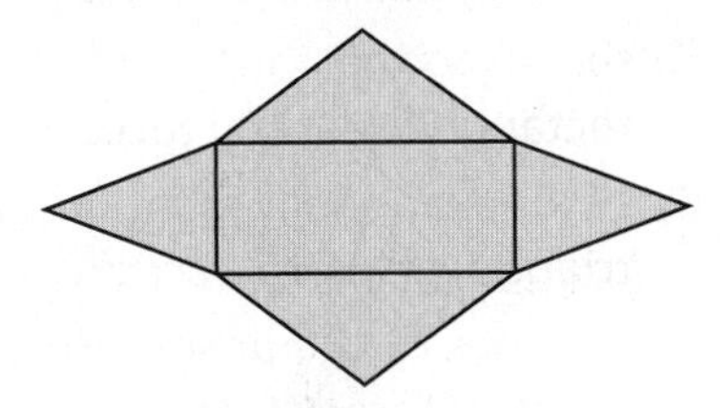

A. triangular pyramid
B. rectangular pyramid
C. cube
D. square pyramid

3. Which of the following describes a net of the octagonal pyramid?

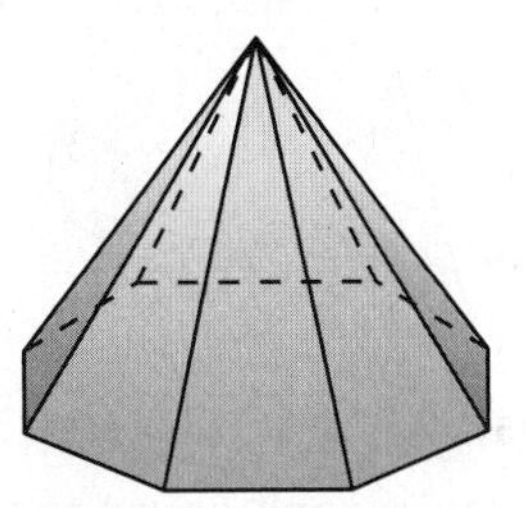

A. one octagonal base and eight triangular lateral faces
B. one rectangular base and eight octagonal lateral faces
C. two octagonal bases and eight rectangular lateral faces
D. eight octagonal bases and eight rectangular lateral faces

4. Jewelry Box A jewelry box has the shape of the net shown. Identify the shape of the jewelry box.

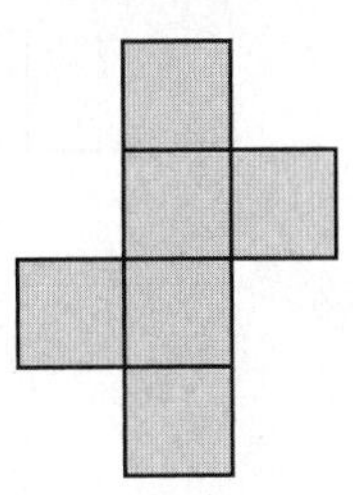

A. cube
B. square pyramid
C. rectangular pyramid
D. rectangular prism

5. **Think About the Process** You have to draw a net of the figure.

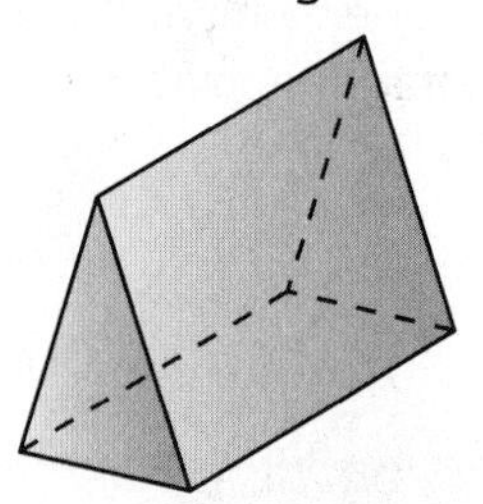

a. What is a good first step?

A. Identify and count the bases and faces.

B. Draw a face connected to the base(s).

C. Identify and count the edges.

D. Identify and count the vertices.

b. Which of the following is a net of the figure?

A.

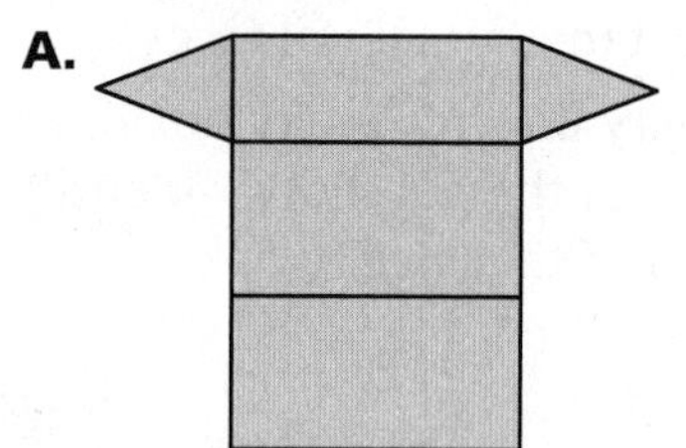

B.

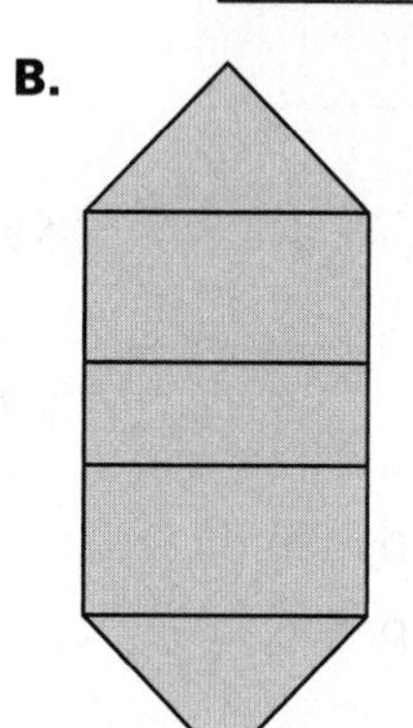

C.

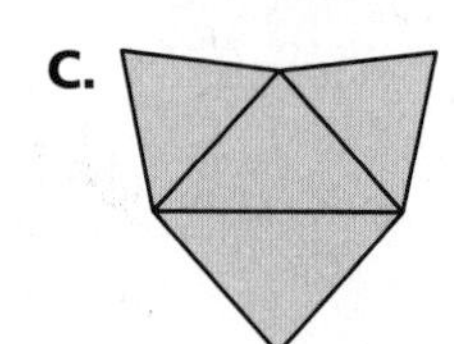

6. Describe a net of each prism.

Figure 1 **Figure 2**

a. Which of the following describes a net of Figure 1?

A. two pairs of rectangular bases and two pairs of rectangular lateral faces

B. two pairs of triangular bases and two pairs of rectangular lateral faces

C. two rectangular bases and two pairs of rectangular lateral faces

D. two rectangular bases and two pairs of triangular lateral faces

b. Which of the following describes a net of Figure 2?

A. six triangular bases and six hexagonal lateral faces

B. two hexagonal bases and six rectangular lateral faces

C. six hexagonal bases and six rectangular lateral faces

D. two hexagonal bases and six triangular lateral faces

c. Draw a net of the prisms. How are the nets different? How are they alike?

7. **Think About the Process** The given net forms a three-dimensional figure.

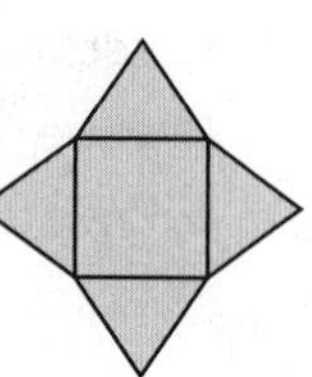

a. How many bases and lateral faces does the three-dimensional figure have?

b. Identify the figure.

8. **Challenge** What figure's net has two pentagonal bases and five rectangular lateral faces? Draw the figure and its net.

14-3 Surface Areas of Prisms

Vocabulary
surface area of a three-dimensional figure

CCSS: 6.G.A.4

Key Concept

The **surface area of a three-dimensional figure** is the sum of the areas of its faces.

You can find the surface area by finding the area of the net of the three-dimensional figure.

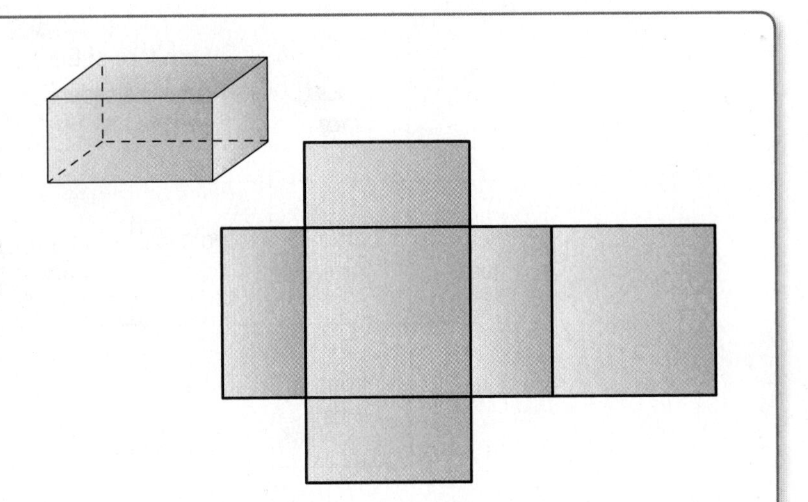

Part 1

Example Finding the Surface Area of Cubes

Use a net to find the surface area of the cube.

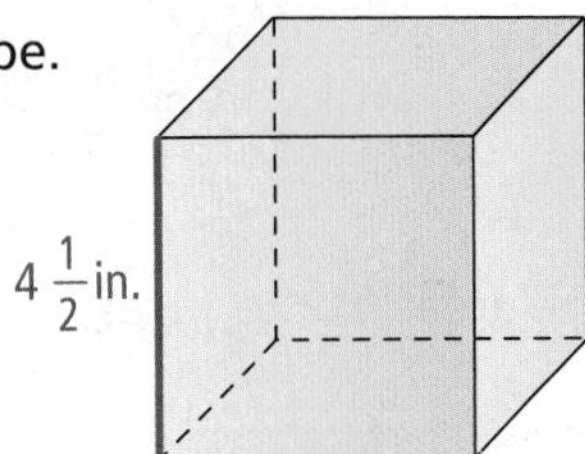

Solution

Know

The three-dimensional figure is a cube.

The cube has edge length $4\frac{1}{2}$ in.

The cube has six faces that are squares of equal size.

Need

You need to find the surface area of the cube.

Plan

Draw and label a net of the cube. Find the area of each face in the net. Then add the areas.

continued on next page >

Part 1

Solution continued

Step 1 Draw and label a net of the cube.

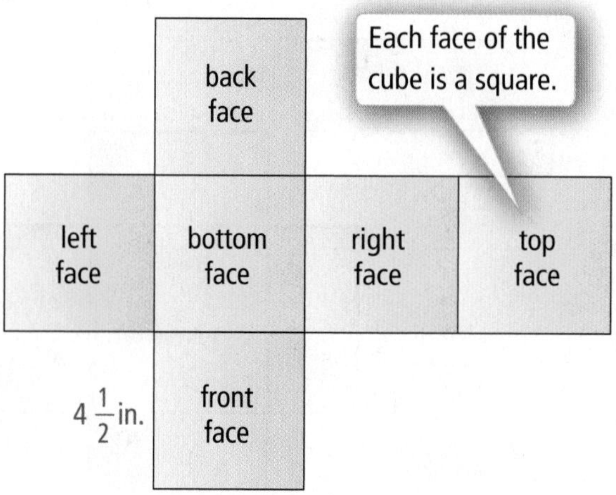

Each face of the cube is a square.

back face

left face | bottom face | right face | top face

front face

$4\frac{1}{2}$ in.

Step 2 Find the area of each face of the cube. Use $A = s^2$.

$$A = s^2$$
$$= \left(4\tfrac{1}{2}\right)^2$$
$$= \left(\frac{9}{2}\right)^2, \text{ or } \frac{81}{4}$$

Each face of the cube has an area of $\frac{81}{4}$ in.^{2}.

Step 3 Add the areas of the faces together.

$$\text{Surface area} = \frac{81}{4} + \frac{81}{4} + \frac{81}{4} + \frac{81}{4} + \frac{81}{4} + \frac{81}{4}$$
$$= \frac{486}{4}$$
$$= 121\tfrac{1}{2}$$

The surface area of the cube is $121\frac{1}{2}$ in.^{2}.

See your complete lesson at MyMathUniverse.com

Part 2

Example Finding the Surface Area of Rectangular Prisms

Find the surface area of the rectangular prism.

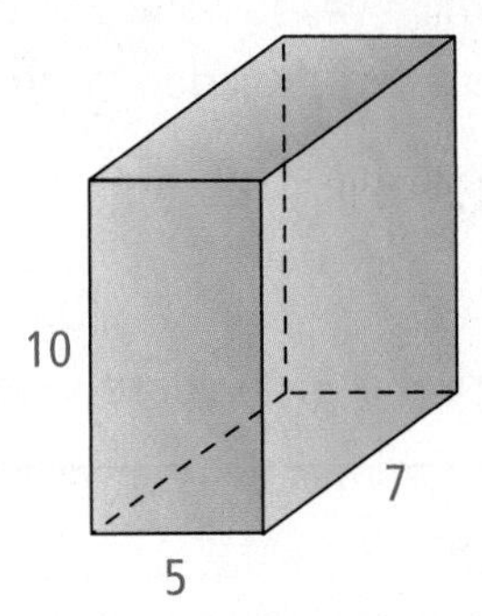

Solution

Step 1 Draw and label a net of the rectangular prism.

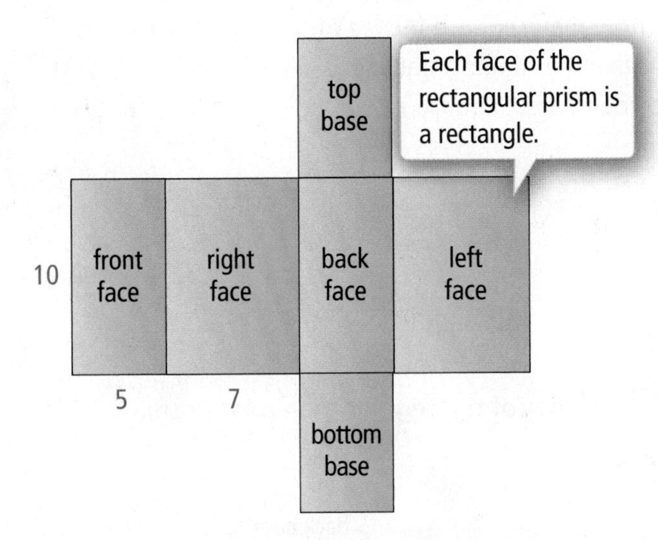

Step 2 Find the area of each face of the rectangular prism.

Opposite faces of a rectangular prism are equal in size. If you find the areas of the front and left faces and a base, you can determine the surface area of the prism.

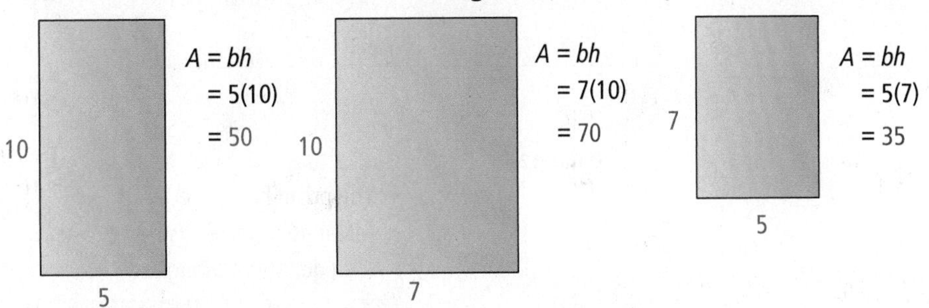

continued on next page >

Part 2

Solution continued

Step 3 Add the areas of the faces together.

$$\text{Surface area} = \text{Area of Front} + \text{Area of back} + \text{Area of left side} + \text{Area of right side} + \text{Area of top} + \text{Area of bottom}$$

$$= 50 + 50 + 70 + 70 + 35 + 35$$

$$= 310$$

The surface area of the rectangular prism is 310 square units.

Part 3

Example Finding the Surface Area of Triangular Prisms

The mailing package has the shape of a regular triangular prism. Find how many square inches of cardboard it takes to make the mailing package. Round your answer to the nearest square inch.

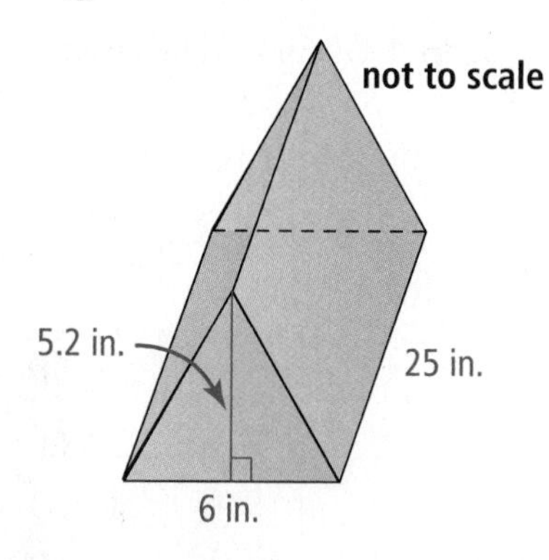

Solution

Step 1 Draw and label a net of the regular triangular prism.

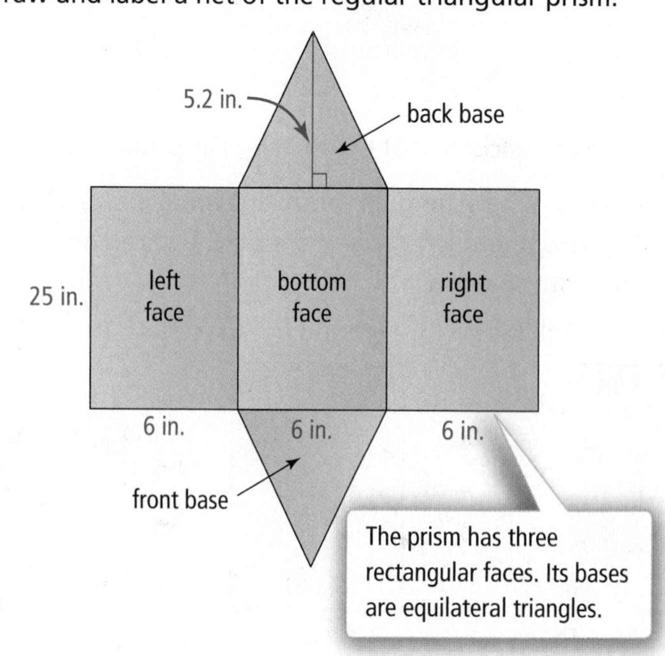

continued on next page >

Part 3

Solution continued

Step 2 Find the area of each face of the triangular prism.

The bases of the triangular prism are equal in size. Since the bases are equilateral triangles, the left, right, and bottom faces of the prism are also equal in size. If you find the area of the left face and a base, you can determine the surface area of the prism.

Front and back bases:

Left, right, and bottom faces:

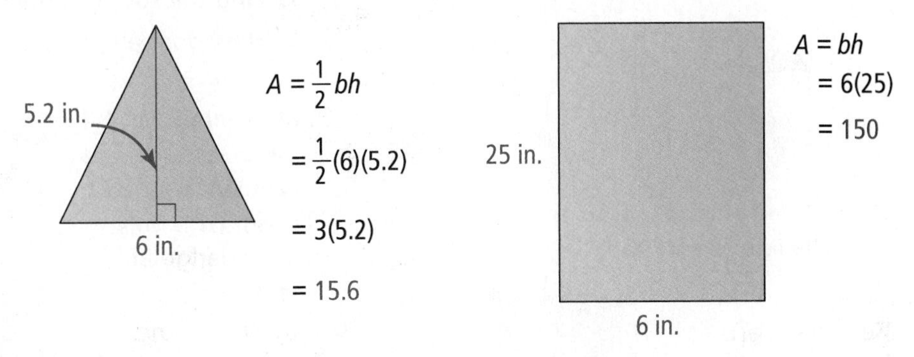

$A = \frac{1}{2}bh$

$= \frac{1}{2}(6)(5.2)$

$= 3(5.2)$

$= 15.6$

$A = bh$

$= 6(25)$

$= 150$

Step 3 Add the areas of the faces together.

$$\text{Surface area} = \text{Area of front} + \text{Area of back} + \text{Area of left side} + \text{Area of right side} + \text{Area of bottom}$$

$$= 15.6 + 15.6 + 150 + 150 + 150$$

$$= 481.2$$

It takes about 481 in.^{2} of cardboard to make the mailing package.

Digital Resources    

1. Use a net to find the surface area of the cube.

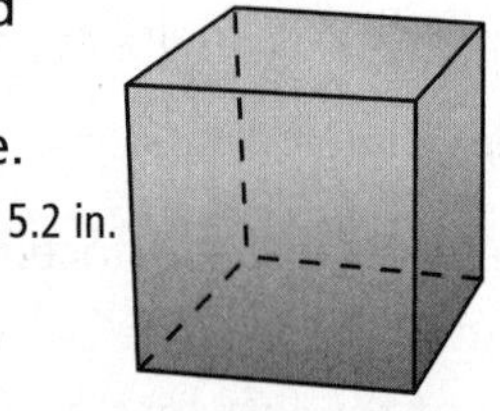

(The figure is not to scale.)

2. Use a net to find the surface area of the cube.

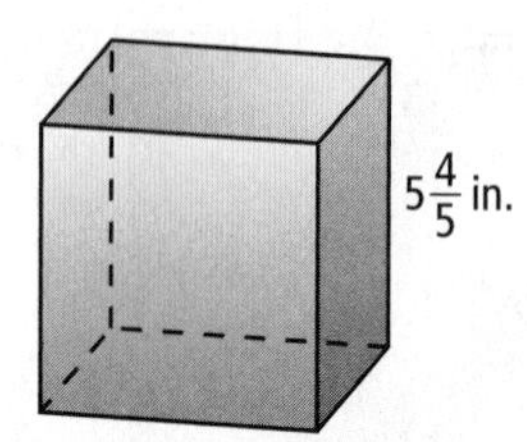

(The figure is not to scale.)

3. Use a net to find the surface area of the rectangular prism.

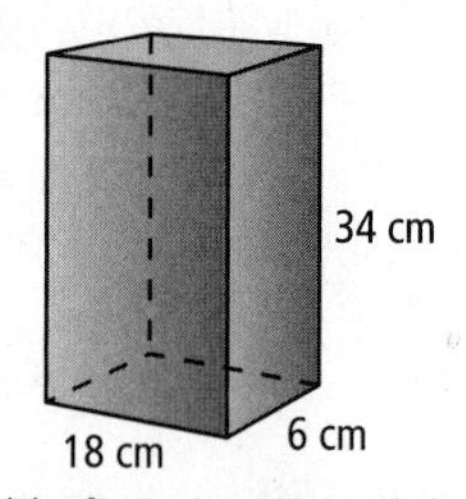

(The figure is not to scale.)

4. Find the surface area of the triangular prism, using a net if necessary.

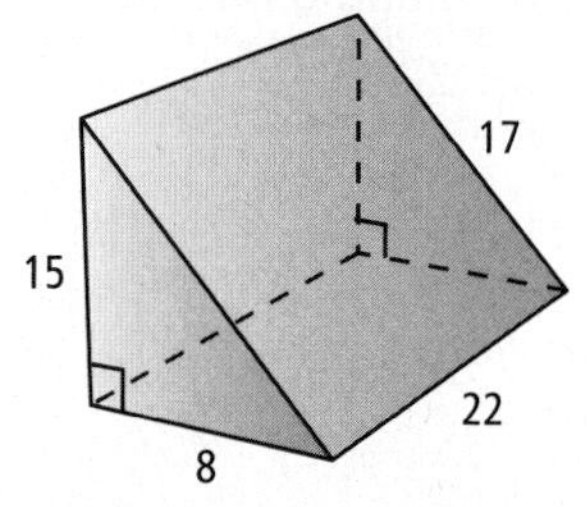

(The figure is not to scale.)

5. The triangular faces of the prism shown are equilateral triangles with perimeter 42 cm. Use a net to find the surface area of the prism.

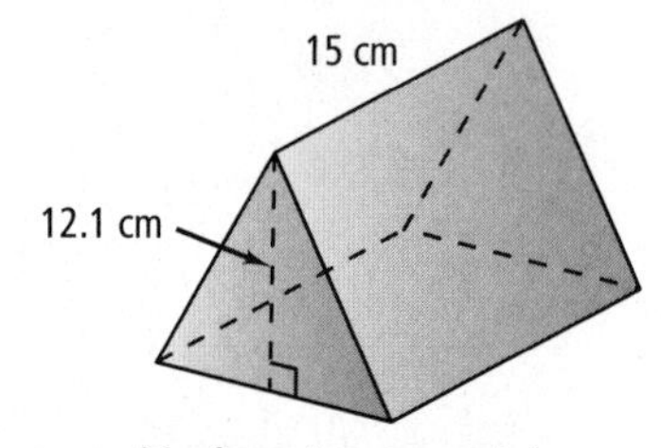

(The figure is not to scale.)

6. Writing A patio is made up of stones shaped like the figure.

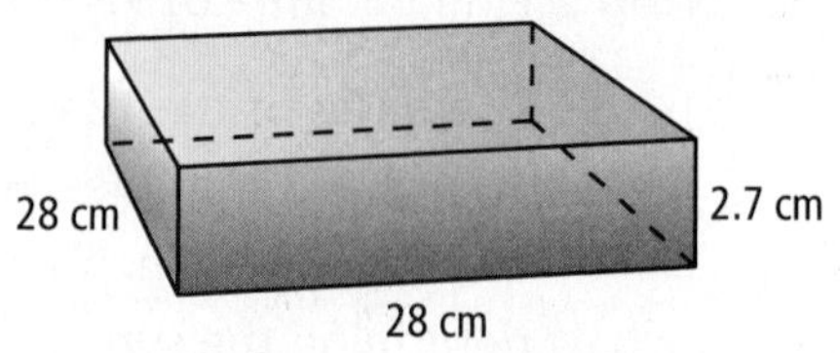

(The figure is not to scale.)

a. Find the surface area of one stone.

b. How does a net help you find the surface area?

7. Reasoning Mr. Jones has a vase that is a regular triangular prism with only one triangular face.

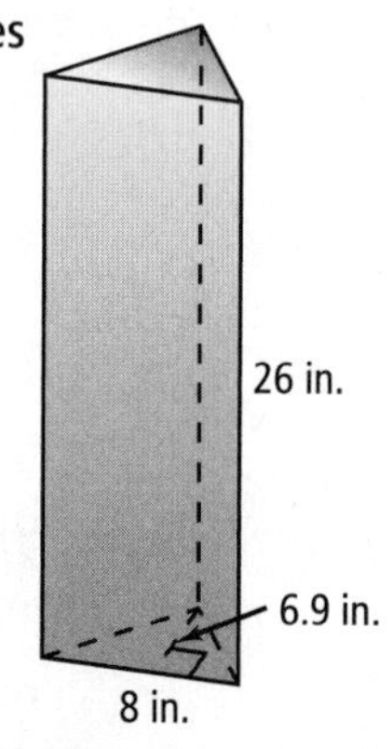

(The figure is not to scale.)

a. What is the surface area of the vase?

b. Which figure shows a net for the vase?

A.

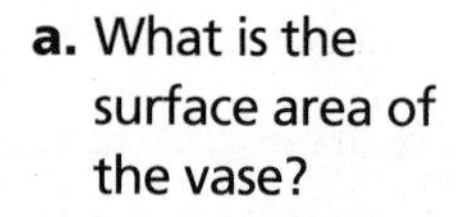

B.

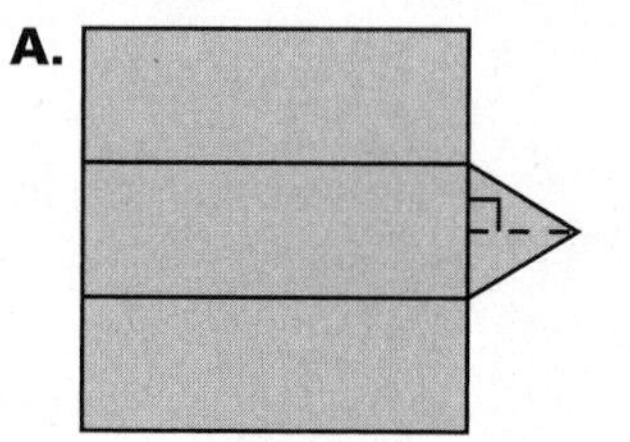

C.

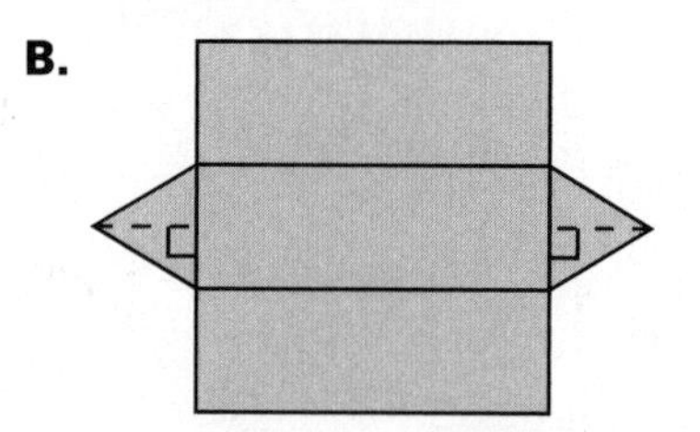

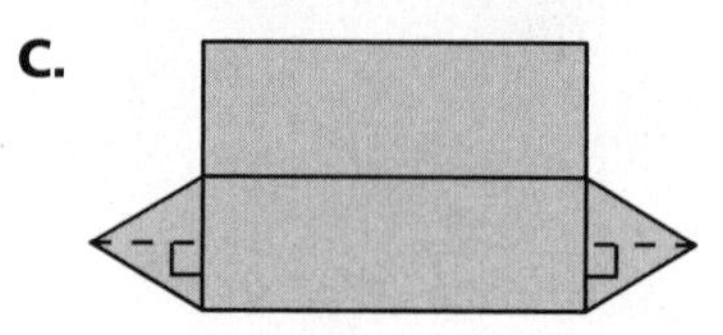

c. Explain why the net you chose above represents the vase accurately.

See your complete lesson at MyMathUniverse.com

8. Set Construction For a school play, you are making plastic cubes that are 1.5 feet on each side.

a. How much plastic is needed to make one cube?

b. If you want to make two cubes, how much plastic is needed?

9. Mental Math Find the surface area of the rectangular prism.

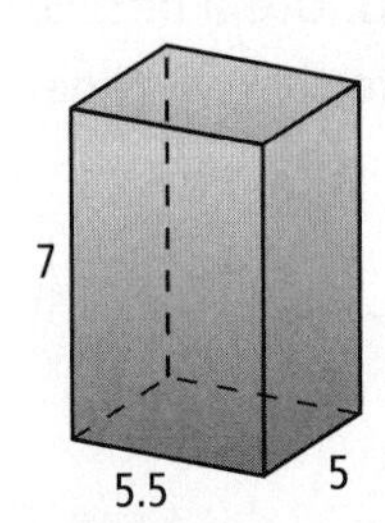

(The figure is not to scale.)

10. Think About the Process

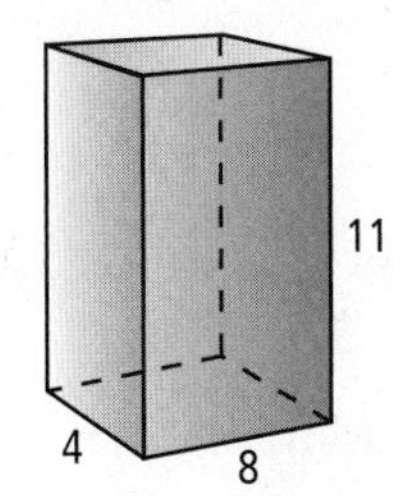

(The figure is not to scale.)

a. Which equation could you use to help you find the surface area of the prism shown?

A. Surface area = 2(88 + 44 + 32)

B. Surface area = 2(88) + 44 + 32

C. Surface area = 88 + 44 + 32

b. What is the surface area of the prism?

11. a. Which expression represents the surface area of the prism shown?

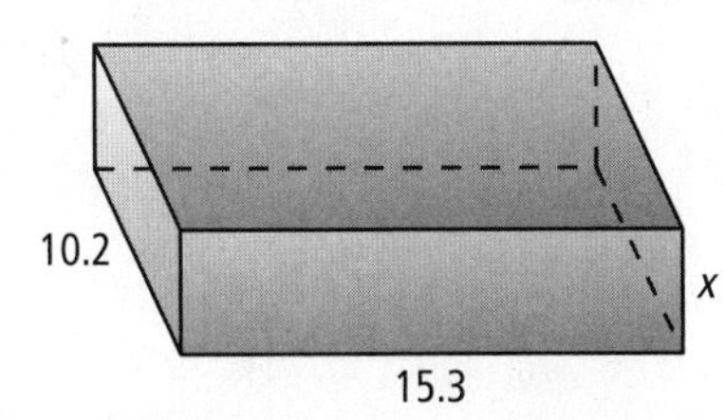

(The figure is not to scale.)

A. 2(10.2 + 15.3 + 78.03)

B. $2(10.2x + 15.3x + 156.06)$

C. 2(10.2 + 15.3 + 156.06)

D. $2(10.2x + 15.3x + 78.03)$

b. If $x = 5.1$, what is the surface area of the rectangular prism?

12. Think About the Process

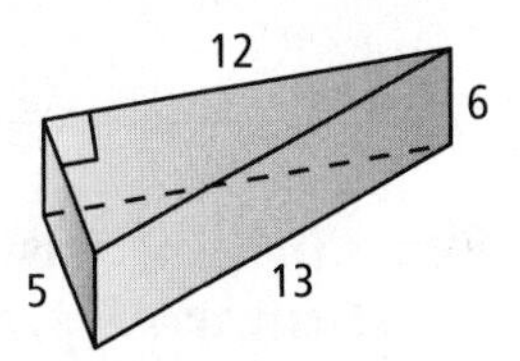

(The figure is not to scale.)

a. Which formula can you use to find the area of one rectangular face of this prism?

A. $A = b + h$ **B.** $A = bh$

C. $A = \frac{1}{3}bh$ **D.** $A = \frac{1}{2}bh$

b. Find the surface area of the triangular prism.

13. Challenge An art exhibit is made by stacking three identical prisms on top of each other end-to-end so their smallest faces overlap. One of the prisms is shown here.

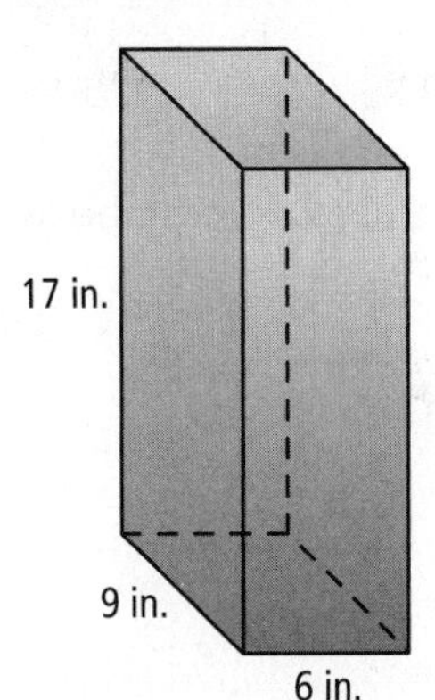

(The figure is not to scale.)

a. Find the surface area of the prism.

b. Find the total surface area of the exhibit.

14-4 Surface Areas of Pyramids

CCSS: 6.G.A.4

Part 1

Example Finding the Surface Area of Square Pyramids

A package for a terrarium has the shape of a square pyramid. Use a net to find how many square feet of cardboard are needed to make the package.

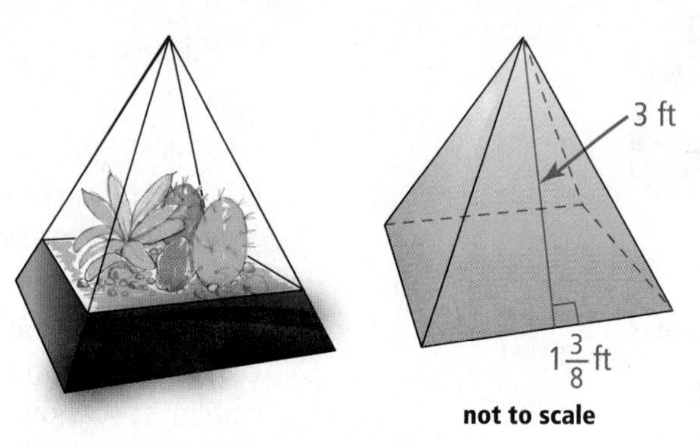

Solution

Step 1 Draw and label a net of the square pyramid.

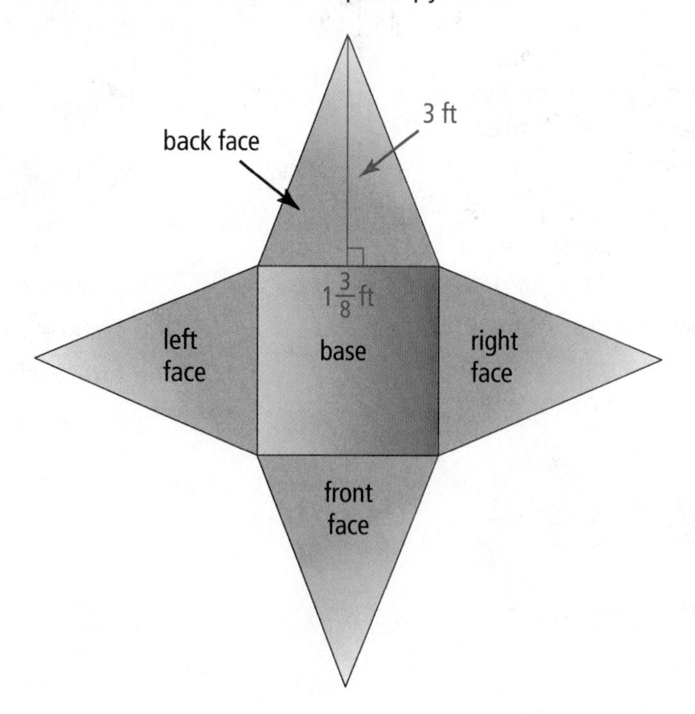

continued on next page >

Part 1

Solution continued

Step 2 Find the area of each face of the square pyramid.

Since this is a regular pyramid with a square base, the four faces of the pyramid are triangles that are equal in size.

Base: Front, back, left, and right faces:

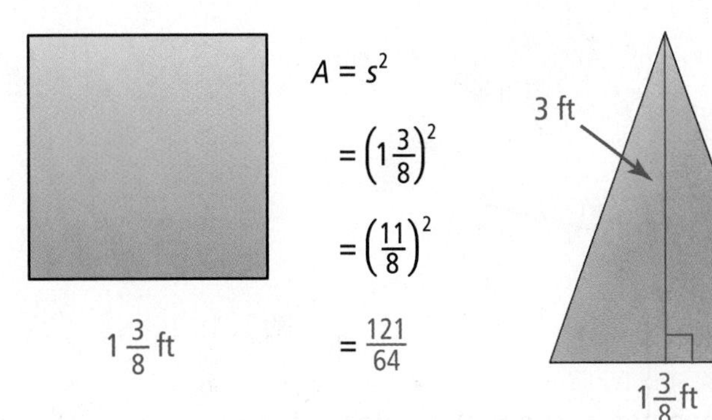

$$A = s^2 = \left(1\frac{3}{8}\right)^2 = \left(\frac{11}{8}\right)^2 = \frac{121}{64}$$

$$A = \frac{1}{2}bh = \frac{1}{2}\left(1\frac{3}{8}\right)3 = \frac{1}{2}\left(\frac{11}{8}\right)3 = \frac{33}{16}$$

Step 3 Add the areas of the faces together.

Surface area = Area of base + Area of front + Area of back + Area of left face + Area of right face

$$= \frac{121}{64} + \frac{33}{16} + \frac{33}{16} + \frac{33}{16} + \frac{33}{16}$$

$$= \frac{121}{64} + \frac{132}{64} + \frac{132}{64} + \frac{132}{64} + \frac{132}{64}$$

The common denominator is 64.

$$= \frac{649}{64}, \text{ or } 10\frac{9}{64}$$

It takes about $10\frac{9}{64}$ ft^2 of cardboard to make the terrarium package.

Part 2

Example Finding the Surface Area of Rectangular Pyramids

Find the surface area of the rectangular pyramid to the nearest square centimeter.

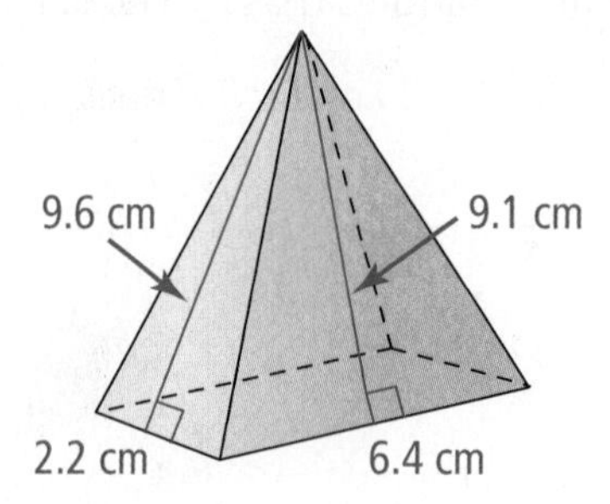

Solution

Step 1 Draw and label a net of the rectangular pyramid.

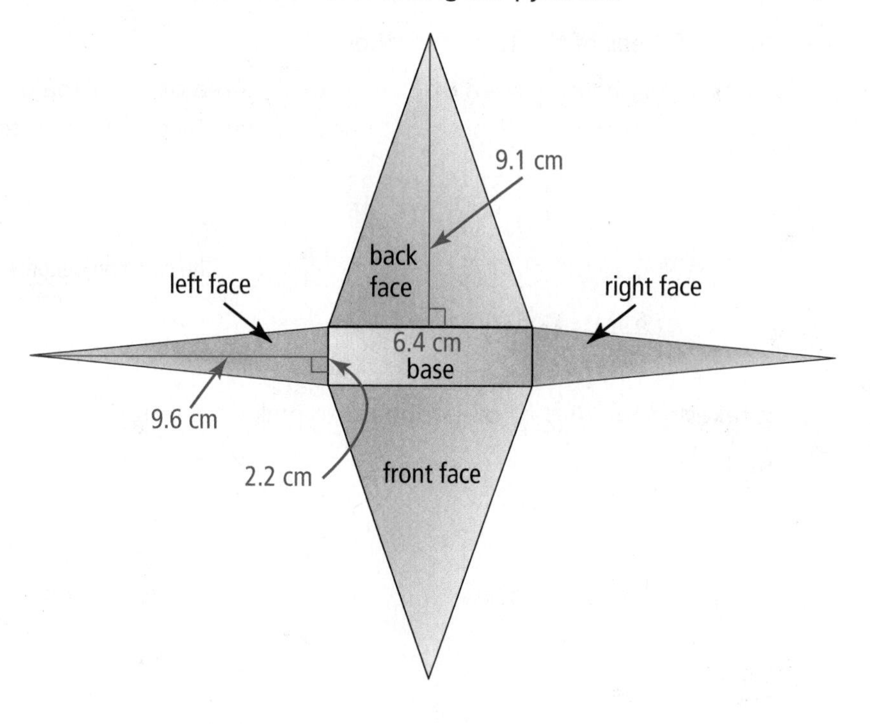

continued on next page >

Part 2

Solution continued

Step 2 Find the area of each face of the rectangular pyramid.

Since this is a pyramid with a rectangular base, opposite faces of the pyramid are triangles that are equal in size. If you find the areas of the base, front face, and left face, you can determine the surface area of the pyramid.

Base:

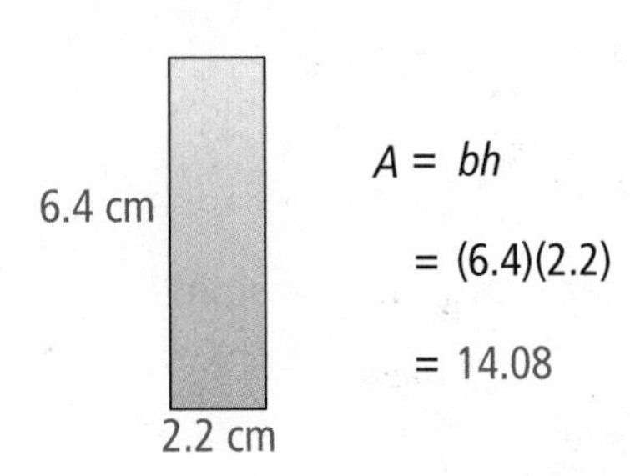

$$A = bh$$
$$= (6.4)(2.2)$$
$$= 14.08$$

Front and back faces:

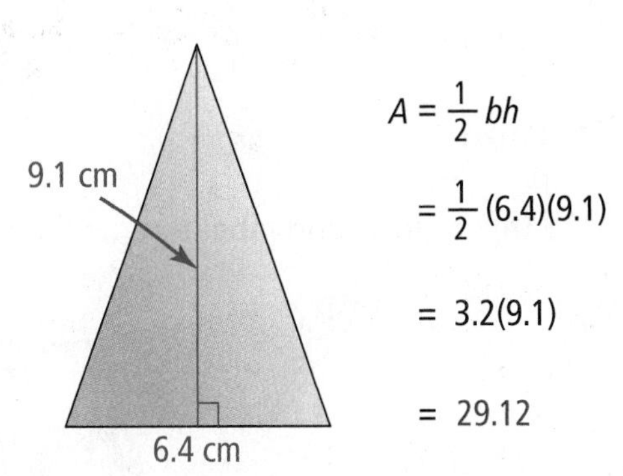

$$A = \frac{1}{2}bh$$
$$= \frac{1}{2}(6.4)(9.1)$$
$$= 3.2(9.1)$$
$$= 29.12$$

Left and right faces:

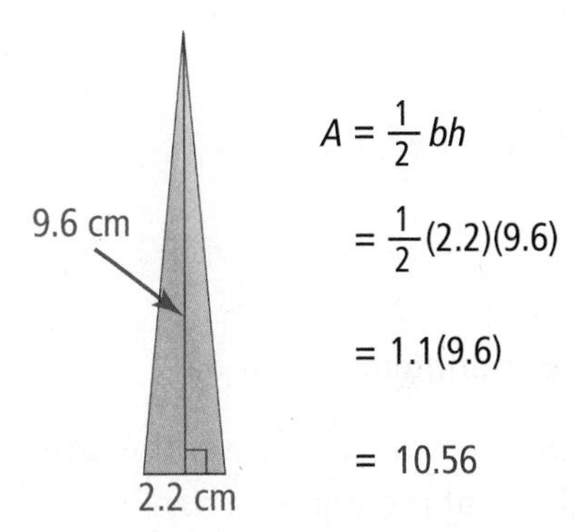

$$A = \frac{1}{2}bh$$
$$= \frac{1}{2}(2.2)(9.6)$$
$$= 1.1(9.6)$$
$$= 10.56$$

Step 3 Add the areas of the faces together.

$$\text{Surface area} = \text{Area of base} + \text{Area of front} + \text{Area of back} + \text{Area of left face} + \text{Area of right face}$$
$$= 14.08 + 29.12 + 29.12 + 10.56 + 10.56$$
$$= 93.44$$

The surface of the area of the rectangular pyramid is about 93 cm^2.

Part 3

Example Finding the Surface Area of Rectangular Pyramids

Find the surface area of the regular triangular pyramid to the nearest square unit.

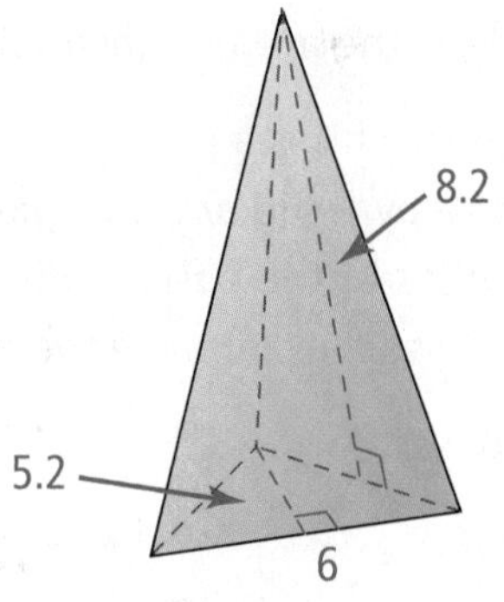

Solution

Step 1 Draw and label a net of the regular triangular pyramid.

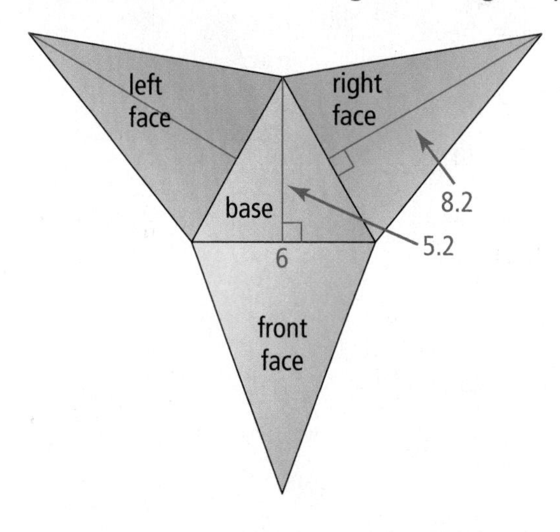

Step 2 Find the area of each face of the triangular pyramid.

Since this is a regular pyramid with a triangular base, the lateral faces of the pyramid are triangles that are equal in size. If you find the area of the base and a lateral face you can determine the surface area of the pyramid.

Base:

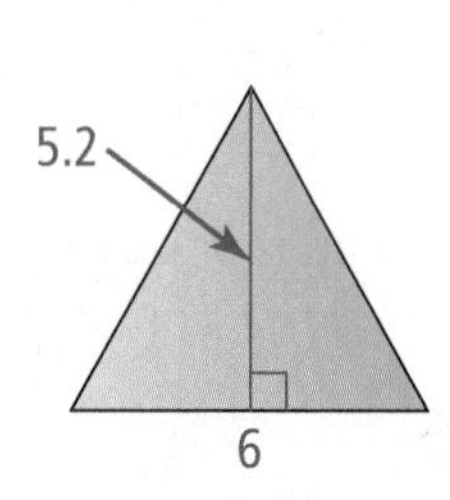

$A = \frac{1}{2}bh$

$= \frac{1}{2}(6)(5.2)$

$= 3(5.2)$

$= 15.6$

Left, right, and front faces:

$A = \frac{1}{2}bh$

$= \frac{1}{2}(6)(8.2)$

$= 3(8.2)$

$= 24.6$

continued on next page >

Part 3

Solution continued

Step 3 Add the areas of the faces together.

$$\text{Surface area} = \text{Area of base} + \text{Area of left face} + \text{Area of right face} + \text{Area of front face}$$

$$= 15.6 + 24.6 + 24.6 + 24.6$$

$$= 89.4$$

The surface of the area of the triangular pyramid is about 89 square units.

1. Find the surface area of the square pyramid using a net.

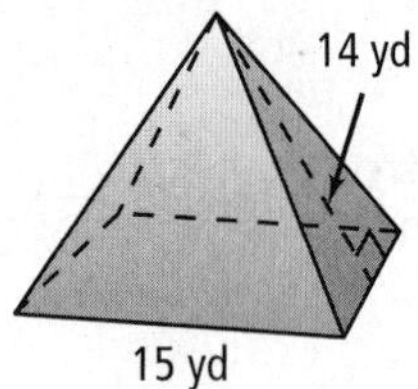

2. Think About the Process A regular triangular pyramid is shown.

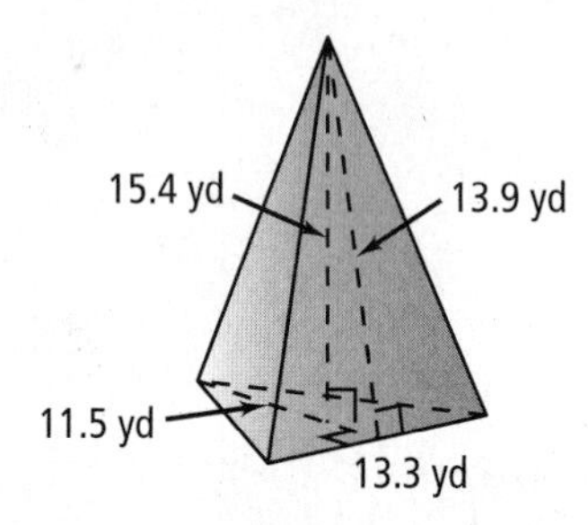

a. Which of the given values do you need to find its surface area? Select all that apply.

A. 11.5

B. 13.9

C. 13.3

D. 15.4

b. Find the surface area.

3. The packaging for an item is in the shape of a square pyramid. Each side of the base is 14.8 cm. The height of each triangular face is 13.5 cm. Use a net to find how many square centimeters of packaging you need for 25 items.

4. a. Reasoning Use a net to find the surface area of the regular triangular pyramid.

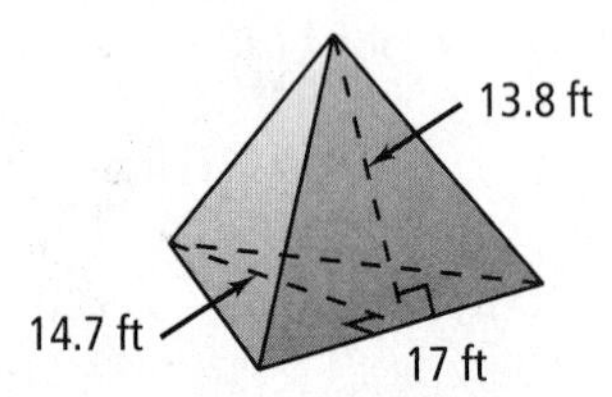

b. What must be true about the lateral faces of the triangular pyramid in order to find the surface area?

5. Manufacturing A company manufactures candles in the shape of rectangular pyramids. The candles are made in plastic containers. The manager of the company wants to find the surface area of one candle to approximate the cost of the plastic needed.

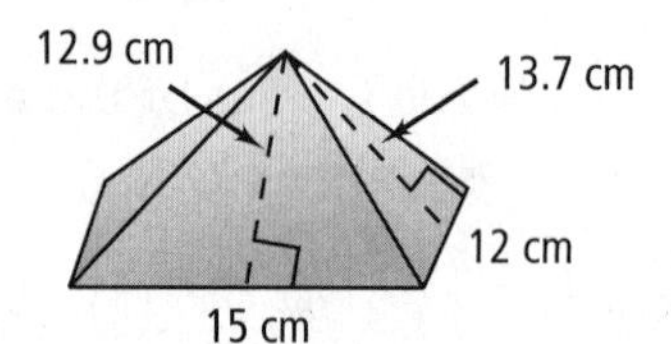

a. Find the surface area of one candle.

b. What is the minimum amount of plastic needed for 49 of these candles?

6. A teacher wants to make a regular triangular pyramid for his classroom. He has 335 cm^2 of cardboard to make the pyramid. He wants the side lengths of the base of the pyramid to be 14 cm, the height of the base to be 12.1 cm, and the height of each lateral face to be 11.3 cm.

a. Find the surface area of the pyramid the teacher wants to make.

b. Does he have enough cardboard to make this pyramid if he uses all of the cardboard?

7. a. Open-Ended Use the net to find the surface area of the regular triangular pyramid.

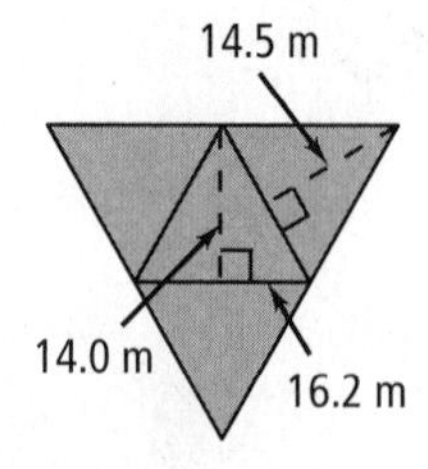

b. Can you fold this net to result in a different shape? Explain.

8. A group of friends wants to build a tree house in the shape of a square pyramid. The plywood they want to use costs $1.25 per square foot.

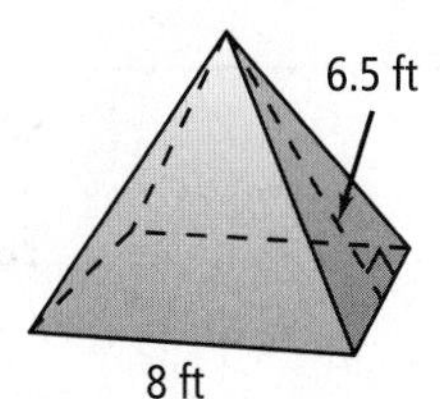

a. Use a net to find how much it will cost if they need to completely cover each face of the pyramid with the plywood.

b. If they split the cost of the plywood evenly, how much will it cost each friend?

9. A net of a rectangular pyramid is shown. The rectangular base has length 24 cm and width 21 cm. The net of the pyramid has length 69.2 cm and width 64.6 cm. Find the surface area of the pyramid.

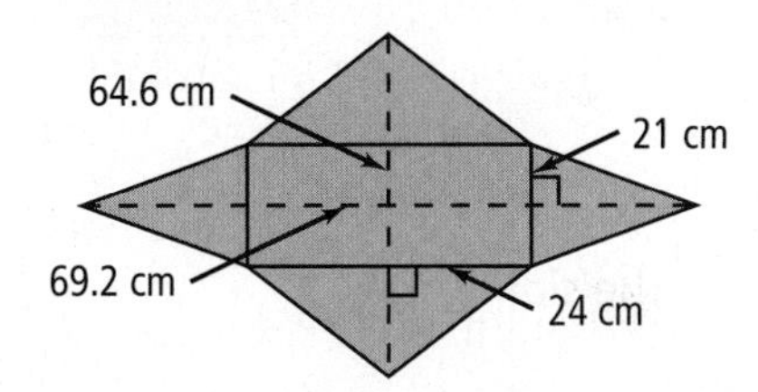

10. **Think About the Process**

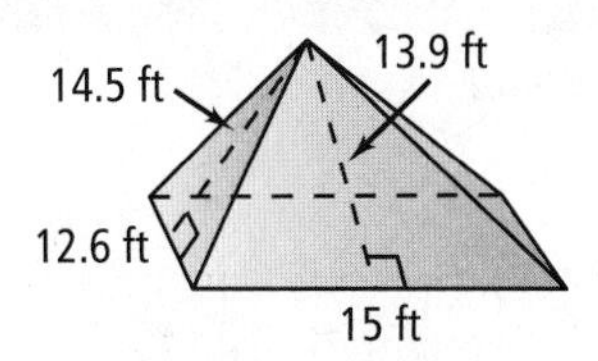

a. Which of the following shows a net of the rectangular pyramid labeled correctly?

A.

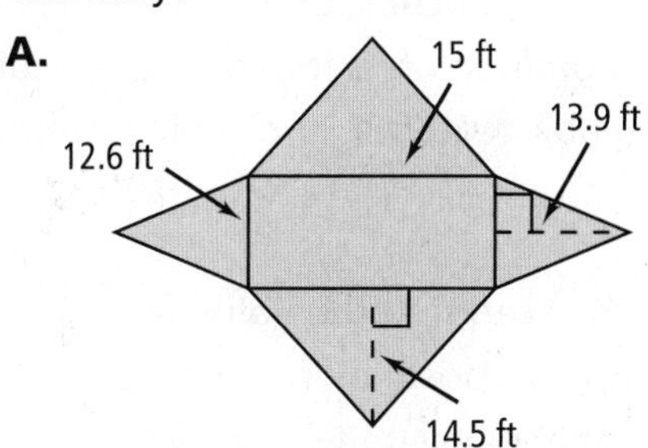

B.

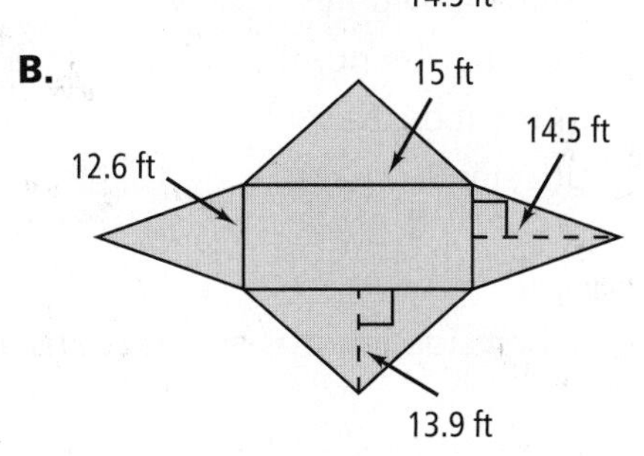

C.

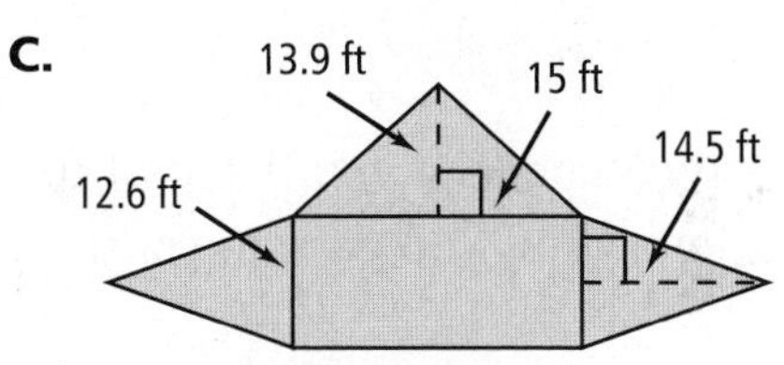

b. Find the surface area.

11. **Challenge** A hotel is the shape of a rectangular pyramid with approximate dimensions as show. The hotel's landscaping company needs to know the length of each side of the base for designing purposes. The manger of the company is given the dimensions shown and the surface area of the hotel, which is approximately 30,098.4 m^2. Find the unknown length, x.

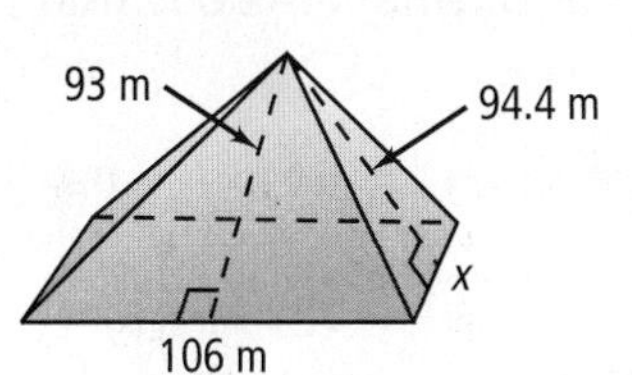

14-5 Volumes of Rectangular Prisms

Vocabulary
volume of a prism

CCSS: 6.G.A.2

Part 1

Intro

The **volume of a prism** is the number of unit cubes, or cubic units, needed to fill the prism. Common units for volume are cubic inches (in.^{3}), cubic feet (ft^3), and cubic meters (m^3).

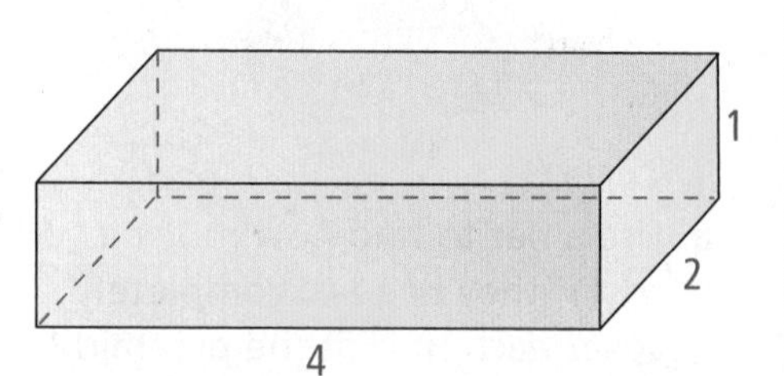

You can find the volume of this prism by finding how many unit cubes will fit in it. The number of unit cubes that fill the prism is 8.

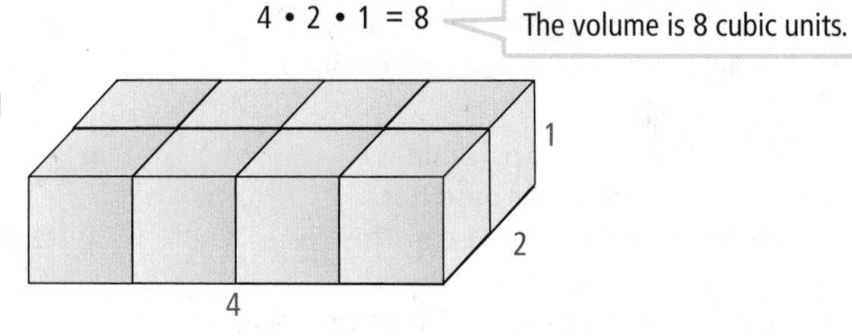

When side lengths are fractions, unit cubes may not fit.

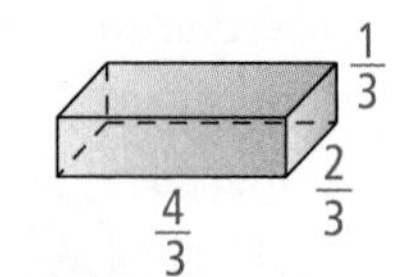

Try a smaller cube. The least common denominator of the side lengths is 3. So pack the prism with smaller cubes.

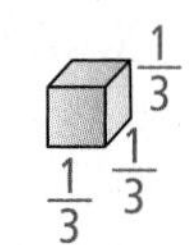

The number of smaller cubes that fill the prism is:

$4 \cdot 2 \cdot 1 = 8$ smaller cubes

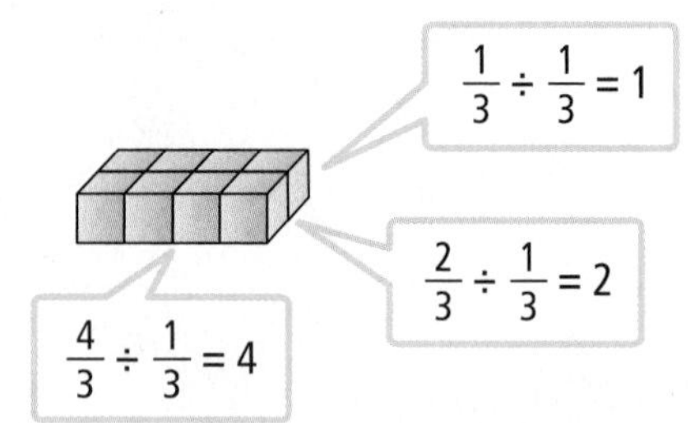

The volume is the number of unit cubes that fill the prism. Find the number of smaller cubes that fit in a unit cube.

$3 \cdot 3 \cdot 3 = 27$ smaller cubes in a unit cube

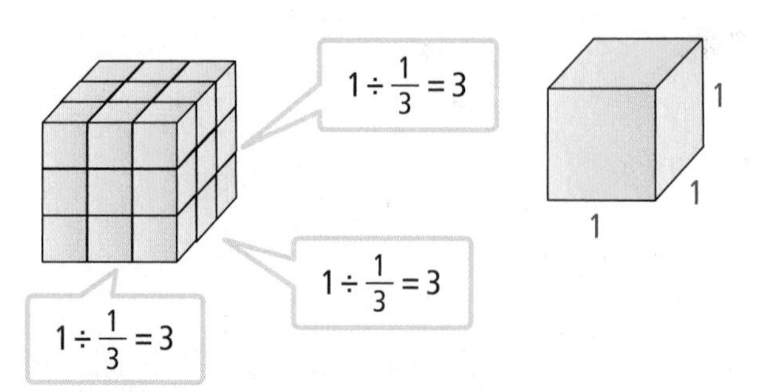

continued on next page >

Part 1

Intro continued

Each smaller cube is $\frac{1}{27}$ of a unit cube.

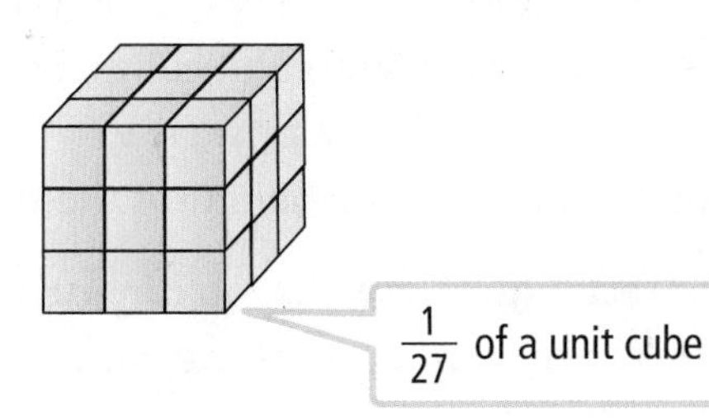

Look at the original prism again.

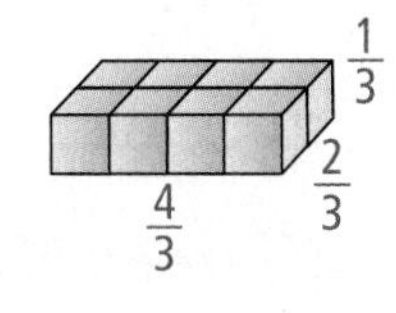

8 of the smaller cubes fit in the prism.

Each smaller cube is $\frac{1}{27}$ of a unit cube.

So the volume of the prism is $8 \cdot \frac{1}{27} = \frac{8}{27}$ cubic units.

Example Using Unit Cubes to Find the Area of Rectangular Prisms

Use cubes with fractional edge lengths to find the volume of the rectangular prism.

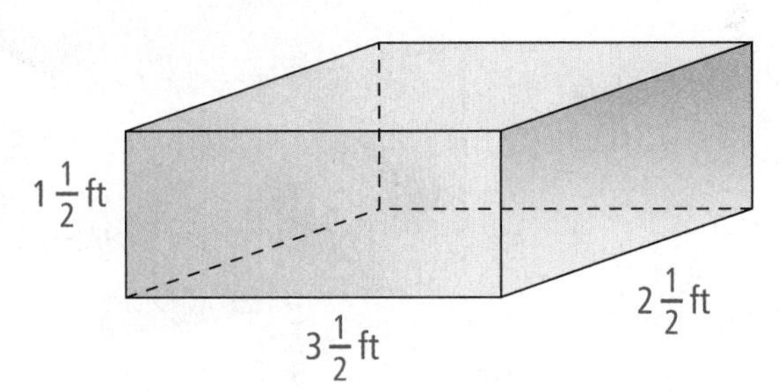

Solution

Step 1 Fill the prism with cubes of $\frac{1}{2}$ ft by $\frac{1}{2}$ ft by $\frac{1}{2}$ ft.

The front layer of the prism has 7×3, or 21, cubes.

The prism is 5 cubes deep, so there are 21×5, or 105 cubes in the prism.

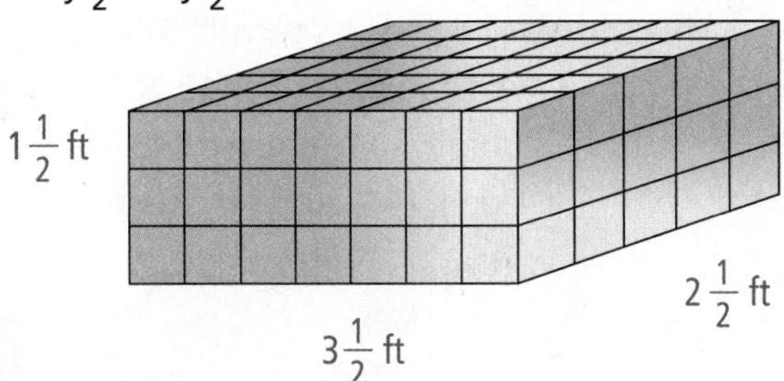

Step 2 Fill a unit cube with cubes of $\frac{1}{2}$ ft by $\frac{1}{2}$ ft by $\frac{1}{2}$ ft.

The front layer of the unit cube has 4 smaller cubes.

The unit cube is 2 smaller cubes deep, so there are 4×2, or 8, smaller cubes in the unit code.

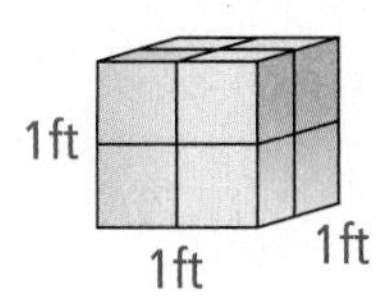

Step 3 Calculate the volume of the rectangular prism in cubic feet.

Each smaller cube is $\frac{1}{8}$ of a unit cube. So the volume of the rectangular prism is $105 \cdot \frac{1}{8}$ ft^3, or $\frac{105}{8}$ ft^3.

Key Concept

There is more than one way to find the volume of a prism. You can pack a prism with unit cubes, or you can use a formula. The formula for the volume V of a prism is $V = Bh$, where B represents the area of a base and h represents the height of the prism.

For rectangular prisms, you can use the formula $V = \ell wh$, where ℓ represents the length, w represents the width, and h represents the height of the prism.

Part 2

Example Using Different Methods to Find the Area of Rectangular Prisms

Use two different methods to find the volume of the rectangular prism.

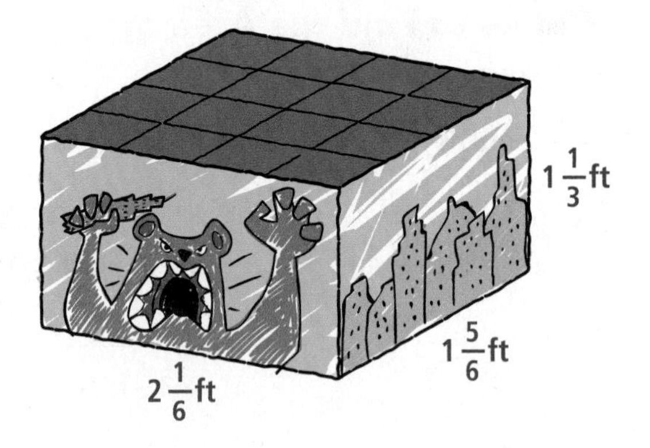

Solution

Method 1 Fill the prism with cubes of $\frac{1}{6}$ ft by $\frac{1}{6}$ ft by $\frac{1}{6}$ ft. The top layer of the prism has 13 × 11, or 143, cubes. The prism is 8 cubes high, so there are 143 × 8 cubes high, so there are 143 × 8, or 1,144, cubes in the prism.

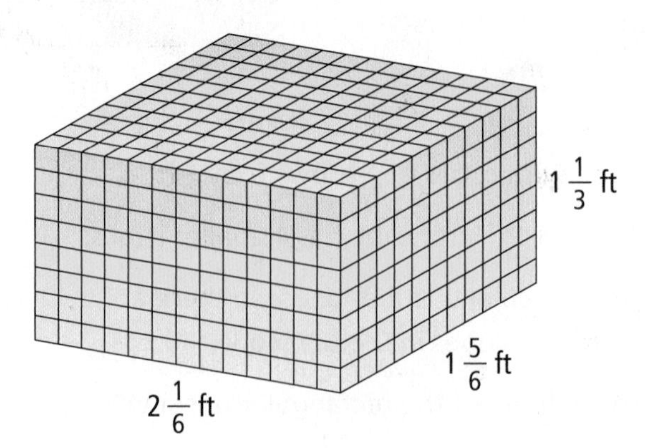

continued on next page >

Part 2

Solution continued

Now fill a unit cube with cubes of $\frac{1}{6}$ ft by $\frac{1}{6}$ ft by $\frac{1}{6}$ ft. The top layer of the unit cube has 6×6, or 36, smaller cubes.

The unit cube is 6 smaller cubes high, so there are 36×6, or 216, smaller cubes in the unit cube.

Each of the smaller cubes is $\frac{1}{216}$ of a unit cube.

So the volume of the rectangular prism is $1{,}144 \cdot \frac{1}{216}$, which equals $\frac{1{,}144}{216}$ or $5\frac{8}{27}$ ft^3.

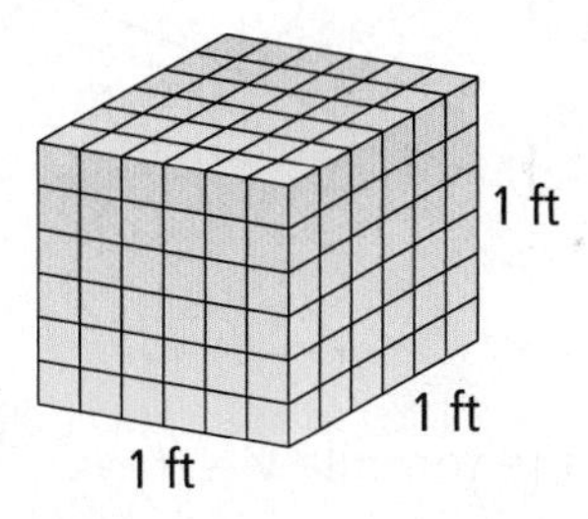

Method 2 Use the formula $V = Bh$ or the formula $V = \ell wh$.

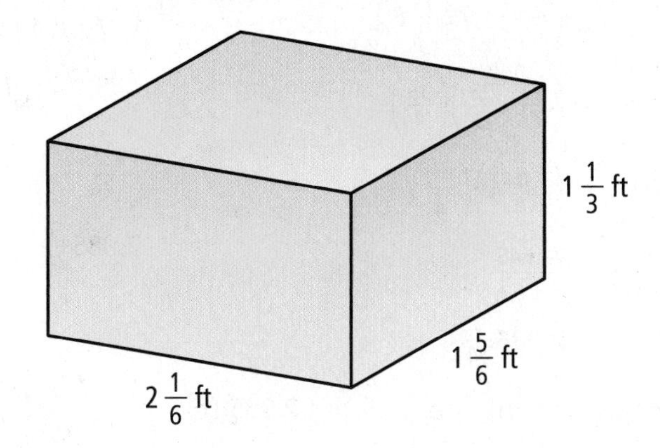

$$\begin{aligned} V &= Bh \\ &= \left(2\tfrac{1}{6} \cdot 1\tfrac{5}{6}\right)\left(1\tfrac{1}{3}\right) \\ &= \left(\tfrac{13}{6} \cdot \tfrac{11}{6}\right)\left(\tfrac{4}{3}\right) \\ &= \left(\tfrac{143}{36}\right)\left(\tfrac{4}{3}\right) \\ &= \tfrac{572}{108} \\ &= 5\tfrac{8}{27} \end{aligned}$$

$$\begin{aligned} V &= \ell wh \\ &= \left(2\tfrac{1}{6}\right)\left(1\tfrac{5}{6}\right)\left(1\tfrac{1}{3}\right) \\ &= \left(\tfrac{13}{6}\right)\left(\tfrac{11}{6}\right)\left(\tfrac{4}{3}\right) \\ &= \tfrac{572}{108} \\ &= 5\tfrac{8}{27} \end{aligned}$$

Both formulas give the same result.

The volume of the rectangular prism is $5\frac{8}{27}$ ft^3.

Part 3

Example Using a Formula to Find the Area of Rectangular Prisms

The cargo container has the shape of a rectangular prism. Use a formula to find the volume of the cargo container to the nearest cubic foot.

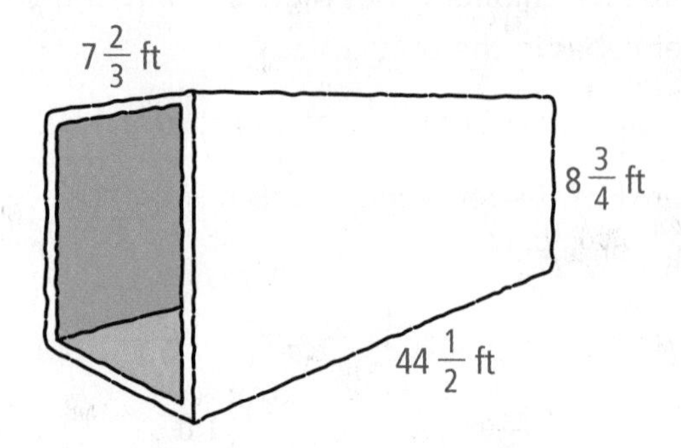

Solution

Use the formula $V = Bh$ or the formula $V = \ell wh$.

$$\begin{aligned} V &= Bh \\ &= \left(44\tfrac{1}{2} \cdot 7\tfrac{2}{3}\right)\left(8\tfrac{3}{4}\right) \\ &= \left(\tfrac{89}{2} \cdot \tfrac{23}{3}\right)\left(\tfrac{35}{4}\right) \\ &= \left(\tfrac{2{,}047}{6}\right)\left(\tfrac{35}{4}\right) \\ &= \tfrac{71{,}645}{24} \\ &= 2{,}985\tfrac{5}{24} \end{aligned}$$

$$\begin{aligned} V &= \ell wh \\ &= \left(44\tfrac{1}{2}\right)\left(7\tfrac{2}{3}\right)\left(8\tfrac{3}{4}\right) \\ &= \left(\tfrac{89}{2}\right)\left(\tfrac{23}{3}\right)\left(\tfrac{35}{4}\right) \\ &= \tfrac{71{,}645}{24} \\ &= 2{,}985\tfrac{5}{24} \end{aligned}$$

The volume of the cargo container is about 2,985 ft^3.

Digital Resources   

1. Use unit cubes to find the volume of the right rectangular prism.

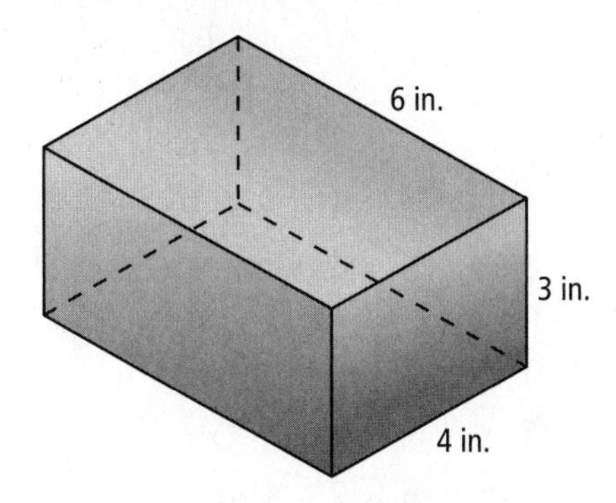

2. Think About the Process A right rectangular prism has length $2\frac{1}{2}$ yd, width $1\frac{1}{2}$ yd, and height $1\frac{1}{2}$ yd. You use cubes with fractional edge length $\frac{1}{2}$ yd to find the volume.

a. How many cubes are there for each of the length, width, and height of the prism? Complete the sentence below.

The length has ■ cubes, the width has ■ cubes, and the height has ■ cubes.

b. Find the volume.

3. Find the volume of a rectangular block of ice 1 ft by $2\frac{1}{2}$ ft by $\frac{1}{2}$ ft.

4. a. Writing Find the volume of the right rectangular prism using unit cubes.

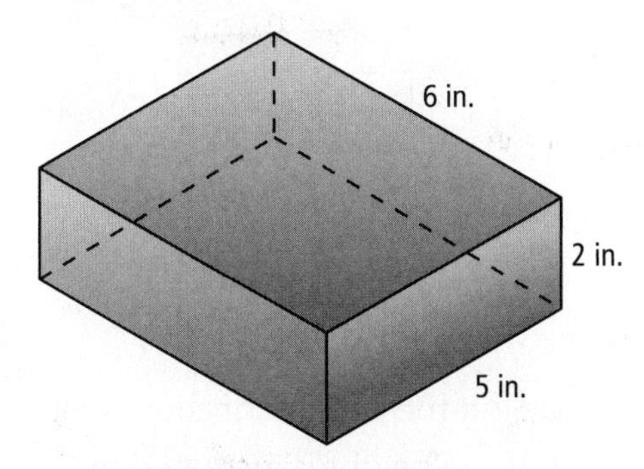

b. Use a formula to find the volume.

c. Explain how to use unit cubes to find the volume in ft^3.

5. Multiple Representations

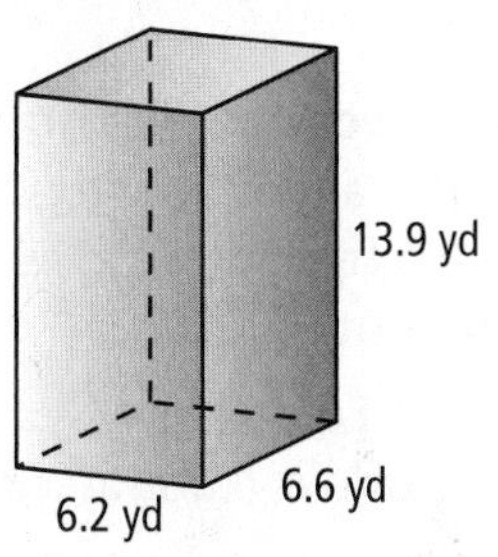

(The figure is not to scale.)

a. Find the volume of the rectangular prism.

b. Can prisms with different dimensions have the same volume? Explain.

6. Error Analysis Jackson claims the volume of the right rectangular prism is 28 in^3.

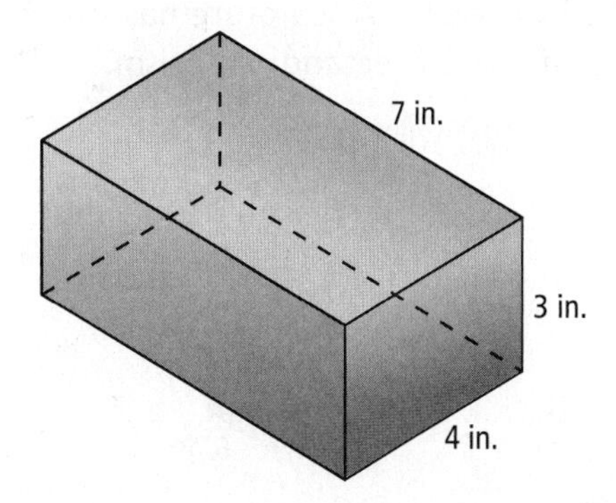

a. Find the correct volume using unit cubes.

b. What mistake might Jackson have made?

A. Jackson counted cubes to fill a prism with length 1 in., instead of length 7 in.

B. Jackson counted cubes to fill a prism with height 1 in., instead of height 3 in.

C. Jackson counted cubes to fill a prism with height 3 in., instead of height 1 in.

D. Jackson counted cubes to fill a prism with width 1 in., instead of width 4 in.

7. a. Use unit cubes to find the volume of a right rectangular prism with width 4 ft, length 5 ft, and height 5 ft.
   b. Find the volume of a right rectangular prism with width 5 ft, length 4 ft, and height 5 ft. What do you notice?

8. **Playground Equipment** A sandbox has the shape of a rectangular prism.

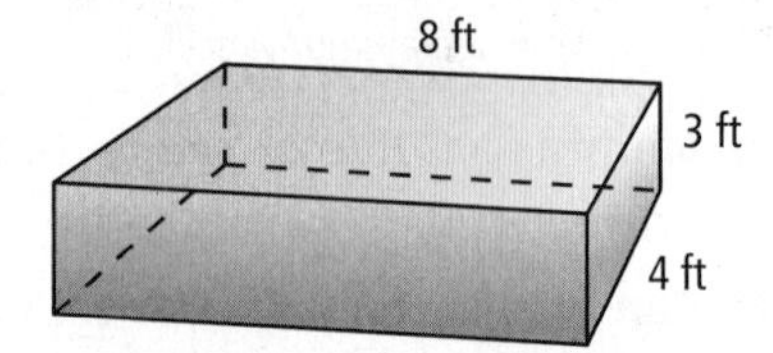

(The figure is not to scale.)

   a. What is the volume?
   b. Would 110 ft^3 of sand fit inside the sandbox?

9. **Estimation** A sculpture has the shape of a right rectangular prism.

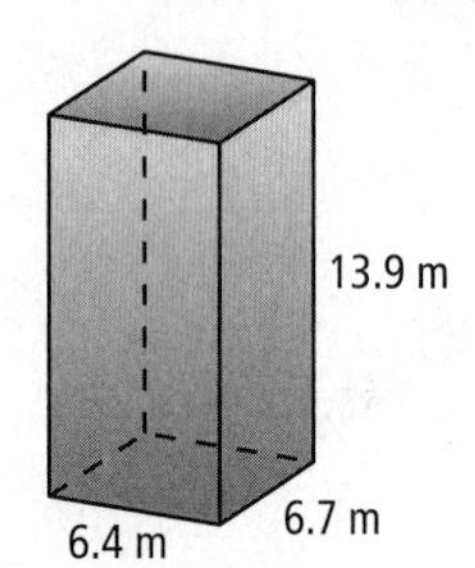

(The figure is not to scale.)

   a. Estimate the volume by rounding each dimension to the nearest whole number.
   b. Find the exact volume of the sculpture.

10. **Think About the Process**

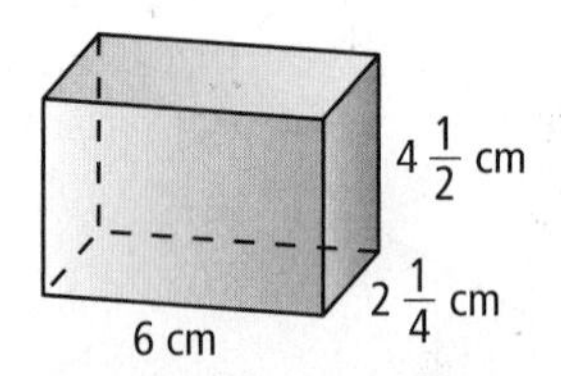

(The figure is not to scale.)

   a. What equation can you use to find the volume of the rectangular prism?
      A. $V = 6 \times 2\frac{1}{4} \div 4\frac{1}{2}$
      B. $V = 6 \times 2\frac{1}{4} \times 4\frac{1}{2}$
      C. $V = 6 + 2\frac{1}{4} + 4\frac{1}{2}$
      D. $V = 6\frac{1}{4} \times 2\frac{1}{2} \times 4$
   b. Find the volume.

11. **Challenge** Find the volume, in ft^3, of the figure shown.

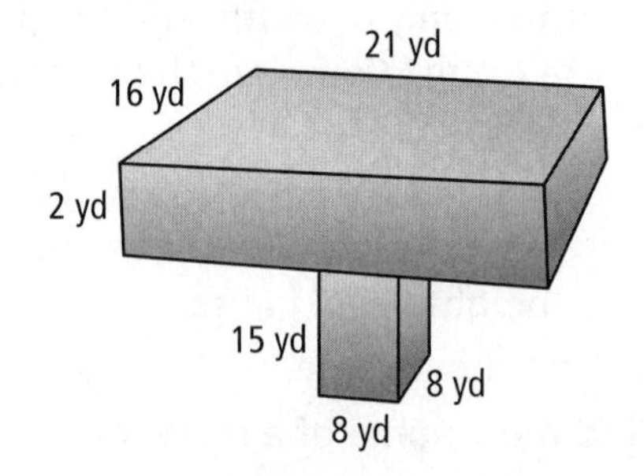

(The figure is not to scale.)

12. **Challenge** A jewelry box has the shape of a rectangular prism.

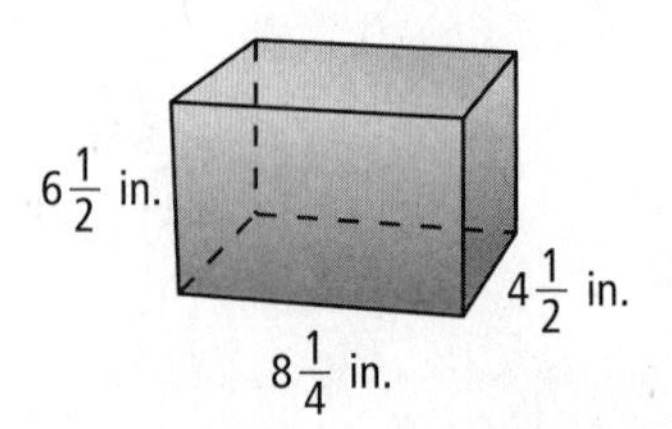

(The figure is not to scale.)

   a. Find the volume of the jewelry box.
   b. If the height is increased by 2 in., by how much does the volume increase?

14-6 Problem Solving

CCSS: 6.G.A.2, 6.G.A.4

Part 1

Example Using Surface Area and Volume to Solve Real-World Problems

The two cereal boxes have the shape of rectangular prisms. The company cares about its customers, so it wants the box to hold as much cereal as possible. The company also wants to help save the environment, so it wants to use the least amount of cardboard possible. Which box should the company choose to make? Explain.

Box A

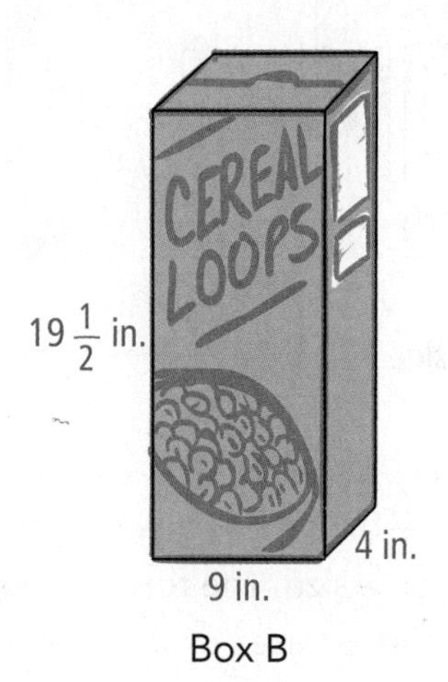

Box B

Solution

To find out how much cereal each box holds and how much material is needed to make each box, you will need to find the volume and surface area of each box.

$$\text{Amount of cereal the box holds} = \text{Volume of the box}$$

The boxes are each rectangular prisms. Use the formula $V = Bh$.

Volume of Box A

$V = Bh$

$= \left(10 \cdot 4\frac{1}{2}\right)\left(15\frac{3}{5}\right)$

$= 702$

Volume of Box B

$V = Bh$

$= (9 \cdot 4)\left(19\frac{1}{2}\right)$

$= 702$

continued on next page >

Part 1

Solution continued

Box A and Box B both have a volume of 702 in.^{3}, so they hold the same amount of cereal.

$$\text{Amount of cardboard used to make box} = \text{Surface area of the box}$$

Use the nets to help find the surface area.

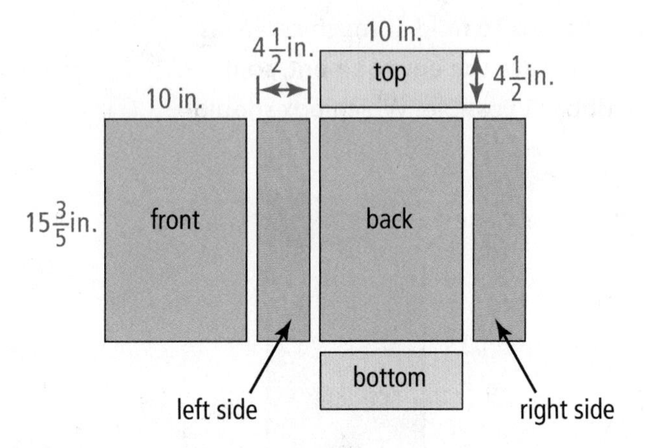

Box A

The front and back of the box are the same size. The right and left sides of the box are the same size. The top and bottom of the box are also the same size. To find the surface area of the box, add the areas of the sides of the box together.

front, back, left side, right side, top, bottom

$$\text{Surface area} = 10\left(15\tfrac{3}{5}\right) + 10\left(15\tfrac{3}{5}\right) + \left(4\tfrac{1}{2}\right)\left(15\tfrac{3}{5}\right) + \left(4\tfrac{1}{2}\right)\left(15\tfrac{3}{5}\right) + 10\left(4\tfrac{1}{2}\right) + 10\left(4\tfrac{1}{2}\right)$$

$$= 156 + 156 + \frac{351}{5} + \frac{351}{5} + 45 + 45$$

A common denominator is 5.

$$= \frac{2{,}712}{5}$$

$$= 542\tfrac{2}{5}$$

continued on next page >

Part 1

Solution continued

The surface area of Box A is $542\frac{2}{5}$ in.^{2}.

Similarly,

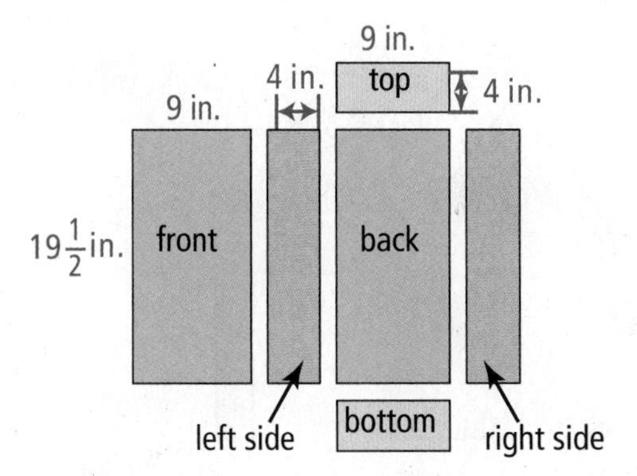

Box B

$$\text{Surface area} = 9\left(19\tfrac{1}{2}\right) + 9\left(19\tfrac{1}{2}\right) + 4\left(19\tfrac{1}{2}\right) + 4\left(19\tfrac{1}{2}\right) + 9 \cdot 4 + 9 \cdot 4$$

$$= \frac{351}{2} + \frac{351}{2} + 78 + 78 + 36 + 36$$

$$= 351 + 78 + 78 + 36 + 36$$

$$= 579$$

The surface area of Box B is 579 in.^{2}.

You have already found that the surface area of Box A is $542\frac{2}{5}$ in.^{2}. Since the surface area of Box A is less than the surface area of Box B, Box A uses less cardboard. The company should choose Box A because Box A holds the same amount of cereal as Box B, but it uses less cardboard.

Part 2

Example Using Surface Area to Solve Real-World Problems

An amusement park entrance has the shape of a cube with a square pyramid on top. Guests pass through two matching doorways in the structure. One gallon of paint covers 350 square feet. How many gallons of paint does the park staff need to paint the entrance?

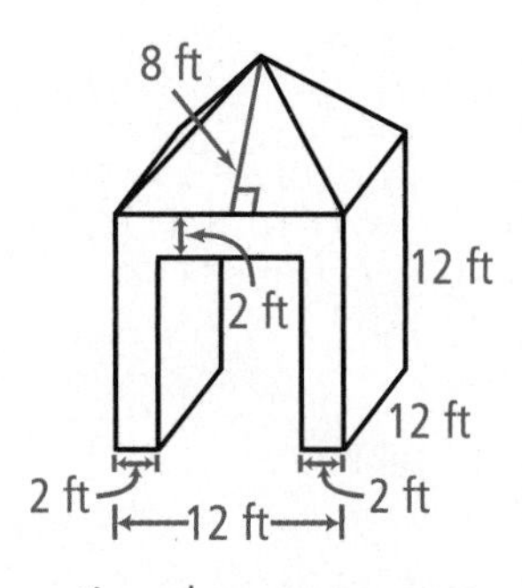

continued on next page >

Part 2

Example continued

Solution

Step 1 Draw and label a net of the entrance.

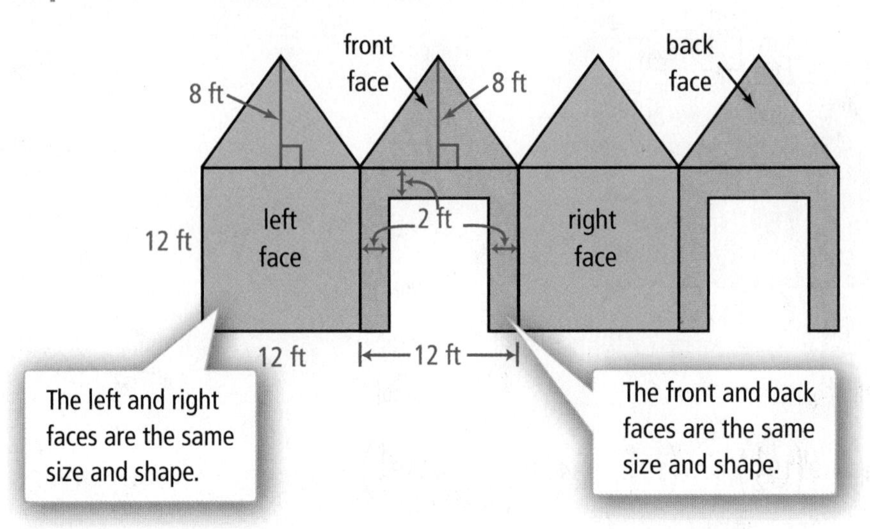

Step 2 Find the area of each face of the entrance.

Area of the front and back:

Area of triangle $= \frac{1}{2}bh$

$= \frac{1}{2}(12)(8)$

$= 6(8)$

$= 48$

Area of square $= s^2$

$= 12^2$, or 144

Area of opening $= bh$

$= (12 - 2 - 2)(12 - 2)$

$= (8)(10)$

$= 80$

Area of front and back = Area of triangle + Area of square − opening

$= 48 + 144 - 80$

$= 112$

continued on next page >

Part 2

Solution continued

Area of the left and right sides:

Area of triangle $= \frac{1}{2}bh$
$= \frac{1}{2}(12)(8)$
$= 6(8)$
$= 48$

Area of square $= s^2$
$= 12^2$, or 144

Area of left and right sides = Area of triangle + Area of square
$= 48 + 144$
$= 192$

Step 3 Add the areas of the faces together.

Surface of area = Area of front + Area of back + Area of left side + Area of right side

$= 112 + 112 + 192 + 192$

$= 608$

The surface area of the entrance is 608 ft^2.

Step 4 Find the number of gallons of paint needed.

$$\text{Gallons of paint needed} = \frac{\text{Surface area in square feet}}{\text{Number of square feet one gallon covers}}$$

$$= \frac{608}{350}$$

$$= 1\frac{129}{175}$$

The company needs 2 gallons of paint to paint the entrance.

Digital Resources    

1. You baked brownies for a friend and are going to put them in the given canister as a gift.

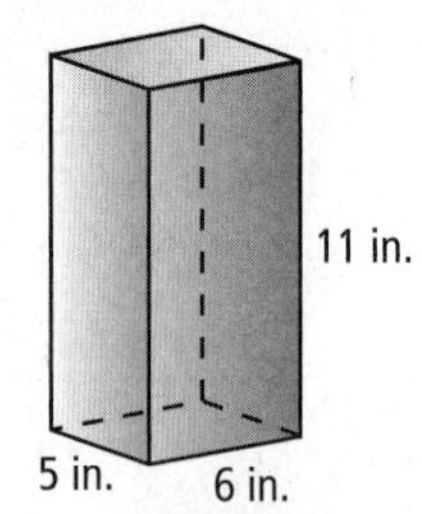

(The figure is not to scale.)

   a. Find the volume of the canister to find the amount of brownies you can fit in it.
   b. Find the surface area of the canister to find the amount of decorative wrap you need to wrap the canister.

2. You plan to build a step stool with two steps as shown. How many square inches of wood do you need to build this step stool?

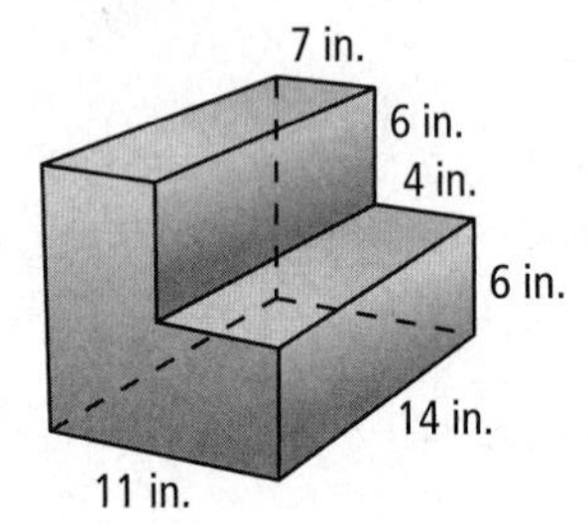

(The figure is not to scale.)

3. **Think About the Process** You are going to wrap the block in paper for a project.

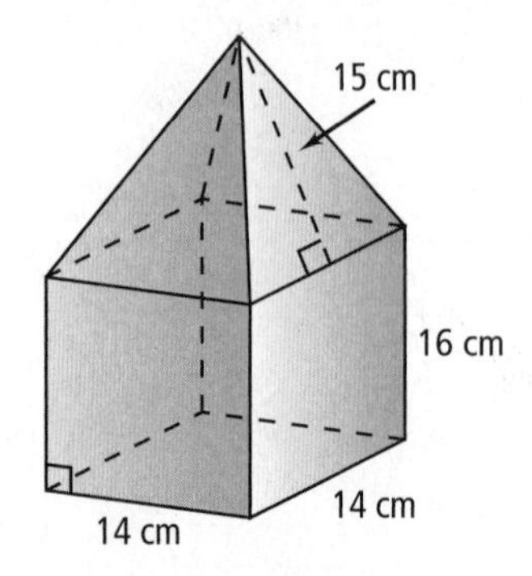

(The figure is not to scale.)

   a. How can you find the amount of paper you will need to wrap the block?
      A. Find the difference of the surface area and the volume of the block.
      B. Find the surface area and volume of the block.
      C. Find the surface area of the block.
      D. Find the volume of the block.
   b. How much paper do you need to wrap the block?

4. You are using wood to build and open-topped sandbox in the shape of a right rectangular prism.

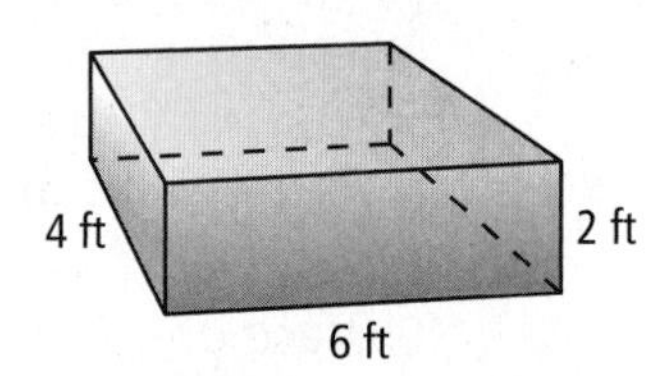

(The figure is not to scale.)

   a. Find the volume of the sandbox to find the amount of sand needed to fill the sandbox.
   b. Find the surface area of the sandbox to find the amount of wood needed to build the sandbox.

5. You are building a shed using the exact measurements shown.

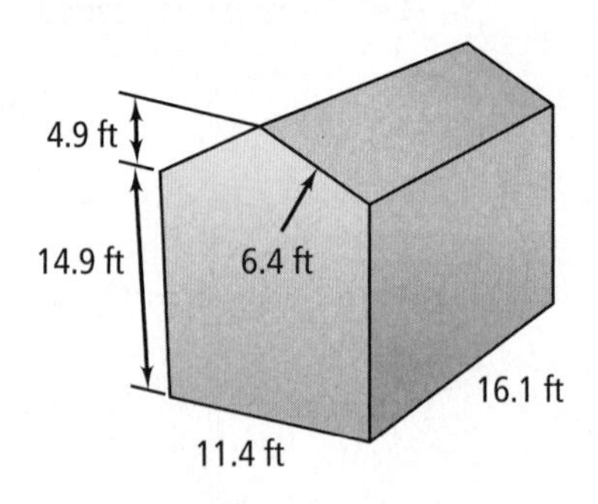

(The figure is not to scale.)

   a. Estimate the amount of wood you will need to build the shed by rounding each value to the nearest whole number.
   b. Find the exact amount of wood you will need to build the shed.

6. Think About the Process You want to buy a plastic container to store flour in. You want the container that holds the most flour and uses the least plastic.

Container F 15 cm, 12 cm, 4 cm

Container G 15 cm, 8 cm, 6 cm

(These figures are not to scale.)

a. How will you decide which container to buy?

A. Find the container with the greater volume and the greater surface area.

B. Find the container with the lesser volume and the greater surface area.

C. Find the container with the lesser volume and the lesser surface area.

D. Find the container with the greater volume and the lesser surface area.

b. Which container should you buy?

7. Challenge You are going to frost the two layers of this cake except where the layers meet. You can frost 100 square inches with one jar of frosting.

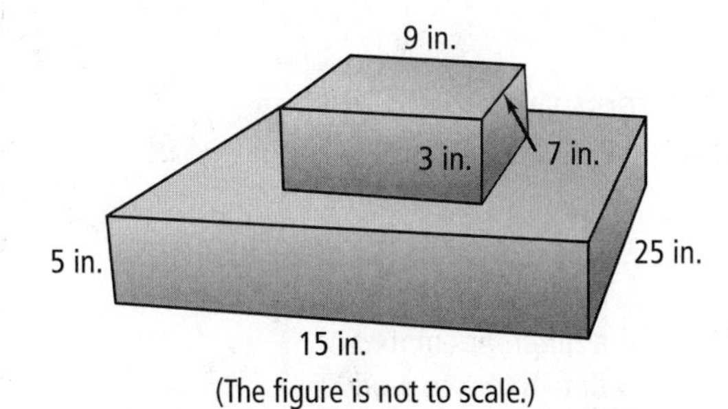

(The figure is not to scale.)

How many jars of frosting do you need to frost the cake?

8. Challenge A cracker company cares about the environment so they would like to buy boxes that use the least amount of cardboard, but hold the most crackers.

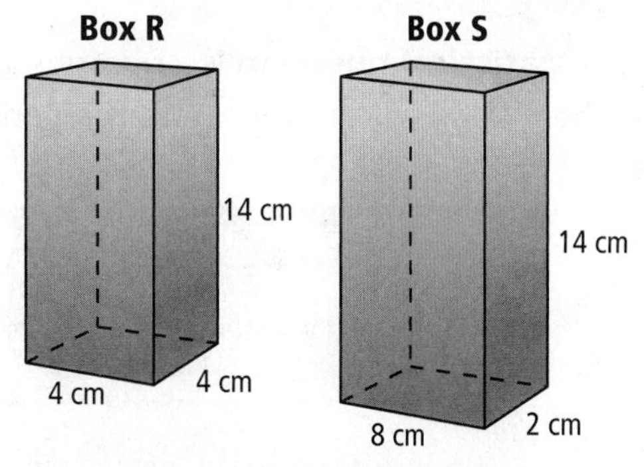

(These figures are not to scale.)

a. Which box should the company buy?

b. Find two boxes that use the same amount of cardboard but cannot hold the same amount of crackers.

See your complete lesson at MyMathUniverse.com

15-1 Statistical Questions

Vocabulary
data, statistical question

CCSS: 6.SP.A.1, 6.SP.B.5b

Key Concept

A **statistical question** is a question that investigates an aspect of the world and can have more than one possible response.

Statistical Questions	Answer
How old are students in my class?	They are 10, 11, and 12 years old.
How do my friends get to school?	They walk, ride a bike, take the bus, and take the train.

Questions That are Not Statistical	Answer
How old am I?	I am 11 years old.
How did I get to school today?	I walked to school today.

Part 1

Example Understanding Statistical Questions

Why is *"How long does it take people to commute to work?"* a statistical question?

Solution

The question *"How long does it take people to commute to work?"* is a statistical question because the answers can vary from person to person. For example,

Person A takes 20 minutes to get to work.

Person B takes 1.5 hours to get to work.

Person C takes 45 minutes to get to work.

... ...

One person can take a different amount of time to get to work from another person.

Part 2

Example Identifying Statistical Questions

Which questions are statistical? Which are not? Why?

a. How many plastic bottles did I use last month?
b. Do shoppers in my town use paper bags or plastic bags?
c. How many computers does my school have?
d. How much do drivers spend on gasoline per month?

Solution

Statistical: Statistical questions have many possible answers.

b. Do shoppers in my town use paper bags or plastic bags?

There is more than one person who shops in your town, so you can expect to get a different answer depending on whom you ask.
For example,

Shopper A: paper bags

Shopper B: plastic bags

... ...

The question is statistical.

d. How much do drivers spend on gasoline per month?

There is more than one driver who spends money on gasoline, and you can expect that each driver uses a different amount. For example,

Driver A: $98.00
Driver B: $55.00
... ...

The question is statistical.

Not Statistical: Questions that are not statistical only have only one possible answer.

a. How many plastic bottles did I use last month?

The question asks only one person, so only one answer is expected. The question is not statistical.

c. How many computers does my school have?

The question asks only about one place, so only one answer is expected. The question is not statistical.

Part 3

Intro

When you ask a statistical question, the responses that you get are *data*.

Data are numbers or other pieces of information collected by asking questions, measuring, or making observations about the real world.

Example Analyzing Results of Statistical Questions

The data shown reflect answers to the statistical question *"What kinds of relics were found at the dig site of an ancient village?"*

Describe the way you think this village lived. Explain your reasoning.

Solution

Sample: The set of data contains a greater number of pottery objects than things like arrowheads.

This could mean that this village was more focused on arts than on hunting.

Digital Resources   

1. Why is the following a statistical question?

   How many plays do students see in a year?

   A. Some students might not like seeing plays.

   B. Different students can see different numbers of plays in a year.

   C. Some students might not see any plays in a year.

   D. The question asks about only one year.

2. You want to learn about the recycling habits of people in your neighborhood. Which of the following is a statistical question for this situation?

   A. How many cans did your family recycle last week?

   B. How many cans did your family recycle last month?

   C. How many times did your neighbors recycle cardboard last month?

3. **a.** Which of the following are statistical questions? Select all that apply.

   A. How many pages do textbooks have?

   B. How many monkeys does the nearest zoo have?

   C. How much do drivers spend on oil each month?

   D. How many e-mails did you receive last week?

   b. Explain why the others are not statistical questions.

4. Is the following question statistical? Explain.

   How do shoppers in a town pay for their groceries?

5. Some children were playing at the park yesterday. A parent later recalled that some of the children were wearing the kinds of clothing listed at the right. Which of the following questions could the parent answer? Select all that apply.

light jacket
light jacket
short sleeves
heavy jacket
sweater
light jacket
heavy jacket
long pants

   A. Were there more boys than girls at the park?

   B. What was the weather like at the park yesterday?

   C. How long was each child playing at the park?

   D. What time of day were the children playing at the park?

6. You and some of your friends are experiencing growth spurts. Which of the following are statistical questions for this situation?

   1. How tall were your friends last month?

   2. How tall are you now?

   3. How tall are your friends now?

   A. Only question 3

   B. Only questions 1 and 3

   C. Only questions 2 and 3

   D. Only question 1

   E. Only questions 1 and 2

   F. Only question 2

   G. All three questions

   H. None of the questions

7. A factory processes tomatoes from several farms. A manager at the factory wants to know whether the harvest from these farms will be good this year. Which of the following could the manager statistically study to get useful information about this? Select all that apply.

   A. the number of fields the farms have

   B. the geography of the farms

   C. the amount of rain the farms get

   D. the amount of fertilizer the farmers use

8. Writing You want to study how the students in your class spend their free time.

a. Give three examples of questions that are statistical.

b. Give three examples of questions that are not statistical.

c. Describe how the two kinds of questions are different.

9. a. Reasoning Which of the following are statistical questions? Select all that apply.

A. How did your classmates get to school yesterday?

B. Does your family get a daily newspaper?

C. How did you get to school yesterday?

D. How many computers do schools have?

b. Explain why the others are not statistical questions.

10. Think About the Process Your teacher asks, "At what temperature does water freeze?" To answer this question, you freeze twelve trays of water. Then you record the temperature of the water in each tray when the water starts to freeze. These data are shown in the table. What should you do to answer your teacher's question?

Temperature of Water in Each Tray (°C)					
−0.7	−1.2	−0.7	−0.9	−0.9	−0.7
−1.2	−0.7	−1.2	−0.9	−1.2	−0.7

A. Find the temperature that occurs the most.

B. Find the highest temperature.

C. Find the difference between the highest and lowest temperatures.

D. Find the lowest temperature.

11. Think About the Process You want to find whether the question shown below is statistical. What questions should you ask to do this? Select all that apply.

In what month were your classmates born?

A. Could the birth month vary from student to student?

B. Could a student have more than one birth month?

C. Are there as many boys as girls in the class?

D. How many students are there in the class?

12. a. Challenge Which of the following questions are statistical? Select all that apply.

A. How many e-mails did you get each day last month?

B. Which radio station do you like the most?

C. How many desks are there in your classroom?

D. How long are popular songs?

E. How much do shoes cost?

F. None of the questions are statistical.

b. Explain why each of the other questions is not statistical. Rewrite them as statistical questions.

15-2 Dot Plots

Vocabulary
dot plot,
frequency

CCSS: 6.SP.B.4, 6.SP.B.5, 6.SP.B.5c

Key Concept

A **dot plot** shows the shape of a data set by representing each data point as a dot over its corresponding value on a number line.

The values in the data set must be numerical to be displayed on a dot plot. This data set has 12 values.

My Friends' Siblings: 2, 0, 1, 3, 2, 4, 1, 6, 2, 2, 1, 3

The scale is made up of a number line and a unit label. The least value in this data set is 0. The greatest value is 6. So the scale can be a number line from 0 to 6.

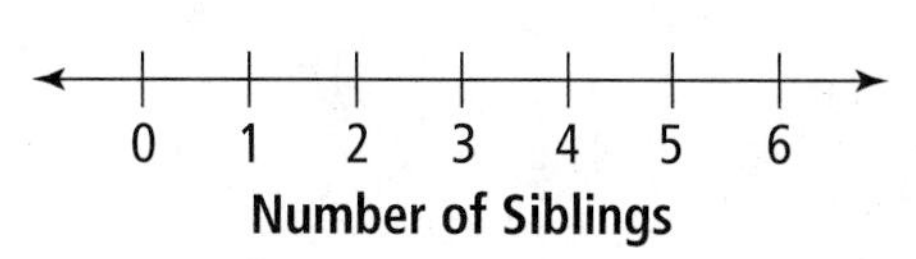

Each dot represents one value in the data set.

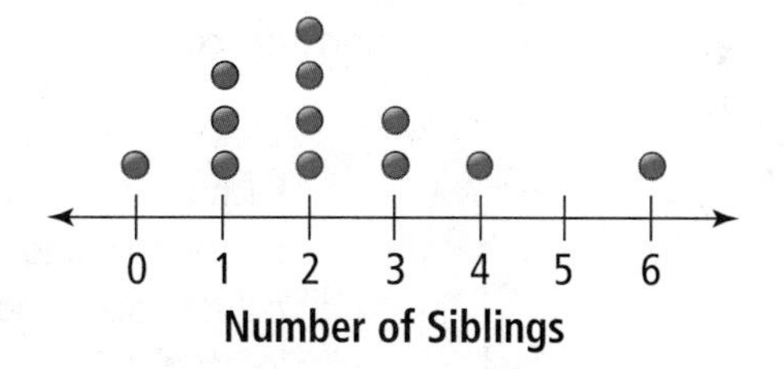

The frequency describes how often a data value occurs. The number of dots above a value on the scale shows the frequency of that value in the data set. There are three dots above the number 1, so the frequency of 1 in this data set is three.

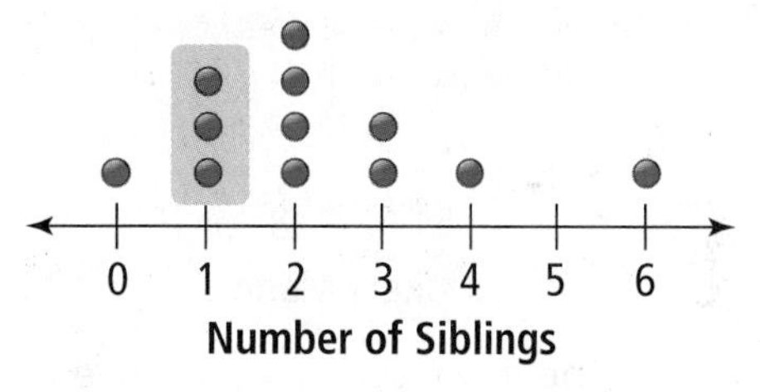

Part 1

Example Using Dot Plots

Your friends hold a basketball-shooting contest. The person who makes the most baskets in one minute wins. Use the dot plot to answer the questions.

a. How many people made eight baskets?

b. How many baskets did the most people make?

c. What is the least number of baskets that a person made?

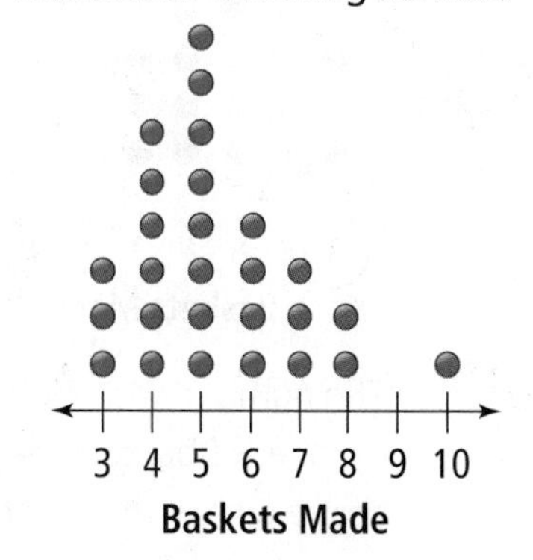

continued on next page >

Part 1

Example continued

Solution

a. Basketball-shooting contest

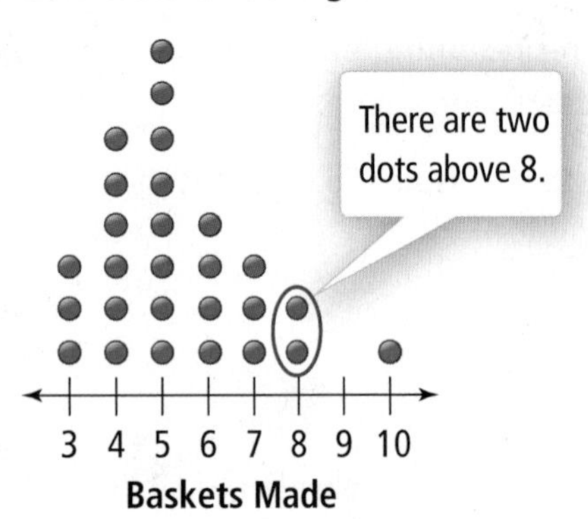

There were two people who made eight baskets.

b. Basketball-shooting contest

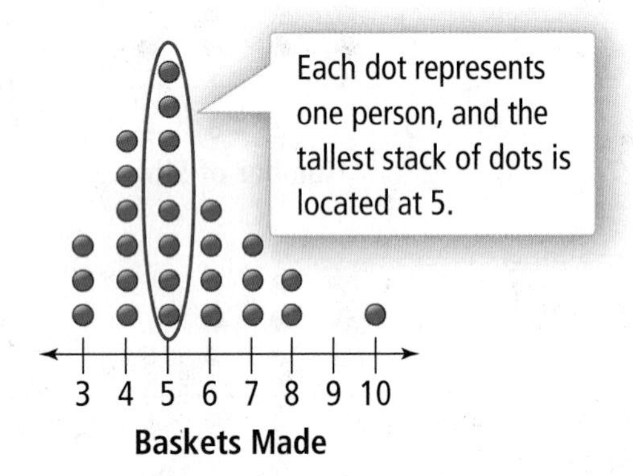

The most people made five baskets.

c. Basketball-shooting contest

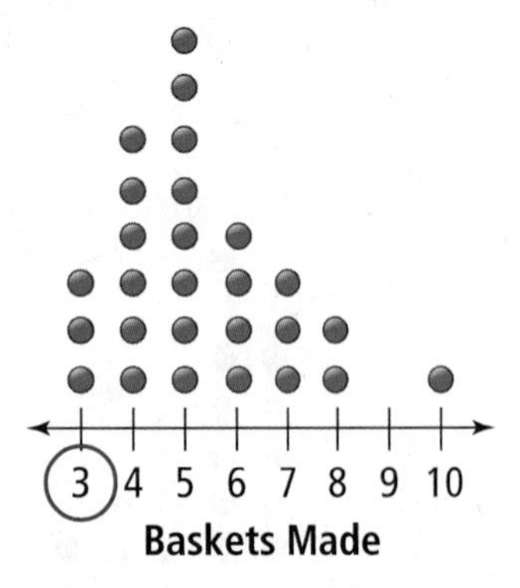

The number at the left end of the number line represents the fewest number of baskets that a person made. The fewest number of baskets that a person made is three.

Part 2

Example Making Dot Plots

The data show the ages of the dancers on a dance team. Make a dot plot of the data to find out which age is most common on the team.

Dancer Ages

11	12	14	12
10	13	12	12
11	12	12	
12	12	13	
11	11	11	
12	12	12	

Solution

Graph the ages of the dancers. The youngest dancer is 10 years old. The oldest dancer is 14 years old. So the scale should go from 10 to 14 years. Represent each data value with a dot above the corresponding age on the number line.

Age of Dancers on a Dance Team

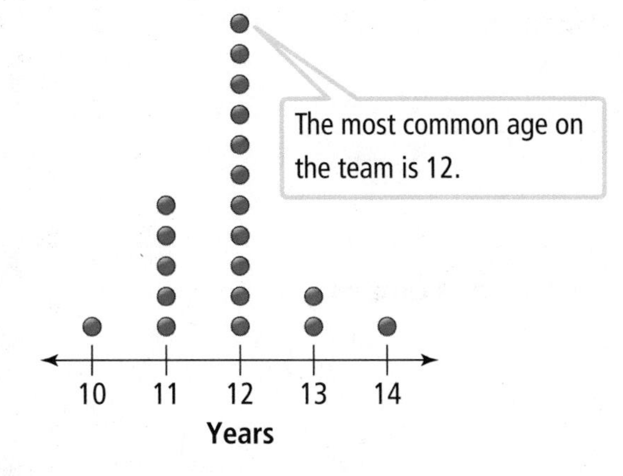

Part 3

Intro

Dot plots are useful for seeing clusters and gaps in the data set. They are also useful for seeing values that stray from the general shape of the data.

Ages of Cats at a Local Shelter

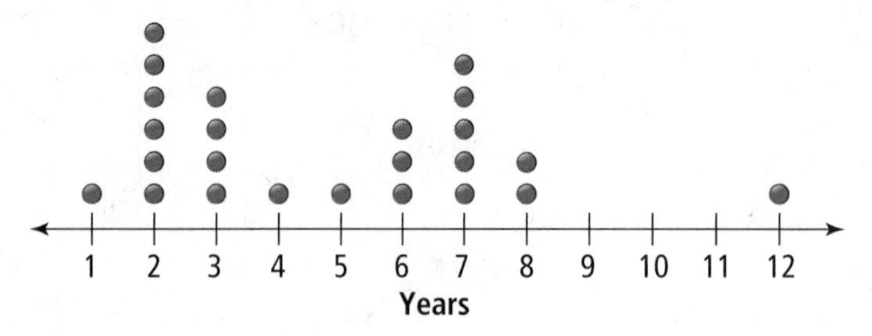

The distribution describes the way that the data is spread out over all possible values. You can use words like "cluster" and "gap" to describe distribution.

Ages of Cats at a Local Shelter

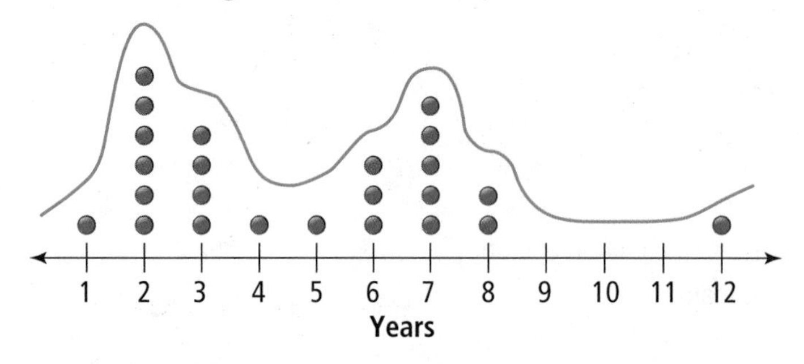

Areas where most of the dots are stacked are known as clusters.

Ages of Cats at a Local Shelter

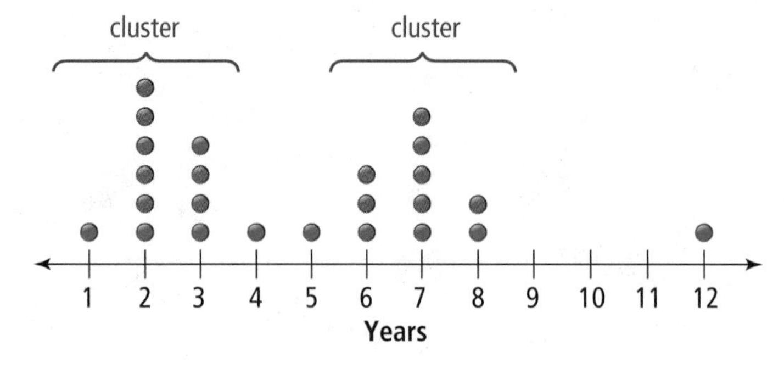

continued on next page >

Part 3

Intro continued

Areas where there are a significantly smaller number of dots are known as gaps.

Ages of Cats at a Local Shelter

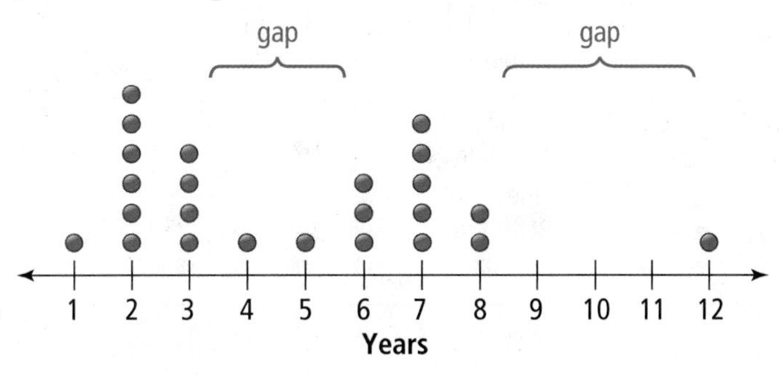

Dots that are located far away from the main set of data are known as stray data values.

Ages of Cats at a Local Shelter

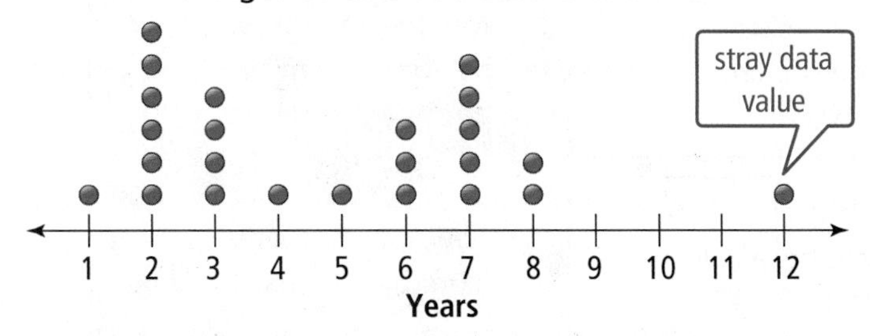

Example Finding Clusters, Gaps, and Stray Values on Dot Plots

The dot plot shows the heights of plants in a research laboratory. Identify the clusters, the gaps, and any data values that stray. What do they tell you about the heights of the plants?

Plant Heights

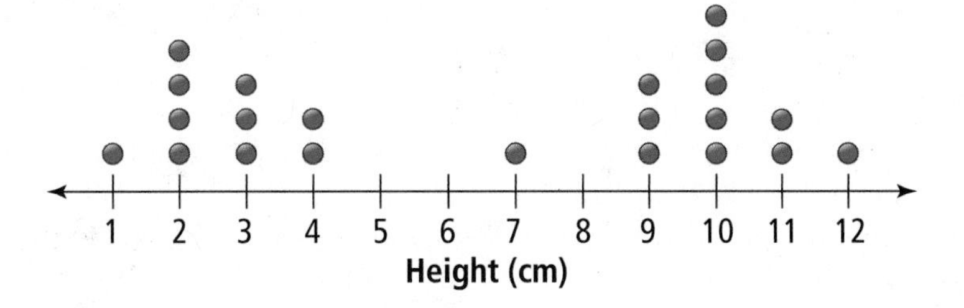

continued on next page >

Part 3

Example continued

Solution

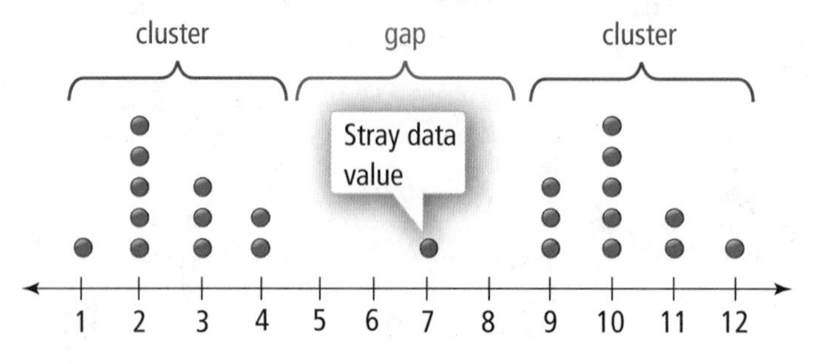

Think	Write
There are two clusters: one at around 2 cm, and one at around 10 cm.	Most plants grew either to about 2 cm or to about 10 cm.
There is a big gap from 5 to 8 cm where there is little data plotted.	Few plants grew from 5 to 8 cm.
One dot at 7 cm seems like a stray data value because it falls in between the two clusters.	There was only one plant that grew to 7 cm.

1. A teacher asked 20 students how many books they read last summer. The dot plot displays the data. What is the greatest number of books a student read?

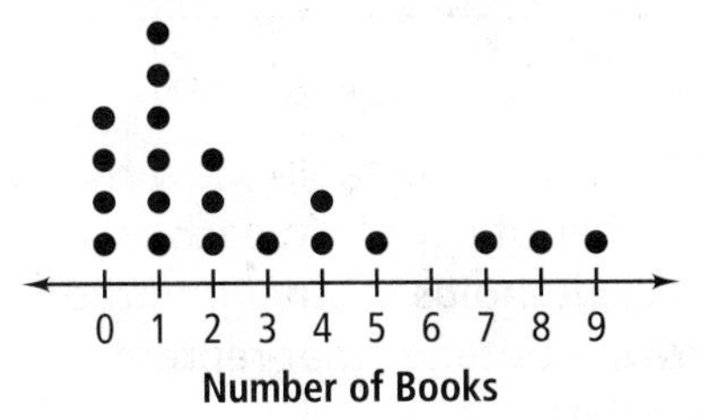

2. A scientist measured the temperature at which water boils. The table shows the results for 10 measurements. Which dot plot represents the data?

Boiling Point of Water (°F)				
211.6	211.5	211.6	211.4	211.5
211.7	211.6	211.6	211.6	211.8

A.
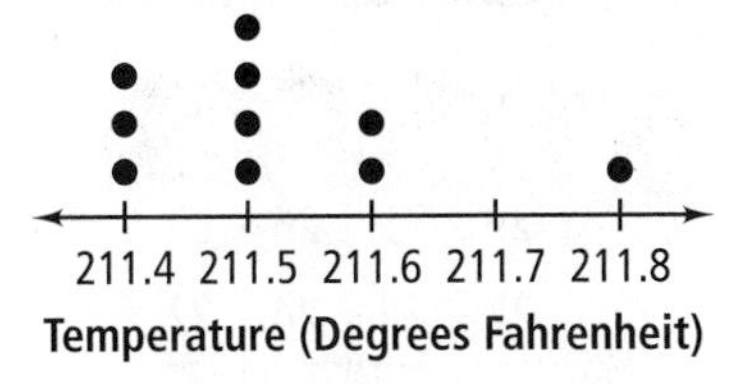

B.
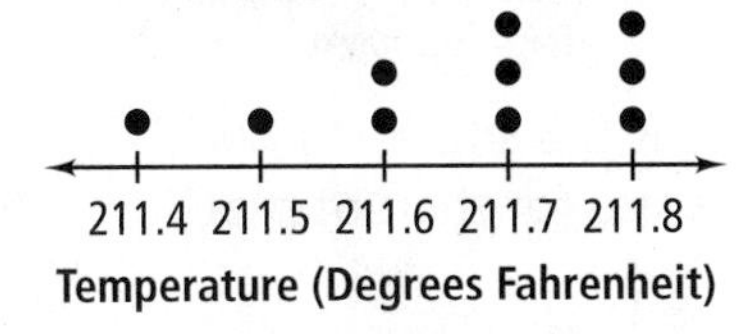

C.
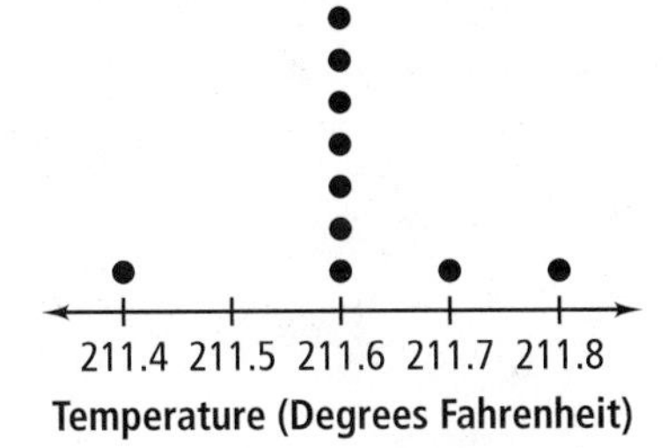

D.
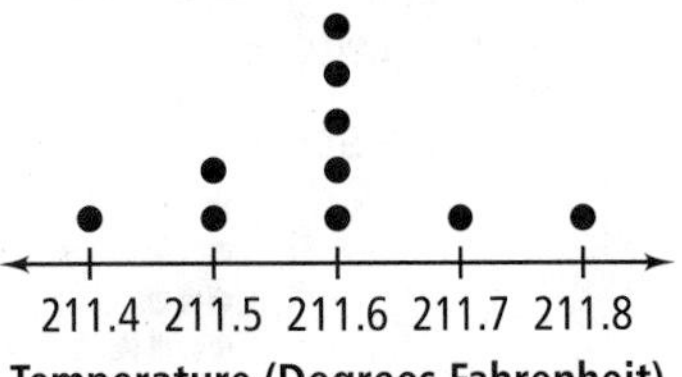

3. A doctor asked 15 people how many hours they spend exercising each week. The dot plot displays the data. What do any clusters and gaps in the dot plot tell you about the exercise habits of these people?

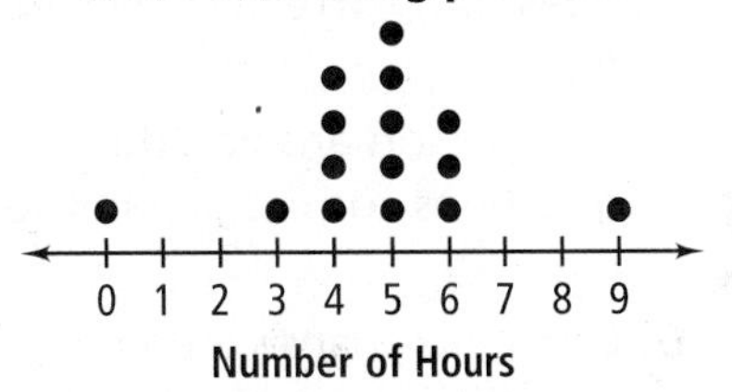

4. **Think About the Process** In an experiment, some people answered 20 True/False questions without reading the questions. A researcher recorded the number of correct answers for each person. The dot plot displays the data.

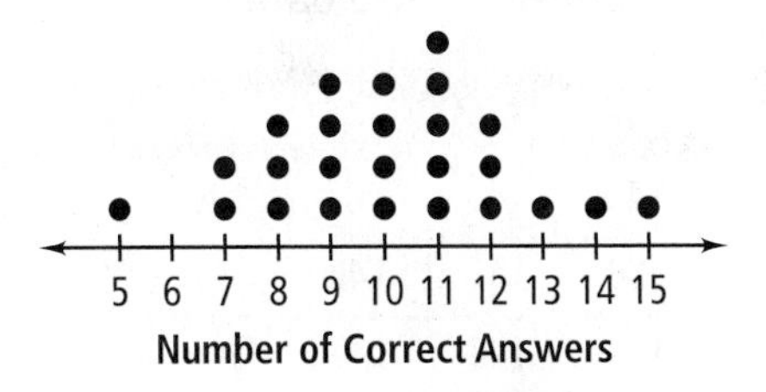

a. What values do you need from the dot plot to find the percentage of people who had exactly 7 correct answers? Check all that apply.

A. The number of dots above 7

B. The number of dots over 100

C. The total number of dots

D. The number of dots above values other than 7

b. What percentage of people had exactly 7 correct answers?

5. Open-Ended The people applying for a job took a test. The dot plot shows the number of questions each person answered correctly.

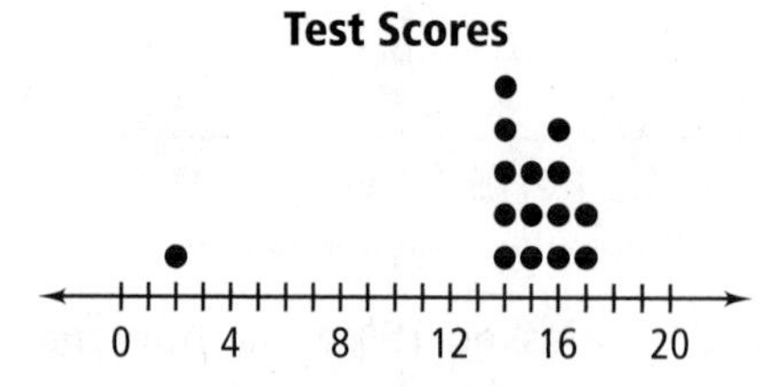

a. Which statement best describes any stray values?

A. One person answered half of the questions correctly.

B. One person answered more questions correctly than the rest did.

C. One person answered fewer questions correctly than the rest did.

D. One person answered no questions correctly. Another answered them all correctly.

b. Draw a dot plot showing that 5 of the 15 people should get the job. Explain your dot plot.

6. Heights A science class measured the heights of 15 students in centimeters. The table shows the data. Which dot plot represents the data?

Heights of Students in Centimeters				
148	146	147	145	147
150	147	146	147	149
148	148	147	144	148

A.

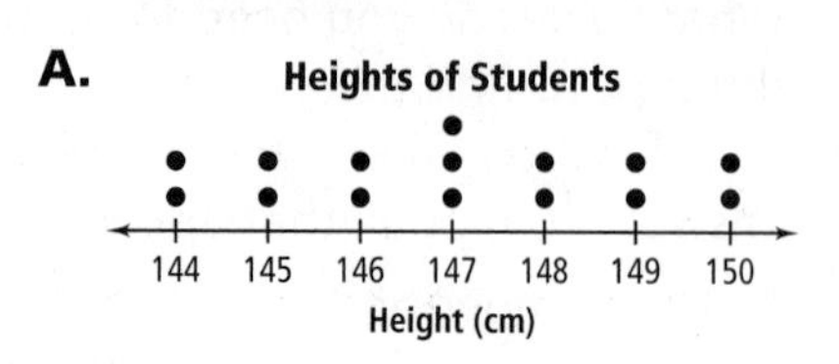

B.

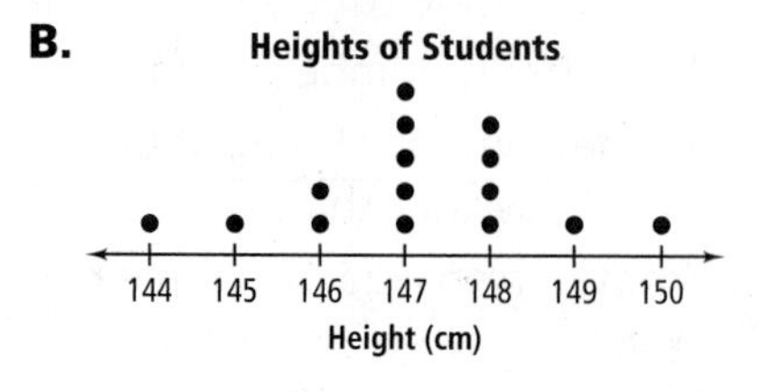

C.

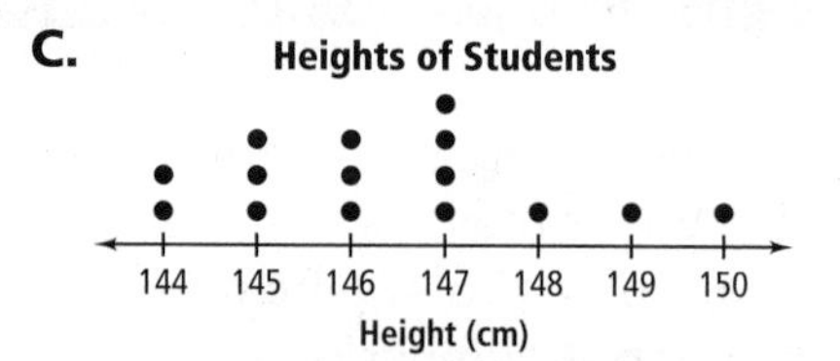

D.

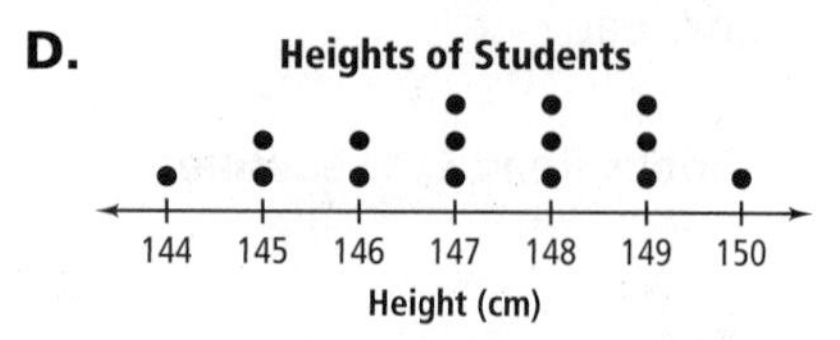

7. The data in the table show the number of people in each of 20 households in a neighborhood. Draw a dot plot that represents the data.

People per Household				
4	5	7	5	6
3	3	1	2	2
6	7	5	1	3
2	6	5	4	4

8. Think About the Process The table shows the number of eggs from 16 hens in one month. You want to make a dot plot of the data.

Numbers of Eggs			
29	25	26	23
22	28	24	22
24	29	25	25
28	27	25	27

What is the shortest possible number-line scale for the dot plot?

15-3 Histograms

Vocabulary
histogram

CCSS: 6.SP.B.4, 6.SP.B.5, 6.SP.B.5c

Key Concept

A **histogram** shows the shape of a data set with vertical bars above intervals of values on a number line.

The values in the data set must be numerical to be graphed on a histogram. This data set has ten data values. There is one for each park visitor.

Ages of Water Park Visitors: 21, 15, 78, 79, 24, 20, 6, 20, 16, 41

The horizontal scale is made up of a number line divided into intervals, and a unit label. The least value in this data set is 6. The greatest value in this data set is 79. So the horizontal scale can be a number line from 0 to 80. Set the width of the intervals to 20 years. Label the scale in units of years.

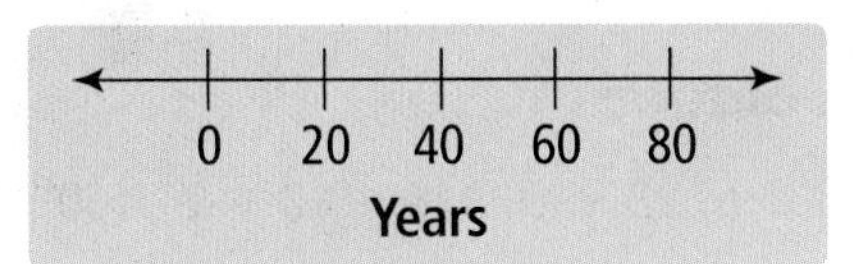

The vertical scale measures the frequency of data values that occur within intervals on the horizontal scale. For this data set, the vertical scale measures the number of visitors whose ages fall into each interval.

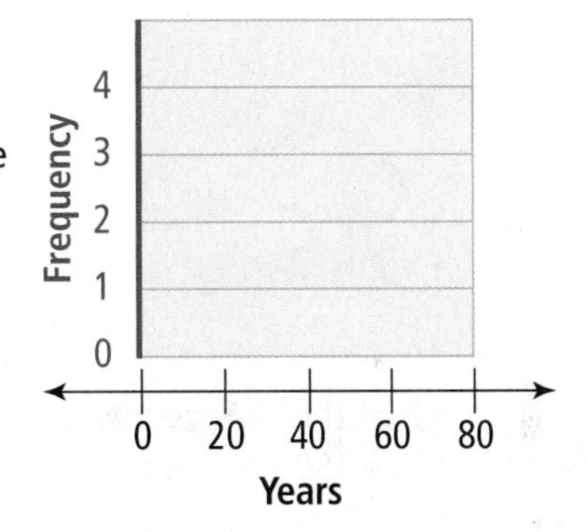

The bars organize the data into groups, and show the frequencies at which each group of data values occur in each interval on the horizontal scale.

Ages of Water Park Visitors:
21, 15, 78, 79, 24, 20, 6, 20, 16, 41

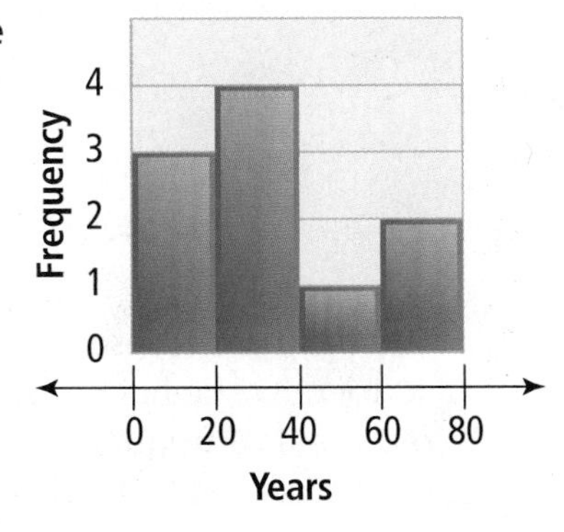

See your complete lesson at MyMathUniverse.com

Part 1

Example Using Histograms

You are helping a new social networking website company analyze data. Use the histogram to answer the questions.

a. How many users were surveyed?

b. How many users surveyed have 150 friends or more.

c. How many of the users surveyed have between 0 and 49 friends?

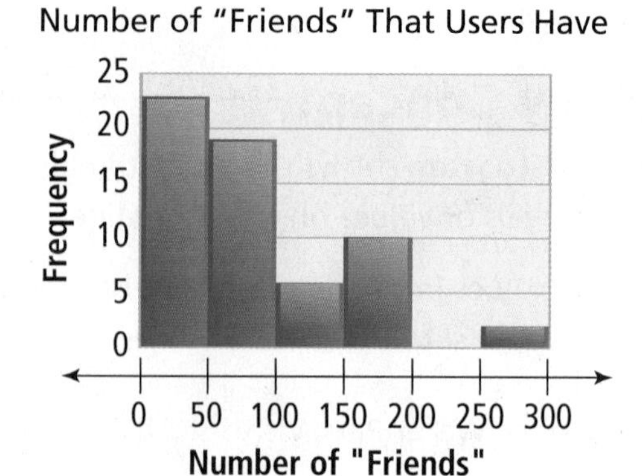

Solution

a. $23 + 19 + 6 + 10 + 2 = 60$

60 users were surveyed.

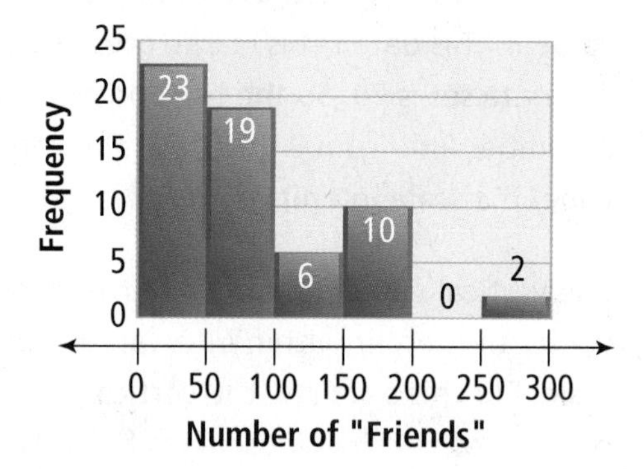

b. $10 + 0 + 2 = 12$

12 of the users surveyed have 150 friends or more.

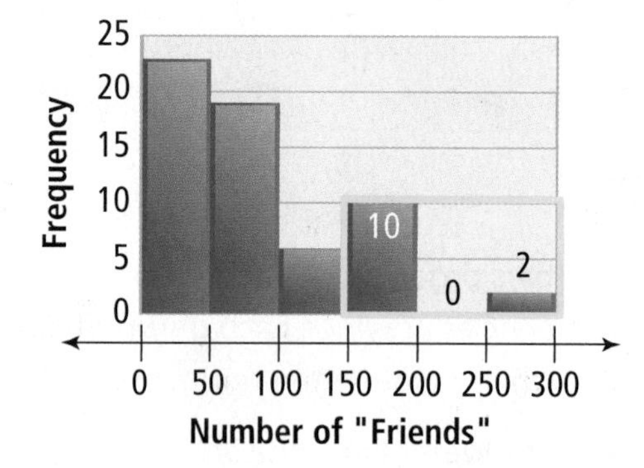

c. The first bar represents users with 0 to 49 friends. The height of the bar represents a frequency of 23, so 23 users surveyed have between 0 and 49 friends.

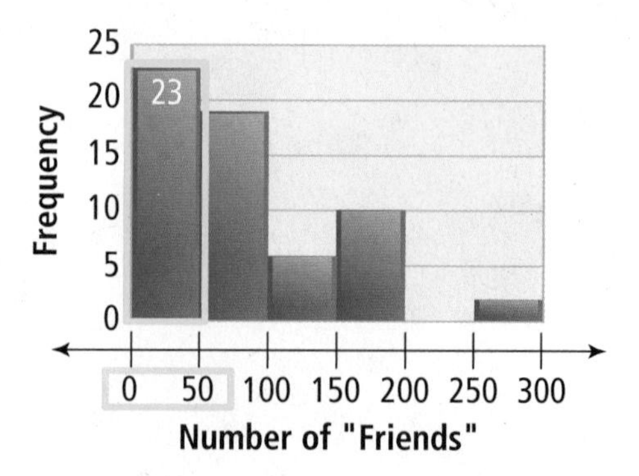

Part 2

Example Making Histograms

The participants in a ski race are divided into four groups of six skiers each. The table shows the results of the races.

Make a histogram to show how the race times are distributed among all of the participants.

Ski Race Results

	Times (s)
Group 1	89.4, 89.8, 90.3, 91.4, 94.3, 97.4
Group 2	87.9, 88.0, 90.6, 92.7, 96.8, 97.3
Group 3	89.7, 90.5, 91.3, 92.8, 92.9, 100.4
Group 4	90.1, 91.8, 92.9, 93.7, 95.2, 96.8

Solution

The fastest times is 87.9 seconds. The slowest time is 100.4 seconds. You can use a horizontal scale that runs from 86 seconds to 102 seconds to display all of the data.

These values differ by only tenths of a second, so using smaller intervals will help keep the bars from getting too tall.

Add a vertical scale. Count the number of data values that fall into each interval.

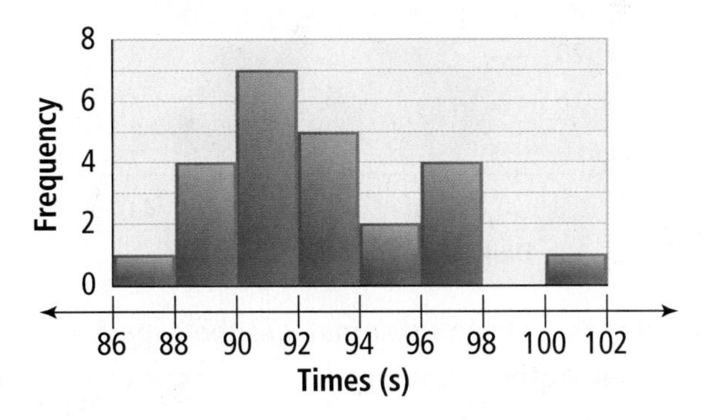

Part 3

Example Analyzing Data from Histograms

Three wind turbines were constructed in your town. Each one is expected to generate 3,000 kilowatts (kW) per day. During the testing phase, engineers recorded the daily amount of energy produced by each turbine. What does the histogram show about the test results?

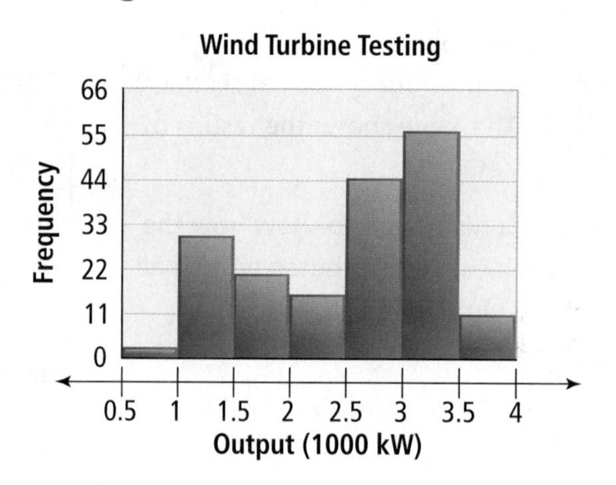

Solution

There are two clusters in the test data.

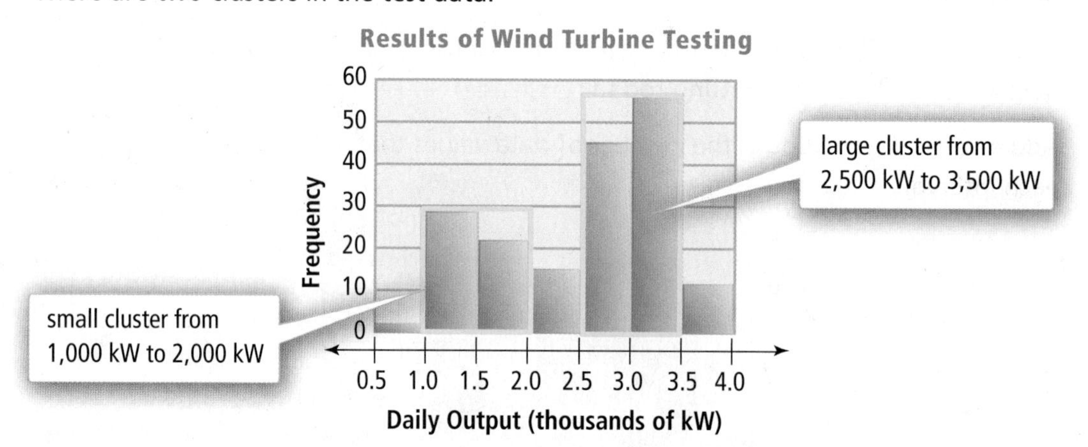

The energy generated in the large cluster matches the expected result of 3,000 kW. The energy generated in the smaller cluster does not match the expected result.

1. A survey asked 250 people how far they drive to work. The histogram shows the results of the survey. One bar in the histogram stands out. What might it tell you about the drives?

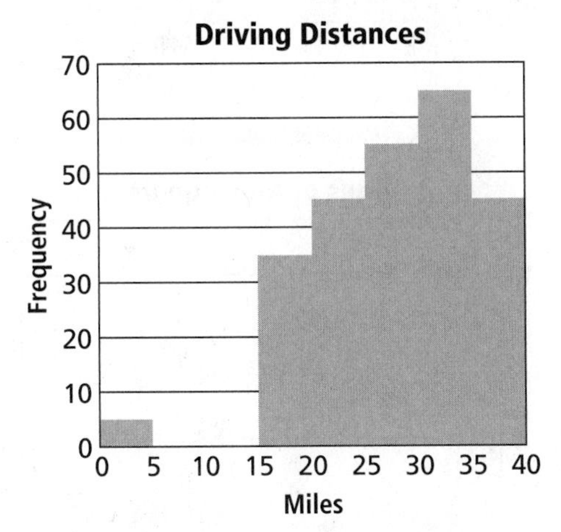

2. **Mental Math** The table shows the number of paid holidays for 15 companies.

Number of Paid Holidays				
2	11	8	14	10
8	5	14	2	10
2	14	11	4	7

a. Which histogram shows the data?

A.

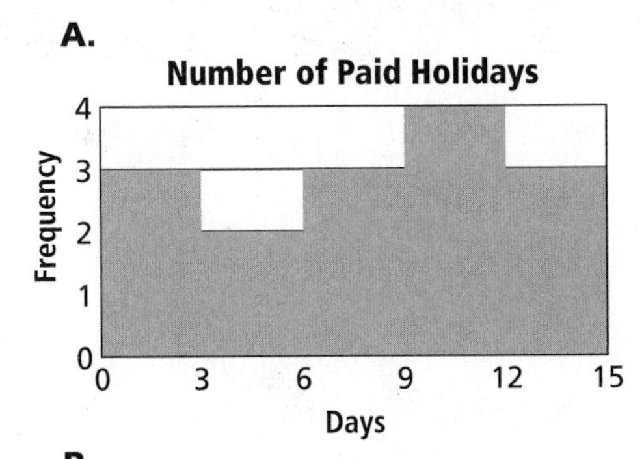

B.

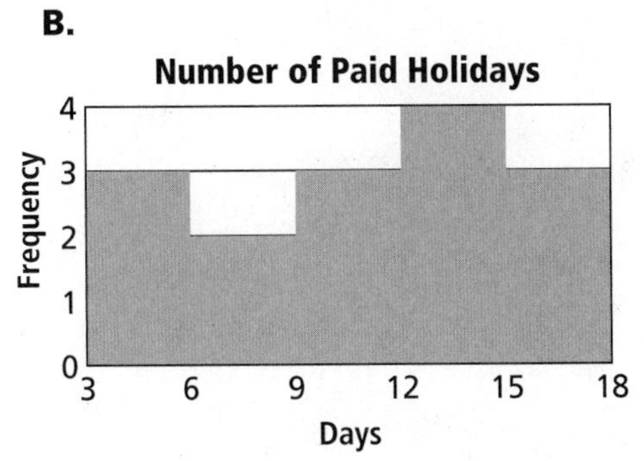

C.

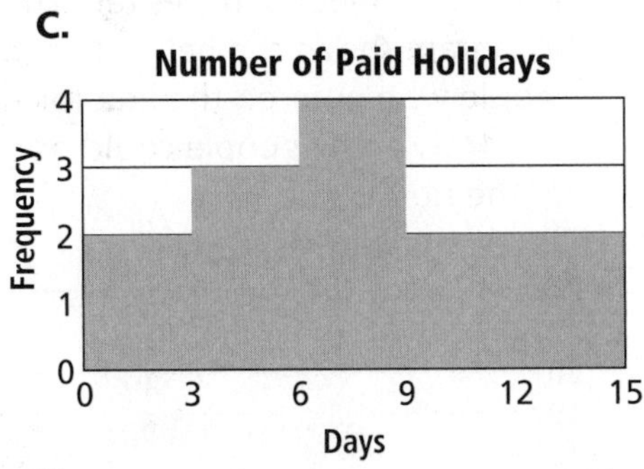

D.

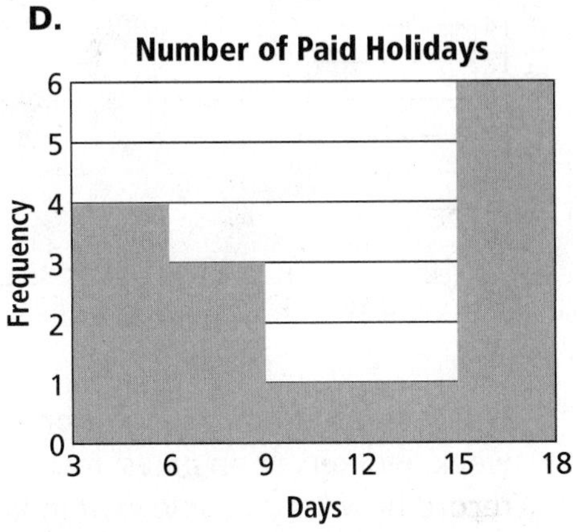

b. How many of these companies do not fall in the interval for the least frequency or the greatest frequency?

3. The histogram shows the rainfall amounts from last week for several cities. No city had exactly 1 inch of rain. How many cities had less than 1 inch of rain?

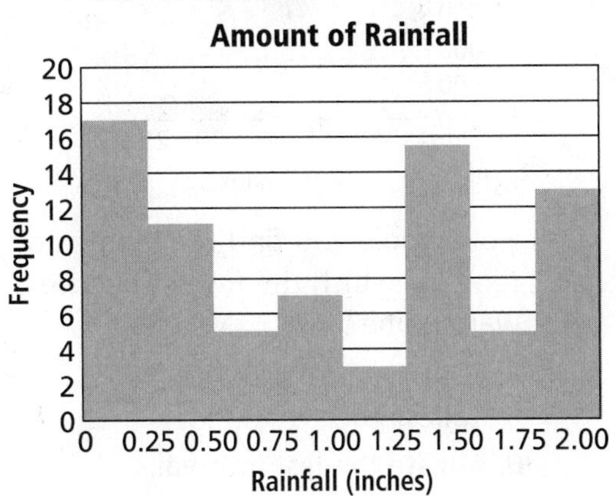

4. For a ride at the county fair, you must be at least 4 feet 6 inches tall. The histogram shows the heights of people who entered the line for this ride. How many people could not go on the ride?

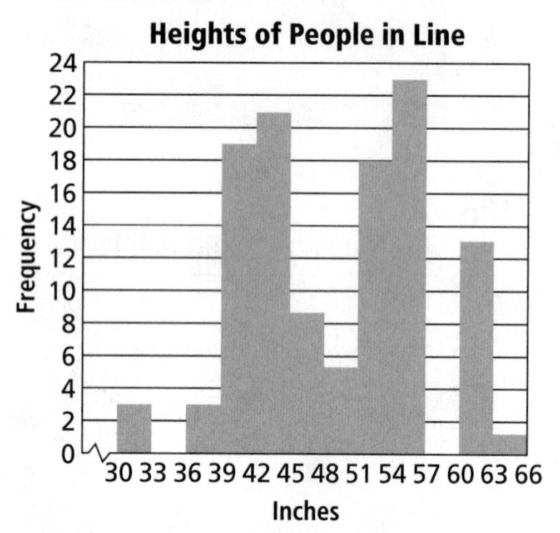

5. **Think About the Process** For one week, workers at an amusement park record how long people wait in line for one of the rides. The histogram shows these wait times.

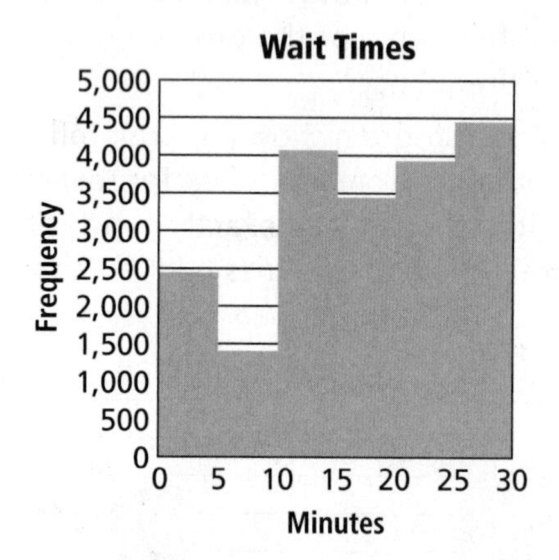

a. How would you find the lengths of time for which the fewest people wait in line?

A. Find the interval with the tallest bar.

B. Locate the last interval.

C. Locate the first interval.

D. Find the interval with the shortest bar.

b. The interval of wait times for the fewest people is ■ minutes.

6. **Challenge** The histogram shows the ages of people at a movie. For the ticket prices shown, what was the total value of ticket sales?

Ticket Prices	
Under 10	$7
Regular Price	$10
Aged 60 or Over	$5

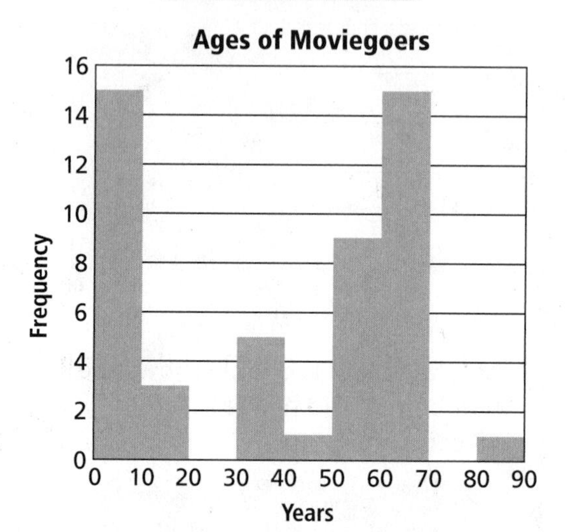

15-4 Box Plots

Vocabulary
box plot

CCSS: 6.SP.B.4, 6.SP.B.5, 6.SP.B.5c

Part 1

Intro

A box plot shows five boundary values. To find the boundary values, first put the data values in numerical order.

Basket Points Scored Per Game: 5, 28, 32, 39, 45, 47, 56, 63, 74, 76, 80

The least value in a data set is the minimum.

Basket Points Scored Per Game: 5, 28, 32, 39, 45, 47, 56, 63, 74, 76, 80

The minimum is 5.

The greatest value in a data set is the maximum.

Basket Points Scored Per Game: 5, 28, 32, 39, 45, 47, 56, 63, 74, 76, 80

The maximum is 80.

The middle value of the ordered data set is the value with the same number of values on either side.

Basket Points Scored Per Game: 5, 28, 32, 39, 45, 47, 56, 63, 74, 76, 80

The middle value of the data set is 47.

The middle value of the lower half of the ordered data set is the value with the same number of values on either side in the lower half.

Basket Points Scored Per Game: 5, 28, 32, 39, 45, **47**, 56, 63, 74, 76, 80

The middle value of the lower half is 32.

The middle value of the upper half of the ordered data set is the value with the same number of values on either side in the lower half.

Basket Points Scored Per Game: 5, 28, 32, 39, 45, **47**, 56, 63, 74, 76, 80

The middle value of the upper half is 74.

Part 1

Example Finding Boundary Values of Data Sets

Order the data set. Then label the five boundary values.

30 16 68 35 57 5 27 76 21 91 44

Solution

Know	**Need**	**Plan**
The values in the data set.	To label the boundary values of the data set.	Order the data set. Then identify the boundary values.

Step 1 Order the data set from least to greatest.

5 16 21 27 30 35 44 57 68 76 91

Step 2 Identify the boundary values.

5 16 21 27 30 35 44 57 68 76 91

- 5: Minimum
- 16: Middle of Lower Half
- 35: Middle of Data Set
- 68: Middle of Upper Half
- 91: Maximum

Key Concept

A **box plot** shows the distribution of a data set by making five boundary points where data occur along a number line. Unlike a dot plot or histogram, a box plot does not show frequency.

Football Game Scores: 32, 17, 21, 35, 19, 39, 30, 29, 6, 23, 37

The values in the data set must be numerical to be graphed on a box plot.

Football Game Scores: 6, 17, 18, 21, 23, 29, 30, 32, 35, 37, 39

The scale consists of one section of a number line and the unit label of the data values. The minimum value in this data set is 6. The maximum value in this data set is 39. You can make the scale a number line from 0 to 40.

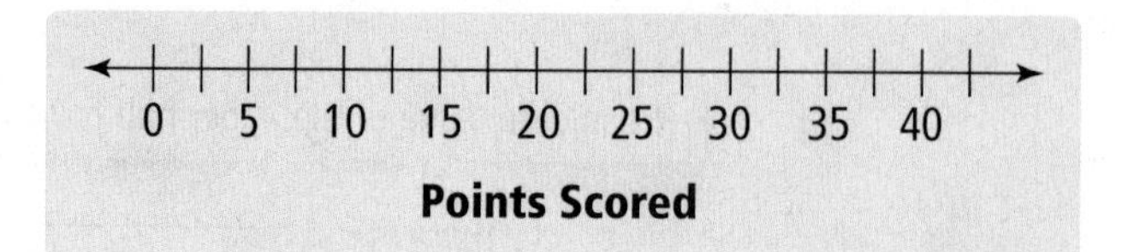

continued on next page >

Key Concept

continued

The two end points represent the minimum and maximum of the data set.

Football Game Scores: 6, 17, 18, 21, 23, 29, 30, 32, 35, 37, 39

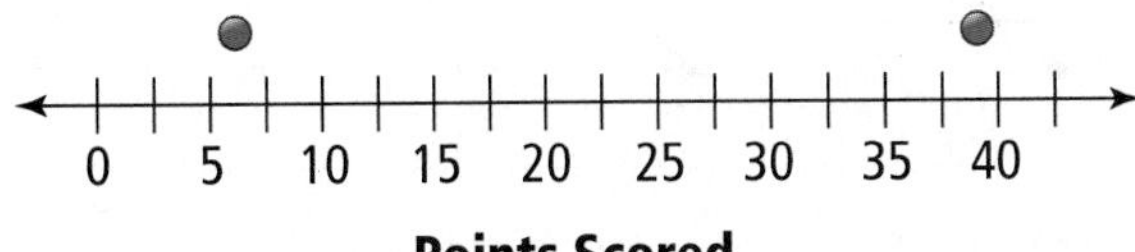

Points Scored

The line inside the box represents the middle value of the data set. The middle score is 29 points. Make a dot on the scale above 29.

The left edge represents the middle value of the lower half of the data set. The middle of the lower scores is 18 points. Make a dot on the scale above 18.

The right edge represents the middle value of the upper half of the data set. The middle of the higher scores is 35 points. Make a dot on the scale above 35.

Football Game Scores: 6, 17, 18, 21, 23, 29, 30, 32, 35, 37, 39

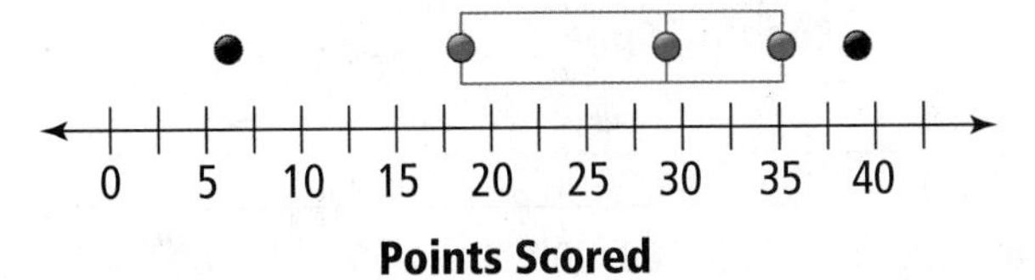

Points Scored

The whiskers are two horizontal lines that connect the edges of the box to the end points.

Football Game Scores: 6, 17, 18, 21, 23, 29, 30, 32, 35, 37, 39

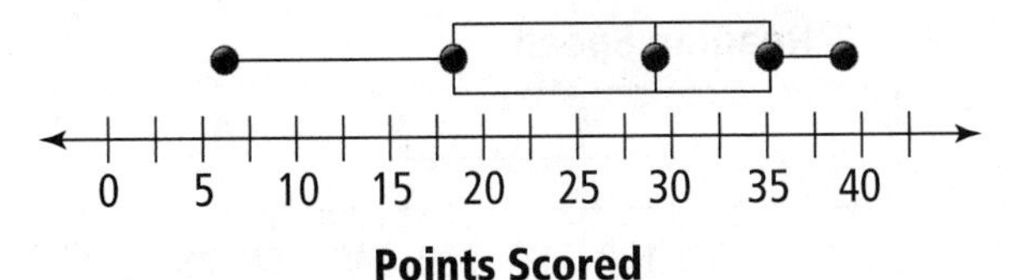

Points Scored

Even though the horizontal sections of the box plot are different lengths, each section represents a quarter of the data. The box plot divides the scale into four sections.

Football Game Scores

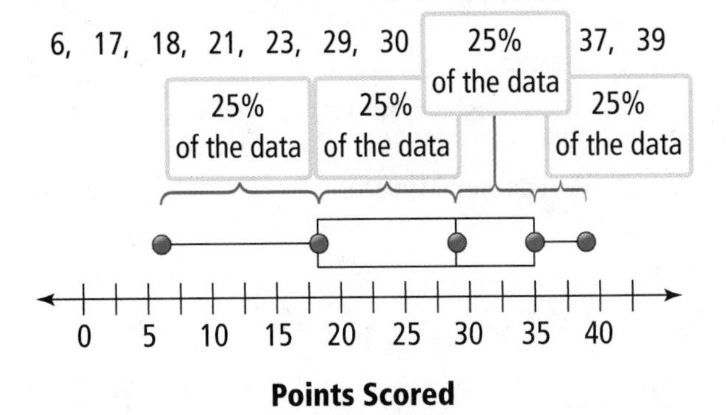

Points Scored

Part 2

Example Using Box Plots

Use the box plot to answer the questions.

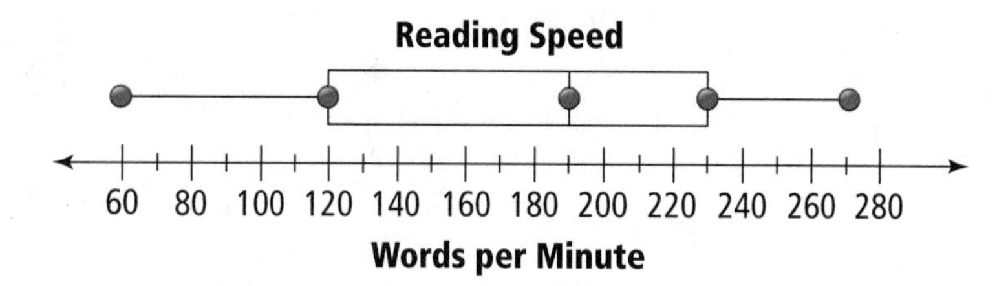

a. What is the reading speed in the exact middle of the data?

b. How many words does the slowest reader read per minute?

c. How many words do the middle 50% of readers read per minute?

Solution

a. The reading speed in the exact middle of the data is 190 words per minute.

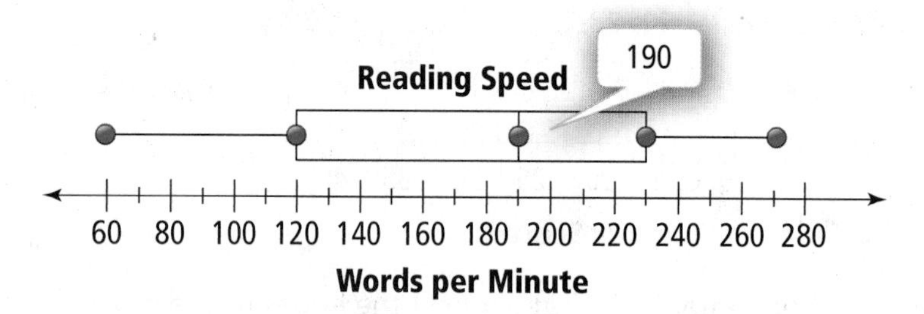

b. The slowest reader reads 60 words per minute.

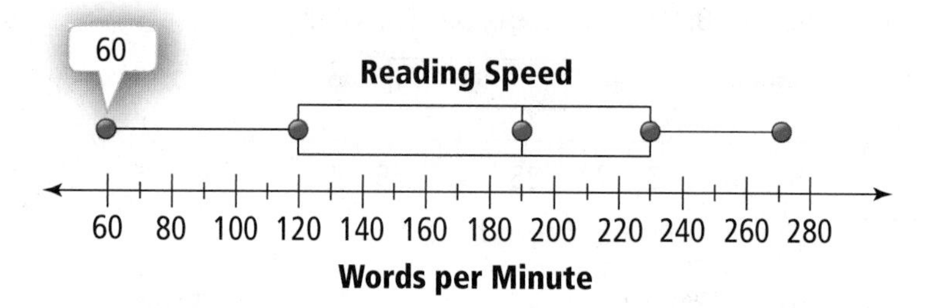

c. The middle 50% of readers read between 120 and 230 words per minute.

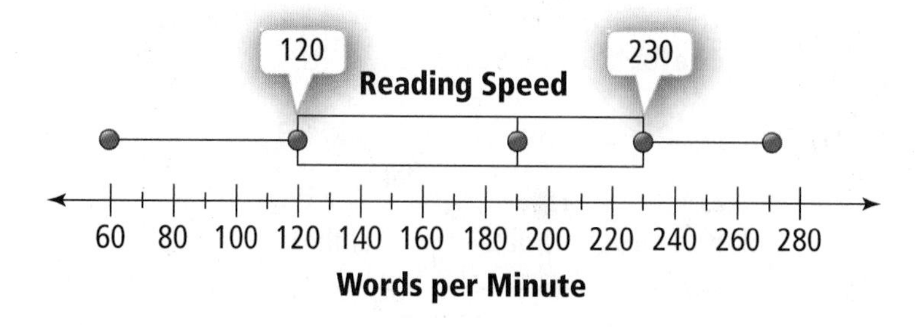

Part 3

Example Making Box Plots

The measure of an athlete's heart rate while performing a sport is important. The lower the heart rate, the more efficiently the body uses the oxygen that is breathed in. A doctor records the heart rates of 15 athletes. Make a box plot that shows the distribution of heart rates.

84 95 93 92 91 101 89 95 98

118 90 100 98 96 105

Solution

Step 1 Order the data.

84 89 90 91 92 93 95 95 96 98 100 101 105 118

Step 2 Find the boundary points.

Minimum: 84

Maximum: 118

Middle Value: 95

Middle Value of Lower Half: 91

Middle Value of Upper Half: 100

Step 3 Draw the box plot.

Heart Rates of Athletes

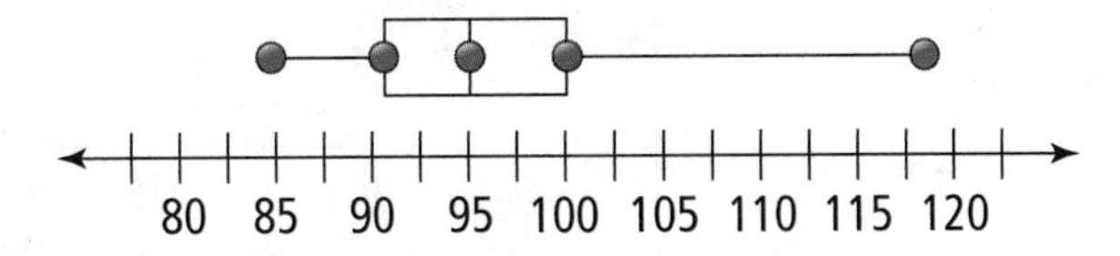

Heartbeats per Minute

Step 4 Check your answer.

Make a dot plot. The distribution of dots confirms what the box plot shows.

Heart Rates of Athletes

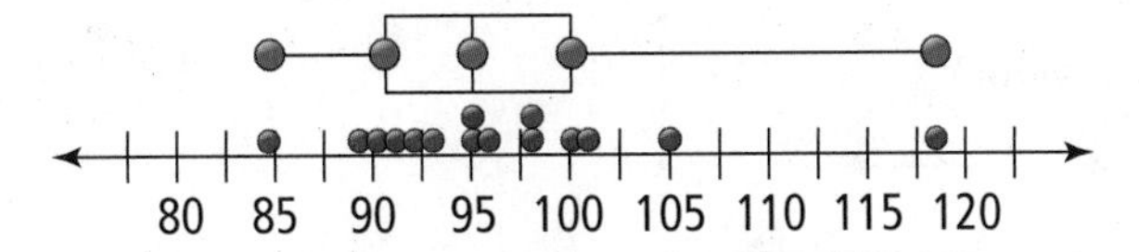

Heartbeats per Minute

1. What is the middle value of the data set 21, 49, 46, 57, 22, 37, and 58?
2. Find the five boundary values of the data set 5, 25, 53, 27, 18, 28, 32, 47, 19, 45, 29, 34, 38, 48, and 46.
3. What is the middle value of the lower half of the data set? Use the box plot to answer the question.

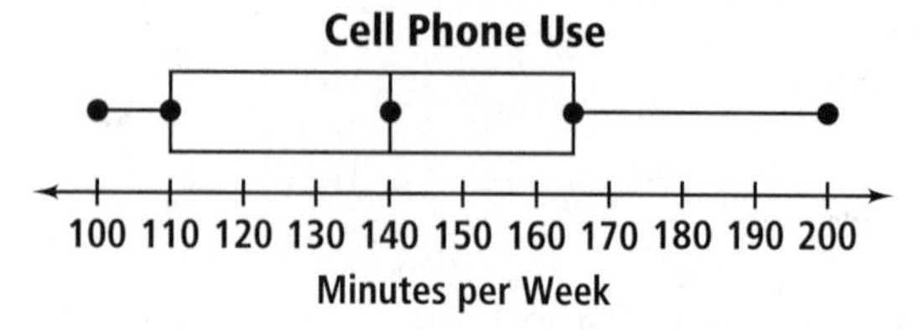

4. Use the box plot to answer the following question. How many words does the fastest keyboarder type per minute?

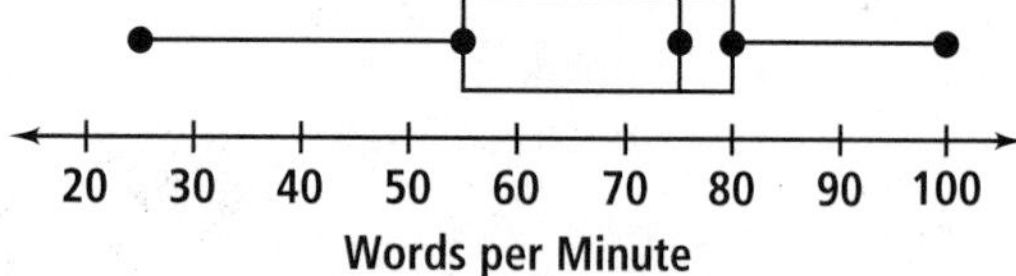

5. Use the box plot to answer the following question. How many words do the fastest 50% of keyboarders type per minute?

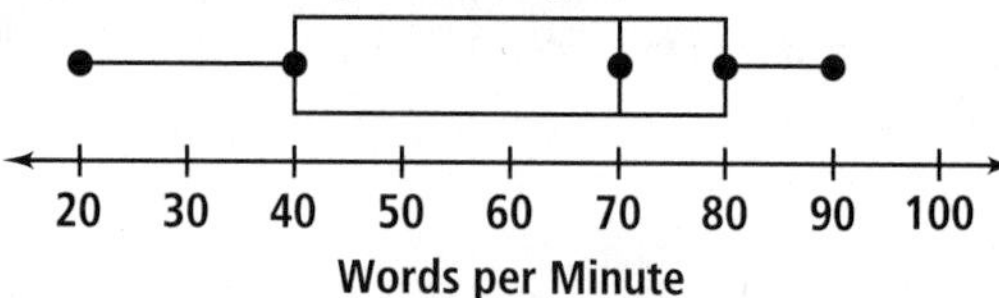

6. **Reasoning** Suppose you spend 75 minutes per day on homework. Do you spend more or less time on homework than most of the students represented by this box plot? Explain your reasoning.

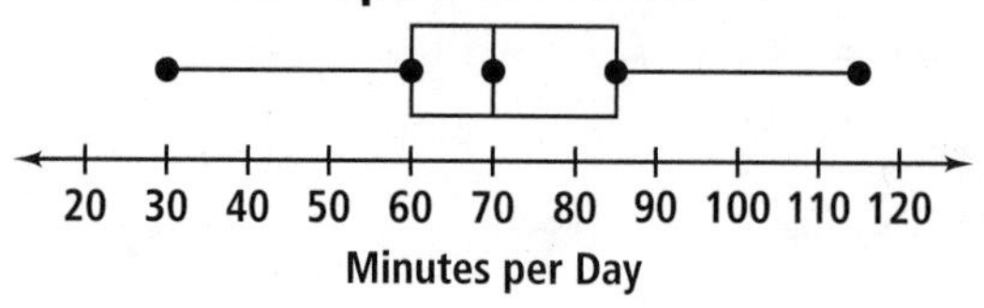

7. These data show the temperatures (in degrees Fahrenheit) of 15 different patients in a hospital. Select the box plot that shows the distribution of temperatures.

101.4	102.9	104.3	100.5	104.4
104.1	102.4	104.6	106.8	101.9
101.6	106.9	100.1	101.5	101.3

A.

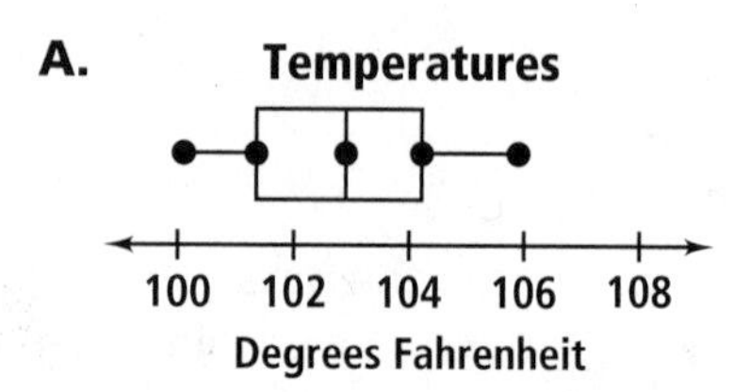

B.

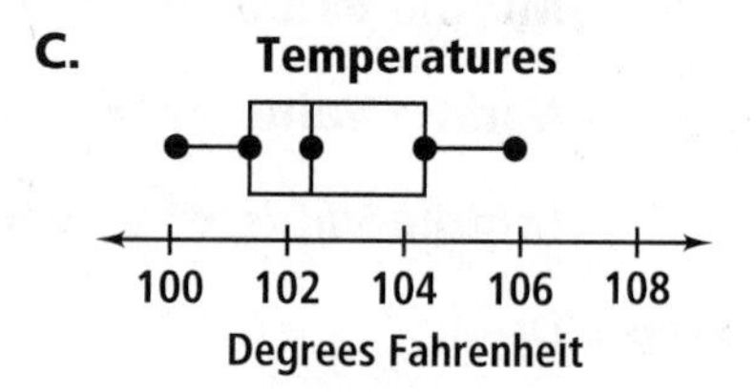

C.

Temperatures

100 102 104 106 108

Degrees Fahrenheit

D.

Temperatures

100 102 104 106 108

Degrees Fahrenheit

8. **Age Survey** Judy recorded the names and ages of seven people she chose at random at a concert. Using the data set Priya (67), Tom (39), Joyce (58), Mark (69), Sofia (50), Bill (90), and Jorge (35), find the middle value of the data set.

9. Think About the Process A basketball team played 11 games. The following data set shows the number of points the team scored in each game.

32, 30, 80, 69, 25, 45,

51, 73, 57, 29, 53

a. What is the first step in finding the middle value of the data set?

A. Find the value in the middle of the given list.

B. Order the data set.

C. Find the first value in the given list.

D. Find the last value in the given list.

b. What is the middle value of the data set?

10. a. The data set 255, 219, 211, 206, 228, 295, 223, 243, 259, 201, and 283 represents cave lengths, in miles. Make a box plot that shows the distribution of cave lengths.

b. Is the 283-mile long cave in the shortest 25%, the longest 25%, or the middle 50% of the cave lengths?

A. the middle 50%

B. the longest 25%

C. the shortest 25%

11. Think About the Process On a school trip, 11 students bought a snack. The data show how much each student spent.

\$1.30, \$1.80, \$1.60, \$2.00, \$1.75, \$1.20, \$1.40, \$1.90, \$1.05, \$1.70, \$1.45

a. After ordering the data set, what is the next step in drawing a box plot that shows the distribution of the amounts spent?

A. Make a dot plot for comparing.

B. Find the five boundary values.

C. Write a title for the box plot.

D. Plot and connect the end points.

b. Which box plot correctly shows the distribution of the amounts spent?

A.

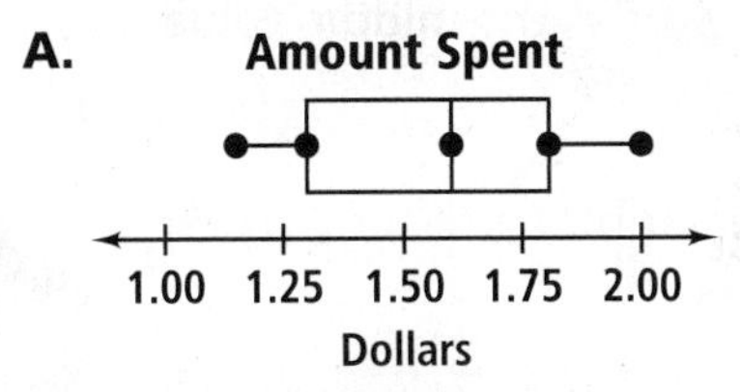

B.

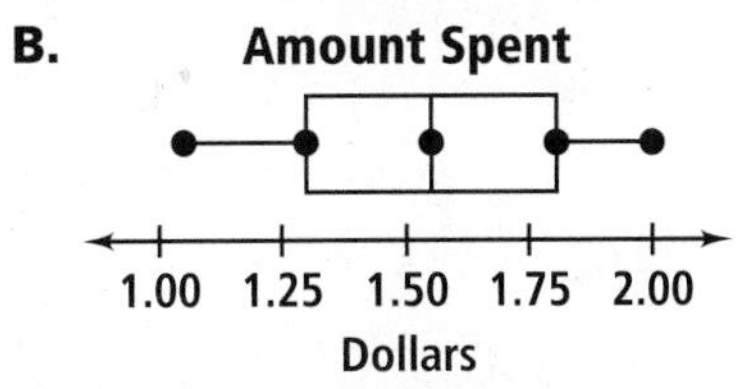

C.

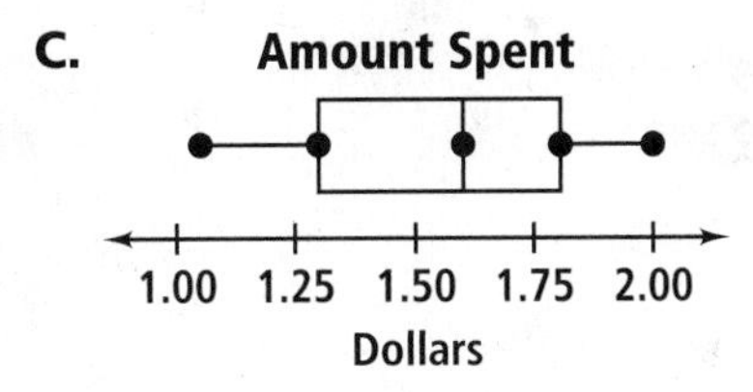

15-5 Choosing an Appropriate Display

CCSS: 6.SP.B.4

Key Concept

There are many data displays. You can choose which display to use based on what you are investigating and the aspects of the data you need to see.

A	each data value	D	clusters and gaps
B	frequencies of data	E	small data sets
C	the middle value	F	large data sets

A dot plot is helpful to see...

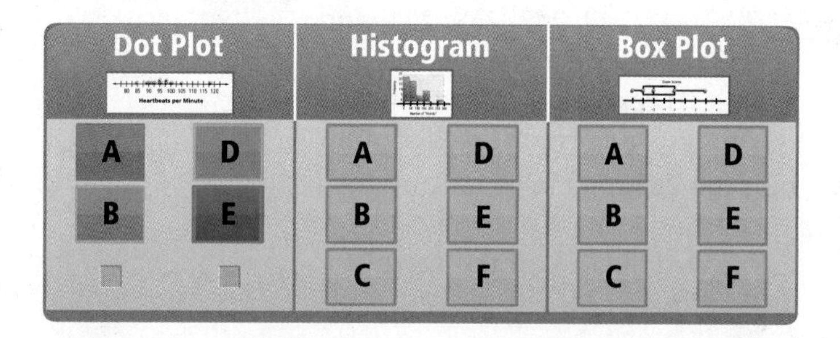

A histogram is helpful to see...

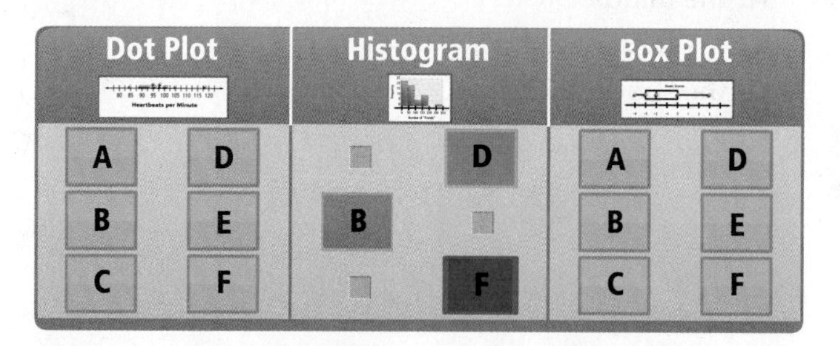

A box plot is helpful to see...

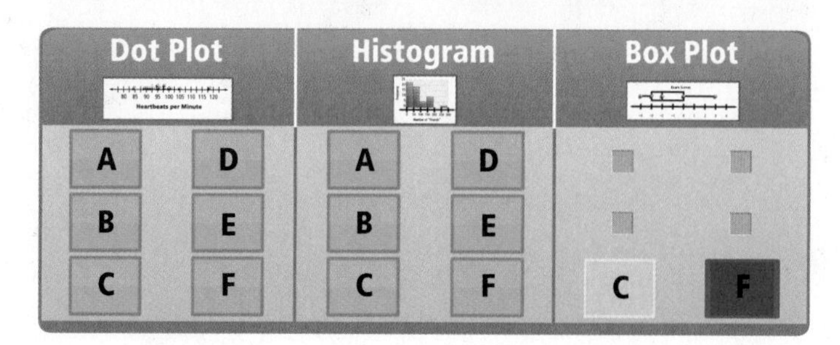

Part 1

Example Understanding Different Data Displays

Which data display(s) can help you answer each question? Which CANNOT help you? Why?

a. "In the results of an online quiz, how many people scored 78?"
b. "In the results of a health study, what was the middle data value?"
c. "In the results of a national survey, where did most of the responses fall?"

Solution

a. "In the results of an online quiz, how many people scored 78?"

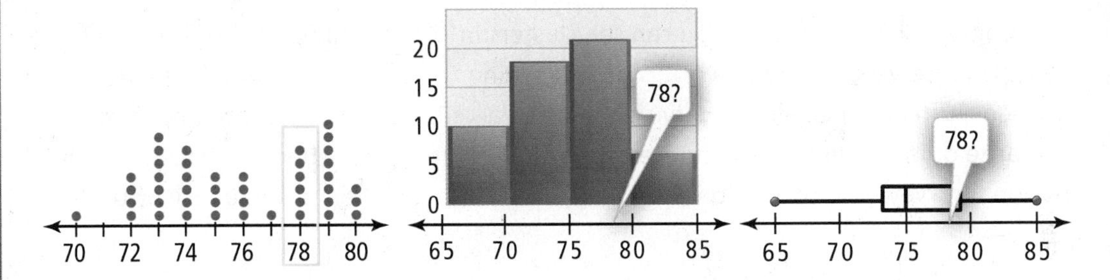

A **dot plot** is the only display that allows you to see each value that occurs in a data set.

The data values in a histogram are grouped together in intervals, so you cannot see the frequency of any one value.

A box plot does not show the frequency of the data values, so you cannot see how many people scored 78.

b. "In the results of a health study, what was the middle data value?"

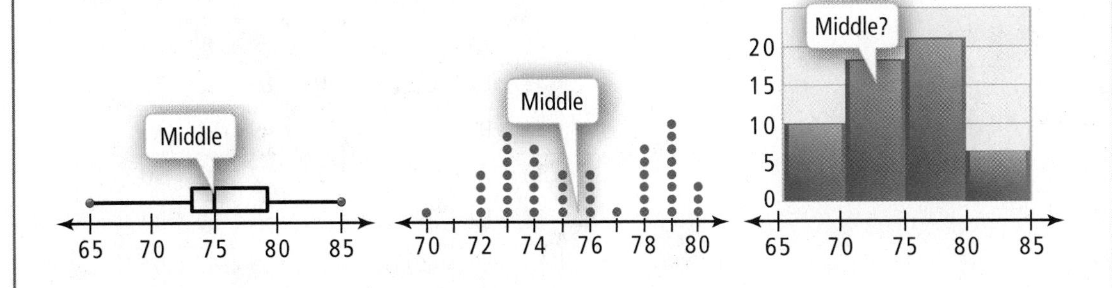

A box plot shows the middle value of a data set as the line inside its box.

A dot plot also shows the middle value, but you would need to count each dot to find it.

A histogram does not show any exact data values, so you cannot see the exact middle value.

continued on next page >

Part 1

Solution continued

c. "In the results of a national survey, where did most of the responses fall?"

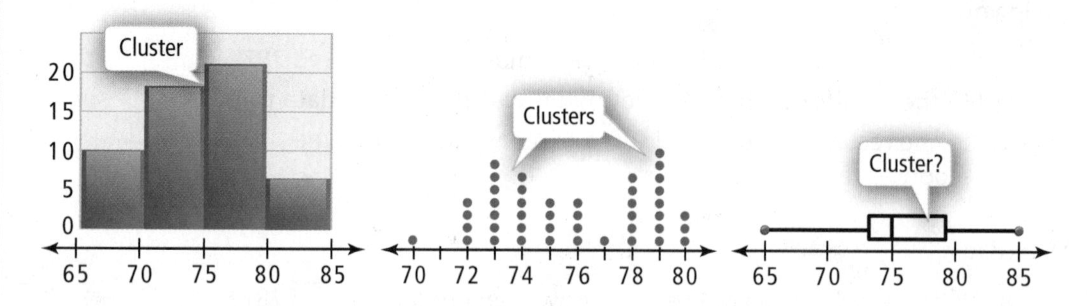

A histogram shows data values in intervals, but you can see clusters, especially for large data sets like a national survey.

You can see clusters in a dot plot, but seeing every single data value is unnecessary in such a large data set.

A box plot can show generally how data are distributed, but it is not as clear because you cannot see the frequency of the data.

Part 2

Example Choosing Data Displays to Solve Problems

You need to be in the top 25% to pass to the second round. Use a data display to determine the lowest score you can get and still move on.

Round 1 Results								
56	71	81	93	67	62	38	44	36
68	42	59	45	24	58	47	51	41
48	58	45	39	49	52	56	83	54
29	48	60	67	19	61	94	54	63
32	73	49	61	29	48	40	39	40
46	87	61	64	55	60	88	58	75
34	90	43	49	91	49	81	46	48
38	68	77	53	88	52	23	50	
10	52	28	61	79	50	56	39	
65	35	41	37	62	55	43	51	
59	40	50	79	43	51	67	47	
51	84	78	80	68	85	92	82	
84	96	92	36	57	70	76	46	
42	32	44	54	68	62	20	72	
63	57	56	87	91	79	49	58	

continued on next page >

Part 2

Example continued

Solution

Think

A dot plot shows too much information. I only need to see general sections of the data.

A histogram doesn't clearly indicate the top 25% of values.

A box plot shows the data values at 25%, 50%, and 75%. I need the value at 75%.

I will use the Data and Graphs tool to display the data as a box plot.

I will use the box plot to find the value at the 75% mark.

Write

I will use the box plot because it shows the value that marks the top 25% of the scores.

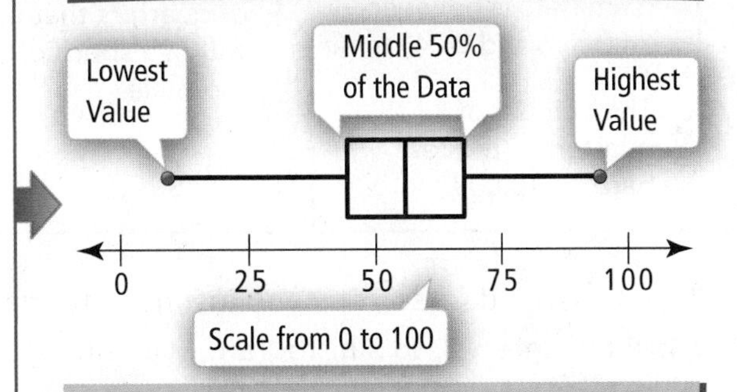

The value at the 75% mark is 68, so I need to score at least 68 to move on to the second round.

Part 3

Example Choosing Appropriate Data Displays

All coins minted in the United States must pass several inspections before they ship out to banks. A quarter coin must have a diameter between 24.0 mm and 24.49 mm. Which data display(s) can show you the number of quarters that are and are not acceptable in a test batch of 10,000 quarters? Explain.

Solution

Know
- The acceptable measure of quarter diameters is between 24.0 mm and 24.49 mm.
- The number of quarters in the test batch is 10,000.

Need
The data display that best shows the number of quarters that fall within a specific span on the scale

Plan
Determine which data display(s) can show you exact data frequencies between two values on the scale for a large data set.

This is a large data set, and you just need to see what is and is not in the 24.0 mm to 24.49 mm interval, so a histogram with intervals of 0.5 mm is the best display to use in this information.

Digital Resources   

1. Which data display(s) can you use to find the middle score on a quiz? Select all that apply.

   A. box plot **B.** dot plot

   C. histogram

2. The box plot shows the test scores for a student. What question(s) can you answer using the box plot? Select all that apply.

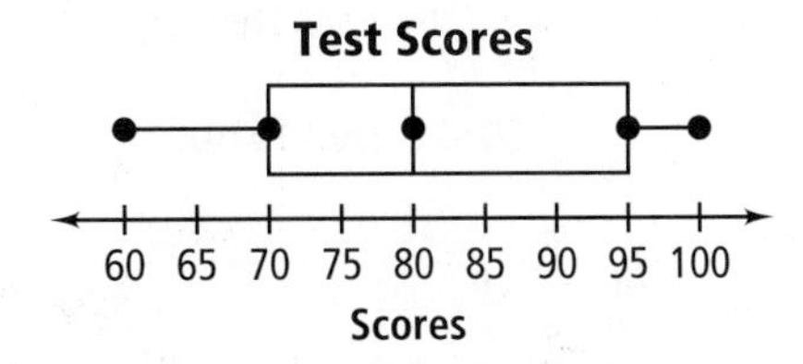

   A. How many test scores were less than 79?

   B. How many test scores were between 79 and 86?

   C. How many test scores were greater than 79?

   D. What was the middle test score?

   E. What was the lowest test sore?

3. Students who score 50 or greater on a qualifying exam can join an academic team. The table shows exam scores.

Exam Scores			
77	78	48	51
65	88	87	92
56	91	57	64

   a. Which histogram shows the correct data?

   A.

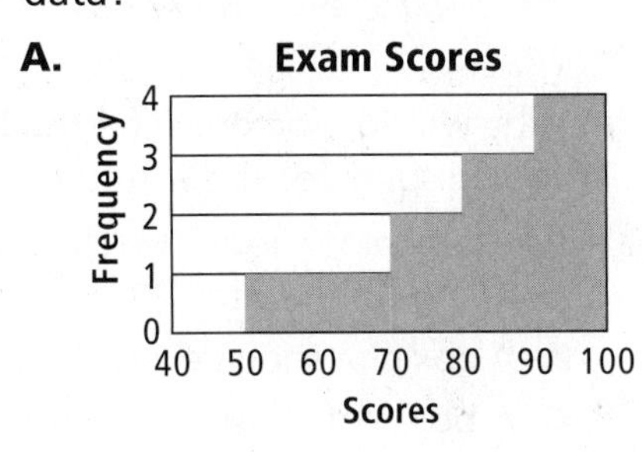

   B.

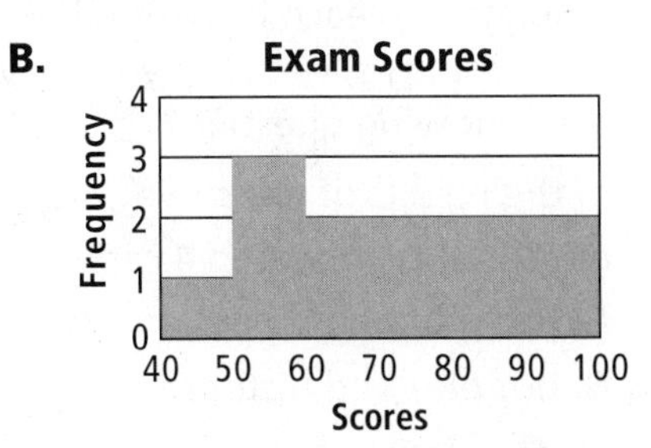

   C.

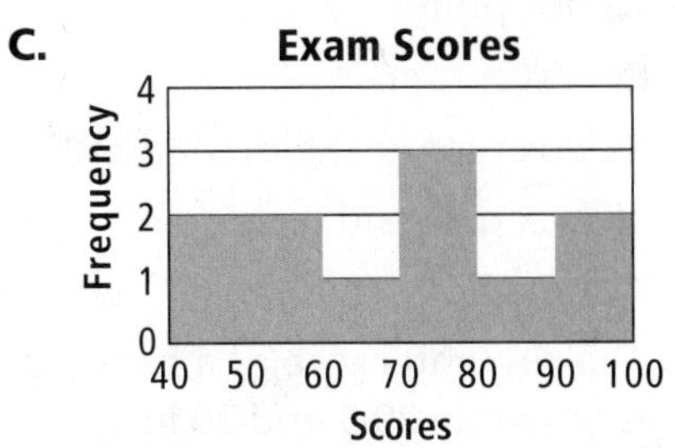

   b. How many students can join the team?

4. **Think About the Process** The table shows the monthly interest earned in a savings account. You want to see how many months you earned less than $7.87. You decide to make a dot plot. How would you start making the dot plot?

Interest Earned (Dollars)					
7.62	7.37	7.12	7.12	7.62	7.87
7.37	7.12	8.12	7.62	7.62	7.87

   A. Use the greatest and least data values to organize the data into intervals.

   B. Construct a number line from the minimum and maximum values of the data set.

   C. Find the middle value of the data set.

   D. Mark the five boundary points where data occur along a number line.

See your complete lesson at MyMathUniverse.com

5. A survey studied how many cars belonged to each household. Which data display(s) can help you answer the following question?

In the results of the survey, how many households answered 4 cars?

A. dot plot and box plot
B. dot plot and histogram
C. dot plot
D. histogram
E. box plot, dot plot, and histogram
F. box plot and histogram
G. box plot

6. The circumference of a basketball is between 29.5 and 30 inches. A manufacturer measures 39 basketballs. Which data display(s) can help him display his results?

A. box plot
B. dot plot and histogram
C. dot plot and box plot
D. box plot and histogram
E. dot plot, box plot, and histogram
F. histogram
G. dot plot

7. **Estimation** The dot plot and histogram represent the numbers of defective products in 35 shipments.

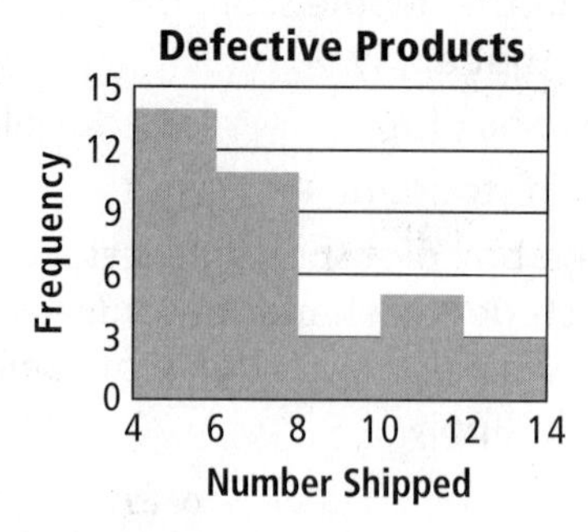

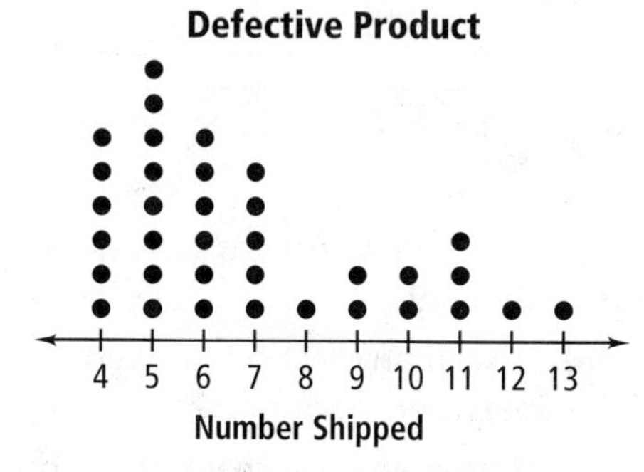

a. Which data display can you use to estimate the number of defective products in any given shipment?

A. histogram only
B. dot plot only
C. histogram and dot plot

Estimate the number of defective products in any given shipment.

b. Explain how you would use the display(s) to make the estimate.

8. **Think About the Process** The top 25% in a talent competition move on to the final round. Here are the scores of the 11 contestants.

70, 74, 75, 84, 68, 77, 81, 76, 73, 79, 78

a. Why would a box plot be the best data display for the results?

A. A box plot shows the clusters and gaps in data.
B. A box plot shows every data value.
C. A box plot shows frequencies of data values.
D. A box plot shows the five boundary values of a data set.

b. What are the scores of the top 25%?

15-6 Problem Solving

CCSS: 6.SP.B.4

Part 1

Example Making Conclusions from Histograms

Your friend is allowed to play video games if he gets mostly A's. He made a histogram to show his test results. Should your friend be able to play video games? Why?

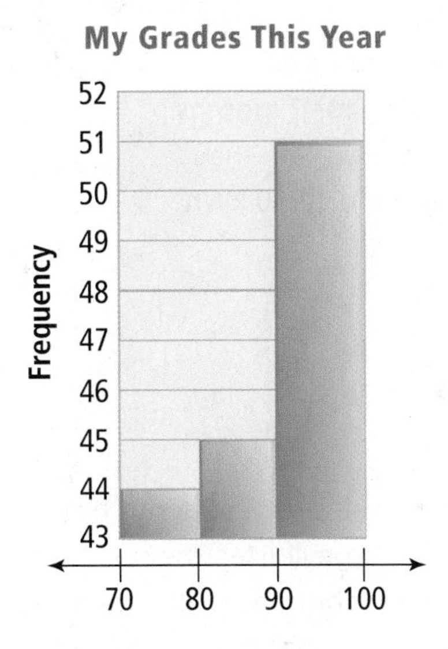

Solution

Notice that the vertical scale of the graph starts at 43. An accurate histogram always starts at 0. See what happens when the data are graphed with a vertical scale that starts at 0.

There is not a big difference between the scores that your friend got after all. Your friend should redraw his histogram accurately.

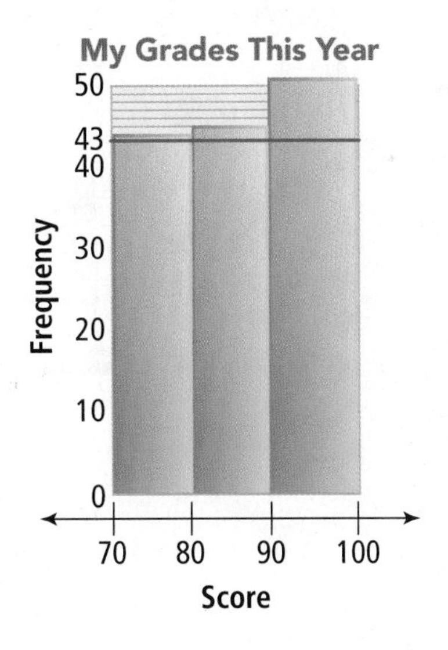

Part 2

Example Analyzing Clusters in Histograms

Each wind turbine is expected to generate 3,000 kilowatts (kW) per day. The histogram shows the daily amount of energy produced by each turbine for 2 months. What might explain the cluster around 1,000 kWh the histogram?

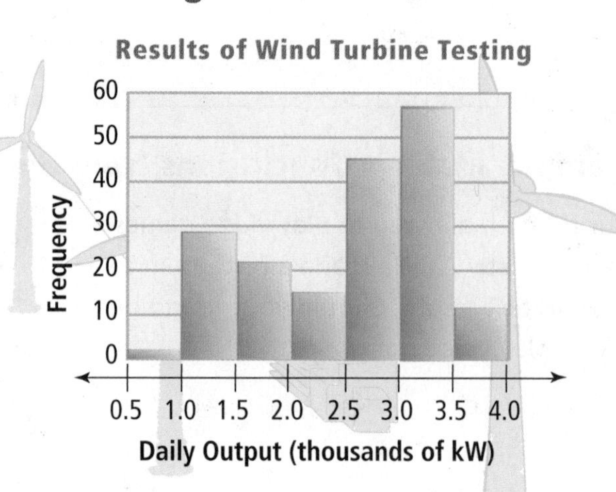

Solution

Since the small cluster is about half the size of the large cluster, the small cluster may indicate that one of the three wind turbines is not operating correctly.

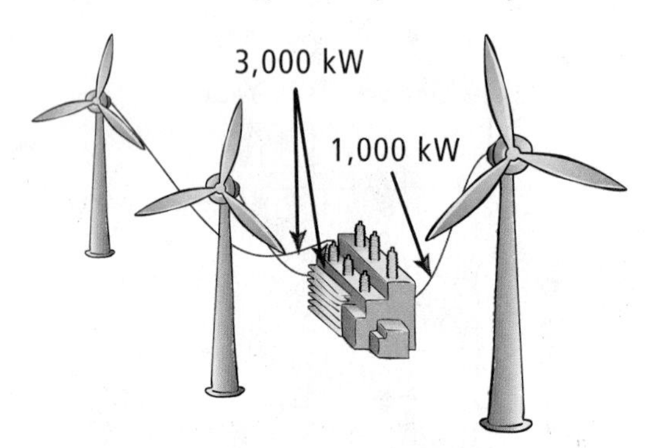

Results of Wind Turbine Testing

60
50
40
30
20
10
0

0.5 1.0 1.5 2.0 2.5 3.0 3.5 4.0

Daily Output (thousands of kW)

Digital Resources  

1. Mr. Perkins gave a test to the 24 students in his class. He made this histogram to represent the students' scores. Why is the histogram misleading?

Test Scores

Frequency: 0, 11, 12, 13, 14
Points: 85, 90, 95

2. Ben asked 19 of his classmates how many books they read last summer. He made this dot plot to represent their replies. Why is his dot plot misleading?

Books Read Last Summer

2 3 4 5 6 7 8 9 10 11 12
Number of Books

3. At your school's field day, 30 students run a race. Some of them are runners on the track team and others are not. The histogram represents the students' times. How many of the 30 students, at most, are likely runners on the track team?

Race Times

Frequency: 0 1 2 3 4 5 6 7 8 9 10
20 25 30 35 40 45 50 55 60 65
Seconds

4. **Think About the Process** For a school project, Alex asks people how long they slept last night. She makes a histogram to represent the data she collects. What questions could you ask about the histogram to see if it is misleading? Select all that apply.

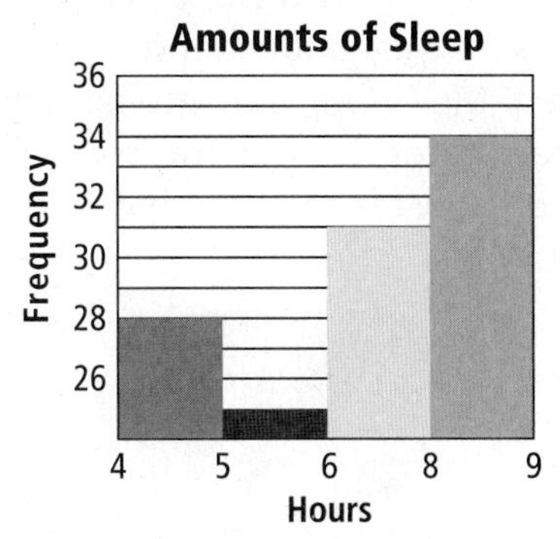

A. Are all of the intervals equal in size?

B. Does the vertical scale start at 0?

C. Does the horizontal scale start at 0?

D. Are any of the bars much taller than the others?

5. A fair coin is just as likely to show heads as it is to show tails when you toss it. Pedro wants to see if a coin is fair. He asks each of 25 friends to toss the coin 22 times. Each friend records the number of tails. Pedro makes this dot plot.

Results of Coin Tosses

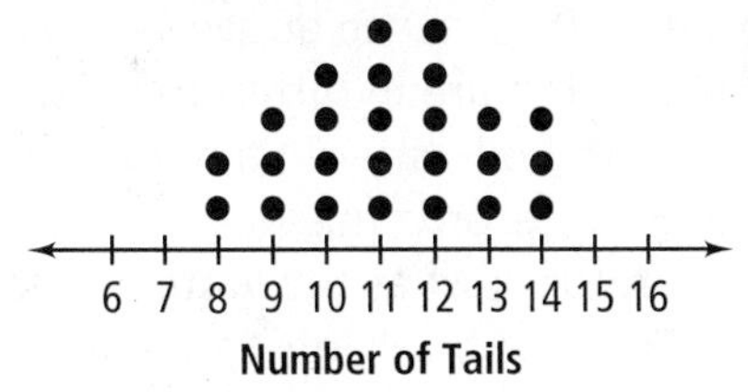

a. Is the coin likely a fair coin?

A. No, the coin is likely not fair. It shows tails much more often than it shows heads.

B. Yes, the coin is likely fair. It shows tails about as often as it shows heads.

C. No, the coin is likely not fair. It shows tails much less often than it shows heads.

b. Draw or describe the dot plot that would represent the numbers of heads that Pedro's friends tossed.

6. Think About the Process There are 15 students in Mr. Gupta's math class. He gives them a test with 100 points. Students who score less than 75 will need to do an extra worksheet to make sure they understand the subject. Mr. Gupta wants to display the results for the students so they will see how many of them will get worksheets.

Points		
67	72	73
83	77	83
72	94	89
69	86	93
88	76	71

a. What data display(s) could Mr. Gupta use? Select all that apply.

A. Dot plot **B.** Histogram
C. Box plot

b. How many students will get worksheets?

c. Explain how you would prefer to see these results and tell why.

7. Water boils at different temperatures based on its distance above sea level. Ann and Rob are in different cities. They both boil water in a number of pots. Each records the water temperature just as the water starts to boil. They use box plots to display their data.

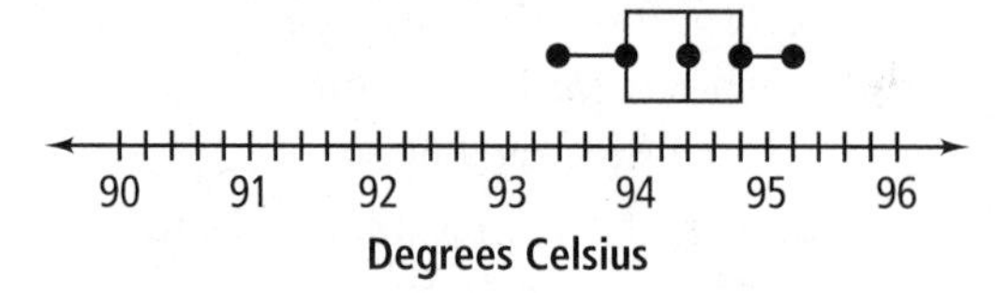

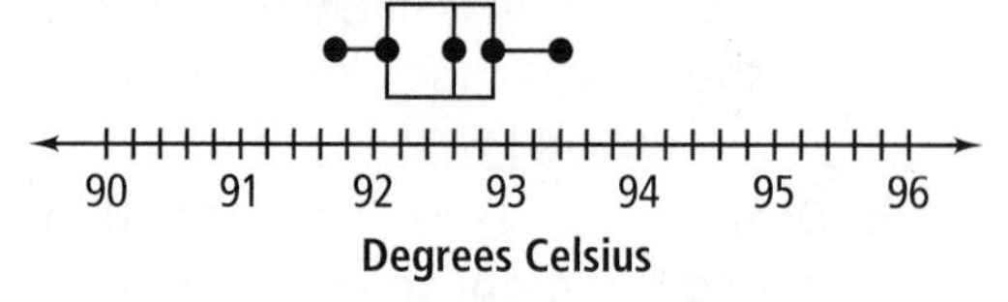

a. Are the two cities at about the same distance above sea level?

b. How might this problem and your answer change if Ann and Rob had used degrees Fahrenheit instead?

8. Challenge Ms. Gessel teaches 63 students in her four history classes. She asked each of them to write a short essay. After reading each essay, she counted its words. She made this histogram to show the results.

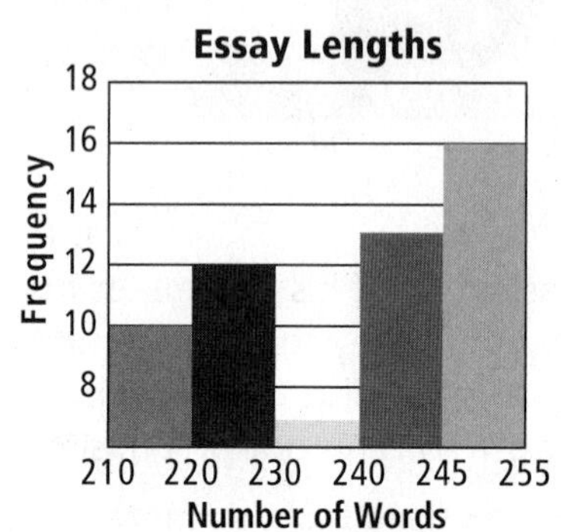

a. Why is her histogram misleading? Select all that apply.

A. The intervals are not equal in size.

B. The vertical scale does not start at 0.

C. The horizontal scale does not start at 0.

D. The bars have different colors.

b. For each reason the histogram is misleading, tell or show how you could fix it. If you would need additional information, tell what it would be.

16-1 Median

Vocabulary
measures of center, median

CCSS: 6.SP.A.3, 6.SP.B.4, 6.SP.B.5, 6.SP.B.5c

Key Concept

You have a data set of the ages of dancers on a drill team. You can describe this data set by graphing it on a data display, like a dot plot.

Ages of Dancers: 8, 10, 11, 12, 12, 13, 13, 15, 16

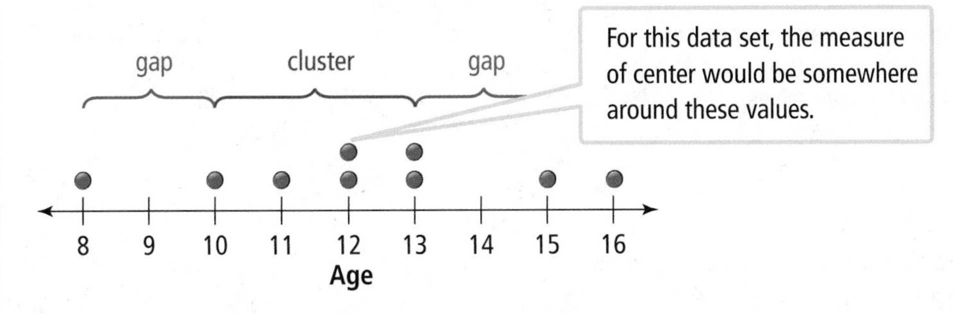

A measure of center is a value that represents the middle of a data set.

The **median** is measure of center of a numerical data set.

For an odd number of data values, the **median** is the middle value when the data values are arranged in numerical order.

Ages of Dancers: 8, 10, 11, 12, 12, 13, 13, 15, 16 — 9 data values

The median is 12.

For an even number of data values, the **median** is the average of the two middle items when the data values are arranged in numerical order.

Ages of Dancers: 8, 10, 11, 12, 13, 13, 15, 16 — 8 data values

$$\text{median} = \frac{12 + 13}{2}$$
$$= 12.5$$

The median is 12.5.

See your complete lesson at MyMathUniverse.com

Part 1

Example Finding Medians of Data Sets

What is the median of each data set?

a. 7, 8, 9, 12, 14, 16, 17, 19, 20, 50
b. −132, −105, −19, 15, 16, 17, 17, 22, 25
c. 13, 21, 10, 23, 15, 9, 22

Solution

a. 7, 8, 9, 12, 14, 16, 17, 19, 20, 50

When there is an even number of values, take the average of the two middle values.

$$\frac{14 + 16}{2} = 15$$

The median of this data set is 15.

b. −132, −105, −19, 15, 16, 17, 17, 22, 25

When there is an odd number of values, find the middle value.

The median of this data set is 16.

c. 13, 21, 10, 23, 15, 9, 22

A data set must be in numerical order to find the median.

9, 10, 13, 15, 21, 22, 23

To find the median of a data set with an odd number of values, find the middle value.

The median of this data set is 15.

Part 2

Intro

20, 21, 25, 27, 33, 36, 39, 42

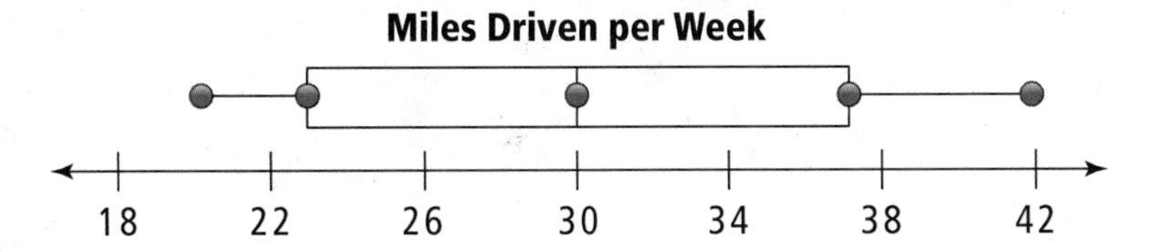

The line inside the box is the median of the data set.

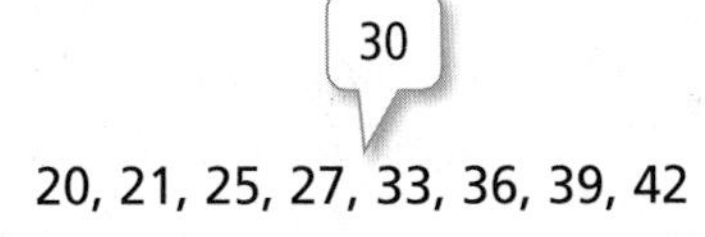

20, 21, 25, 27, 33, 36, 39, 42

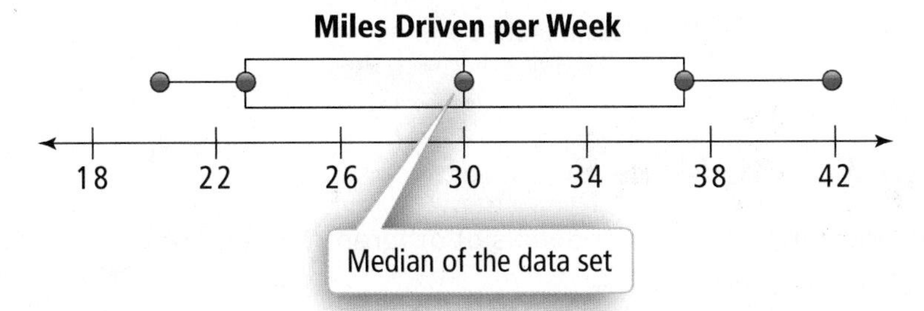

The left edge of the box is the median of the lower half of the data set. If the data set has an even number of values, the lower half includes the lower middle value.

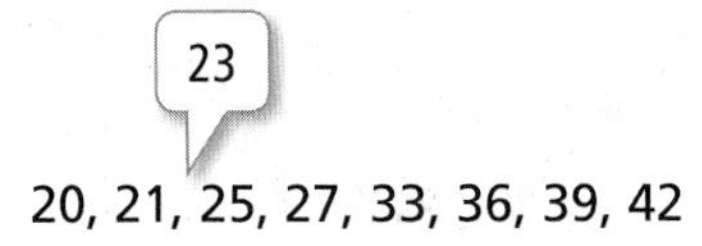

20, 21, 25, 27, 33, 36, 39, 42

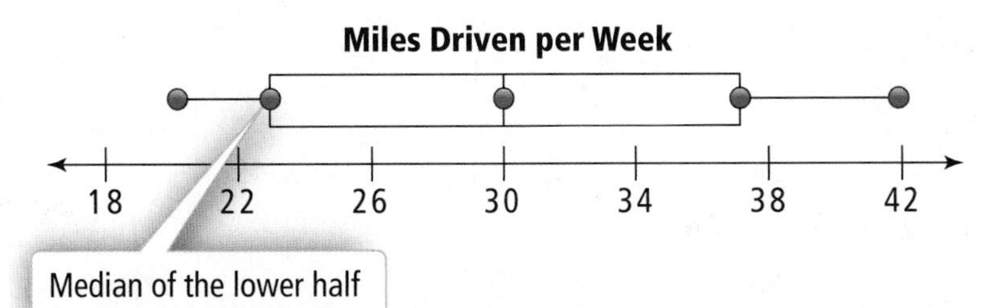

continued on next page >

Part 2

Intro continued

The right edge of the box is the median of the upper half of the data set. If the data set has an even number of values, the upper half includes the upper middle value.

20, 21, 25, 27, 33, 36, 39, 42

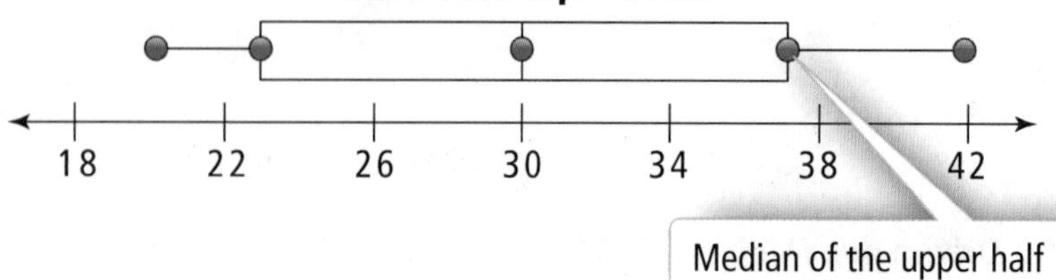

Example Using Medians to Make Box Plots

The data set shows the prices in thousands of dollars of different types of cars. Make a box plot of the data set.

Type H: $112.5	Type D: $27.2
Type B: $37.5	Type A: $21.5
Type F: $61.8	Type G: $67.3
Type C: $26.4	Type E: $28.9

Solution

First order the data set.

21.5, 26.4, 27.2, 28.9, 35.7, 61.8, 67.3, 112.5

$$\frac{28.9 + 35.7}{2} = \frac{64.6}{2}$$
$$= 32.3$$

The median of the data set is 32.3.

median: 32.3

21.5, 26.4, 27.2, 28.9, ↓ 35.7, 61.8, 67.3, 112.5

lower half — upper half

Find the median of the lower half.

$$\frac{26.4 + 27.2}{2} = \frac{53.6}{2}$$
$$= 26.8$$

The median of the lower half of the data set is 26.8.

continued on next page >

Part 2

Solution continued

Find the median of the upper half.

$$\frac{61.8 + 67.3}{2} = \frac{129.1}{2}$$
$$= 64.55$$

The median of the upper half of the data set is 64.55.

Draw the box plot. First, plot the minimum, maximum, median, and the medians of the lower and upper halves of the data on the number line. Then draw the box plot lines.

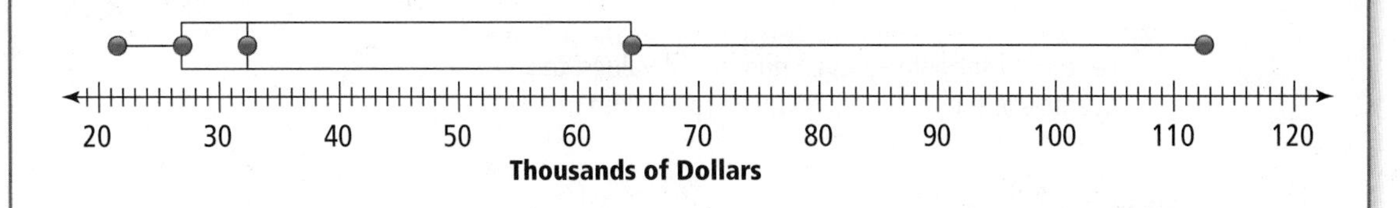

Part 3

Intro

When choosing a measure of center to represent your data, keep in mind that a sometimes an appropriate measure of center should not be strongly affected by extreme data values.

It is easier to see the effect of extreme data values on the medium by graphing the data. Here the track coach salary of $100,000 is an extreme value that does not represent the group.

Track Coach Salaries: $14,000, $15,500, $16,000, $17,500, $18,500, $20,500, $24,500, $27,000, $100,000

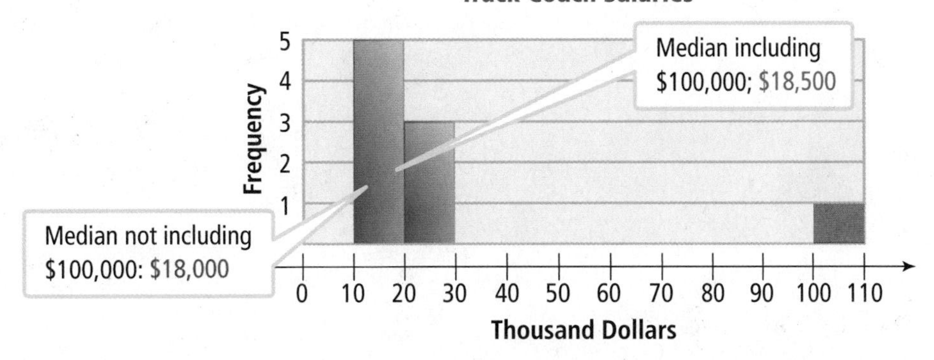

The median is the measure of center that is not drastically affected by extreme data values.

Part 3

Example Determining If Medians are Appropriate Measures of Center

A track coach wants to know how fast his runners typically run. During practice, he uses a radar gun to measure the running speeds in miles per hour of ten of his runners. Is the median an appropriate measure of center for this data set? Use a graph to justify your reasoning.

Solution

Order the data set and find the median.

12.9 13.3, 13.4, 13.5, 14.4, 14.6, 14.8, 15.1, 15.2, 37.0

For a data set with an even number of values, take the average of the middle two values to find the median.

$$\text{median} = \frac{14.4 + 14.6}{2}$$

$$= 14.5$$

Graph the data on a dot plot.

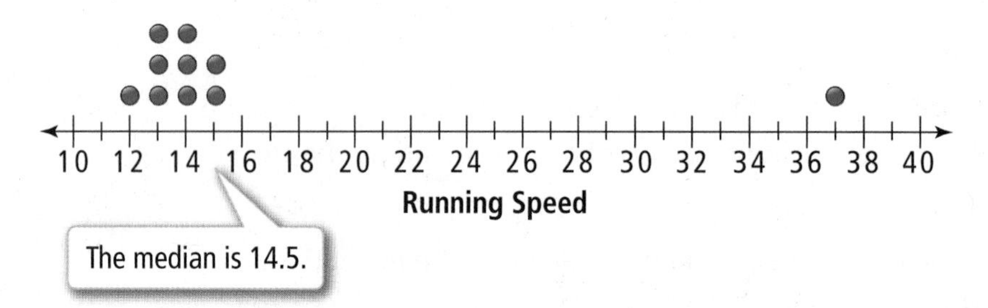

Yes, the median, 14.5 miles per hour, is an appropriate measure of the center because it is close to all of the values except 37.0 mph. A stray data value like 37.0 mph may be an error in measurement and should not be considered a realistic data value.

16-1 Homework

1. Find the median value of the data set 46, 41, 34, 64, 57, 48, and 32.

2. Find the median for the data set 27, 24, 23, 22, 28, 25, 21, and 23.

3. Find the median value.
   1379, 1157, 1397, 941, 1170, 1027

4. Which is the box plot of the data set 17, 15, 18, 13, 11, and 12?

A.

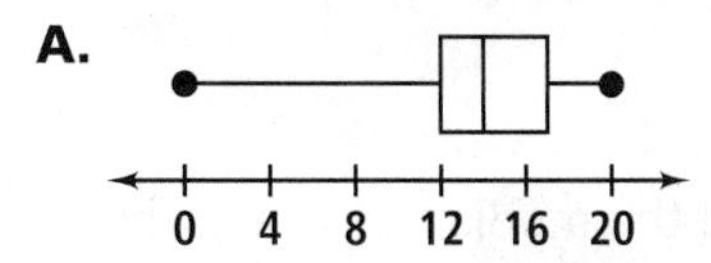

B.

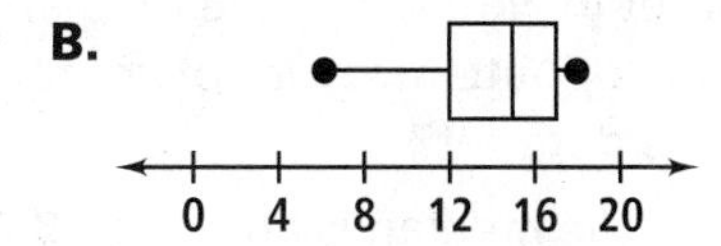

C.

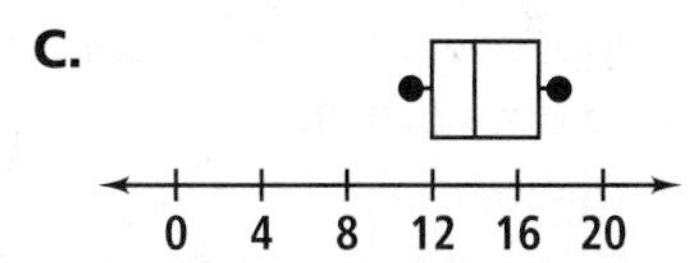

5. Which is the box plot of the data set 5, 12, 8, 1, 9, 6, 4, 1, 13, and 14?

A.

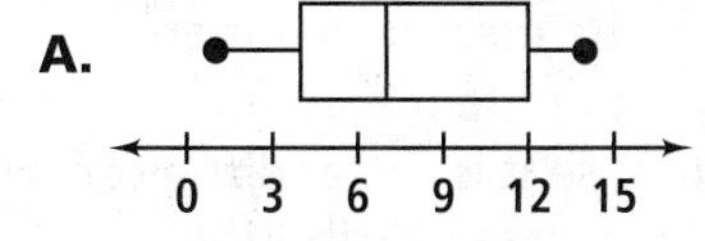

B.

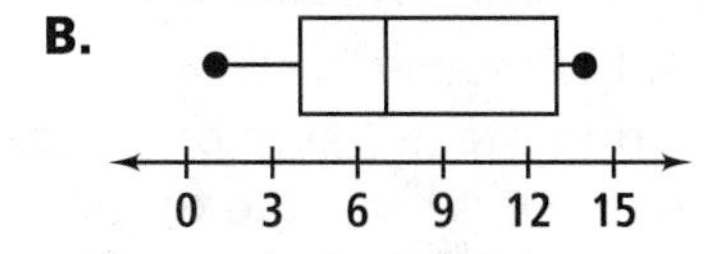

C.

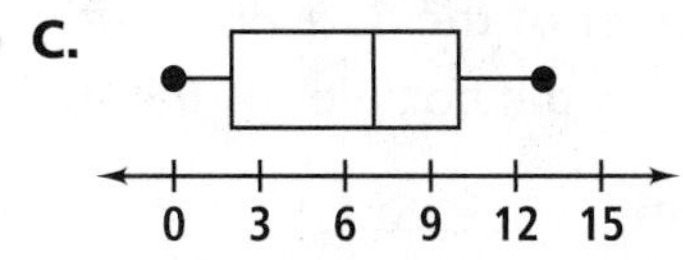

6. **a.** Find the median of the data set 16, 17, 12, 15, 14, 31, and 18.

   b. Is the median an appropriate measure of center for this data set?

   A. Yes, the median is an appropriate measure of center because it is close to all of the values except 31, which may be an error in data collection.

   B. Yes, the median is an appropriate measure of center because it is not close to the center of the data distribution.

   C. No, the median is not an appropriate measure of center because it is not close to the center of the data distribution.

   D. No, the median is not an appropriate measure of center because it is close to all of the values except 31, which may be an error in data collection.

7. **a.** Find the median of the data set 4, 33, 40, 1, 6, 38, and 7.

   b. Is the median an appropriate measure of center for this data set?

   A. Yes, the median is an appropriate measure of center because it is close to the center of the data distribution.

   B. No, the median is not an appropriate measure of center because it is not close to the center of the data distribution.

   C. No, the median is not an appropriate measure of center because it is close to the center of the data distribution.

   D. Yes, the median is an appropriate measure of center because it is not close to the center of the data distribution.

8. **a. Reasoning** What is the median of the data set 171, 182, 197, 175, 205, 177, and 203?

   b. How is using the median to represent a set of numbers helpful? How is using the median not helpful? Explain your reasoning.

9. The annual salaries of the workers at a local cable television office are \$23,100; \$43,300; \$36,800; \$32,600; \$42,500; \$41,700; \$21,400; \$29,800; \$10,400; and \$11,100. Find the median value.

10. Think About the Process The following data set shows the final scores for a basketball team for 8 games.

60, 59, 47, 63, 53, 65, 56, 61

a. What is the first step in finding the median of a data set?

A. Find the last value of the given list.

B. Find the value in the middle of the given list.

C. Find the first value of the given list.

D. Put the values in numerical order.

b. Find the median of the data set.

11. Think About the Process In a recent survey, students were asked how many hours of television they watch per week. The data show the number of hours each student spends watching television in one week.

5, 19, 16, 4, 11, 12, 13, 2, 15

a. What do you need to do to draw a box plot, after putting the data values in numerical order?

A. You need to find all five boundary values.

B. You only need the median of the data set.

C. You only need the minimum and maximum values.

D. None of these

b. Which is the box plot of the data set?

A.

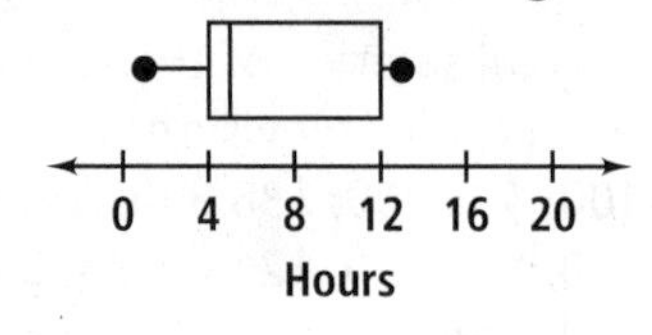

B.

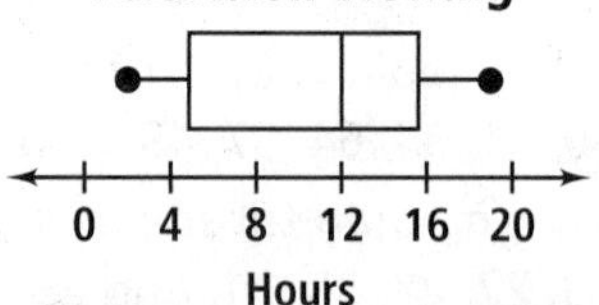

C.

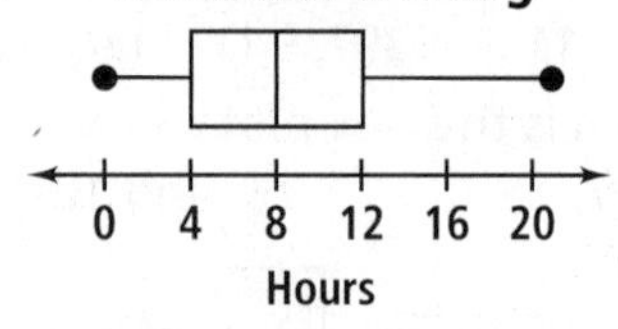

12. Multiple Representations

a. Find the median of the graphed data set in **Figure 1.** Is the median an appropriate measure of center for this data set?

A. Yes, the median is an appropriate measure of center of the data distribution.

B. No, the median is not an appropriate measure of center because it is not close to the center of the data distribution.

C. No, the median is not an appropriate measure of center because it is close to the center of the data distribution.

D. Yes, the median is an appropriate measure of center because it is not close to the center of the data distribution.

b. Which is the box plot of the data set?

A.

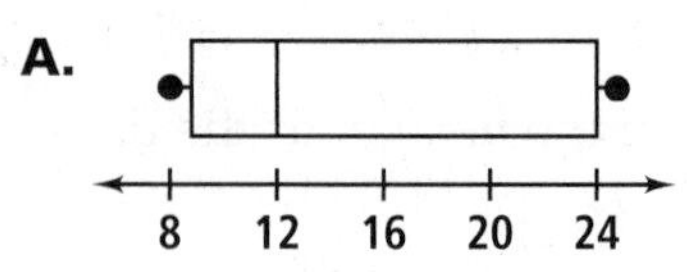

B.

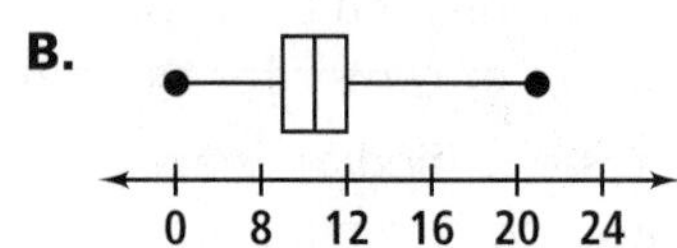

C.

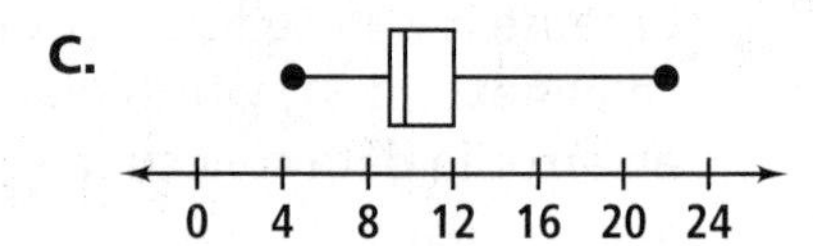

(Figure 1)

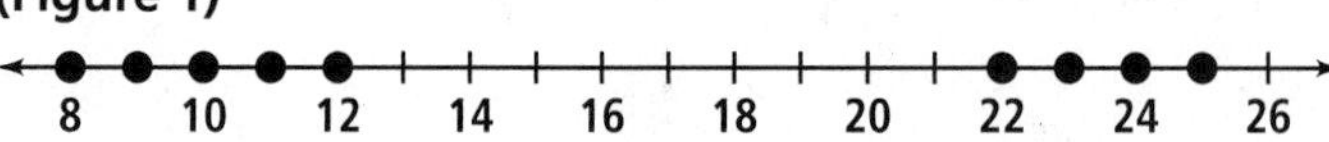

16-2 Mean

Vocabulary
mean

CCSS: 6.SP.A.3, 6.SP.B.5, 6.SP.B.5c

Key Concept

Visual Model You can use a visual model to represent the mean of a data set. You can use blocks to model the values. The mean is the value you get if you redistribute the blocks equally.

Number of Inches of Snow: 2, 4, 5, 1

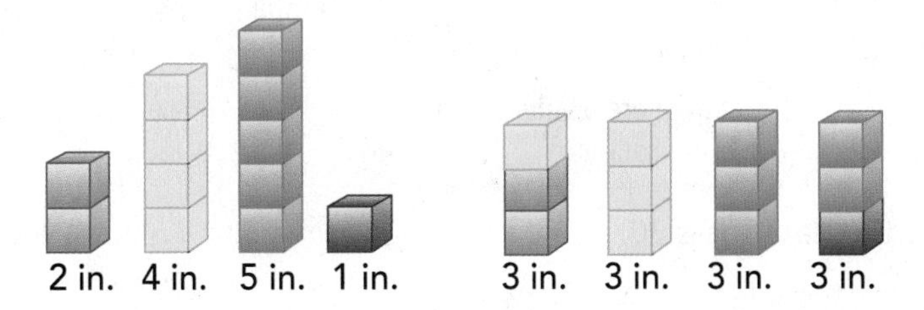

The mean is 3 inches.

Definition and Formula The **mean** is a measure of center in a set of numerical data. You calculate the mean by adding all the data values together and dividing the sum by the total number of data values.

Number of Inches of Snow: 2, 4, 5, 1

These are 4 data values in this data set.

$$\text{mean} = \frac{\text{sum of the data values}}{\text{total number of values}}$$

$$\text{mean} = \frac{2 + 4 + 5 + 1}{4}$$

$$= 3$$

The mean of the data set is 3. The calculated mean of 3 inches agrees with the visual model.

Part 1

Example Finding Means of Data Sets

What is the mean of each data set?

a. 24, 27, 30, 31, 33, 35
b. 43, 1, 89, 0, 11, 2, 64
c. 33, 9, 34, 28, 41

Solution

a. $\text{mean} = \frac{24 + 27 + 30 + 31 + 33 + 35}{6}$

$= \frac{180}{6}$

$= 30$

Calculate the mean by adding together all of the data values and then dividing by the total number of data values.

There are 6 values in this data set.

The mean of the data set is 30.

b. $\text{mean} = \frac{43 + 1 + 89 + 0 + 11 + 2 + 64}{7}$

$= \frac{210}{7}$

$= 30$

There are 7 values in this data set.

The mean of the data set is 30.

c. $\text{mean} = \frac{33 + 9 + 34 + 28 + 41}{5}$

$= \frac{145}{5}$

$= 29$

There are 5 values in this data set.

The mean of the data set is 29.

Part 2

Example Using Means to Find Missing Data Values

A tourist company is hiring three new tour guides. The mean wage of the new guides must be $15 per hour. Two guides have been hired at $16.50 and $17.50 per hour. What must the wage of the third guide be?

Solution

Know
- Three new tour guides
- Two hired at $16.50 and $17.50 per hour
- The mean is $15

Need
Find the wage of the third tour guide.

Plan
Use the formula for the mean, substituting the values you know. Then, solve for the unknown value.

$$\text{mean} = \frac{\text{sum of the data values}}{\text{total number of values}}$$

$$15.00 = \frac{16.50 + 17.50 + ?}{3}$$

$$15.00 = \frac{16.50 + 17.50 + ?}{3}$$

3 times the mean

Sum of the wages

$$3 \times 15 = 16.5 + 17.50 + x$$

Simplify. $45 = 34 + x$

Subtract 34 from each side. $45 - 34 = 34 - 34 + x$

Simplify. $11 = x$

In order for the mean of all three new employees to be $15 per hour, the wage of the third employee must be $11 per hour.

continued on next page >

Part 2

Solution continued

Check that the answer is reasonable. The mean wage is $15 and the other two tour guides get more than that. The third tour guide's wage must balance the data around the mean. The third tour guide must get less than $15 per hour, so the answer is reasonable.

Part 3

Intro

A median is not strongly affected by extreme data values. But sometimes, extreme values can give an inaccurate picture of what the typical data values are. In the data below, the mean is strongly affected by the extreme data value.

Track Coach Salaries:

$14,000	$15,500	$16,000	$17,500	$18,500
$20,500	$24,500	$27,000	$100,000	

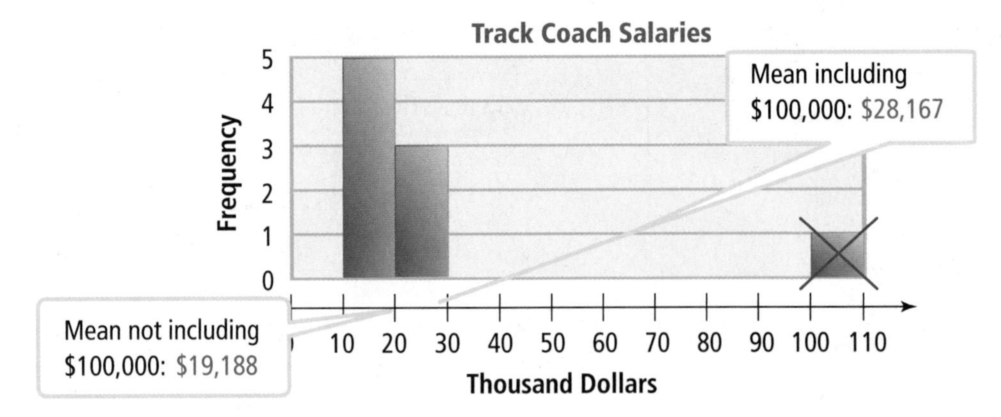

Part 3

Example Determining If Means Are Appropriate Measures of Center for a Data Set

A track coach wants to know how fast his runners typically run. During practice, he uses a radar gun to measure the running speeds in miles per hour of ten of his runners. Is the mean an appropriate measure of center for this data set? Use a graph to justify your reasoning.

12.9	13.3	13.4	13.5	14.4
14.6	14.8	15.1	15.2	37.0

Solution

There are 10 values in the data set. Calculate the mean.

$$\text{mean} = \frac{\text{sum of the data values}}{\text{total number of values}}$$

$$= \frac{12.9 + 13.3 + 13.4 + 13.5 + 14.4 + 14.6 + 14.8 + 15.1 + 15.2 + 37.0}{10}$$

$$= \frac{164.2}{10}$$

$$= 16.42$$

No, the mean 16.42 miles per hour is not an appropriate measure of center because it is greater than 9 of the 10 values in the data set.

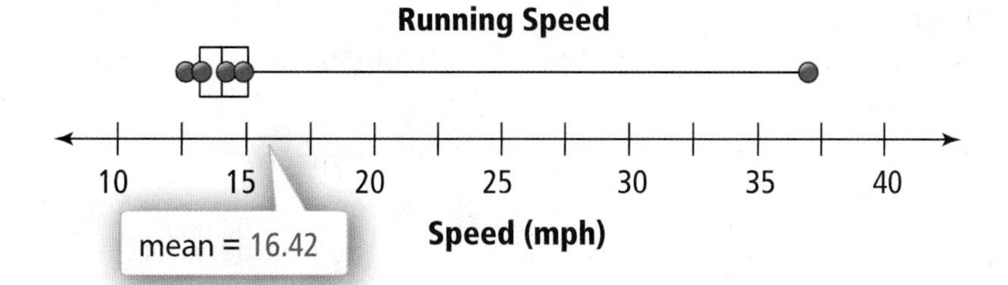

Digital Resources    

1. Find the mean of the data set 10, 0, 2, and 8.

2. A student received grades of 86, 88, 97, 82, and 60 on math quizzes. Find the mean.

3. Find the mean of the following set of numbers.

193, 153, 103, 120, 173

4. Find the mean of the following set of numbers.

109, 399, 422, 570

5. Find the value of x such that the data set 102, 119, 106, 114, 108, and x has a mean of 119.

6. Three cars are driving on a racetrack. The mean speed of the three cars is 100 miles per hour. Car X drives 103 miles per hour and Car Y drives 116 miles per hour.

a. Use the mean to estimate the speed of Car Z.

A. The speed of Car Z is about 100 miles per hour.

B. The speed of Car Z is greater than 100 miles per hour.

C. The speed of Car Z is less then 100 miles per hour.

D. It is impossible to estimate the speed of Car Z.

b. Find the actual speed of Car Z.

7. a. Find the mean of the data set 0, 5, 7, 9, and 59.

b. Is the mean an appropriate measure of center?

A. No, because it is close to the center of the data distribution.

B. Yes, because it is not close to any of the values in the data set.

C. No, because it is not close to any of the values in the data set.

D. Yes, because it is close to the center of the data distribution.

8. Writing The last five houses built in town sold for the prices $189,000; $167,000; $170,000; $146,000; and $167,000.

a. What is the mean price of the houses?

b. If a new house built in town sold for $130,000, how would that affect the mean?

9. a. Reasoning Find the mean of the data set 10, 16, 48, 49, 71, and 79.

b. Is the mean an appropriate measure of center?

A. No, because it is not close to any of the values in the data set.

B. Yes, because it is close to the center of the data distribution.

C. No, because it is close to the center of the data distribution.

D. Yes, because it is close to one of the values in the data set.

10. Error Analysis The mean of the data set 100, 121, 107, 114, 110, and x is 114. Your friend says that the value of x is 110.4.

a. What is the correct value of x?

b. What mistake might your friend have made?

A. Your friend found the median of the numbers, not the mean.

B. Your friend found the mean of the five numbers listed.

C. Your friend did not divide the sum of the values.

D. Your friend divided the sum of 6 numbers by 5, not 6.

11. Track Team The coach of a track team measures the time it takes each member of her team to run 100 m. The times for five runners are shown in the table in seconds.

Time to Run 100 m

Runner	Time (seconds)
1	13.5
2	25.9
3	11.8
4	12.1
5	12.7

a. Find the mean time for the five runners.

b. Is the mean an appropriate measure of center?

A. Yes

B. No

12. Think About the Process

99, 120, 104, 111, 110, x

a. What is a good first step to find the value of x in this data set?

A. Find the mean of the other numbers in the data set.

B. Divide the mean by 5.

C. Find the sum of the other numbers in the data set.

D. Multiply each number in the data set by 5.

b. Find the value of x such that the data set has a mean of 116.

13. Think About the Process

102, 109, 182, 185, 187

a. How can you tell if the mean of a data set is an appropriate measure of center?

A. Subtract the mean from each value in the data set.

B. Graph the mean on a number line and look at points near it.

C. Multiply the mean by the number of values in the data set and compare it to the sum of the values.

D. Graph the data set and the mean on a number line and compare.

b. Find the mean of the data set above.

c. Is the mean an appropriate measure of center?

A. No, because it is not close to any of the values in the data set.

B. Yes, because it is close to one of the values in the data set.

C. Yes, because it is close to the center of the data distribution.

D. No, because it is close to the center of the data distribution.

14. Estimation The mean of the data set 264, x, 277, and 237 is 250.

a. Use the mean to estimate the value of x.

A. The value of x is less than 250.

B. The value of x is about 250.

C. The value of x is greater than 250.

D. It is impossible to estimate the value of x.

b. What is the value of x?

15. Two groups of people worked together collecting morel mushrooms. A group of 2 people collected 25 mushrooms. A second group of 6 people collected 55 mushrooms. If all of the mushrooms were shared equally, how many mushrooms did each person get?

16. Challenge The costs of four different bicycles are shown in the table.

Bicycle Costs

Bicycle	Cost
A.	$184
B.	$195
C.	$187
D.	$214

a. What is the mean cost of the four bicycles?

b. If a fifth bicycle costs $141, what is the mean cost of all five bicycles?

16-3 Variability

Vocabulary
measure of variability, range, variability

CCSS: 6.SP.A.2, 6.SP.A.3, Also 6.SP.B.5, 6.SP.B.5c

Key Concept

Measures of center can help describe a data set. Another way to describe a data set is using measures of variability. Variability describes how much the data sets differ, or vary, from each other.

High Variability The more spread out, or varied, the data values are, the higher the variability in the data set.

The median of this data set is 6. It has high variability.

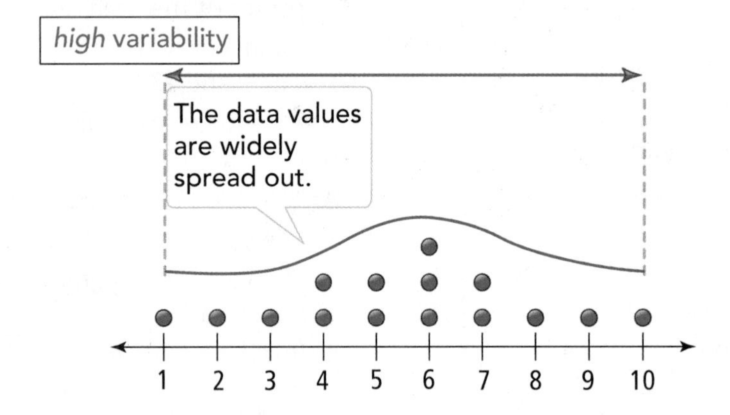

Low Variability The more similar the data values are, the less variability there is in the data set.

The median of this data set is also 6. It has low variability.

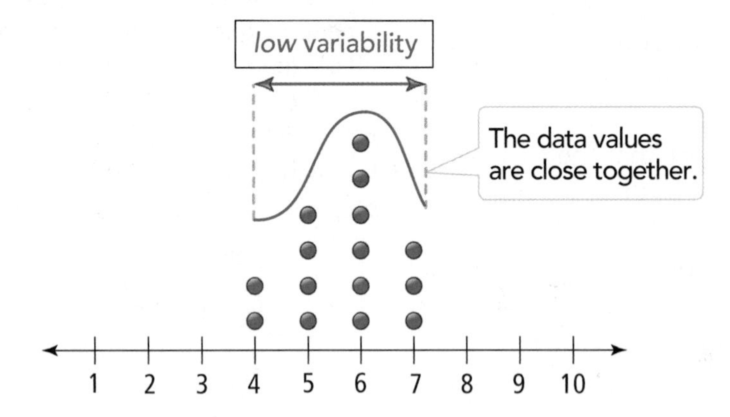

continued on next page >

Key Concept

continued

No Variability If all of the data values are the same, there is no variability in the data set.

The median of this data set is also 6. It has no variability.

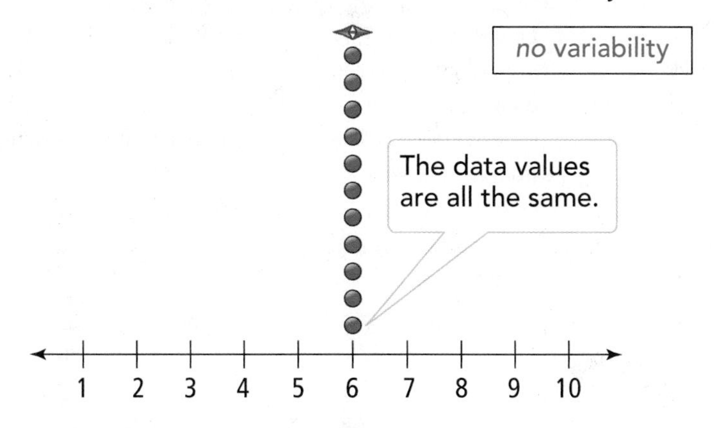

Part 1

Example Describing Variability

Determine which data displays show *high variability, low variability,* or *no variability*.

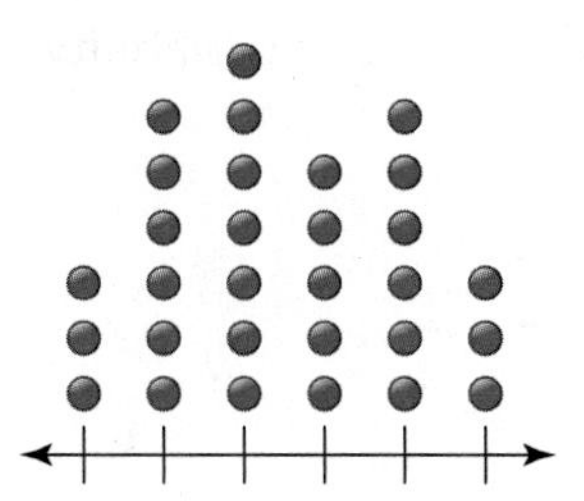

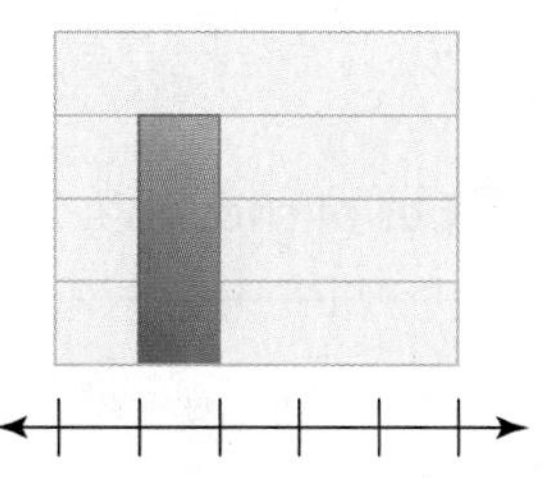

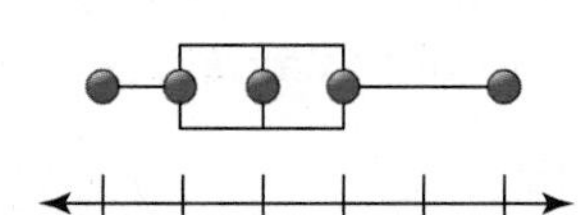

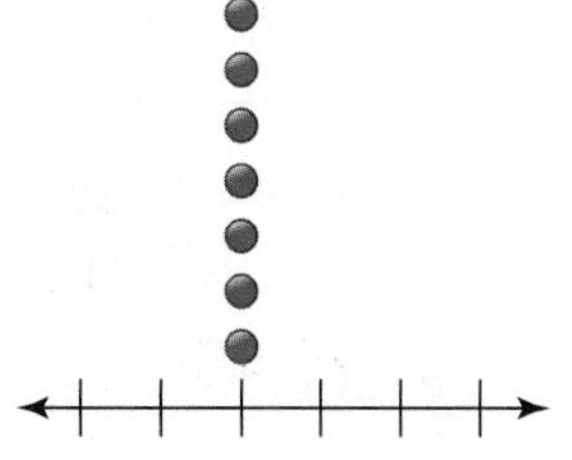

continued on next page >

Part 1

Example continued

Solution

Answers may vary. Sample:

High Variability These displays show that the data values in each data set vary a lot from each other.

Low Variability This display shows that the data values in the data set vary only a little from each other.

No Variability This display shows that the data values in the data set don't vary at all. That is, the data values are all the same.

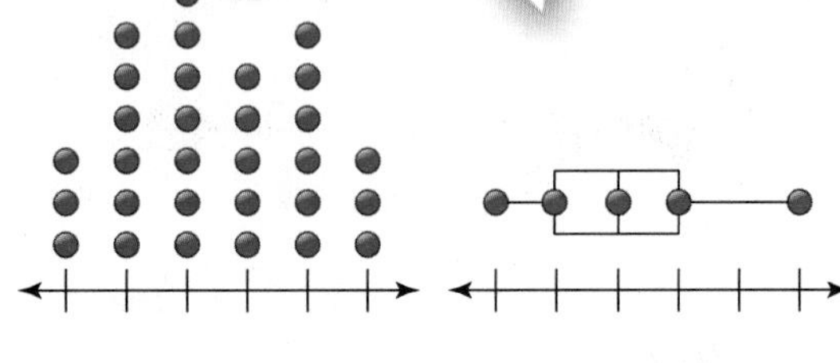

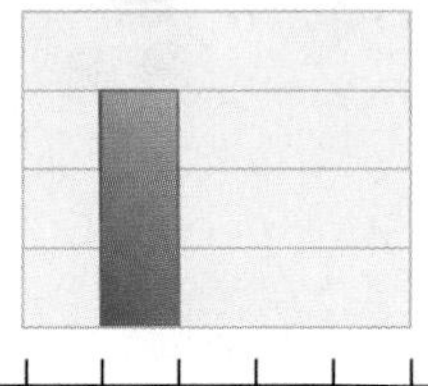

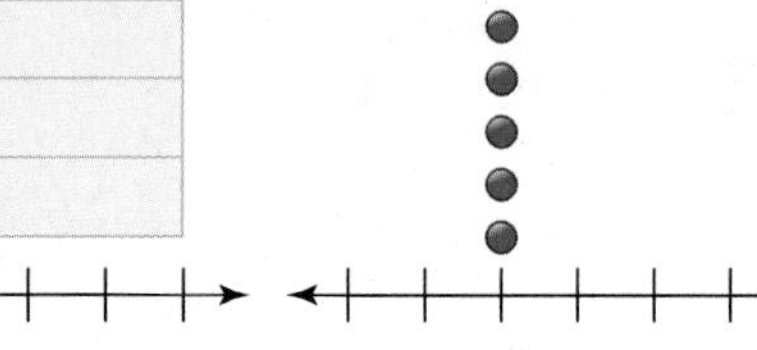

Part 2

Intro

A **measure of variability** is a value that describes the amount of variability in a data set.

Daily number of inches of snowfall: 2, 3, 4, 4, 7, 10, 12, 15, 40

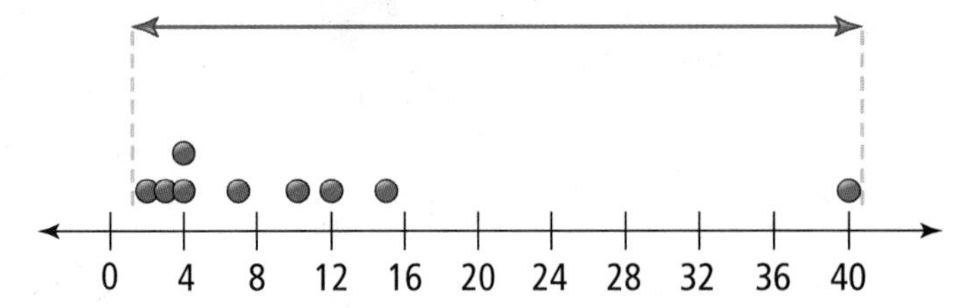

The **range** is a measure of variability of a numerical data set. The range of a data set is the difference between the greatest and least values in a data set.

Daily number of inches of snowfall: 2, 3, 4, 4, 7, 10, 12, 15, 40

$$\begin{aligned} \text{range} &= \text{maximum} - \text{minimum} \\ &= 40 - 2 \\ &= 38 \end{aligned}$$

Part 2

Example Finding Ranges of Data Sets

Find the range of each data set.

a. 24, 27, 30, 30, 31, 32

b. 43, 1, 89, 0, 11, 2, 64

c. 33, 10, 34, 33, 35

Solution

a. 24, 27, 30, 30, 31, 32

The data values are arranged from least to greatest value.

range = maximum − minimum
= 32 − 24
= 8

b. 43, 1, 89, 0, 11, 2, 64 → 0, 1, 2, 11, 43, 64, 89

These data values must be ordered from least to greatest.

range = maximum − minimum
= 89 − 0
= 89

c. 3,10, 34, 33, 35 → 10, 33, 33, 34, 35

range = maximum − minimum
= 35 − 10
= 25

Part 3

Example Describing the Variability of Data Sets

In a science experiment about the surface tension of water, each team of students uses a dropper to drop water onto the surface of a penny. Each team records the number of water droplets that its penny is able to hold. Find the range of the results. Then describe the variability of the data set.

Team	Drops of Water
Team 1	23
Team 2	26
Team 3	19
Team 4	26
Team 5	21
Team 6	20
Team 7	24
Team 8	26
Team 9	22
Team 10	25
Team 11	12
Team 12	21
Team 13	22
Team 14	26
Team 15	24
Team 16	23

Solution

The range of the data set is the maximum value minus the minimum value.

12, 19, 20, 21, 21, 22, 22, 23, 23, 24, 24, 25, 26, 26, 26, 26

$$\begin{aligned} \text{range} &= \text{maximum} - \text{minimum} \\ &= 26 - 12 \\ &= 14 \end{aligned}$$

A range of 14 drops of water is a wide range in this situation. So the data set has high variability.

1. Describe the level of variability for the given data display.

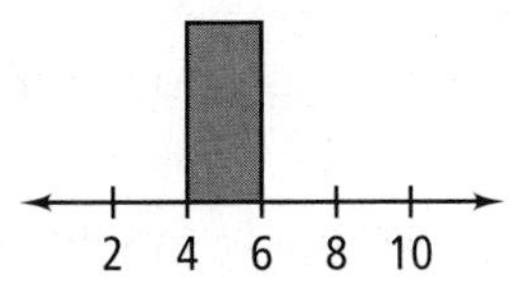

2. Which data displays show a data set with no variability?

A.
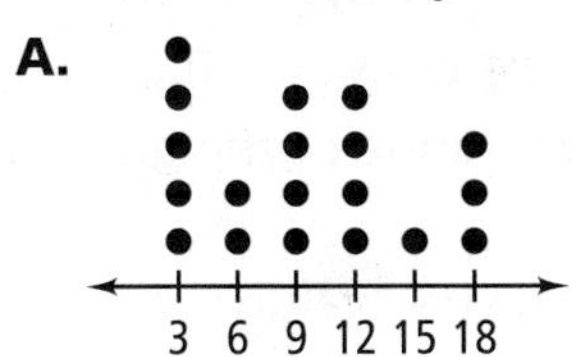

B.
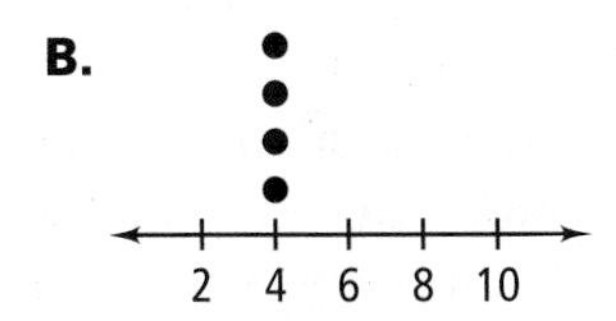

C.
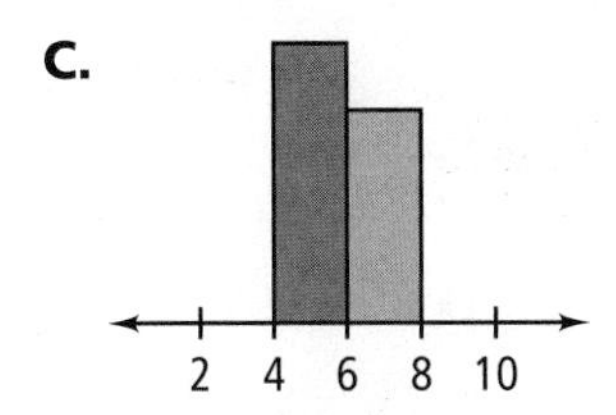

3. Find the range of the data set.
171, 169, 166, 177, 159, 178, 156

4. For a project, the teacher asked seven students to each count the number of pedestrians that cross the street where they live on a certain day. The data collected had a range of 36. Six of the seven data values are 30, 13, 17, 10, 35, and 13. Find the missing data value.

5. Reasoning Which data displays show a data set with high variability? Select all that apply.

A.
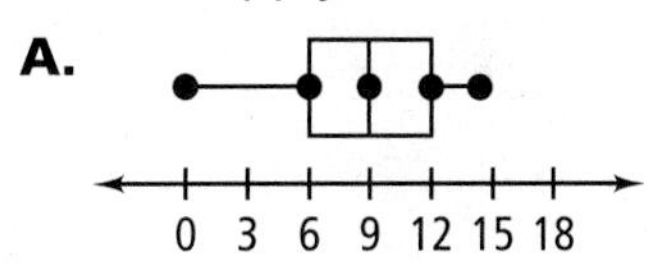

B.
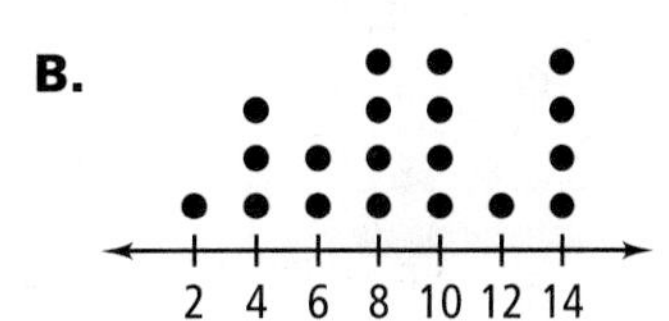

C.
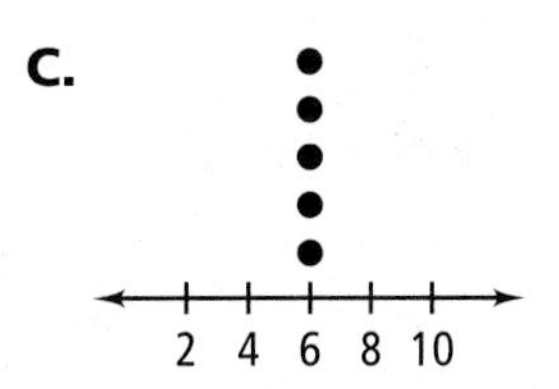

6. Rainfall The annual rainfall in six towns is recorded, but one of the data values is missing. If the range of the data set is 64.5, what was the annual rainfall in Town X?

Annual Rainfall

Town	Rainfall (cm)
V	52.5
W	28.8
X	x
Y	46.6
Z	30.5

7. Find the range of the data set $6\frac{7}{9}$, $9\frac{8}{9}$, $5\frac{8}{9}$, $7\frac{4}{9}$, 13, $7\frac{5}{9}$, and $6\frac{2}{9}$.

8. Think About the Process
22, 27, x, 29, 26

a. Given the range, which formula can you use to find a missing value in a data set of positive values?

A. Range = maximum − minimum

B. Range = maximum + minimum

C. Range = minimum − maximum

b. If the range of this data set of positive values is 34, what is the missing value?

9. The data set shows the number of seconds it takes a race car to complete one lap of a race track.

Racing Times

29.70	38.81
36.21	29.92
31.14	35.72
38.82	33.25
34.16	36.58

a. Find the range of the data set in the table.

b. Describe the variability of the data.

A. The data set has no variability.

B. The date set has low variability.

C. The data set has high variability.

c. What is the mean time it takes the race car to complete one lap?

10. While learning to use thermometers, ten students heat water and record the temperature at the point when the water begins to boil.

Boiling Point of Water (°C)

Student 1: 99.39	Student 6: 99.16
Student 2: 99.65	Student 7: 104.33
Student 3: 98.81	Student 8: 100.67
Student 4: 100.67	Student 9: 99.65
Student 5: 99.59	Student 10: 99.59

a. Which data value is relatively far from the other values?

b. If this stray value is removed from the data set, how is the range affected?

A. The range of the data increases from ■ to ■.

B. The range of the data decreases from ■ to ■.

C. The range does not change.

11. **Think About the Process**

155, 121, 110, 56, 149, 173, 104, 110, 155, 131

a. When a stray data value is removed from a data set, how does the range change?

A. The range always decreases.

B. The range either increases or decreases.

C. The range always increases.

D. The range does not change.

b. What is the range of the given data set?

c. What is the stray value?

d. What is the range of the data set after the stray value is removed?

12. **a.** **Challenge** The range of the data set 130, x, 168, 192, 138, 114, and 176 is 90. What is the range of the known values?

b. Which two values could be the missing value?

A. 102

B. −102

C. 114

D. 204

16-4 Interquartile Range

Vocabulary
first quartile,
interquartile range,
third quartile

CCSS: 6.SP.A.3, 6.SP.B.5, 6.SP.B.5c

Part 1

Intro

A box plot can be described by different parts.

The minimum is the least value in the data set.

Points Scored Per Football Game
6, 17, 18, 21, 23, 29, 30, 32, 35, 37, 39

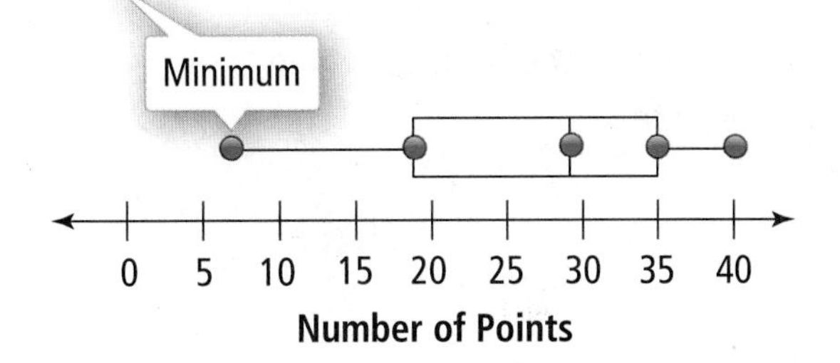

The first quartile is the median of the values in the lower half of the data set.

Points Scored Per Football Game
6, 17, **18**, 21, 23, 29, 30, 32, 35, 37, 39

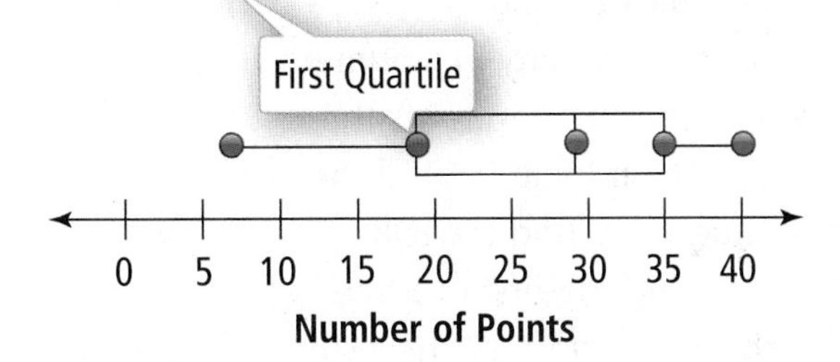

The median is the middle of the data set.

Points Scored Per Football Game
6, 17, 18, 21, 23, **29**, 30, 32, 35, 37, 39

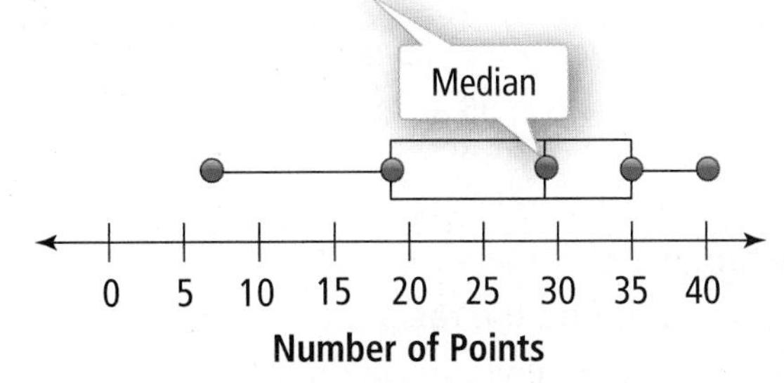

continued on next page >

Part 1

Intro continued

The third quartile is the median of the values in the upper half of the data set.

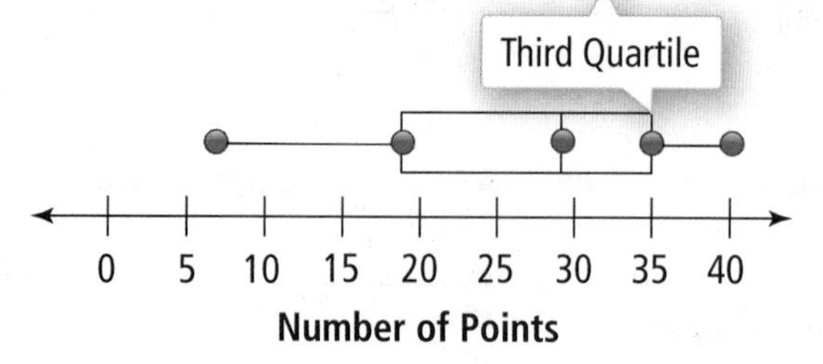

The maximum is the greatest value in the data set.

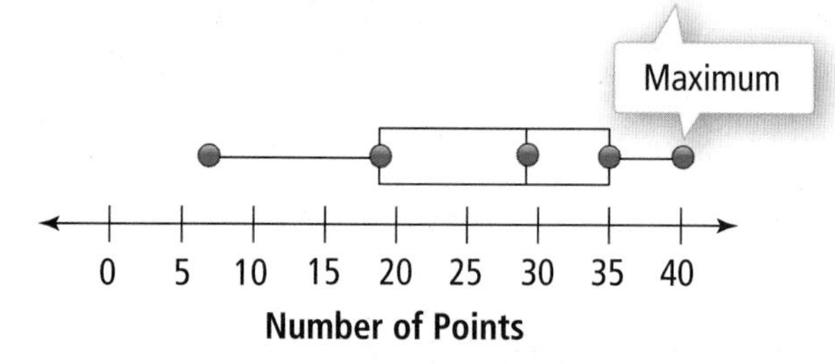

The interquartile range (IQR) is a measure of variability in a numerical data set. The IQR represents the spread of the middle 50% of the data values. You find the IQR by subtracting the first quartile from the third quartile. The lesser the interquartile range, the more consistent or close the values in the data set are to the median.

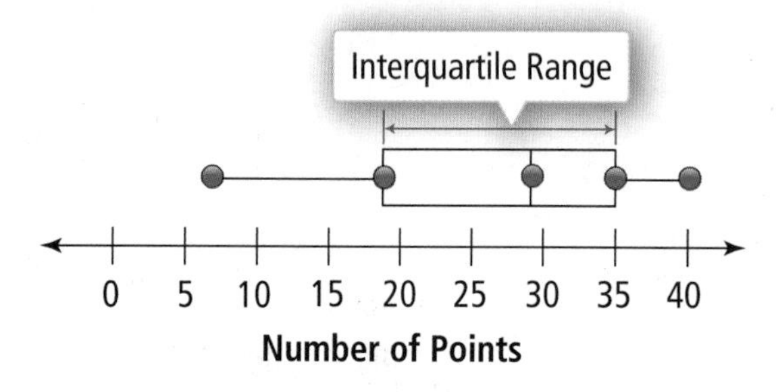

Interquartile Range = Third Quartile − First Quartile
= 35 − 18
= 17

The range is the span of the entire data set. You find the range by subtracting the minimum value from the maximum value.

Range = Maximum − Minimum
= 39 − 6
= 33

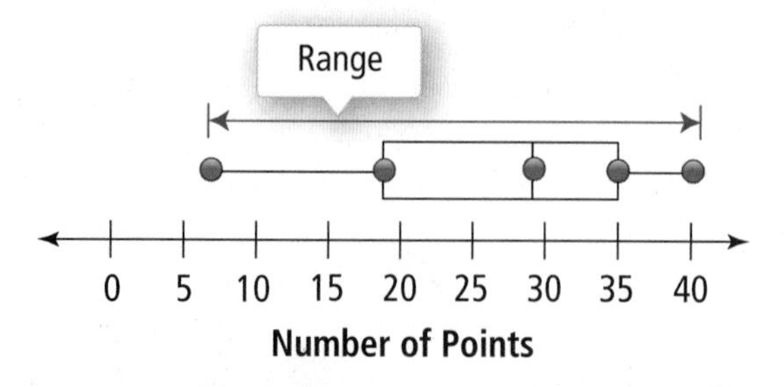

Part 1

Example Understanding Interquartile Range

Does the data set have an interquartile range of 16?

a. 

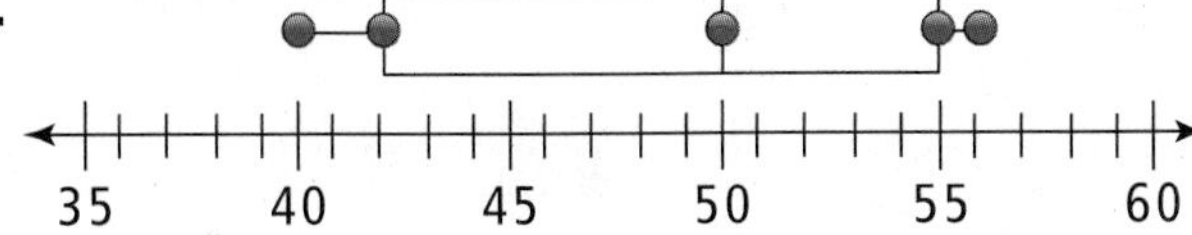

b.

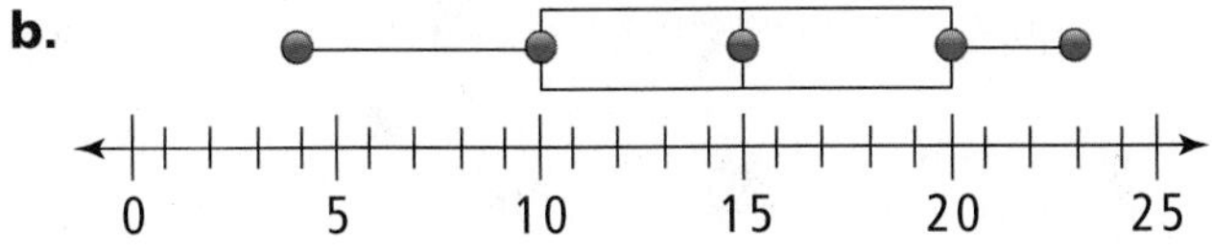

c.

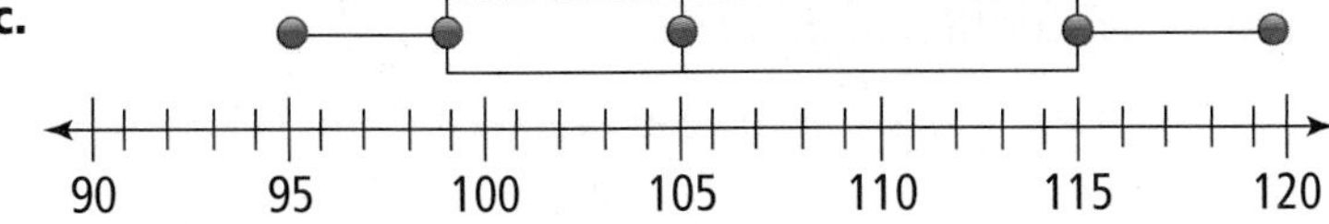

Solution

a.

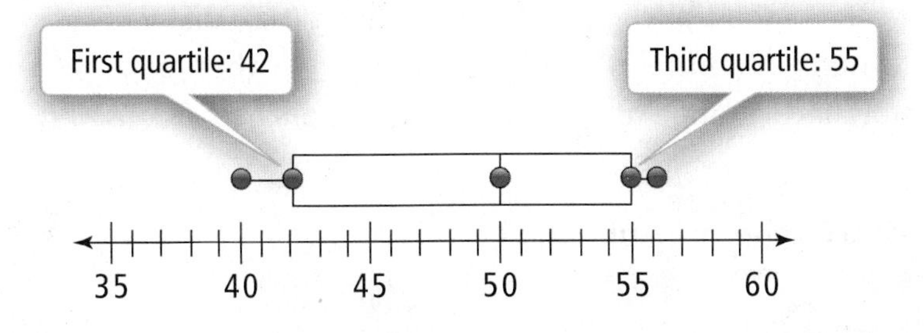

$$\begin{aligned} \text{IQR} &= \text{Third quartile} - \text{First quartile} \\ &= 55 - 42 \\ &= 13 \end{aligned}$$

This data set has an interquartile range of 13, not 16.

b.

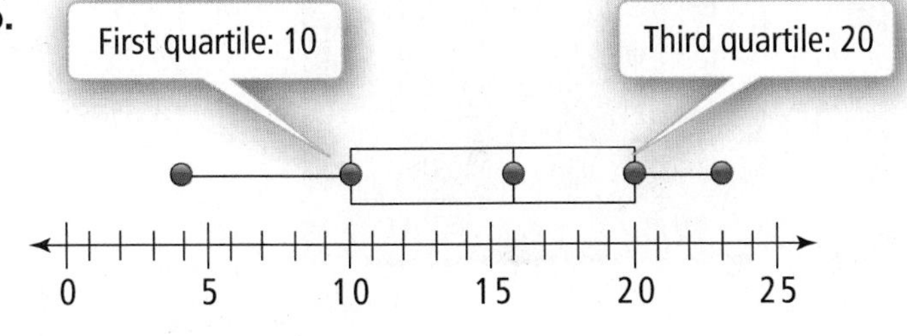

$$\begin{aligned} \text{IQR} &= 20 - 10 \\ &= 10 \end{aligned}$$

This data set has an interquartile range of 10, not 16.

continued on next page >

Part 1

Solution continued

c.

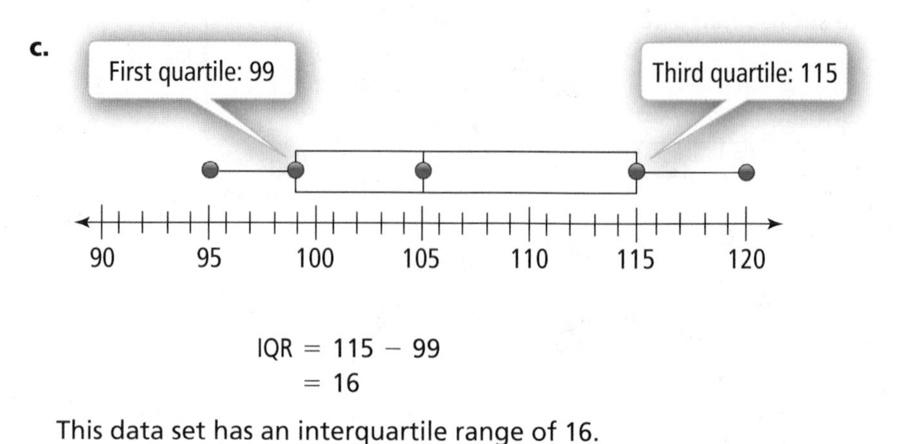

$$IQR = 115 - 99$$
$$= 16$$

This data set has an interquartile range of 16.

Part 2

Example Finding Interquartile Ranges

The data set shows the highest pitches, measured in hertz (Hz), that various animals can hear. Find the interquartile range of the set of highest pitches. What does the interquartile range tell about the highest pitches various animals can hear?

Hearing Ranges of Animals

Animal	Highest Pitch (Hz)
bat	110,000
beluga whale	123,000
bullfrog	3,000
canary	8,000
cat	64,000
chicken	2,000
cow	35,000
dog	45,000
elephant	12,000
goldfish	3,000

Animal	Highest Pitch (Hz)
horse	33,500
human	23,000
mouse	91,000
opossum	64,000
owl	12,000
parakeet	8,500
porpoise	150,000
rabbit	42,000
racoon	40,000
rat	76,000

continued on next page >

Part 2

Example continued

Solution

Put the data in numerical order. Find the median of the data set.

Animal	Highest Pitch (Hz)
chicken	2,000
bullfrog	3,000
goldfish	3,000
canary	8,000
parakeet	8,500
elephant	12,000
owl	12,000

Animal	Highest Pitch (Hz)
human	23,000
horse	33,500
cow	35,000
raccoon	40,000
rabbit	42,000
dog	45,000
cat	64,000

Animal	Highest Pitch (Hz)
opossum	64,000
rat	76,000
mouse	91,000
bat	110,000
beluga whale	123,000
porpoise	150,000

Median

$\frac{35{,}000 + 40{,}000}{2}$

$\frac{75{,}000}{2}$

37,500

Look at the lower half of the data to find the first quartile.

Animal	Highest Pitch (Hz)
chicken	2,000
bullfrog	3,000
goldfish	3,000
canary	8,000
parakeet	8,500
elephant	12,000
owl	12,000

Animal	Highest Pitch (Hz)
human	23,000
horse	33,500
cow	35,000
raccoon	40,000
rabbit	42,000
dog	45,000
cat	64,000

Animal	Highest Pitch (Hz)
opossum	64,000
rat	76,000
mouse	91,000
bat	110,000
beluga whale	123,000
porpoise	150,000

First quartile

$\frac{8{,}500 + 12{,}000}{2}$

$\frac{20{,}500}{2}$

10,250

continued on next page >

Part 2

Solution continued

Look at the upper half of the data to find the third quartile.

Animal	Highest Pitch (Hz)
chicken	2,000
bullfrog	3,000
goldfish	3,000
canary	8,000
parakeet	8,500
elephant	12,000
owl	12,000

Animal	Highest Pitch (Hz)
human	23,000
horse	33,500
cow	35,000
raccoon	40,000
rabbit	42,000
dog	45,000
cat	64,000

Animal	Highest Pitch (Hz)
opossum	64,000
rat	76,000
mouse	91,000
bat	110,000
beluga whale	123,000
porpoise	150,000

Third quartile

$\frac{64{,}000 + 76{,}000}{2}$

$\frac{140{,}000}{2}$

70,000

Use the formula for the interquartile range.

Animal	Highest Pitch (Hz)
chicken	2,000
bullfrog	3,000
goldfish	3,000
canary	8,000
parakeet	8,500
elephant	12,000
owl	12,000

Animal	Highest Pitch (Hz)
human	23,000
horse	33,500
cow	35,000
raccoon	40,000
rabbit	42,000
dog	45,000
cat	64,000

Animal	Highest Pitch (Hz)
opossum	64,000
rat	76,000
mouse	91,000
bat	110,000
beluga whale	123,000
porpoise	150,000

Interquartile range

Third − First

70,000 − 10,250

59,750

continued on next page >

Part 2

Solution continued

This means that the highest pitches heard by the middle 50% of the animals are within 59,750 hertz of each other.

Animal	Highest Pitch (Hz)
chicken	2,000
bullfrog	3,000
goldfish	3,000
canary	8,000
parakeet	8,500
elephant	12,000
owl	12,000
human	23,000
horse	33,500
cow	35,000
raccoon	40,000
rabbit	42,000
dog	45,000
cat	64,000
opossum	64,000
rat	76,000
mouse	91,000
bat	110,000
beluga whale	123,000
porpoise	150,000

Median
37,500

First quartile
10,250

Third quartile
70,000

Interquartile range
59,750

Part 3

Example Determining Characteristics of Data Sets

The data set shows the maximum lifespan of various animals. Determine whether each statement is *true* or *false*.

a. The median lifespan is 12.5 years.
b. The first quartile is 52.
c. The third quartile is 65.
d. The interquartile range is 44.

Maximum Lifespan

Animal	Years
Cat	30
Dog	24
Dolphin	52
Elephant	65
Gorilla	21
Mouse	4
Rabbit	9
Tiger	26
Turtle	138
Whale	211

Solution

First, order the data set. The table to the right shows the ordered data.

Maximum Lifespan

Animal	Years
Mouse	4
Rabbit	9
Gorilla	21
Dog	24
Tiger	26
Cat	30
Dolphin	52
Elephant	65
Turtle	138
Whale	211

a. Since there are an even number of data points, the median lifespan is the average of the middle two animals' lifespans.

$$\text{Median} = \frac{\text{Tiger} + \text{Cat}}{2} = \frac{26 + 30}{2} = 28$$

The median lifespan is 28 years, not 12.5 years, so the statement is false.

b. The first quartile is the middle of the lower half of the data. In this case the first quartile is 21, not 52, so the statement is false.

c. The third quartile is the middle of the upper half of the data. In this case the third quartile is 65, so the statement is true.

d. The interquartile range is the difference of the third quartile and the first quartile.

$$\text{Interquartile range} = 65 - 21 = 44$$

The interquartile range is 44, so the statement is true.

Digital Resources   

1. Use the box plot to find the interquartile range.

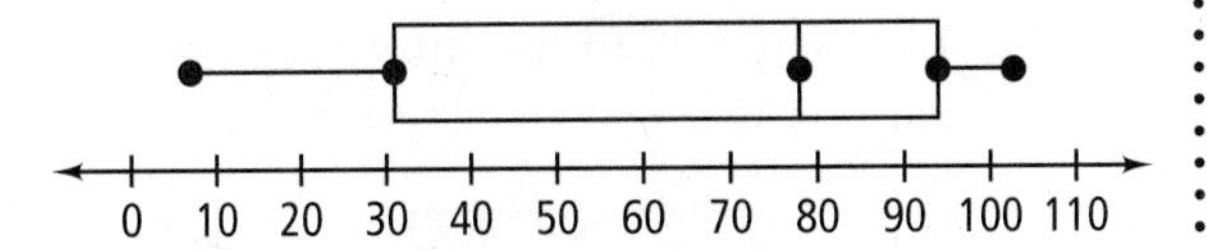

2. **Think About the Process**
   a. What is the first step to find the interquartile range of the given data set?

      50 18 35 70 37 41 47 69 9 27

      A. Find the mean of the data set.
      B. Find the maximum of the data set.
      C. Order the data set from least to greatest.
      D. Find the sum of the values in the data set.

   b. Find the interquartile range of the given data set.

3. a. Find the interquartile range for each data set in **Figure 1**.
   b. Which set of data values is more consistent?
      A. Data Set Z is more consistent.
      B. Data Set Y and Data Set Z are equally consistent.
      C. Data Set Y is more consistent.

4. The **Figure 2** contains data on the cost of attending a play at 10 different theaters in the United States.
   a. Find the interquartile range for this data set.
   b. Explain what the interquartile range represents for this data set.
      A. The top 50% of prices range from $25 to $43.
      B. The top 25% of prices range from $25 to $39.
      C. The bottom 50% of prices range from $43 to $65.
      D. The middle 50% of prices range from $39 to $57.

5. You collect a data set of the heights of the students in your mathematics class. What does it mean if the interquartile range is 2 inches?
   A. The data set has a lot of variability.
   B. The data set does not have any variability.
   C. The data set has very little variability.

6. Given the five boundary values of a data set, find the interquartile range (IQR).

   Minimum = 20
   First quartile = 60
   Median = 104
   Third quartile = 118
   Maximum = 128

(Figure 1)

Data Set Y	24	29	49	50	54	55	57	63	64	68
Data Set Z	12	13	14	22	24	26	28	33	36	38

(Figure 2)

Cost of Attending a Play										
Theater	Q	R	S	T	U	V	W	X	Y	Z
Cost ($)	57	64	43	40	25	52	65	43	37	39

See your complete lesson at MyMathUniverse.com

7. Error Analysis A student was asked to use the five boundary values (Minimum = 14, First quartile = 56, Median = 69, Third quartile = 109, and Maximum = 207) to find the interquartile range (IQR). He incorrectly said the IQR is 193.

a. Find the correct IQR.

b. What mistake might he have made?

A. He found the sum of the first and third quartiles of the data set instead of the difference.

B. He found the difference between the maximum and minimum values instead of the first and third quartiles of the data set.

C. He found the sum of the maximum and minimum values instead of the first and third quartiles of the data set.

D. He found the sum of the maximum and minimum values instead of the difference.

8. Figure 3 shows the home team's score from ten basketball games throughout a season.

a. Find the interquartile range (IQR) of the set.

b. How do the middle 50% of the scores vary?

A. The middle 50% of the scores vary from 41 to 64.

B. The middle 50% of the scores vary from 55 to 66.

C. The middle 50% of the scores vary from 23 to 53.

D. The middle 50% of the scores vary from 23 to 66.

9. a. Challenge Find the interquartile range (IQR) of the data set.

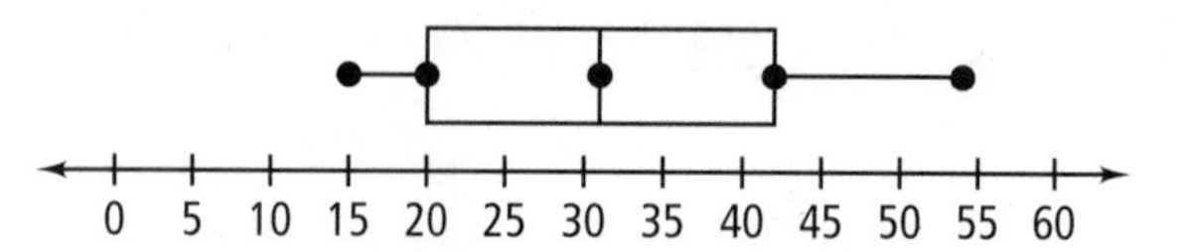

b. Create a set of values for this data set.

10. Think About the Process The data sets in **Figure 4** represent times (in minutes) for Yara and Andrea at nine different 2-mile races.

a. How can you decide who is a more consistent runner?

A. Compare the mean of their race times.

B. Compare the third quartile of their race times.

C. Compare the interquartile range of their race times.

D. Compare the first quartile of their race times.

E. Compare the median of their race times.

b. Which person is a more consistent runner?

A. Yara is a more consistent runner.

B. Andrea is a more consistent runner.

C. Yara and Andrea are equally consistent runners.

(Figure 3)

Basketball Scores

Game	1	2	3	4	5	6	7	8	9	10
Score	65	23	42	53	57	41	66	24	55	64

(Figure 4)

Yara	13.9	13.6	12.2	14.3	12.8	13.8	13.3	14.4	11.8
Andrea	12.7	11.4	10.7	12.8	13.5	10.6	11.1	13.3	12.5

16-5 Mean Absolute Deviation

Vocabulary
absolute deviation from the mean, deviation from the mean, mean absolute deviation

CCSS: 6.SP.B.5, 6.SP.B.5c, Also 6.SP.A.3

Part 1

Intro

Weights of Cats in a Local Shelter (lb): 9, 7, 11, 8, 13, 10, 8, 11, 13

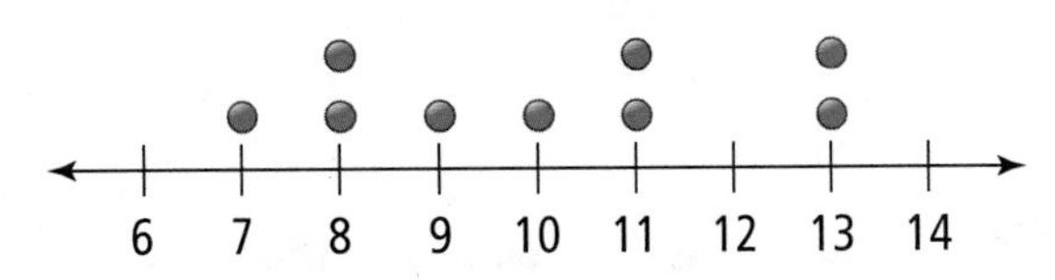

The mean represents the center of the data set. The mean is used as a reference point to measure how much each data value in the data set deviates, or strays, from it.

To calculate the mean, divide the sum of the data values by the number of data values.

$$\text{mean} = \frac{90}{9}$$
$$= 10$$

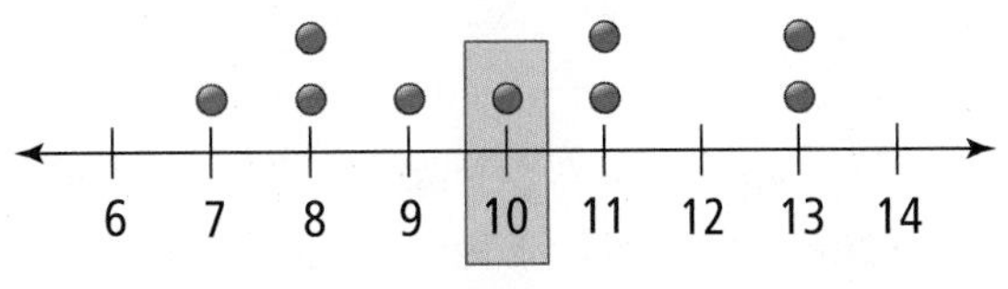

The **deviation of a data value from the mean** measures how far away and in which direction the data value is from the mean. Data values that are less than the mean have a negative deviation. Data values that are greater than the mean have a positive deviation.

To find the deviation of a data value from the mean, count how far the data value is from the mean.

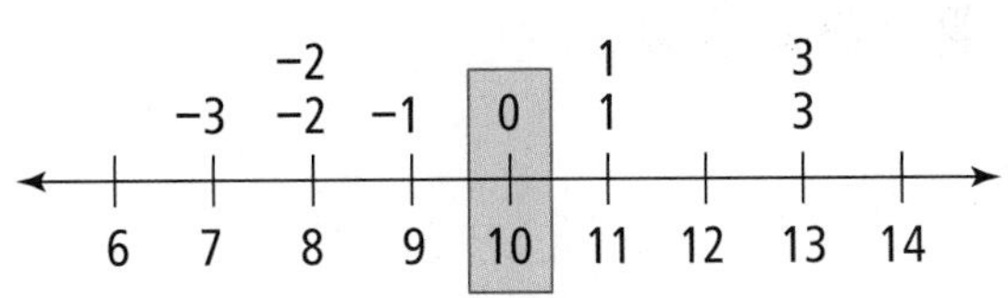

Part 1

Example Finding Deviations from the Mean

You are starting a dog walking business. The dot plot shows how many dogs you walked per day for 12 days. The mean is 2. Find the deviation for each data value from the mean.

Dogs Walked Per Day, With Deviations

0 1 2 3 4 5 6

Number of Dogs

Solution

The mean of the data set is 2. The data values of 2 are equal to the mean, so their deviation is 0. The data values of 1 deviate from the mean by 1 in the negative direction, so the deviation of these data values is −1.

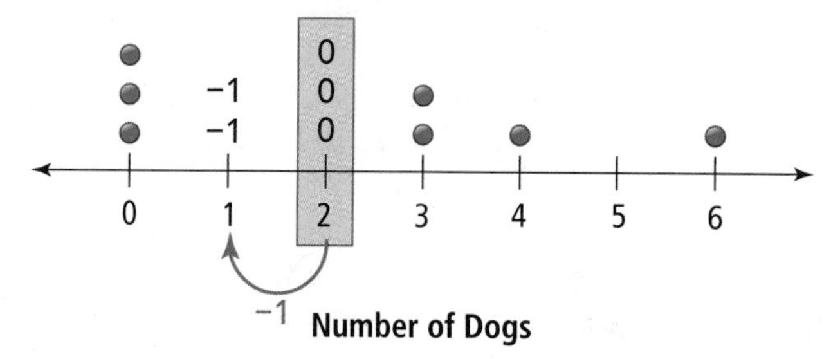

The data values of 0 deviate from the mean by 2 in the negative direction, so the deviation of these data values is −2.

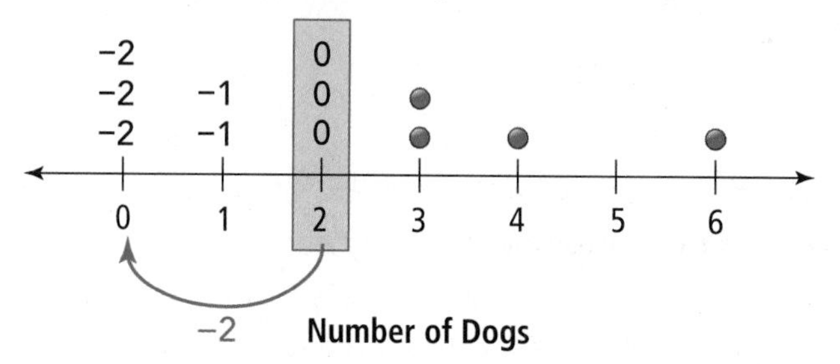

The data values of 3 deviate from the mean by 1 in the positive direction, so the deviation of these data values is 1.

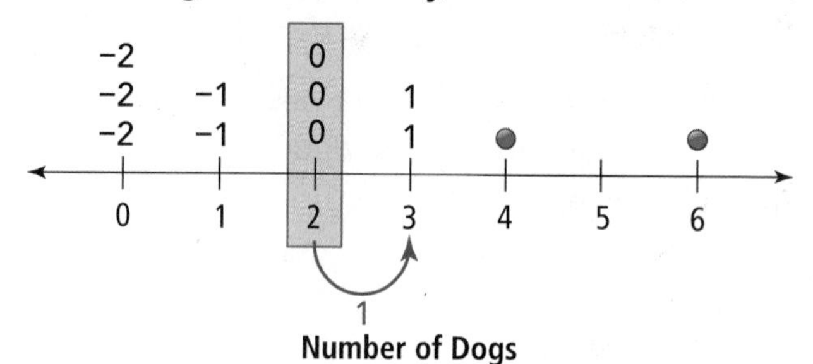

continued on next page >

Part 1

Solution continued

The deviation of the data value at 4 is 2 in the positive direction, so the deviation of this data value is 2.

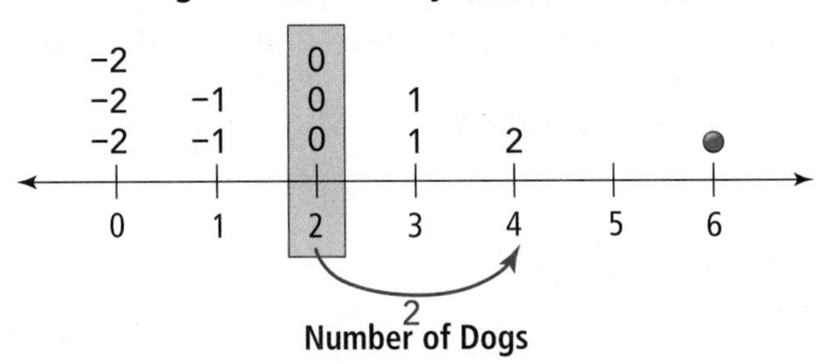

The deviation of the data value at 6 is 4 in the positive direction, so the deviation of this data value is 4.

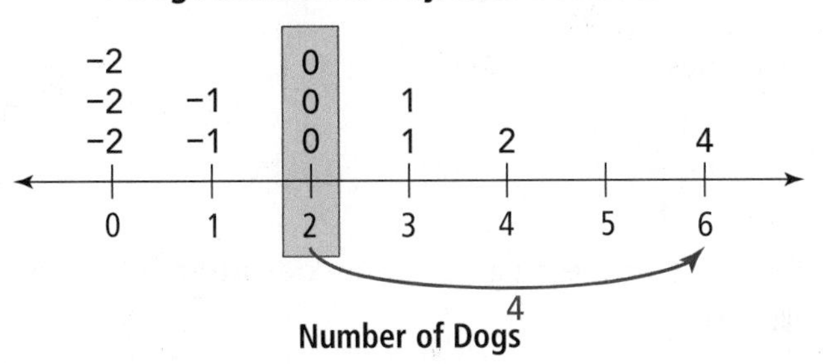

Part 2

Intro

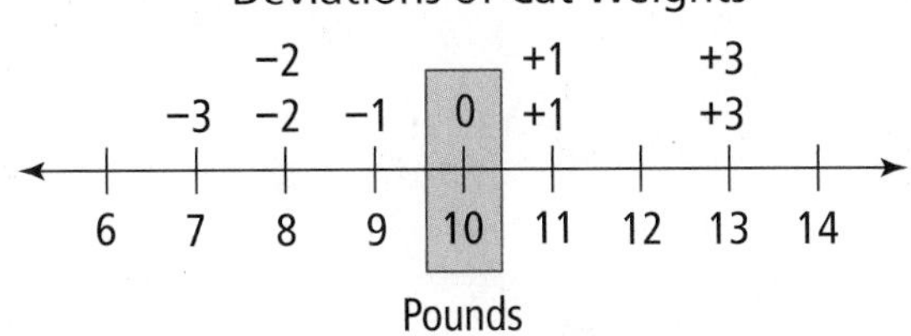

The **absolute deviation of a data value from the mean** is the distance that the data value is away from the mean of the data set. Because it is a distance, absolute deviation cannot be negative.

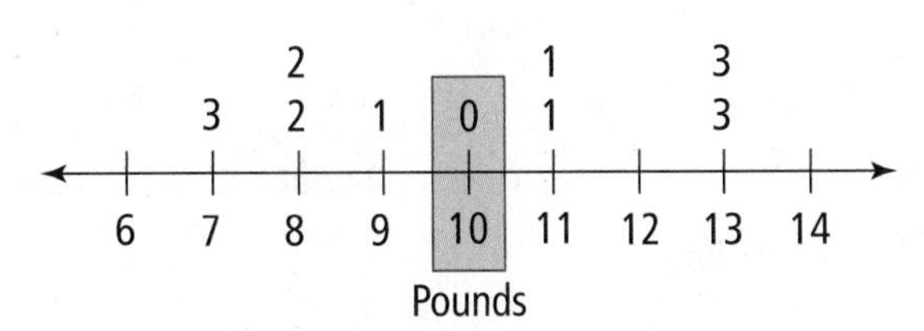

To find the absolute deviation of a data value from the mean, take the absolute value of the deviation of the data value from the mean.

$$\text{absolute deviation} = |\text{deviation}|$$

The **mean absolute deviation** is a measure of variability that describes how much the data values are spread out from the mean of a data set. The mean absolute deviation is the average distance that the data values are spread around the mean.

continued on next page >

Part 2

Intro continued

To find the mean absolute deviation, find the sum of the absolute deviations. Then divide by the number of data values.

Sum of the absolute deviations:

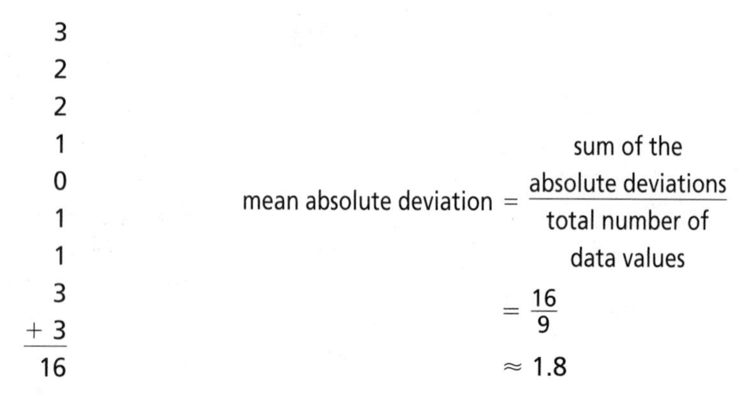

The greater the mean absolute deviation, the higher the variability in the data set.

The mean absolute deviation is 1.8, which means that the average distance the data values are spread around the mean is 1.8 units away from the mean.

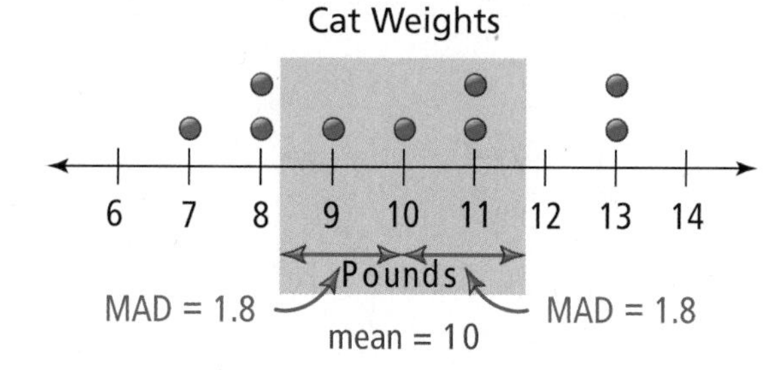

Example Finding Mean Absolute Deviations

You are starting a dog-walking business. The dot plot shows the deviations of the data values from the mean. Find the absolute deviation of each data value from the mean. Then find the mean absolute deviation of the data set.

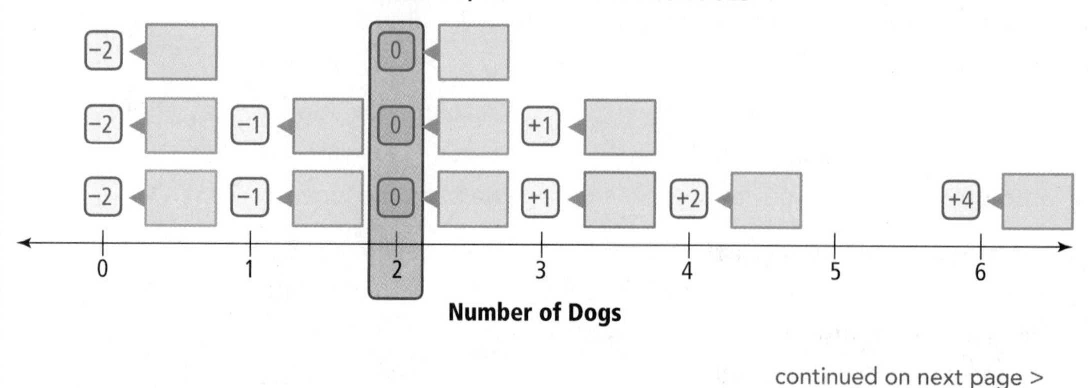

continued on next page >

Part 2

Example continued

Solution

Step 1 To find the absolute deviations from the mean, take the absolute value of the deviation of each data value.

Deviations, With Absolute Deviations

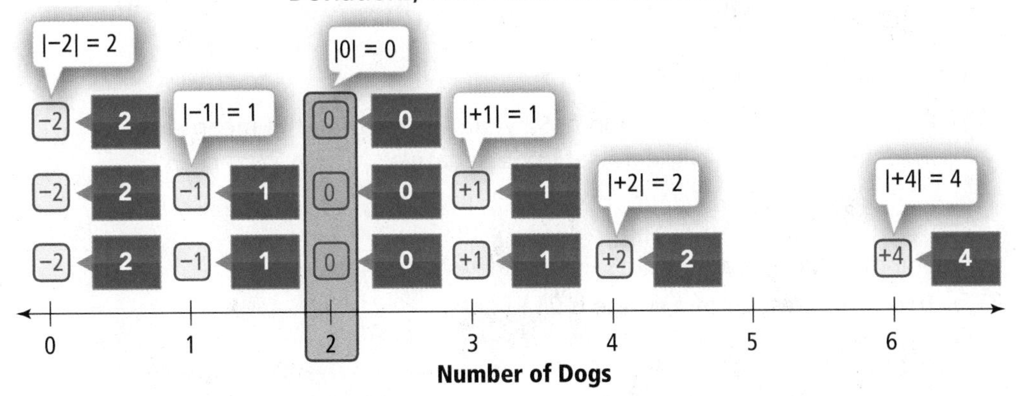

Step 2 Find the mean absolute deviation.

$$\text{mean absolute deviation} = \frac{\text{sum of the absolute deviations}}{\text{total number of data values}}$$

$$= \frac{2 + 2 + 2 + 1 + 1 + 0 + 0 + 0 + 1 + 1 + 2 + 4}{12}$$

$$= \frac{16}{12}$$

$$\approx 1.33$$

The mean absolute deviation of this data set is about 1.33.

Part 3

Example Analyzing Deviations of Data Sets

The table shows the maximum lifespan of various animals. The mean absolute deviation is 48. Determine whether each statement is *true* or *false*.

a. The mean lifespan is 58 years.

b. The deviation of a dolphin's lifespan from the mean is +6.

c. The absolute deviation of a whale's lifespan from the mean is greater than the absolute deviation of a mouse's lifespan from the mean.

d. A cat's lifespan deviates from the mean more than average.

Maximum Lifespan

Animal	Years
Cat	30
Dog	24
Dolphin	52
Elephant	65
Gorilla	21
Mouse	4
Rabbit	9
Tiger	26
Turtle	138
Whale	211

continued on next page >

Part 3

Example continued

Solution

a. True.

$$\text{mean lifespan} = \frac{30 + 24 + 52 + 65 + 21 + 4 + 9 + 26 + 138 + 211}{10}$$
$$= \frac{580}{10}$$
$$= 58$$

b. False. The lifespan of a dolphin, 52 years, is less than the mean lifespan, 58 years, so the deviation is negative.

$52 - 58 = -6$

The deviation of a dolphin's lifespan from the mean is -6.

c. True. The lifespan of a whale is 211 years.

$|211 - 58| = 153$

So the absolute deviation of a whale's lifespan from the mean is 153.

The lifespan of a mouse is 4 years.

$$|4 - 58| = |-54|$$
$$= 54$$

So the absolute deviation of a mouse's lifespan from the mean is 54. The absolute deviation of a whale's lifespan from the mean is greater than the absolute deviation of a mouse's lifespan from the mean.

d. False. The mean absolute deviation is 48. So a lifespan that has an average deviation from the mean is 48 years away from the mean, which is 58.

$58 - 48 = 10$

$58 + 48 = 106$

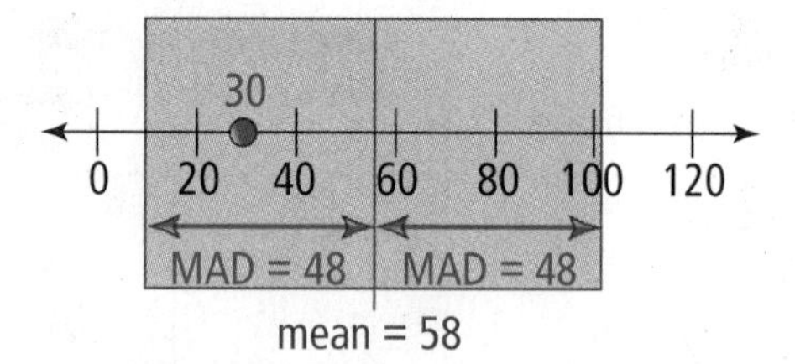

Since a cat has a lifespan of 30 years, its lifespan deviates from the mean less than average.

16-5 | Homework

Digital Resources   

1. The mean of the data set shown in the dot plot is 3. What is the deviation of 7?

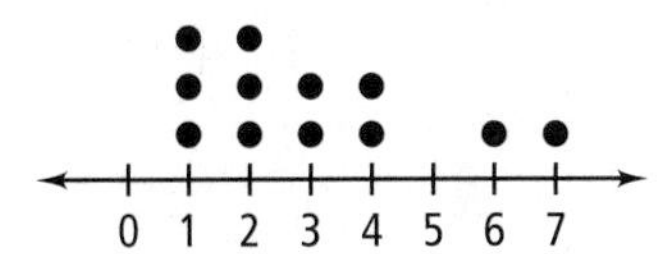

2. During the summer, Marissa walks dogs to earn extra money. The dot plot shows the number of dogs she walked per day for the last 11 days. The mean number of dogs walked is 2. Marissa plans to walk 5 dogs tomorrow. What is the deviation of 5?

Dogs Walked per Day

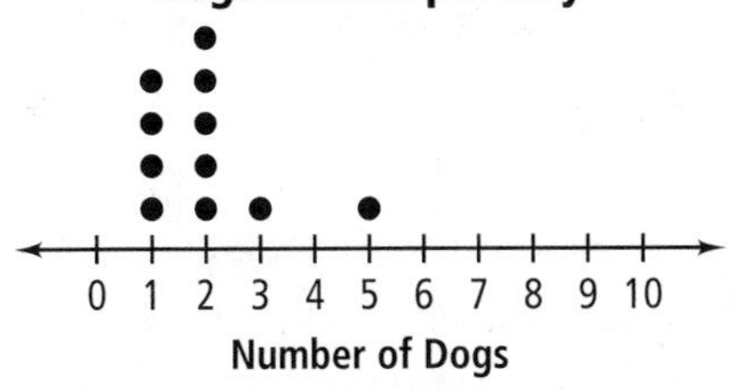

3. The mean of the data set is 3. Find the absolute deviation of 1.

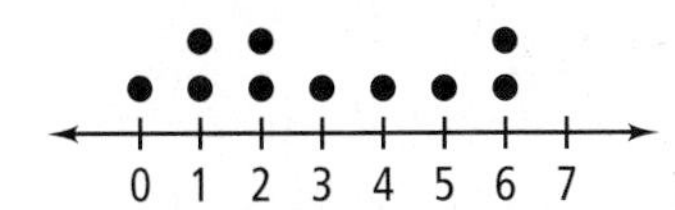

4. The mean of the data set is 3. Find the absolute deviation of each of the light gray data values.

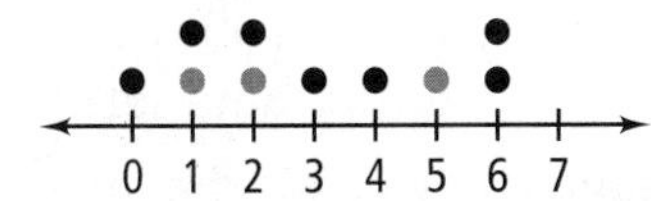

a. The absolute deviation of 1 is ■.

b. The absolute deviation of 2 is ■.

c. The absolute deviation of 5 is ■.

5. You measure the temperature on the first day of the month for six months. What is the mean absolute deviation of the temperatures?

First Day Temperatures

Month	Temperature (°F)
January	6
February	12
March	21
April	18
May	21
June	30

6. The mean absolute deviation of this data set is about 12.4. Which value below deviates from the mean by more than most of the values?

4	50	44
32	10	22
27	38	16

7. The mean absolute deviation of the data set in the table is about 3.3. Does the value 9 deviate more or less than most values?

1	9	7	8
6	2	10	15

A. The data value 9 deviates less than most values.

B. The data value 9 deviates more than most values.

C. The deviation of the data value 9 is equal to the mean absolute deviation.

8. Reasoning The mean absolute deviation of the data set in the table is about 6.7.

4	28	25
19	7	13
16	22	10

a. Does the value 4 deviate more or less than most values?

b. Explain.

9. Your class creates a dot plot to show the number of books each student read over summer vacation. The mean number of books read by your class is 5. The star represents the number of books you read. What is the deviation of the number of books you read?

Summer Reading

1 2 3 4 5 6 7 8 9 10

Number of Books Read

10. Think About the Process This dot plot shows the number of glasses of water a group of people drink in one day.

Glasses of Water

1 2 3 4 5 6 7 8 9 10

Number of Glasses of Water

a. What is the first step to find the deviation of a data value?

A. Find the mean of the data set.

B. Count how far the data value is from the greatest data value.

C. Find the median of the data set.

D. Find the range of the data set.

b. If you drink 1 glass of water in one day, what is the deviation of the number of glasses of water you drink?

11. Mental Math The mean of a data set is 20. What is the deviation of 15?

12.

16	12	10	16
20	18	19	13
14	19	18	15
15	18	19	14

a. Find the mean of the data set shown above.

b. What is the absolute deviation of 10?

c. What is the absolute deviation of 15?

d. What is the absolute deviation of 19?

13. The data set shows the batting average of several baseball players.

Batting Averages

Player	Average
1	0.261
2	0.213
3	0.231
4	0.246
5	0.279

a. Find the mean absolute deviation of the data set.

b. Which players' batting average deviates from the mean more than most? Select all that apply.

A. Player 3 **B.** Player 2

C. Player 4 **D.** Player 1

E. Player 5

14. Think About the Process

36 32 46 49 40 37 33 47

a. What information do you need to find the mean absolute deviation of a given data set? Select all that apply.

A. The range of the data set

B. The median of the data set

C. The absolute deviation of each data value

D. The mean of the data set

b. What is the mean absolute deviation of this data set?

15. a. Challenge What is the mean of the data set shown in the dot plot?

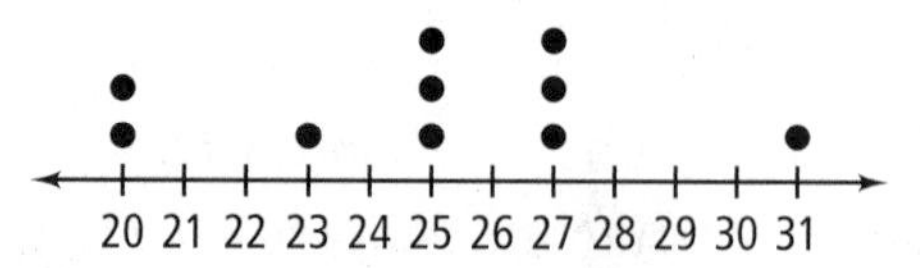

b. What is the deviation of 27?

c. What is the deviation of 23?

See your complete lesson at MyMathUniverse.com

16-6 Problem Solving

CCSS: 6.SP.B.5, 6.SP.B.5d, Also 6.SP.A.3

Part 1

Example Making Conclusions from Mean Absolute Deviations

You found the mean absolute deviation of the year-round temperatures in Anaheim, California to be 6°F, and the mean absolute deviation of the temperatures in Boston, Massachusetts to be 14°F. If you wanted to go to college in a place with low variability in temperatures, which city would you choose to live in? Why?

Solution

Sample answer: You might choose to live in Anaheim, California because the mean absolute deviation is only 6°F.

That means that the temperature in Anaheim changes by an average of 6°F from the mean temperature there.

Part 2

Example Making Conclusions from Medians

The student council is determining the winner of a two-classroom running race. The table shows the race times of the students of Classroom A and Classroom B. The student council wants to give the prize to the faster class. Compare the median of both classes to determine the winner.

Race Times (seconds)

Classroom A	12.7	13.0	13.3	13.4	14.0	14.1	15.2	15.4	15.4	15.5	15.8	17.2	18.3	20.0
Classroom B	13.2	13.5	13.8	13.9	13.9	14.1	14.2	14.7	15.6	15.9	16.4	17.9	18.1	18.3

continued on next page >

Part 2

Example continued

Solution

There are 14 data values for Classroom A, so the median is the average of the two middle values.

Race Times (seconds)

Classroom A	12.7	13.0	13.3	13.4	14.0	14.1	15.2	15.4	15.4	15.5	15.8	17.2	18.3	20.0

The median of Classroom A is 15.3.

$$\text{median} = \frac{15.2 + 15.4}{2} = \frac{30.6}{2} = 15.3$$

There are also 14 data values for Classroom B, so the median is the average of the two middle values.

Race Times (seconds)

Classroom B	13.2	13.5	13.8	13.9	13.9	14.1	14.2	14.7	15.6	15.9	16.4	17.9	18.1	18.3

The median of Classroom B is 14.45.

$$\text{median} = \frac{14.2 + 14.7}{2} = \frac{28.9}{2} = 14.45$$

The median race time of Classroom A is greater than the median race time of Classroom B, so Classroom A was slower. The winner is Classroom B.

Part 3

Example Making Conclusions from Ranges

The student council is determining the winner of a two-classroom running race. The table shows the race times of the students of Classroom A and Classroom B. The student council wants to give the prize to the class that is the most consistent. Compare the range of both classes to determine the winner.

Race Times (seconds)

Classroom A	12.7	13.0	13.3	13.4	14.0	14.1	15.2	15.4	15.4	15.5	15.8	17.2	18.3	20.0
Classroom B	13.2	13.5	13.8	13.9	13.9	14.1	14.2	14.7	15.6	15.9	16.4	17.9	18.1	18.3

Solution

Use the formula for the range for Classroom A.

Race Times (seconds)

Classroom A	12.7	13.0	13.3	13.4	14.0	14.1	15.2	15.4	15.4	15.5	15.8	17.2	18.3	20.0

$$\begin{aligned}\text{range} &= \text{maximum} - \text{minimum}\\ &= 20.0 - 12.7\\ &= 7.3\end{aligned}$$

The range of times for Classroom A is 7.3 s.

Use the formula for the range for Classroom B.

Race Times (seconds)

Classroom B	13.2	13.5	13.8	13.9	13.9	14.1	14.2	14.7	15.6	15.9	16.4	17.9	18.1	18.3

$$\begin{aligned}\text{range} &= \text{maximum} - \text{minimum}\\ &= 18.3 - 13.2\\ &= 5.1\end{aligned}$$

The range of times for Classroom B is 5.1 s.

The range of times for Classroom A is greater than the range of times for Classroom B, so the winner is Classroom B.

1. Hector found the mean absolute deviation of the year-round temperatures in State X to be 8°F, and the mean absolute deviation of the temperatures in State Y to be 14°F. If he wanted to go to college in a place with low variability in temperatures, which state should he choose and why?

2. Jim works as a waitperson on the weekend. The table shows the tips he received in dollars over one weekend. He wants to know whether he received better tips on Friday night or Saturday night. Compare the mean tip of both nights to find the answer.

Tips ($)										
Friday	7	6	8	4	6	5	8	4	5	4
Saturday	11	11	3	11	5	11	7	4	6	5

3. The student council is deciding on the winner of a two-classroom running race. The given table shows the race times of the students of Classroom X and Classroom Y. The student council wants to give the prize to the class that is more consistent. Compare the range of times of both classes to choose the winner. **(Figure 1)**

4. Peggy polled her class to find out how many siblings and pets each student has. Is there a lower variability in number of siblings or pets? Why?

Absolute Deviation of Number of Siblings and Pets										
Siblings	0	2	0	4	1	0	1	0	0	2
Pets	1	1	1	1	0	1	0	2	3	2

5. You recorded the humidity level in two cities over ten days. Which city has a lower variability in humidity level over these ten days? Why? **(Figure 2)**

6. You went to a baseball game to see your favorite player pitch. You recorded the speed of his fastballs during the first two innings. The table shows the fastball speeds in miles per hour. Compare the range of speed for each inning to decide which was more consistent. **(Figure 3)**

(Figure 1)

Race Times (s)										
Classroom X	27.4	28.6	29.4	29.4	30.2	31.3	31.9	32.0	32.1	33.5
Classroom Y	26.1	26.2	26.4	27.2	28.3	28.6	28.8	29.1	29.1	29.4

(Figure 2)

Humidity Levels (%)										
City X	28	48	61	23	35	55	40	55	50	62
City Y	35	27	23	34	25	24	31	25	36	26

(Figure 3)

Fastball Speeds (mi/hr)												
Inning 1	91.7	95.8	97.6	91.1	91.7	90.2	95.4	90.3	94.7	97.7	97.6	91.6
Inning 2	93.8	92.2	90.9	94.9	94.6	92.3	92.3	93.6	92.2	92.8	93.0	■

7. Think About the Process The student council is deciding the winner of a two-classroom running race. The given table shows the race times of the students of Classroom *X* and Classroom *Y*. The student council wants to give the prize to the faster class. **(Figure 4)**

a. How can the student council use the medians to find the winner?

A. In a race, the winning time is the shorter time, so the winner is the classroom with the lesser median race time.

B. In a race, the winning time is the longer time, so the winner is the classroom with the lesser median race time.

C. In a race, the winning time is the shorter time, so the winner is the classroom with the greater median race time.

D. In a race, the winning time is the longer time, so the winner is the classroom with the greater median race time.

b. Compare the medians of both classes to find the winner. What number is needed to complete your choice?

A. Classroom *Y* is the winner because its median race time, ■ s, is less than the median race time for Classroom *X*, ■ s.

B. Classroom *X* is the winner because its median race time, ■ s, is less than the median race time for Classroom *Y*, ■ s.

C. Classroom *Y* is the winner because its median race time, ■ s, is greater than the median race time for Classroom *X*, ■ s.

D. Classroom *X* is the winner because its median race time, ■ s, is greater than the median race time for Classroom *Y*, ■ s.

8. Think About the Process Your teacher Ms. Ortiz gives the same biology midterm to two different classes. The table shows the scores for each class. Use interquartile range to compare the consistency of the two classes. **(Figure 5)**

a. Which of these are steps in finding interquartile range? Select all that apply.

A. Order the data set from least to greatest.

B. Find the first quartile.

C. Find the maximum data value.

D. Find the median.

E. Find the minimum data value.

F. Find the third quartile.

b. Which class received more consistent scores? Explain your answer.

(Figure 4)

Race Times (s)										
Classroom *X*	13.7	14.8	14.8	14.9	14.9	15.4	16.0	16.1	16.2	16.4
Classroom *Y*	11.4	11.5	11.7	11.7	11.8	12.1	12.7	12.8	13.6	13.6

(Figure 5)

Test Scores													
Period 2	88	80	95	88	82	92	85	91	82	85	92	■	■
Period 5	85	80	76	83	82	91	90	86	80	82	77	93	91

English/Spanish Glossary

A

Absolute deviation from the mean Absolute deviation measures the distance that the data value is from the mean. You find the absolute deviation by taking the absolute value of the deviation of a data value. Absolute deviations are always nonnegative.

Desviación absoluta de la media La desviación absoluta mide la distancia a la que un valor se encuentra de la media. Para hallar la desviación absoluta, tomas el valor absoluto de la desviación de un valor. Las desviaciones absolutas siempre son no negativas.

Absolute value The absolute value of a number a is the distance between a and zero on a number line. The absolute value of a is written as $|a|$.

Valor absoluto El valor absoluto de un número a es la distancia entre a y cero en la recta numérica. El valor absoluto de a se escribe como $|a|$.

Accuracy The accuracy of an estimate or measurement is the degree to which it agrees with an accepted or actual value of that measurement.

Exactitud La exactitud de una estimación o medición es el grado de concordancia con un valor aceptado o real de esa medición.

Action In a probability situation, an action is a process with an uncertain result.

Acción En una situación de probabilidad, una acción es el proceso con un resultado incierto.

Acute angle An acute angle is an angle with a measure between 0° and 90°.

Ángulo agudo Un ángulo agudo es un ángulo que mide entre 0° y 90°.

Acute triangle An acute triangle is a triangle with three acute angles.

Triángulo acutángulo Un triángulo acutángulo es un triángulo que tiene tres ángulos agudos.

Addend Addends are the numbers that are added together to find a sum.

Sumando Los sumandos son los números que se suman para hallar un total.

English/Spanish Glossary

Additive inverses Two numbers that have a sum of 0.

Inversos de suma Dos números cuya suma es 0.

Adjacent angles Two angles are adjacent angles if they share a vertex and a side, but have no interior points in common.

Ángulos adyacentes Dos ángulos son adyacentes si tienen un vértice y un lado en común, pero no comparten puntos internos.

Algebraic expression An algebraic expression is a mathematical phrase that consists of variables, numbers, and operation symbols.

Expresión algebraica Una expresión algebraica es una frase matemática que consiste en variables, números y símbolos de operaciones.

Analyze To analyze is to think about and understand facts and details about a given set of information. Analyzing can involve providing a written summary supported by factual information, diagrams, charts, tables, or any combination of these.

Analizar Analizar es pensar en los datos y detalles de cierta información y comprenderlos. El análisis puede incluir la presentación de un resumen escrito sustentado por información objetiva, diagramas, tablas o una combinación de esos elementos.

Angle An angle is a figure formed by two rays with a common endpoint.

Ángulo Un ángulo es una figura formada por dos semirrectas que tienen un extremo en común.

Angle of rotation The angle of rotation is the number of degrees a figure is rotated.

Ángulo de rotación El ángulo de rotación es el número de grados que se rota una figura.

Annual salary The amount of money earned at a job in one year.

Salario annual La cantidad de dinero ganó en un trabajo en un año.

Area The area of a figure is the number of square units the figure encloses.

Área El área de una figura es el número de unidades cuadradas que ocupa.

English/Spanish Glossary

Area of a circle The formula for the area of a circle is $A = \pi r^2$, where A represents the area and r represents the radius of the circle.

Área de un círculo La fórmula del área de un círculo es $A = \pi r^2$, donde A representa el área y r representa el radio del círculo.

Area of a parallelogram The formula for the area of a parallelogram is $A = bh$, where A represents the area, b represents a base, and h is the corresponding height.

Área de un paralelogramo La fórmula del área de un paralelogramo es $A = bh$, donde A representa el área, b representa una base y h es la altura correspondiente.

Area of a rectangle The formula for the area of a rectangle is $A = bh$, where A represents the area, b represents the base, and h represents the height of the rectangle.

Área de un rectángulo La fórmula del área de un rectángulo es $A = bh$, donde A representa el área, b representa la base y h representa la altura del rectángulo.

Area of a square The formula for the area of a square is $A = s^2$, where A represents the area and s represents a side length.

Área de un cuadrado La fórmula del área de un cuadrado es $A = s^2$, donde A representa el área y l representa la longitud de un lado.

Area of a trapezoid The formula for the area of a trapezoid is $A = \frac{1}{2}h(b_1 + b_2)$, where A represents the area, b_1 and b_2 represent the bases, and h represents the height between the bases.

El área de un trapezoide La fórmula para el área de un trapezoide es $A = \frac{1}{2}h(b_1 + b_2)$, donde A representa el área, b_1 y b_2 representan las bases, y h representa la altura entre las bases.

Area of a triangle The formula for the area of a triangle is $A = \frac{1}{2}bh$, where A represents the area, b represents the length of a base, and h represents the corresponding height.

Área de un triángulo La fórmula del área de un triángulo es $A = \frac{1}{2}bh$, donde A representa el área, b representa la longitud de una base y h representa la altura correspondiente.

Asset An asset is money you have or property of value that you own.

Ventaja Una ventaja es dinero que tiene o la propiedad de valor que usted posee.

English/Spanish Glossary

Associative Property of Addition For any numbers *a*, *b*, and *c*: $(a + b) + c = a + (b + c)$

Propiedad asociativa de la suma Para los números cualesquiera *a*, *b* y *c*: $(a + b) + c = a + (b + c)$

Associative Property of Multiplication For any numbers *a*, *b*, and *c*: $(a \cdot b) \cdot c = a \cdot (b \cdot c)$

Propiedad asociativa de la multiplicación Para los números cualesquiera *a*, *b* y *c*: $(a \cdot b) \cdot c = a \cdot (b \cdot c)$

Average of two numbers The average of two numbers is the value that represents the middle of two numbers. It is found by adding the two numbers together and dividing by 2.

Promedio de dos números El promedio de dos números es el valor que está justo en el medio de esos dos números. Se halla sumando los dos números y dividiendo el resultado por 2.

B

Balance The balance in an account is the principal amount plus the interest earned.

Saldo El saldo de una cuenta es el capital más el interés ganado.

Balance of a checking account The balance of a checking account is the amount of money in the checking account.

El equilibrio de una Cuenta Corriente Bancaria El equilibrio de una cuenta corriente bancaria es la cantidad de dinero en la cuenta corriente bancaria.

Balance of a loan The balance of a loan is the remaining unpaid principal.

El equilibrio de un préstamo El equilibrio de un préstamo es el director impagado restante.

Bar diagram A bar diagram is a way to represent part to whole relationships.

Diagrama de barras Un diagrama de barras es una forma de representar una relación de parte a entero.

Base The base is the repeated factor of a number written in exponential form.

Base La base es el factor repetido de un número escrito en forma exponencial.

English/Spanish Glossary

Base area of a cone The base area of a cone is the area of a circle. Base Area $= \pi r^2$.

Área de la base de un cono El área de la base de un cono es el área de un círculo. El área de la base $= \pi r^2$.

Base of a cone The base of a cone is a circle with radius *r*.

Base de un cono La base de un cono es un círculo con radio *r*.

Base of a cylinder A base of a cylinder is one of a pair of parallel circular faces that are the same size.

Base de un cilindro Una base de un cilindro es una de dos caras circulares paralelas que tienen el mismo tamaño.

Base of a parallelogram A base of a parallelogram is any side of the parallelogram.

Base de un paralelogramo La base de un paralelogramo es cualquiera de los lados del paralelogramo.

Base of a prism A base of a prism is one of a pair of parallel polygonal faces that are the same size and shape. A prism is named for the shape of its bases.

Base de un prisma La base de un prisma es una de las dos caras poligonales paralelas que tienen el mismo tamaño y la misma forma. El nombre de un prisma depende de la forma de sus bases.

Base of a pyramid A base of a pyramid is a polygonal face that does not connect to the vertex.

Base de una pirámide La base de una pirámide es una cara poligonal que no se conecta con el vértice.

Base of a triangle The base of a triangle is any side of the triangle.

Base de un triángulo La base de un triángulo es cualquiera de los lados del triángulo.

Benchmark A benchmark is a number you can use as a reference point for other numbers.

Referencia Una referencia es un número que usted puede utilizar como un punto de referencia para otros números.

English/Spanish Glossary

Bias A bias is a tendency toward a particular perspective that is different from the overall perspective of the population.

Sesgo Un sesgo es una tendencia hacia una perspectiva particular que es diferente de la perspectiva general de la población.

Biased sample In a biased sample, the number of subjects in the sample with the trait that you are studying is not proportional to the number of members in the population with that trait. A biased sample does not accurately represent the population.

Muestra sesgada En una muestra sesgada, el número de sujetos de la muestra que tiene la característica que se está estudiando no es proporcional al número de miembros de la población que tienen esa característica. Una muestra sesgada no representa con exactitud la población.

Bivariate categorical data Bivariate categorical data pairs categorical data collected about two variables of the same population.

Datos bivariados por categorías Los datos bivariados por categorías agrupan pares de datos obtenidos acerca de dos variables de la misma población.

Bivariate data Bivariate data is comprised of pairs of linked observations about a population.

Datos bivariados Los datos bivariados se forman a partir de pares de observaciones relacionadas sobre una población.

Box plot A box plot is a statistical graph that shows the distribution of a data set by marking five boundary points where data occur along a number line. Unlike a dot plot or a histogram, a box plot does not show frequency.

Diagrama de cajas Un diagrama de cajas es un diagrama de estadísticas que muestra la distribución de un conjunto de datos al marcar cinco puntos de frontera donde se hallan los datos sobre una recta numérica. A diferencia del diagrama de puntos o el histograma, el diagrama de cajas no muestra la frecuencia.

Budget A budget is a plan for how you will spend your money.

Presupuesto Un presupuesto es un plan para cómo gastará su dinero.

C

Categorical data Categorical data consist of data that fall into categories.

Datos por categorías Los datos por categorías son datos que se pueden clasificar en categorías.

Center of a circle The center of a circle is the point inside the circle that is the same distance from all points on the circle. Name a circle by its center.

Centro de un círculo El centro de un círculo es el punto dentro del círculo que está a la misma distancia de todos los puntos del círculo. Un círculo se identifica por su centro.

Center of a regular polygon The center of a regular polygon is the point that is equidistant from its vertices.

Centro de un polígono regular El centro de un polígono regular es el punto equidistante de todos sus vértices.

Center of rotation The center of rotation is a fixed point about which a figure is rotated.

Centro de rotación El centro de rotación es el punto fijo alrededor del cual se rota una figura.

Check register A record that shows all of the transactions for a bank account, including withdrawals, deposits, and transfers. It also shows the balance of the account after each transaction.

Verifique registro Un registro que muestra todas las transacciones para una cuenta bancaria, inclusive retiradas, los depósitos, y las transferencias. También muestra el equilibrio de la cuenta después de cada transacción.

Circle A circle is the set of all points in a plane that are the same distance from a given point, called the center.

Círculo Un círculo es el conjunto de todos los puntos de un plano que están a la misma distancia de un punto dado, llamado centro.

Circle graph A circle graph is a graph that represents a whole divided into parts.

Gráfica circular Una gráfica circular es una gráfica que representa un todo dividido en partes.

English/Spanish Glossary

Circumference of a circle The circumference of a circle is the distance around the circle. The formula for the circumference of a circle is $C = \pi d$, where C represents the circumference and d represents the diameter of the circle.	**Circunferencia de un círculo** La circunferencia de un círculo es la distancia alrededor del círculo. La fórmula de la circunferencia de un círculo es $C = \pi d$, donde C representa la circunferencia y d representa el diámetro del círculo.
Cluster A cluster is a group of points that lie close together on a scatter plot.	**Grupo** Un grupo es un conjunto de puntos que están agrupados en un diagrama de dispersión.
Coefficient A coefficient is the number part of a term that contains a variable.	**Coeficiente** Un coeficiente es la parte numérica de un término que contiene una variable.
Common denominator A common denominator is a number that is the denominator of two or more fractions.	**Común denominador** Un común denominador es un número que es el denominador de dos o más fracciones.
Common multiple A common multiple is a multiple that two or more numbers share.	**Múltiplo común** Un múltiplo común es un múltiplo que comparten dos o más números.
Commutative Property of Addition For any numbers a and b: $a + b = b + a$	**Propiedad conmutativa de la suma** Para los números cualesquiera a y b: $a + b = b + a$
Commutative Property of Multiplication For any numbers a and b: $a \cdot b = b \cdot a$	**Propiedad conmutativa de la multiplicación** Para los números cualesquiera a y b: $a \cdot b = b \cdot a$
Comparative inference A comparative inference is an inference made by interpreting and comparing two sets of data.	**Inferencia comparativa** Una inferencia comparativa es una inferencia que se hace al interpretar y comparar dos conjuntos de datos.

English/Spanish Glossary

Compare To compare is to tell or show how two things are alike or different.

Comparar Comparar es describir o mostrar en qué se parecen o en qué se diferencian dos cosas.

Compatible numbers Compatible numbers are numbers that are easy to compute mentally.

Números compatibles Los números compatibles son números fáciles de calcular mentalmente.

Complementary angles Two angles are complementary angles if the sum of their measures is 90°. Complementary angles that are adjacent form a right angle.

Ángulos complementarios Dos ángulos son complementarios si la suma de sus medidas es 90°. Los ángulos complementarios que son adyacentes forman un ángulo recto.

Complex fraction A complex fraction is a fraction $\frac{A}{B}$ where A and/or B are fractions and B is not zero.

Fracción compleja Una fracción compleja es una fracción $\frac{A}{B}$ donde A y/o B son fracciones y B es distinto de cero.

Compose a shape To compose a shape, join two (or more) shapes so that there is no gap or overlap.

Componer una figura Para componer una figura, debes unir dos (o más) figuras de modo que entre ellas no queden espacios ni superposiciones.

Composite figure A composite figure is the combination of two or more figures into one object.

Figura compuesta Una figura compuesta es la combinación de dos o más figuras en un objeto.

Composite number A composite number is a whole number greater than 1 with more than two factors.

Número compuesto Un número compuesto es un número entero mayor que 1 con más de dos factores.

Compound event A compound event is an event associated with a multi-step action. A compound event is composed of events that are the outcomes of the steps of the action.

Evento compuesto Un evento compuesto es un evento que se relaciona con una acción de varios pasos. Un evento compuesto se compone de eventos que son los resultados de los pasos de una acción.

English/Spanish Glossary

Compound interest Compound interest is interest paid on both the principal and the interest earned in previous interest periods. To calculate compound interest, use the formula $B = p(1 + r)^n$, where B is the balance in the account, p is the principal, r is the annual interest rate, and n is the time in years that the account earns interest.

Interés compuesto El interés compuesto es el interés que se paga sobre el capital y el interés obtenido en períodos de interés anteriores. Para calcular el interés compuesto, usa la fórmula $B = c(1 + r)^n$ donde B es el saldo de la cuenta, c es el capital, r es la tasa de interés anual y n es el tiempo en años en que la cuenta obtiene un interés.

Cone A cone is a three-dimensional figure with one circular base and one vertex.

Cono Un cono es una figura tridimensional con una base circular y un vértice.

Congruent figures Two two-dimensional figures are congruent $\cong$ if the second can be obtained from the first by a sequence of rotations, reflections, and translations.

Figuras congruentes Dos figuras bidimensionales son congruentes $\cong$ si la segunda puede obtenerse a partir de la primera mediante una secuencia de rotaciones, reflexiones y traslaciones.

Conjecture A conjecture is a statement that you believe to be true but have not yet proved to be true.

Conjetura Una conjetura es un enunciado que crees que es verdadero, pero que todavía no has comprobado que sea verdadero.

Constant A constant is a term that only contains a number.

Constante Una constante es un término que solamente contiene un número.

Constant of proportionality In a proportional relationship, one quantity y is a constant multiple of the other quantity x. The constant multiple is called the constant of proportionality. The constant of proportionality is equal to the ratio $\frac{y}{x}$.

Constante de proporcionalidad En una relación proporcional, una cantidad y es un múltiplo constante de la otra cantidad x. El múltiplo constante se llama constante de proporcionalidad. La constante de proporcionalidad es igual a la razón $\frac{y}{x}$.

Construct To construct is to make something, such as an argument, by organizing ideas. Constructing an argument can involve a written response, equations, diagrams, charts, tables, or a combination of these.

Construir Construir es hacer o crear algo, como se construye un argumento al organizar ideas. Para construir un argumento puede usarse una respuesta escrita, ecuaciones, diagramas, tablas o una combinación de esos elementos.

Convenience sampling Convenience sampling is a sampling method in which a researcher chooses members of the population that are convenient and available. Many researchers use this sampling technique because it is fast and inexpensive. It does not require the researcher to keep track of everyone in the population.

Muestra de conveniencia Una muestra de conveniencia es un método de muestreo en el que un investigador escoge miembros de la población que están convenientemente disponibles. Muchos investigadores usan esta técnica de muestreo porque es rápida y no es costosa. No requiere que el investigador lleve un registro de cada miembro de la población.

Cost of attendance The cost of attendance of one year of college is the sum of all of your expenses during the year.

El costo de asistencia El costo de asistencia de un año del colegio es la suma de todos sus gastos durante el año.

Cost of credit The cost of credit for a loan is the difference between the total cost and the principal.

El costo de crédito El costo de crédito para un préstamo es la diferencia entre el coste total y el director.

Converse of the Pythagorean Theorem If the sum of the squares of the lengths of two sides of a triangle equals the square of the length of the third side, then the triangle is a right triangle. If $a^2 + b^2 = c^2$, then the triangle is a right triangle.

Expresión recíproca del Teorema de Pitágoras Si la suma del cuadrado de la longitud de dos lados de un triángulo es igual al cuadrado de la longitud del tercer lado, entonces el triángulo es un triángulo rectángulo. $a^2 + b^2 = c^2$, entonces el triángulo es un triángulo rectángulo.

Conversion factor A conversion factor is a rate that equals 1.

Factor de conversión Un factor de conversión es una tasa que es igual a 1.

English/Spanish Glossary

Coordinate plane A coordinate plane is formed by a horizontal number line called the *x*-axis and a vertical number line called the *y*-axis.

Plano de coordenadas Un plano de coordenadas está formado por una recta numérica horizontal llamada eje de las *x* y una recta numérica vertical llamada eje de las *y*.

Corresponding angles Corresponding angles lie on the same side of a transversal and in corresponding positions.

Ángulos correspondientes Los ángulos correspondientes se ubican al mismo lado de una secante y en posiciones correspondientes.

Counterexample A counterexample is a specific example that shows that a conjecture is false.

Contraejemplo Un contraejemplo es un ejemplo específico que muestra que una conjetura es falsa.

Counting Principle If there are m possible outcomes of one action and n possible outcomes of a second action, then there are $m \cdot n$ outcomes of the first action followed by the second action.

Principio de conteo Si hay m resultados posibles de una acción y n resultados posibles de una segunda acción, entonces hay $m \cdot n$ resultados de la primera acción seguida de la segunda acción.

Coupon A coupon is part of a printed or online advertisement entitling the holder to a discount at checkout.

Cupón Un cupón forma parte de un anuncio impreso o en línea que permite al poseedor a un descuento en comprueba.

Credit card A credit card is a card issued by a lender that can be used to borrow money or make purchases on credit.

Tarjeta de crédito Una tarjeta de crédito es una tarjeta publicada por un prestamista que puede ser utilizado para pedir dinero prestado o compras de marca a cuenta.

Credit history A credit history shows how a consumer has managed credit in the past.

Acredite la historia Una historia del crédito muestra cómo un consumidor ha manejado crédito en el pasado.

English/Spanish Glossary

Credit report A report that shows personal information about a consumer and details about the consumer's credit history.

Acredite reporte Un reporte que muestra información personal sobre un consumidor y detalles acerca de la historia del crédito del consumidor.

Critique A critique is a careful judgment in which you give your opinion about the good and bad parts of something, such as how a problem was solved.

Crítica Una crítica es una evaluación cuidadosa en la que das tu opinión acerca de las partes positivas y negativas de algo, como la manera en la que se resolvió un problema.

Cross section A cross section is the intersection of a three-dimensional figure and a plane.

Corte transversal Un corte transversal es la intersección de una figura tridimensional y un plano.

Cube A cube is a rectangular prism whose faces are all squares.

Cubo Un cubo es un prisma rectangular cuyas caras son todas cuadrados.

Cube root The cube root of a number, n, is a number whose cube equals n.

Raíz cúbica La raíz cúbica de un número, n, es un número que elevado al cubo es igual a n.

Cubic unit A cubic unit is the volume of a cube that measures 1 unit on each edge.

Unidad cúbica Una unidad cúbica es el volumen de un cubo en el que cada arista mide 1 unidad.

Cylinder A cylinder is a three-dimensional figure with two parallel circular bases that are the same size.

Cilindro Un cilindro es una figura tridimensional con dos bases circulares paralelas que tienen el mismo tamaño.

D

Data Data are pieces of information collected by asking questions, measuring, or making observations about the real world.

Datos Los datos son información reunida mediante preguntas, mediciones u observaciones sobre la vida diaria.

English/Spanish Glossary

Debit card A debit card is a card issued by a bank that is linked a customer's bank account, normally a checking account. A debit card can normally be used to withdraw money from an ATM or to make a purchase.

Tarjeta de débito Una tarjeta de débito es una tarjeta publicada por un banco que es ligado la cuenta bancaria de un cliente, normalmente una cuenta corriente bancaria. Una tarjeta de débito puede ser utilizada normalmente retirar dinero de una ATM o para hacer una compra.

Decimal A decimal is a number with one or more places to the right of a decimal point.

Decimal Un decimal es un número que tiene uno o más lugares a la derecha del punto decimal.

Decimal places The digits after the decimal point are called decimal places.

Lugares decimales Los dígitos que están después del punto decimal se llaman lugares decimales.

Decompose a shape To decompose a shape, break it up to form other shapes.

Descomponer una figura Para descomponer una figura, debes separarla para formar otras figuras.

Deductive reasoning Deductive reasoning is a process of reasoning logically from given facts to a conclusion.

Razonamiento deductivo El razonamiento deductivo es un proceso de razonamiento lógico que parte de hechos dados hasta llegar a una conclusión.

Denominator The denominator is the number below the fraction bar in a fraction.

Denominador El denominador es el número que está debajo de la barra de fracción en una fracción.

Dependent events Two events are dependent events if the occurrence of the first event affects the probability of the second event.

Eventos dependientes Dos eventos son dependientes si el resultado del primer evento afecta la probabilidad del segundo evento.

Deposit A transaction that adds money to a bank account is a deposit.

Depósito Una transacción que agrega dinero a una cuenta bancaria es un depósito.

English/Spanish Glossary

Dependent variable A dependent variable is a variable whose value changes in response to another (independent) variable.

Variable dependiente Una variable dependiente es una variable cuyo valor cambia en respuesta a otra variable (independiente).

Describe To describe is to explain or tell in detail. A written description can contain facts and other information needed to communicate your answer. A diagram or a graph may also be included.

Describir Describir es explicar o indicar algo en detalle. Una descripción escrita puede incluir hechos y otra información necesaria para comunicar tu respuesta. También puede incluir un diagrama o una gráfica.

Design To design is to make using specific criteria.

Diseñar Diseñar es crear algo a partir de criterios específicos.

Determine To determine is to use the given information and any related facts to find a value or make a decision.

Determinar Determinar es usar la información dada y cualquier otro dato relacionado para hallar un valor o tomar una decisión.

Deviation from the mean Deviation indicates how far away and in which direction a data value is from the mean. Data values that are less than the mean have a negative deviation. Data values that are greater than the mean have a positive deviation.

Desviación de la media La desviación indica a qué distancia y en qué dirección un valor se aleja de la media. Los valores menores que la media tienen una desviación negativa. Los valores mayores que la media tienen una desviación positiva.

Diagonal A diagonal of a figure is a segment that connects two nonconsecutive vertices of the figure.

Diagonal La diagonal de una figura es un segmento que conecta dos vértices no consecutivos de la figura.

Diameter A diameter is a segment that passes through the center of a circle and has both endpoints on the circle. The term diameter can also mean the length of this segment.

Diámetro Un diámetro es un segmento que atraviesa el centro de un círculo y tiene sus dos extremos en el círculo. El término diámetro también puede referirse a la longitud de este segmento.

Difference The difference is the answer you get when subtracting two numbers.

Diferencia La diferencia es la respuesta que obtienes cuando restas dos números.

Dilation A dilation is a transformation that moves each point along the ray through the point, starting from a fixed center, and multiplies distances from the center by a common scale factor. If a vertex of a figure is the center of dilation, then the vertex and its image after the dilation are the same point.

Dilatación Una dilatación es una transformación que mueve cada punto a lo largo de la semirrecta a través del punto, a partir de un centro fijo, y multiplica las distancias desde el centro por un factor de escala común. Si un vértice de una figura es el centro de dilatación, entonces el vértice y su imagen después de la dilatación son el mismo punto.

Direct variation A linear relationship that can be represented by an equation in the form $y = kx$, where $x \neq 0$.

Dirija variación Una relación lineal que puede ser representada por una ecuación en la forma $y = kx$, donde x no iguale 0.

Distribution (of a data set) The distribution of a data set describes the way that its data values are spread out over all possible values. This includes describing the frequencies of each data value. The shape of a data display shows the distribution of a data set.

Distribución (de un conjunto de datos) La distribución de un conjunto de datos describe la manera en que sus valores se esparcen sobre todos los valores posibles. Eso incluye la descripción de las frecuencias de cada valor. La forma de una exhibición de datos muestra la distribución de un conjunto de datos.

Distributive Property Multiplying a number by a sum or difference gives the same result as multiplying that number by each term in the sum or difference and then adding or subtracting the corresponding products.
$a \cdot (b + c) = a \cdot b + a \cdot c$ and
$a \cdot (b - c) = a \cdot b - a \cdot c$

Propiedad distributiva Multiplicar un número por una suma o una diferencia da el mismo resultado que multiplicar ese mismo número por cada uno de los términos de la suma o la diferencia y después sumar o restar los productos obtenidos.
$a \cdot (b + c) = a \cdot b + a \cdot c$ and
$a \cdot (b - c) = a \cdot b - a \cdot c$

Dividend The dividend is the number to be divided.

Dividendo El dividendo es el número que se divide.

Divisible A number is divisible by another number if there is no remainder after dividing.

Divisible Un número es divisible por otro número si no hay residuo después de dividir.

Divisor The divisor is the number used to divide another number.

Divisor El divisor es el número por el cual se divide otro número.

Dot plot A dot plot is a statistical graph that shows the shape of a data set with stacked dots above each data value on a number line. Each dot represents one data value.

Diagrama de puntos Un diagrama de puntos es una gráfica estadística que muestra la forma de un conjunto de datos con puntos marcados sobre cada valor de una recta numérica. Cada punto representa un valor.

E

Earned wages Earned wages are the income you receive from an employer for doing a job. Earned wages are also called gross pay.

Sueldos ganados Los sueldos ganados son los ingresos que usted recibe de un empleador para hacer un trabajo. Los sueldos ganados también son llamados la paga bruta.

Easy-access loan The term easy-access loan refers to a wide variety of loans with a streamlined application process. Many easy-access loans are short-term loans of relatively small amounts of money. They often have high interest rates.

Préstamo de fácil-acceso El préstamo del fácil-acceso del término se refiere a una gran variedad de préstamos con un proceso simplificado de aplicación. Muchos préstamos del fácil-acceso son préstamos a corto plazo de cantidades relativamente pequeñas de dinero. Ellos a menudo tienen los tipos de interés altos.

Edge of a three-dimensional figure An edge of a three-dimensional figure is a segment formed by the intersection of two faces.

Arista de una figura tridimensional Una arista de una figura tridimensional es un segmento formado por la intersección de dos caras.

English/Spanish Glossary

Enlargement An enlargement is a dilation with a scale factor greater than 1. After an enlargement, the image is bigger than the original figure.

Aumento Un aumento es una dilatación con un factor de escala mayor que 1. Después de un aumento, la imagen es más grande que la figura original.

Equation An equation is a mathematical sentence that includes an equals sign to compare two expressions.

Ecuación Una ecuación es una oración matemática que incluye un signo igual para comparar dos expresiones.

Equilateral triangle An equilateral triangle is a triangle whose sides are all the same length.

Triángulo equilátero Un triángulo equilátero es un triángulo que tiene todos sus lados de la misma longitud.

Equivalent equations Equivalent equations are equations that have exactly the same solutions.

Ecuaciones equivalentes Las ecuaciones equivalentes son ecuaciones que tienen exactamente la misma solución.

Equivalent expressions Equivalent expressions are expressions that always have the same value.

Expresiones equivalentes Las expresiones equivalentes son expresiones que siempre tienen el mismo valor.

Equivalent fractions Equivalent fractions are fractions that name the same number.

Fracciones equivalentes Las fracciones equivalentes son fracciones que representan el mismo número.

Equivalent inequalities Equivalent inequalities are inequalities that have the same solution.

Desigualdades equivalentes Las desigualdades equivalentes son desigualdades que tienen la misma solución.

Equivalent ratios Equivalent ratios are ratios that express the same relationship.

Razones equivalentes Las razones equivalentes son razones que expresan la misma relación.

Estimate To estimate is to find a number that is close to an exact answer.

Estimar Estimar es hallar un número cercano a una respuesta exacta.

Evaluate a numerical expression To evaluate a numerical expression is to follow the order of operations.

Evaluar una expresión numérica Evaluar una expresión numérica es seguir el orden de las operaciones.

Evaluate an algebraic expression To evaluate an algebraic expression, replace each variable with a number, and then follow the order of operations.

Evaluar una expresión algebraica Para evaluar una expresión algebraica, reemplaza cada variable con un número y luego sigue el orden de las operaciones.

Event An event is a single outcome or group of outcomes from a sample space.

Evento Un evento es un resultado simple o un grupo de resultados de un espacio muestral.

Expand an algebraic expression To expand an algebraic expression, use the Distributive Property to rewrite a product as a sum or difference of terms.

Desarrollar una expresión algebraica Para desarrollar una expresión algebraica, usa la propiedad distributiva para reescribir el producto como una suma o diferencia de términos.

Expected family contribution The amount of money a student's family is expected to contribute towards the student's cost of attendance for school.

Contribución familiar esperado La cantidad de dinero que la familia de un estudiante es esperada contribuir hacia el estudiante es costado de asistencia para la escuela.

Expense Money that a business or a person needs to spend to pay for or buy something.

Gasto El dinero que un negocio o una persona debe gastar para pagar por o comprar algo.

Experiment To experiment is to try to gather information in several ways.

Experimentar Experimentar es intentar reunir información de varias maneras.

Experimental probability You find the experimental probability of an event by repeating an experiment many times and using this ratio: $P(\text{event}) = \frac{\text{number of times event occurs}}{\text{total number of trials}}$

Probabilidad experimental Para hallar la probabilidad experimental de un evento, debes repetir un experimento muchas veces y usar esta razón: $P(\text{evento}) = \frac{\text{número de veces que sucede el evento}}{\text{número total de pruebas}}$

Explain To explain is to give facts and details that make an idea easier to understand. Explaining can involve a written summary supported by a diagram, chart, table, or a combination of these.

Explicar Explicar es brindar datos y detalles para que una idea sea más fácil de comprender. Para explicar algo se puede usar un resumen escrito sustentado por un diagrama, una tabla o una combinación de esos elementos.

Exponent An exponent is a number that shows how many times a base is used as a factor.

Exponente Un exponente es un número que muestra cuántas veces se usa una base como factor.

Expression An expression is a mathematical phrase that can involve variables, numbers, and operations. See algebraic expression or numerical expression.

Expresión Una expresión es una frase matemática que puede tener variables, números y operaciones. Ver expresión algebraica o expresión numérica.

Exterior angle of a triangle An exterior angle of a triangle is an angle formed by a side and an extension of an adjacent side.

Ángulo externo de un triángulo Un ángulo externo de un triángulo es un ángulo formado por un lado y una extensión de un lado adyacente.

F

Face of a three-dimensional figure A face of a three-dimensional figure is a flat surface shaped like a polygon.

Cara de una figura tridimensional La cara de una figura tridimensional es una superficie plana con forma de polígono.

Factor an algebraic expression To factor an algebraic expression, write the expression as a product.

Descomponer una expresión algebraica en factores Para descomponer una expresión algebraica en factores, escribe la expresión como un producto.

Factors Factors are numbers that are multiplied to give a product.

Factores Los factores son los números que se multiplican para obtener un producto.

False equation A false equation has values that do not equal each other on each side of the equals sign.

Ecuación falsa Una ecuación falsa tiene valores a cada lado del signo igual que no son iguales entre sí.

Financial aid Financial aid is any money offered to a student to assist with the cost of attendance.

Ayuda financiera La ayuda financiera es cualquier dinero ofreció a un estudiante para ayudar con el costo de asistencia.

Financial need A student's financial need is the difference between the student's cost of attendance and the student's expected family contribution.

Necesidad financiera Una necesidad financiera del estudiante es la diferencia entre el estudiante es costada de asistencia y la contribución esperado de familia de estudiante.

Find To find is to calculate or determine.

Hallar Hallar es calcular o determinar.

First quartile For an ordered set of data, the first quartile is the median of the lower half of the data set.

Primer cuartil Para un conjunto ordenado de datos, el primer cuartil es la mediana de la mitad inferior del conjunto de datos.

Fixed expenses Fixed expenses are expenses that do not change from one budget period to the next.

Gastos fijos Los gastos fijos son los gastos que no cambian de un período económico al próximo.

Fraction A fraction is a number that can be written in the form $\frac{a}{b}$, where a is a whole number and b is a positive whole number. A fraction is formed by a parts of size $\frac{1}{b}$.

Fracción Una fracción es un número que puede expresarse de forma $\frac{a}{b}$, donde a es un entero y b es un número entero positivo. La fracción está formada por a partes de tamaño $\frac{1}{b}$.

Frequency Frequency describes the number of times a specific value occurs in a data set.

Frecuencia La frecuencia describe el número de veces que aparece un valor específico en un conjunto de datos.

Function A function is a rule for taking each input value and producing exactly one output value.

Función Una función es una regla por la cual se toma cada valor de entrada y se produce exactamente un valor de salida.

G

Gap A gap is an area of a graph that contains no data points.

Espacio vacío o brecha Un espacio vacío o brecha es un área de una gráfica que no contiene ningún valor.

Grant A type of monetary award a student can use to pay for his or her education. The student does not need to repay this money.

Grant Un tipo de premio monetario que un estudiante puede utilizar para pagar por su educación. El estudiante no debe devolver este dinero.

Greater than $>$ The greater-than symbol shows a comparison of two numbers with the number of greater value shown first, or on the left.

Mayor que $>$ El símbolo de mayor que muestra una comparación de dos números con el número de mayor valor que aparece primero, o a la izquierda.

Greatest common factor The greatest common factor (GCF) of two or more whole numbers is the greatest number that is a factor of all of the numbers.

Máximo común divisor El máximo común divisor (M.C.D.) de dos o más números enteros no negativos es el número mayor que es un factor de todos los números.

H

Height of a cone The height of a cone, *h*, is the length of a segment perpendicular to the base that joins the vertex and the base.

Altura de un cono La altura de un cono, *h*, es la longitud de un segmento perpendicular a la base que une el vértice y la base.

Height of a cylinder The height of a cylinder is the length of a perpendicular segment that joins the planes of the bases.

Altura de un cilindro La altura de un cilindro es la longitud de un segmento perpendicular que une los planos de las bases.

Height of a parallelogram A height of a parallelogram is the perpendicular distance between opposite bases.

Altura de un paralelogramo La altura de un paralelogramo es la distancia perpendicular que existe entre las bases opuestas.

Height of a prism The height of a prism is the length of a perpendicular segment that joins the bases.

Altura de un prisma La altura de un prisma es la longitud de un segmento perpendicular que une a las bases.

Height of a pyramid The height of a pyramid is the length of a segment perpendicular to the base that joins the vertex and the base.

Altura de una pirámide La altura de una pirámide es la longitud de un segmento perpendicular a la base que une al vértice con la base.

Height of a triangle The height of a triangle is the length of the perpendicular segment from a vertex to the base opposite that vertex.

Altura de un triángulo La altura de un triángulo es la longitud del segmento perpendicular desde un vértice hasta la base opuesta a ese vértice.

Hexagon A hexagon is a polygon with six sides.

Hexágono Un hexágono es un polígono de seis lados.

Histogram A histogram is a statistical graph that shows the shape of a data set with vertical bars above intervals of values on a number line. The intervals are equal in size and do not overlap. The height of each bar shows the frequency of data within that interval.

Histograma Un histograma es una gráfica de estadísticas que muestra la forma de un conjunto de datos con barras verticales encima de intervalos de valores en una recta numérica. Los intervalos tienen el mismo tamaño y no se superponen. La altura de cada barra muestra la frecuencia de los datos dentro de ese intervalo.

Hundredths One hundredth is one part of 100 equal parts of a whole.

Centésima Una centésima es 1 de las 100 partes iguales de un todo.

Hypotenuse In a right triangle, the longest side, which is opposite the right angle, is the hypotenuse.

Hipotenusa En un triángulo rectángulo, el lado más largo, que es opuesto al ángulo recto, es la hipotenusa.

I

Identify To identify is to match a definition or description to an object or to recognize something and be able to name it.

Identificar Identificar es unir una definición o una descripción con un objeto, o reconocer algo y poder nombrarlo.

Identity Property of Addition The sum of 0 and any number is that number. For any number n, $n + 0 = n$ and $0 + n = n$.

Propiedad de identidad de la suma La suma de 0 y cualquier número es ese número. Para cualquier número n, $n + 0 = n$ and $0 + n = n$.

Identity Property of Multiplication The product of 1 and any number is that number. For any number n, $n \cdot 1 = n$ and $1 \cdot n = n$.

Propiedad de identidad de la multiplicación El producto de 1 y cualquier número es ese número. Para cualquier número n, $n \cdot 1 = n$ and $1 \cdot n = n$.

Illustrate To illustrate is to show or present information, usually as a drawing or a diagram. You can also illustrate a point using a written explanation.

Ilustrar Ilustrar es mostrar o presentar información, generalmente en forma de dibujo o diagrama. También puedes usar una explicación escrita para ilustrar un punto.

English/Spanish Glossary

Image An image is the result of a transformation of a point, line, or figure.

Imagen Una imagen es el resultado de una transformación de un punto, una recta o una figura.

Improper fraction An improper fraction is a fraction in which the numerator is greater than or equal to its denominator.

Fracción impropia Una fracción impropia es una fracción en la cual el numerador es mayor que o igual a su denominador.

Included angle An included angle is an angle that is between two sides.

Ángulo incluido Un ángulo incluido es un ángulo que está entre dos lados.

Included side An included side is a side that is between two angles.

Lado incluido Un lado incluido es un lado que está entre dos ángulos.

Income Money that a business receives. The money that a person earns from working is also called income.

Ingresos El dinero que un negocio recibe. El dinero que una persona gana de trabajar también es llamado los ingresos.

Income tax Income tax is money collected by the government based on how much you earn.

Impuesto de renta El impuesto de renta es dinero completo por el gobierno basado en cuánto gana.

Independent events Two events are independent events if the occurrence of one event does not affect the probability of the other event.

Eventos independientes Dos eventos son eventos independientes cuando el resultado de un evento no altera la probabilidad del otro.

Independent variable An independent variable is a variable whose value determines the value of another (dependent) variable.

Variable independiente Una variable independiente es una variable cuyo valor determina el valor de otra variable (dependiente).

Indicate To indicate is to point out or show.

Indicar Indicar es señalar o mostrar.

English/Spanish Glossary

Indirect measurement Indirect measurement uses proportions and similar triangles to measure distances that would be difficult to measure directly.

Medición indirecta La medición indirecta usa proporciones y triángulos semejantes para medir distancias que serían difíciles de medir de forma directa.

Inequality An inequality is a mathematical sentence that uses $<$, $\leq$, $>$, $\geq$, or $\neq$ to compare two quantities.

Desigualdad Una desigualdad es una oración matemática que usa $<$, $\leq$, $>$, $\geq$, o $\neq$ para comparar dos cantidades.

Inference An inference is a judgment made by interpreting data.

Inferencia Una inferencia es una opinión que se forma al interpretar datos.

Infinitely many solutions A linear equation in one variable has infinitely many solutions if any value of the variable makes the two sides of the equation equal.

Número infinito de soluciones Una ecuación lineal en una variable tiene un número infinito de soluciones si cualquier valor de la variable hace que los dos lados de la ecuación sean iguales.

Initial value The initial value of a linear function is the value of the output when the input is 0.

Valor inicial El valor inicial de una función lineal es el valor de salida cuando el valor de entrada es 0.

Integers Integers are the set of positive whole numbers, their opposites, and 0.

Enteros Los enteros son el conjunto de los números enteros positivos, sus opuestos y 0.

Interest When you deposit money in a bank account, the bank pays you interest for the right to use your money for a period of time.

Interés Cuando depositas dinero en una cuenta bancaria, el banco te paga un interés por el derecho a usar tu dinero por un período de tiempo.

Interest period The length of time on which compound interest is based. The total number of interest periods that you keep the money in the account is represented by the variable n.

Período de interés La cantidad de tiempo sobre la que se calcula el interés compuesto. El número total de períodos de interés que mantienes el dinero en la cuenta se representa con la variable n.

Interest rate Interest is calculated based on a percent of the principal. That percent is called the interest rate (*r*).

Tasa de interés El interés se calcula con base en un porcentaje del capital. Ese porcentaje se llama tasa de interés, (*r*).

Interest rate for an interest period The interest rate for an interest period is the annual interest rate divided by the number of interest periods per year.

El tipo de interés por un período de interés El tipo de interés por un período de interés es el tipo de interés anual dividido por el número de períodos de interés por año.

Interquartile range The interquartile range (IQR) is the distance between the first and third quartiles of the data set. It represents the spread of the middle 50% of the data values.

Rango intercuartil El rango intercuartil es la distancia entre el primer y el tercer cuartil del conjunto de datos. Representa la ubicación del 50% del medio de los valores.

Interval An interval is a period of time between two points of time or events.

Intervalo Un intervalo es un período de tiempo entre dos puntos en el tiempo o entre dos sucesos.

Invalid inference An invalid inference is false about the population, or does not follow from the available data. A biased sample can lead to invalid inferences.

Inferencia inválida Una inferencia inválida es una inferencia falsa acerca de una población, o no se deduce a partir de los datos disponibles. Una muestra sesgada puede llevar a inferencias inválidas.

Inverse operations Inverse operations are operations that undo each other.

Operaciones inversas Las operaciones inversas son operaciones que se cancelan entre sí.

Inverse Property of Addition Every number has an additive inverse. The sum of a number and its additive inverse is zero.

Propiedad inversa de la suma Todos los números tienen un inverso de suma. La suma de un número y su inverso de suma es cero.

Irrational numbers An irrational number is a number that cannot be written in the form $\frac{a}{b}$, where a and b are integers and $b \neq 0$. In decimal form, an irrational number cannot be written as a terminating or repeating decimal.

Números irracionales Un número irracional es un número que no se puede escribir en la forma $\frac{a}{b}$ donde a y b, son enteros y $b \neq 0$. Los números racionales en forma decimal no son finitos y no son periódicos.

Isolate a variable When solving equations, to isolate a variable means to get a variable with a coefficient of 1 alone on one side of an equation. Use the properties of equality and inverse operations to isolate a variable.

Aislar una variable Cuando resuelves ecuaciones, aislar una variable significa poner una variable con un coeficiente de 1 sola a un lado de la ecuación. Usa las propiedades de igualdad y las operaciones inversas para aislar una variable.

Isosceles triangle An isosceles triangle is a triangle with at least two sides that are the same length.

Triángulo isósceles Un triángulo isósceles es un triángulo que tiene al menos dos lados de la misma longitud.

J

Justify To justify is to support your answer with reasons or examples. A justification may include a written response, diagrams, charts, tables, or a combination of these.

Justificar Justificar es apoyar tu respuesta con razones o ejemplos. Una justificación puede incluir una respuesta escrita, diagramas, tablas o una combinación de esos elementos.

L

Lateral area of a cone The lateral area of a cone is the area of its lateral surface. The formula for the lateral area of a cone is L.A. $= \pi r \ell$, where r represents the radius of the base and ℓ represents the slant height of the cone.

Área lateral de un cono El área lateral de un cono es el área de su superficie lateral. La fórmula del área lateral de un cono es A.L. $= \pi r \ell$, donde r representa el radio de la base y ℓ representa la altura inclinada del cono.

English/Spanish Glossary

Lateral area of a cylinder The lateral area of a cylinder is the area of its lateral surface. The formula for the lateral area of a cylinder is L.A. $= 2\pi rh$, where r represents the radius of a base and h represents the height of the cylinder.

Área lateral de un cilindro El área lateral de un cilindro es el área de su superficie lateral. La fórmula del área lateral de un cilindro es A.L. $= 2\pi rh$, donde r representa el radio de una base y h representa la altura del cilindro.

Lateral area of a prism The lateral area of a prism is the sum of the areas of the lateral faces of the prism. The formula for the lateral area, L.A., of a prism is L.A. $= ph$, where p represents the perimeter of the base and h represents the height of the prism.

Área lateral de un prisma El área lateral de un prisma es la suma de las áreas de las caras laterales del prisma. La fórmula del área lateral, A.L., de un prisma es A.L. $= ph$, donde p representa el perímetro de la base y h representa la altura del prisma.

Lateral area of a pyramid The lateral area of a pyramid is the sum of the areas of the lateral faces of the pyramid. The formula for the lateral area, L.A., of a pyramid is L.A. $= \frac{1}{2}p\ell$ where p represents the perimeter of the base and ℓ represents the slant height of the pyramid.

Área lateral de una pirámide El área lateral de una pirámide es la suma de las áreas de las caras laterales de la pirámide. La fórmula del área lateral, A.L., de una pirámide es A.L. $= \frac{1}{2}p\ell$ donde p representa el perímetro de la base y ℓ representa la altura inclinada de la pirámide.

Lateral face of a prism A lateral face of a prism is a face that joins the bases of the prism.

Cara lateral de un prisma La cara lateral de un prisma es la cara que une a las bases del prisma.

Lateral face of a pyramid A lateral face of a pyramid is a triangular face that joins the base and the vertex.

Cara lateral de una pirámide La cara lateral de una pirámide es una cara lateral que une a la base con el vértice.

Lateral surface of a cone The lateral surface of a cone is the curved surface that is not included in the base.

Superficie lateral de un cono La superficie lateral de un cono es la superficie curva que no está incluida en la base.

English/Spanish Glossary

Lateral surface of a cylinder The lateral surface of a cylinder is the curved surface that is not included in the bases.

Superficie lateral de un cilindro La superficie lateral de un cilindro es la superficie curva que no está incluida en las bases.

Least common multiple The least common multiple (LCM) of two or more numbers is the least multiple shared by all of the numbers.

Mínimo común múltiplo El mínimo común múltiplo (MCM) de dos o más números es el múltiplo menor compartido por todos los números.

Leg of a right triangle In a right triangle, the two shortest sides are legs.

Cateto de un triángulo rectángulo En un triángulo rectángulo, los dos lados más cortos son los catetos.

Less than $<$ The less-than symbol shows a comparison of two numbers with the number of lesser value shown first, or on the left.

Menor que $<$ El símbolo de menor que muestra una comparación de dos números con el número de menor valor que aparece primero, o a la izquierda.

Liability A liability is money that you owe.

Obligación Una obligación es dinero que usted debe.

Lifetime income The amount of money earned over a lifetime of working.

Ingresos para toda la vida La cantidad de dinero ganó sobre una vida de trabajar.

Like terms Terms that have identical variable parts are like terms.

Términos semejantes Los términos que tienen partes variables idénticas son términos semejantes.

Line of reflection A line of reflection is a line across which a figure is reflected.

Eje de reflexión Un eje de reflexión es una línea a través de la cual se refleja una figura.

Linear equation An equation is a linear equation if the graph of all of its solutions is a line.

Ecuación lineal Una ecuación es lineal si la gráfica de todas sus soluciones es una línea recta.

Linear function A linear function is a function whose graph is a straight line. The rate of change for a linear function is constant.

Función lineal Una función lineal es una función cuya gráfica es una línea recta. La tasa de cambio en una función lineal es constante.

Linear function rule A linear function rule is an equation that describes a linear function.

Regla de la función lineal La ecuación que describe una función lineal es la regla de la función lineal.

Loan A loan is an amount of money borrowed for a period of time with the promise of paying it back.

Préstamo Un préstamo es una cantidad de dinero pedido prestaddo por un espacio de tiempo con la promesa de pagarlo apoya.

Loan length Loan length is the period of time set to repay a loan.

Preste longitud La longitud del préstamo es el conjunto de espacio de tiempo de devolver un préstamo.

Loan term The term of a loan is the period of time set to repay the loan.

Preste término El término de un préstamo es el conjunto de espacio de tiempo de devolver el préstamo.

Locate To locate is to find or identify a value, usually on a number line or coordinate graph.

Ubicar Ubicar es hallar o identificar un valor, generalmente en una recta numérica o en una gráfica de coordenadas.

Loss When a business's expenses are greater than the business's income, there is a loss.

Pérdida Cuando los gastos de un negocio son más que los ingresos del negocio, hay una pérdida.

M

Mapping diagram A mapping diagram describes a relation by linking the input values to the corresponding output values using arrows.

Diagrama de correspondencia Un diagrama de correspondencia describe una relación uniendo con flechas los valores de entrada con sus correspondientes valores de salida.

Markdown Markdown is the amount of decrease from the selling price to the sale price. The markdown as a percent decrease of the original selling price is called the percent markdown.

Rebaja La rebaja es la cantidad de disminución de un precio de venta a un precio rebajado. La rebaja como una disminución porcentual del precio de venta original se llama porcentaje de rebaja.

Markup Markup is the amount of increase from the cost to the selling price. The markup as a percent increase of the original cost is called the percent markup.

Margen de ganancia El margen de ganancia es la cantidad de aumento del costo al precio de venta. El margen de ganancia como un aumento porcentual del costo original se llama porcentaje del margen de ganancia.

Mean The mean represents the center of a numerical data set. To find the mean, sum the data values and then divide by the number of values in the data set.

Media La media representa el centro de un conjunto de datos numéricos. Para hallar la media, suma los valores y luego divide por el número de valores del conjunto de datos.

Mean absolute deviation The mean absolute deviation is a measure of variability that describes how much the data values are spread out from the mean of a data set. The mean absolute deviation is the average distance that the data values are spread around the mean. mean absolute deviation $= \frac{\text{sum of the absolute deviations of the data values}}{\text{total number of data values}}$

Desviación absoluta media La desviación absoluta media es una medida de variabilidad que describe cuánto se alejan los valores de la media de un conjunto de datos. La desviación absoluta media es la distancia promedio que los valores se alejan de la media. desviación absoluta media $= \frac{\text{suma de las desviaciones absolutas de los valores}}{\text{número total de valores}}$

Measure of variability A measure of variability describes the spread of values in a data set. There may be more than one measure of variability for a data set.

Medida de variabilidad Una medida de variabilidad describe la distribución de los valores de un conjunto de datos. Puede haber más de una medida de variabilidad para un conjunto de datos.

Measurement data Measurement data consist of data that are measures.

Datos de mediciones Los datos de mediciones son datos que son medidas.

Measures of center A measure of center is a value that represents the middle of a data set. There may be more than one measure of center for a data set.

Medida de tendencia central Una medida de tendencia central es un valor que representa el centro de un conjunto de datos. Puede haber más de una medida de tendencia central para un conjunto de datos.

Median The median represents the center of a numerical data set. For an odd number of data values, the median is the middle value when the data values are arranged in numerical order. For an even number of data values, the median is the average of the two middle values when the data values are arranged in numerical order.

Mediana La mediana representa el centro de un conjunto de datos numéricos. Para un número impar de valores, la mediana es el valor del medio cuando los valores están organizados en orden numérico. Para un número par de valores, la mediana es el promedio de los dos valores del medio cuando los valores están organizados en orden numérico.

Median-median line The median-median line, or median trend line, is a method of finding a fit line for a scatter plot that suggests a linear association. This method involves dividing the data into three subgroups and using medians to find a summary point for each subgroup. The summary points are used to find the equation of the fit line.

Recta mediana-mediana La recta mediana-mediana es un método que se usa para hallar una línea de ajuste para un diagrama de dispersión que sugiere una asociación lineal. Este método implica dividir los datos en tres subgrupos y usar medianas para hallar un punto medio para cada subgrupo. Los puntos medios se usan para hallar la ecuación de la línea de ajuste.

Million Whole numbers in the millions have 7, 8, or 9 digits.

Millón Los números enteros no negativos que están en los millones tienen 7, 8 ó 9 dígitos.

Mixed number A mixed number combines a whole number and a fraction.

Número mixto Un número mixto combina un número entero no negativo con una fracción.

Mode The item, or items, in a data set that occurs most frequently.

Modo El artículo, o los artículos, en un conjunto de datos que ocurre normalmente.

Model To model is to represent a situation using pictures, diagrams, or number sentences.

Demostrar Demostrar es usar ilustraciones, diagramas o enunciados numéricos para representar una situación.

Monetary incentive A monetary incentive is an offer that might encourage customers to buy a product.

Estímulo monetario Un estímulo monetario es una oferta que quizás favorezca a clientes para comprar un producto.

Multiple A multiple of a number is the product of the number and a whole number.

Múltiplo El múltiplo de un número es el producto del número y un número entero no negativo.

N

Natural numbers The natural numbers are the counting numbers.

Números naturales Los números naturales son los números que se usan para contar.

Negative exponent property For every nonzero number a and integer n, $a^{-n} = \frac{1}{a^n}$.

Propiedad del exponente negativo Para todo número distinto de cero a y entero n, $a^{-n} = \frac{1}{a^n}$.

Negative numbers Negative numbers are numbers less than zero.

Números negativos Los números negativos son números menores que cero.

Net A net is a two-dimensional pattern that you can fold to form a three-dimensional figure. A net of a figure shows all of the surfaces of that figure in one view.

Modelo plano Un modelo plano es un diseño bidimensional que puedes doblar para formar una figura tridimensional. Un modelo plano de una figura muestra todas las superficies de la figura en una vista.

Net worth Net worth is the total value of all assets minus the total value of all liabilities.

Patrimonio neto El patrimonio neto es el valor total de todas las ventajas menos el valor total de todas las obligaciones.

Net worth statement Net worth is the total value of all assets minus the total value of all liabilities.

Declaración de patrimonio neto El patrimonio neto es el valor total de todas las ventajas menos el valor total de todas las obligaciones.

No solution A linear equation in one variable has no solution if no value of the variable makes the two sides of the equation equal.

Sin solución Una ecuación lineal en una variable no tiene solución si ningún valor de la variable hace que los dos lados de la ecuación sean iguales.

Nonlinear function A nonlinear function is a function that does not have a constant rate of change.

Función no lineal Una función no lineal es una función que no tiene una tasa de cambio constante.

Numerator The numerator is the number above the fraction bar in a fraction.

Numerador El numerador es el número que está arriba de la barra de fracción en una fracción.

Numerical expression A numerical expression is a mathematical phrase that consists of numbers and operation symbols.

Expresión numérica Una expresión numérica es una frase matemática que contiene números y símbolos de operaciones.

O

Obtuse angle An obtuse angle is an angle with a measure greater than 90° and less than 180°.

Ángulo obtuso Un ángulo obtuso es un ángulo con una medida mayor que 90° y menor que 180°.

Obtuse triangle An obtuse triangle is a triangle with one obtuse angle.

Triángulo obtusángulo Un triángulo obtusángulo es un triángulo que tiene un ángulo obtuso.

Octagon An octagon is a polygon with eight sides.

Octágono Un octágono es un polígono de ocho lados.

Online payment system An online payment system allows money to be exchanged electronically between buyer and seller, usually using credit card or bank account information.

Sistema en línea de pago Un sistema en línea del pago permite dinero para ser cambiado electrónicamente entre comprador y vendedor, utilizando generalmente información de tarjeta de crédito o cuenta bancaria.

Open sentence An open sentence is an equation with one or more variables.

Enunciado abierto Un enunciado abierto es una ecuación con una o más variables.

Opposites Opposites are two numbers that are the same distance from 0 on a number line, but in opposite directions.

Opuestos Los opuestos son dos números que están a la misma distancia de 0 en la recta numérica, pero en direcciones opuestas.

Order of operations The order of operations is the order in which operations should be performed in an expression. Operations inside parentheses are done first, followed by exponents. Then, multiplication and division are done in order from left to right, and finally addition and subtraction are done in order from left to right.

Orden de las operaciones El orden de las operaciones es el orden en el que se deben resolver las operaciones de una expresión. Las operaciones que están entre paréntesis se resuelven primero, seguidas de los exponentes. Luego, se multiplica y se divide en orden de izquierda a derecha, y finalmente se suma y se resta en orden de izquierda a derecha.

English/Spanish Glossary

Ordered pair An ordered pair identifies the location of a point in the coordinate plane. The *x*-coordinate shows a point's position left or right of the *y*-axis. The *y*-coordinate shows a point's position up or down from the *x*-axis.

Par ordenado Un par ordenado identifica la ubicación de un punto en el plano de coordenadas. La coordenada *x* muestra la posición de un punto a la izquierda o a la derecha del eje de las *y*. La coordenada *y* muestra la posición de un punto arriba o abajo del eje de las *x*.

Origin The origin is the point of intersection of the *x*- and *y*-axes on a coordinate plane.

Origen El origen es el punto de intersección del eje de las *x* y el eje de las *y* en un plano de coordenadas.

Outcome An outcome is a possible result of an action.

Resultado Un resultado es un desenlace posible de una acción.

Outlier An outlier is a piece of data that doesn't seem to fit with the rest of a data set.

Valor extremo Un valor extremo es un valor que parece no ajustarse al resto de los datos de un conjunto.

P

Parallel lines Parallel lines are lines in the same plane that never intersect.

Rectas paralelas Las rectas paralelas son rectas que están en el mismo plano y nunca se intersecan.

Parallelogram A parallelogram is a quadrilateral with both pairs of opposite sides parallel.

Paralelogramo Un paralelogramo es un cuadrilátero en el cual los dos pares de lados opuestos son paralelos.

Partial product A partial product is part of the total product. A product is the sum of the partial products.

Producto parcial Un producto parcial es una parte del producto total. Un producto es la suma de los productos parciales.

English	Spanish
Pay period Wages for many jobs are paid at regular intervals, such a weekly, biweekly, semimonthly, or monthly. The interval of time is called a pay period.	**Pague el período** Los sueldos para muchos trabajos son pagados con regularidad, tal semanal, quincenal, quincenal, o mensual. El intervalo de tiempo es llamado un período de la paga.
Payroll deductions Your employer can deduct your income taxes from your wages before you receive your paycheck. The amounts deducted are called payroll deductions.	**Deducciones de nómina** Su empleador puede descontar sus impuestos de renta de sus sueldos antes que reciba su cheque de pago. Las cantidades descontadas son llamadas nómina deducciones.
Percent A percent is a ratio that compares a number to 100.	**Porcentaje** Un porcentaje es una razón que compara un número con 100.
Percent bar graph A percent bar graph is a bar graph that shows each category as a percent of the total number of data items.	**Gráfico de barras de por ciento** Un gráfico de barras del por ciento es un gráfico de barras que muestra cada categoría como un por ciento del número total de artículos de datos.
Percent decrease When a quantity decreases, the percent of change is called a percent decrease. percent decrease $= \frac{\text{amount of decrease}}{\text{original quantity}}$	**Disminución porcentual** Cuando una cantidad disminuye, el porcentaje de cambio se llama disminución porcentual. disminución porcentual $= \frac{\text{cantidad de disminución}}{\text{cantidad original}}$
Percent equation The percent equation describes the relationship between a part and a whole. You can use the percent equation to solve percent problems. part = percent · whole	**Ecuación de porcentaje** La ecuación de porcentaje describe la relación entre una parte y un todo. Puedes usar la ecuación de porcentaje para resolver problemas de porcentaje. parte = por ciento · todo
Percent error Percent error describes the accuracy of a measured or estimated value compared to an actual or accepted value.	**Error porcentual** El error porcentual describe la exactitud de un valor medido o estimado en comparación con un valor real o aceptado.

English	Spanish
Percent increase When a quantity increases, the percent of change is called a percent increase.	**Aumento porcentual** Cuando una cantidad aumenta, el porcentaje de cambio se llama aumento porcentual.
Percent of change Percent of change is the percent something increases or decreases from its original measure or amount. You can find the percent of change by using the equation: percent of change $= \frac{\text{amount of change}}{\text{original quantity}}$	**Porcentaje de cambio** El porcentaje de cambio es el porcentaje en que algo aumenta o disminuye en relación a la medida o cantidad original. Puedes hallar el porcentaje de cambio con la siguiente ecuación: porcentaje de cambio $= \frac{\text{cantidad de cambio}}{\text{cantidad original}}$
Perfect cube A perfect cube is the cube of an integer.	**Cubo perfecto** Un cubo perfecto es el cubo de un entero.
Perfect square A perfect square is a number that is the square of an integer.	**Cuadrado perfecto** Un cuadrado perfecto es un número que es el cuadrado de un entero.
Perimeter Perimeter is the distance around a figure.	**Perímetro** El perímetro es la distancia alrededor de una figura.
Period A period is a group of 3 digits in a number. Periods are separated by a comma and start from the right of a number.	**Período** Un período es un grupo de 3 dígitos en un número. Los períodos están separados por una coma y empiezan a la derecha del número.
Periodic savings plan A periodic savings plan is a method of saving that involves making deposits on a regular basis.	**Plan de ahorros periódico** Un plan de ahorros periódico es un método de guardar que implica depósitos que hace con regularidad.
Perpendicular lines Perpendicular lines intersect to form right angles.	**Rectas perpendiculares** Las rectas perpendiculares se intersecan para formar ángulos rectos.

English/Spanish Glossary

Pi Pi (π) is the ratio of a circle's circumference, *C*, to its diameter, *d*.

Pi Pi (π) es la razón de la circunferencia de un círculo, *C*, a su diámetro, *d*.

Place value Place value is the value given to an individual digit based on its position within a number.

Valor posicional El valor posicional es el valor asignado a determinado dígito según su posición en un número.

Plane A plane is a flat surface that extends indefinitely in all directions.

Plano Un plano es una superficie plana que se extiende indefinidamente en todas direcciones.

Polygon A polygon is a closed figure formed by three or more line segments that do not cross.

Polígono Un polígono es una figura cerrada compuesta por tres o más segmentos que no se cruzan.

Population A population is the complete set of items being studied.

Población Una población es todo el conjunto de elementos que se estudian.

Positive numbers Positive numbers are numbers greater than zero.

Números positivos Los números positivos son números mayores que cero.

Power A power is a number expressed using an exponent.

Potencia Una potencia es un número expresado con un exponente.

Predict To predict is to make an educated guess based on the analysis of real data.

Predecir Predecir es hacer una estimación informada según el análisis de datos reales.

Prime factorization The prime factorization of a composite number is the expression of the number as a product of its prime factors.

Descomposición en factores primos La descomposición en factores primos de un número compuesto es la expresión del número como un producto de sus factores primos.

English/Spanish Glossary

Prime number A prime number is a whole number greater than 1 with exactly two factors, 1 and the number itself.

Número primo Un número primo es un número entero mayor que 1 con exactamente dos factores, 1 y el número mismo.

Principal The original amount of money deposited or borrowed in an account.

Capital La cantidad original de dinero que se deposita o se pide prestada en una cuenta.

Prism A prism is a three-dimensional figure with two parallel polygonal faces that are the same size and shape.

Prisma Un prisma es una figura tridimensional con dos caras poligonales paralelas que tienen el mismo tamaño y la misma forma.

Probability model A probability model consists of an action, its sample space, and a list of events with their probabilities. The events and probabilities in the list have these characteristics: each outcome in the sample space is in exactly one event, and the sum of all of the probabilities must be 1.

Modelo de probabilidad Un modelo de probabilidad consiste en una acción, su espacio muestral y una lista de eventos con sus probabilidades. Los eventos y las probabilidades de la lista tienen estas características: cada resultado del espacio muestral está exactamente en un evento, y la suma de todas las probabilidades debe ser 1.

Probability of an event The probability of an event is a number from 0 to 1 that measures the likelihood that the event will occur. The closer the probability is to 0, the less likely it is that the event will happen. The closer the probability is to 1, the more likely it is that the event will happen. You can express probability as a fraction, decimal, or percent.

Probabilidad de un evento La probabilidad de un evento es un número de 0 a 1 que mide la probabilidad de que suceda el evento. Cuanto más se acerca la probabilidad a 0, menos probable es que suceda el evento. Cuanto más se acerca la probabilidad a 1, más probable es que suceda el evento. Puedes expresar la probabilidad como una fracción, un decimal o un porcentaje.

Product A product is the value of a multiplication or an expression showing multiplication.

Producto Un producto es el valor de una multiplicación o una expresión que representa la multiplicación.

Profit When a business's expenses are less than the business's income, there is a profit.

Ganancia Cuando los gastos de un negocio son menos que los ingresos del negocio, hay una ganancia.

Proof A proof is a logical, deductive argument in which every statement of fact is supported by a reason.

Comprobación Una comprobación es un argumento lógico y deductivo en el que cada enunciado de un hecho está apoyado por una razón.

Proper fraction A proper fraction has a numerator that is less than its denominator.

Fracción propia Una fracción propia tiene un numerador que es menor que su denominador.

Proportion A proportion is an equation stating that two ratios are equal.

Proporción Una proporción es una ecuación que establece que dos razones son iguales.

Proportional relationship Two quantities x and y have a proportional relationship if y is always a constant multiple of x. A relationship is proportional if it can be described by equivalent ratios.

Relación de proporción Dos cantidades x y y tienen una relación de proporción si y es siempre un múltiplo constante de x. Una relación es de proporción si se puede describir con razones equivalentes.

Pyramid A pyramid is a three-dimensional figure with a base that is a polygon and triangular faces that meet at a vertex. A pyramid is named for the shape of its base.

Pirámide Una pirámide es una figura tridimensional con una base que es un polígono y caras triangulares que se unen en un vértice. El nombre de la pirámide depende de la forma de su base.

Pythagorean Theorem In any right triangle, the sum of the squares of the lengths of the legs equals the square of the length of the hypotenuse. If a triangle is a right triangle, then $a^2 + b^2 = c^2$, where a and b represent the lengths of the legs, and c represents the length of the hypotenuse.

Teorema de Pitágoras En cualquier triángulo rectángulo, la suma del cuadrado de la longitud de los catetos es igual al cuadrado de la longitud de la hipotenusa. Si un triángulo es un triángulo rectángulo, entonces $a^2 + b^2 = c^2$, donde a y b representan la longitud de los catetos, y c representa la longitud de la hipotenusa.

Q

Quadrant The x- and y-axes divide the coordinate plane into four regions called quadrants.

Cuadrante Los ejes de las x y de las y dividen el plano de coordenadas en cuatro regiones llamadas cuadrantes.

Quadrilateral A quadrilateral is a polygon with four sides.

Cuadrilátero Un cuadrilátero es un polígono de cuatro lados.

Quarter circle A quarter circle is one fourth of a circle.

Círculo cuarto Un círculo cuarto es la cuarta parte de un círculo.

Quartile The quartiles of a data set divide the data set into four parts with the same number of data values in each part.

Cuartil Los cuartiles de un conjunto de datos dividen el conjunto de datos en cuatro partes que tienen el mismo número de valores cada una.

Quotient The quotient is the answer to a division problem. When there is a remainder, "quotient" sometimes refers to the whole-number portion of the answer.

Cociente El cociente es el resultado de una división. Cuando queda un residuo, "cociente" a veces se refiere a la parte de la solución que es un número entero.

R

Radius A radius of a circle is a segment that has one endpoint at the center and the other endpoint on the circle. The term radius can also mean the length of this segment.

Radio Un radio de un círculo es un segmento que tiene un extremo en el centro y el otro extremo en el círculo. El término radio también puede referirse a la longitud de este segmento.

Radius of a sphere The radius of a sphere, r, is a segment that has one endpoint at the center and the other endpoint on the sphere.

Radio de una esfera El radio de una esfera, r, es un segmento que tiene un extremo en el centro y el otro extremo en la esfera.

Random sample In a random sample, each member in the population has an equal chance of being selected.

Muestra aleatoria En una muestra aleatoria, cada miembro en la población tiene una oportunidad igual de ser seleccionado.

Range The range is a measure of variability of a numerical data set. The range of a data set is the difference between the greatest and least values in a data set.

Rango El rango es una medida de la variabilidad de un conjunto de datos numéricos. El rango de un conjunto de datos es la diferencia que existe entre el mayor y el menor valor del conjunto.

Rate A rate is a ratio involving two quantities measured in different units.

Tasa Una tasa es una razón que relaciona dos cantidades medidas con unidades diferentes.

Rate of change The rate of change of a linear function is the ratio $\frac{\text{vertical change}}{\text{horizontal change}}$ between any two points on the graph of the function.

Tasa de cambio La tasa de cambio de una función lineal es la razón del $\frac{\text{cambio vertical}}{\text{cambio horizontal}}$ que existe entre dos puntos cualesquiera de la gráfica de la función.

Ratio A ratio is a relationship in which for every x units of one quantity there are y units of another quantity.

Razón Una razón es una relación en la cual por cada x unidades de una cantidad hay y unidades de otra cantidad.

Rational numbers A rational number is a number that can be written in the form $\frac{a}{b}$ or $-\frac{a}{b}$, where a is a whole number and b is a positive whole number. The rational numbers include the integers.

Números racionales Un número racional es un número que se puede escribir como $\frac{a}{b}$ or $-\frac{a}{b}$, donde a es un número entero no negativo y b es un número entero positivo. Los números racionales incluyen los enteros.

Real numbers The real numbers are the set of rational and irrational numbers.

Números reales Los números reales son el conjunto de los números racionales e irracionales.

Reason To reason is to think through a problem using facts and information.

Razonar Razonar es usar hechos e información para estudiar detenidamente un problema.

Rebate A rebate returns part of the purchase price of an item after the buyer provides proof of purchase through a mail-in or online form.

Reembolso Un reembolso regresa la parte del precio de compra de un artículo después de que el comprador proporcione comprobante de compra por un correo-en o forma en línea.

Recall To recall is to remember a fact quickly.

Recordar Recordar es traer a la memoria un hecho rápidamente.

Reciprocals Two numbers are reciprocals if their product is 1. If a nonzero number is named as a fraction, $\frac{a}{b}$, then its reciprocal is $\frac{b}{a}$.

Recíprocos Dos números son recíprocos si su producto es 1. Si un número distinto de cero se expresa como una fracción, $\frac{a}{b}$, entonces su recíproco es $\frac{b}{a}$.

Rectangle A rectangle is a quadrilateral with four right angles.

Rectángulo Un rectángulo es un cuadrilátero que tiene cuatro ángulos rectos.

Rectangular prism A rectangular prism is a prism with bases in the shape of a rectangle.

Prisma rectangular Un prisma rectangular es un prisma cuyas bases tienen la forma de un rectángulo.

Reduction A reduction is a dilation with a scale factor less than 1. After a reduction, the image is smaller than the original figure.

Reducción Una reducción es una dilatación con un factor de escala menor que 1. Después de una reducción, la imagen es más pequeña que la figura original.

Reflection A reflection, or flip, is a transformation that flips a figure across a line of reflection.

Reflexión Una reflexión, o inversión, es una transformación que invierte una figura a través de un eje de reflexión.

Regular polygon A regular polygon is a polygon with all sides of equal length and all angles of equal measure.

Polígono regular Un polígono regular es un polígono que tiene todos los lados de la misma longitud y todos los ángulos de la misma medida.

Relate To relate two different things, find a connection between them.

Relacionar Para relacionar dos cosas diferentes, halla una conexión entre ellas.

Relation Any set of ordered pairs is called a relation.

Relación Todo conjunto de pares ordenados se llama relación.

Relative frequency relative frequency of an event $= \frac{\text{number of times event occurs}}{\text{total number of trials}}$

Frecuencia relativa frecuencia relativa de un evento $= \frac{\text{número de veces que sucede el evento}}{\text{número total de pruebas}}$

Relative frequency table A relative frequency table shows the ratio of the number of data in each category to the total number of data items. The ratio can be expressed as a fraction, decimal, or percent.

Mesa relativa de frecuencia Una mesa relativa de la frecuencia muestra la proporción del número de datos en cada categoría al número total de artículos de datos. La proporción puede ser expresada como una fracción, el decimal, o el por ciento.

Remainder In division, the remainder is the number that is left after the division is complete.

Residuo En una división, el residuo es el número que queda después de terminar la operación.

English/Spanish Glossary

Remote interior angles Remote interior angles are the two nonadjacent interior angles corresponding to each exterior angle of a triangle.

Ángulos internos no adyacentes Los ángulos internos no adyacentes son los dos ángulos internos de un triángulo que se corresponden con el ángulo externo que está más alejado de ellos.

Repeating decimal A repeating decimal has a decimal expansion that repeats the same digit, or block of digits, without end.

Decimal periódico Un decimal periódico tiene una expansión decimal que repite el mismo dígito, o grupo de dígitos, sin fin.

Represent To represent is to stand for or take the place of something else. Symbols, equations, charts, and tables are often used to represent particular situations.

Representar Representar es sustituir u ocupar el lugar de otra cosa. A menudo se usan símbolos, ecuaciones y tablas para representar determinadas situaciones.

Representative sample A representative sample is a sample of a population in which the number of subjects in the sample with the trait that you are studying is proportional to the number of members in the population with that trait. A representative sample accurately represents the population and does not have bias.

Muestra representativa Una muestra representativa es una muestra de una población en la que el número de sujetos de la muestra que tiene la característica que se estudia es proporcional al número de miembros de la población que tienen esa característica. Una muestra representativa representa la población con exactitud y no está sesgada.

Rhombus A rhombus is a parallelogram whose sides are all the same length.

Rombo Un rombo es un paralelogramo que tiene todos sus lados de la misma longitud.

Right angle A right angle is an angle with a measure of 90°.

Ángulo recto Un ángulo recto es un ángulo que mide 90°.

Right cone A right cone is a cone in which the segment representing the height connects the vertex and the center of the base.

Cono recto Un cono recto es un cono en el que el segmento que representa la altura une el vértice y el centro de la base.

Right cylinder A right cylinder is a cylinder in which the height joins the centers of the bases.

Cilindro recto Un cilindro recto es un cilindro en el que la altura une los centros de las bases.

Right prism In a right prism, all lateral faces are rectangles.

Prisma recto En un prisma recto, todas las caras laterales son rectángulos.

Right pyramid In a right pyramid, the segment that represents the height intersects the base at its center.

Pirámide recta En una pirámide recta, el segmento que representa la altura interseca la base en el centro.

Right triangle A right triangle is a triangle with one right angle.

Triángulo rectángulo Un triángulo rectángulo es un triángulo que tiene un ángulo recto.

Rigid motion A rigid motion is a transformation that changes only the position of a figure.

Movimiento rígido Un movimiento rígido es una transformación que sólo cambia la posición de una figura.

Rotation A rotation is a rigid motion that turns a figure around a fixed point, called the center of rotation.

Rotación Una rotación es un movimiento rígido que hace girar una figura alrededor de un punto fijo, llamado centro de rotación.

Rounding Rounding a number means replacing the number with a number that tells about how much or how many.

Redondear Redondear un número significa reemplazar ese número por un número que indica más o menos cuánto o cuántos.

S

Sale A sale is a discount offered by a store. A sale does not require the customer to have a coupon.

Venta Una venta es un descuento ofreció por una tienda. Una venta no requiere al cliente a tener un cupón.

Sales tax A tax added to the price of goods and services.

Las ventas tasan Un impuesto añadió al precio de bienes y servicios.

Sample of a population A sample of a population is part of the population. A sample is useful when you want to find out about a population but you do not have the resources to study every member of the population.

Muestra de una población Una muestra de una población es una parte de la población. Una muestra es útil cuando quieres saber algo acerca de una población, pero no tienes los recursos para estudiar a cada miembro de esa población.

Sample space The sample space for an action is the set of all possible outcomes of that action.

Espacio muestral El espacio muestral de una acción es el conjunto de todos los resultados posibles de esa acción.

Sampling method A sampling method is the method by which you choose members of a population to sample.

Método de muestreo Un método de muestreo es el método por el cual escoges miembros de una población para muestrear.

Savings Savings is money that a person puts away for use at a later date.

Ahorros Los ahorros son dinero que una persona guarda para el uso en una fecha posterior.

Scale A scale is a ratio that compares a length in a scale drawing to the corresponding length in the actual object.

Escala Una escala es una razón que compara una longitud en un dibujo a escala con la longitud correspondiente en el objeto real.

Scale drawing A scale drawing is an enlarged or reduced drawing of an object that is proportional to the actual object.

Dibujo a escala Un dibujo a escala es un dibujo ampliado o reducido de un objeto que es proporcional al objeto real.

English/Spanish Glossary

Scale factor The scale factor is the ratio of a length in the image to the corresponding length in the original figure.

Factor de escala El factor de escala es la razón de una longitud de la imagen a la longitud correspondiente en la figura original.

Scalene triangle A scalene triangle is a triangle in which no sides have the same length.

Triángulo escaleno Un triángulo escaleno es un triángulo que no tiene lados de la misma longitud.

Scatter plot A scatter plot is a graph that uses points to display the relationship between two different sets of data. Each point can be represented by an ordered pair.

Diagrama de dispersión Un diagrama de dispersión es una gráfica que usa puntos para mostrar la relación entre dos conjuntos de datos diferentes. Cada punto se puede representar con un par ordenado.

Scholarship A type of monetary award a student can use to pay for his or her education. The student does not need to repay this money.

Beca Un tipo de premio monetario que un estudiante puede utilizar para pagar por su educación. El estudiante no debe devolver este dinero.

Scientific notation A number in scientific notation is written as the product of two factors, one greater than or equal to 1 and less than 10, and the other a power of 10.

Notación científica Un número en notación científica está escrito como el producto de dos factores, uno mayor que o igual a 1 y menor que 10, y el otro una potencia de 10.

Segment A segment is part of a line. It consists of two endpoints and all of the points on the line between the endpoints.

Segmento Un segmento es una parte de una recta. Está formado por dos extremos y todos los puntos de la recta que están entre los extremos.

Semicircle A semicircle is one half of a circle.

Semicírculo Un semicírculo es la mitad de un círculo.

Similar figures A two-dimensional figure is similar (~) to another two-dimensional figure if you can map one figure to the other by a sequence of rotations, reflections, translations, and dilations.

Figuras semejantes Una figura bidimensional es semejante (~) a otra figura bidimensional si puedes hacer corresponder una figura con otra mediante una secuencia de rotaciones, reflexiones, traslaciones y dilataciones.

Simple interest Simple interest is interest paid only on an original deposit. To calculate simple interest, use the formula $I = prt$ where I is the simple interest, p is the principal, r is the annual interest rate, and t is the number of years that the account earns interest.

Interés simple El interés simple es el interés que se paga sobre un depósito original solamente. Para calcular el interés simple, usa la fórmula $I = crt$ donde I es el interés simple, c es el capital, r es la tasa de interés anual y t es el número de años en que la cuenta obtiene un interés.

Simple random sampling Simple random sampling is a sampling method in which every member of the population has an equal chance of being chosen for the sample.

Muestreo aleatorio simple El muestreo aleatorio simple es un método de muestreo en el que cada miembro de la población tiene la misma probabilidad de ser seleccionado para la muestra.

Simpler form A fraction is in simpler form when it is equivalent to a given fraction and has smaller numbers in the numerator and denominator.

Forma simplificada Una fracción está en su forma simplificada cuando es equivalente a otra fracción dada, pero tiene números más pequeños en el numerador y el denominador.

Simplest form A fraction is in simplest form when the only common factor of the numerator and denominator is one.

Mínima expresión Una fracción está en su mínima expresión cuando el único factor común del numerador y el denominador es 1.

Simplify an algebraic expression To simplify an algebraic expression, combine the like terms of the expression.

Simplificar una expresión algebraica Para simplificar una expresión algebraica, combina los términos semejantes de la expresión.

Simulation A simulation is a model of a real-world situation that is used to find probabilities.

Simulación Una simulación es un modelo de una situación de la vida diaria que se usa para hallar probabilidades.

Sketch To sketch a figure, draw a rough outline. When a sketch is asked for, it means that a drawing needs to be included in your response.

Bosquejo Para hacer un bosquejo, dibuja un esquema simple. Si se pide un bosquejo, tu respuesta debe incluir un dibujo.

Slant height of a cone The slant height of a cone, ℓ, is the length of its lateral surface from base to vertex.

Altura inclinada de un cono La altura inclinada de un cono, ℓ, es la longitud de su superficie lateral desde la base hasta el vértice.

Slant height of a pyramid The slant height of a pyramid is the height of a lateral face.

Altura inclinada de una pirámide La altura inclinada de una pirámide es la altura de una cara lateral.

Slope Slope is a ratio that describes steepness.

$$\text{slope} = \frac{\text{vertical change}}{\text{horizontal change}} = \frac{\text{rise}}{\text{run}}$$

Pendiente La pendiente es una razón que describe la inclinación.

$$\text{pendiente} = \frac{\text{cambio vertical}}{\text{cambio horizontal}}$$

$$= \frac{\text{distancia vertical}}{\text{distancia horizontal}}$$

Slope of a line slope =

$$\frac{\text{change in } y\text{-coordinates}}{\text{change in } x\text{-coordinates}} = \frac{\text{rise}}{\text{run}}$$

Pendiente de una recta pendiente =

$$\frac{\text{cambio en las coordenadas } y}{\text{cambio en las coordenadas } x}$$

$$= \frac{\text{distancia vertical}}{\text{distancia horizontal}}$$

Slope-intercept form An equation written in the form $y = mx + b$ is in slope-intercept form. The graph is a line with slope m and y-intercept b.

Forma pendiente-intercepto Una ecuación escrita en la forma $y = mx + b$ está en forma de pendiente-intercepto. La gráfica es una línea recta con pendiente m e intercepto en y b.

English/Spanish Glossary

Solution of a system of linear equations A solution of a system of linear equations is any ordered pair that makes all the equations of that system true.

Solución de un sistema de ecuaciones lineales Una solución de un sistema de ecuaciones lineales es cualquier par ordenado que hace que todas las ecuaciones de ese sistema sean verdaderas.

Solution of an equation A solution of an equation is a value of the variable that makes the equation true.

Solución de una ecuación Una solución de una ecuación es un valor de la variable que hace que la ecuación sea verdadera.

Solution of an inequality The solutions of an inequality are the values of the variable that make the inequality true.

Solución de una desigualdad Las soluciones de una desigualdad son los valores de la variable que hacen que la desigualdad sea verdadera.

Solution set A solution set contains all of the numbers that satisfy an equation or inequality.

Conjunto solución Un conjunto solución contiene todos los números que satisfacen una ecuación o desigualdad.

Solve To solve a given statement, determine the value or values that make the statement true. Several methods and strategies can be used to solve a problem, including estimating, isolating the variable, drawing a graph, or using a table of values.

Resolver Para resolver un enunciado dado, determina el valor o los valores que hacen que ese enunciado sea verdadero. Para resolver un problema se pueden usar varios métodos y estrategias, como estimar, aislar la variable, dibujar una gráfica o usar una tabla de valores.

Sphere A sphere is the set of all points in space that are the same distance from a center point.

Esfera Una esfera es el conjunto de todos los puntos en el espacio que están a la misma distancia de un punto central.

Square A square is a quadrilateral with four right angles and all sides the same length.

Cuadrado Un cuadrado es un cuadrilátero que tiene cuatro ángulos rectos y todos los lados de la misma longitud.

Square root A square root of a number is a number that, when multiplied by itself, equals the original number.

Raíz cuadrada La raíz cuadrada de un número es un número que, cuando se multiplica por sí mismo, es igual al número original.

Square unit A square unit is the area of a square that has sides that are 1 unit long.

Unidad cuadrada Una unidad cuadrada es el área de un cuadrado en el que cada lado mide 1 unidad de longitud.

Standard form A number written using digits and place value is in standard form.

Forma estándar Un número escrito con dígitos y valor posicional está escrito en forma estándar.

Statistical question A statistical question is a question that investigates an aspect of the real world and can have variety in the responses.

Pregunta estadística Una pregunta estadística es una pregunta que investiga un aspecto de la vida diaria y puede tener varias respuestas.

Statistics Statistics is the study of collecting, organizing, graphing, and analyzing data to draw conclusions about the real world.

Estadística La estadística es el estudio de la recolección, organización, representación gráfica y análisis de datos para sacar conclusiones sobre la vida diaria.

Stem-and-leaf plot A stem-and-leaf plot is a graph that uses the digits of each number to show the data distribution. Each data item is broken into a stem and into a leaf. The leaf is the last digit of the data value. The stem is the other digit or digits of the data value.

Complot de tallo y hoja Un complot del tallo y la hoja es un gráfico que utiliza los dígitos de cada número para mostrar la distribución de datos. Cada artículo de datos es roto en un tallo y en una hoja. La hoja es el último dígito de los datos valora. El tallo es el otro dígito o los dígitos de los datos valoran.

Stored-value card A stored-value card is a prepaid card electronically coded to be worth a specified amount of money.

Tarjeta de almacenado-valor Una tarjeta del almacenado-valor es una tarjeta pagada por adelantado codificó electrónicamente valer una cantidad especificado de dinero.

Straight angle A straight angle is an angle with a measure of 180°.

Ángulo llano Un ángulo llano es un ángulo que mide 180°.

Student loan A student loan provides money to a student to pay for college. The student needs to repay the loan after leaving college. Often the student will need to pay interest on the amount of the loan.

Crédito personal para estudiantes Un crédito personal para estudiantes le proporciona dinero a un estudiante para pagar por el colegio. El estudiante debe devolver el préstamo después de dejar el colegio. A menudo el estudiante deberá pagar interés en la cantidad del préstamo.

Subject Each member in a sample is a subject.

Sujeto Cada miembro de una muestra es un sujeto.

Sum The sum is the answer to an addition problem.

Suma o total La suma o total es el resultado de una operación de suma.

Summarize To summarize an explanation or solution, go over or review the most important points.

Resumir Para resumir una explicación o solución, revisa o repasa los puntos más importantes.

Supplementary angles Two angles are supplementary angles if the sum of their measures is 180°. Supplementary angles that are adjacent form a straight angle.

Ángulos suplementarios Dos ángulos son suplementarios si la suma de sus medidas es 180°. Los ángulos suplementarios que son adyacentes forman un ángulo llano.

Surface area of a cone The surface area of a cone is the sum of the lateral area and the area of the base. The formula for the surface area of a cone is S.A. = L.A. + B.

Área total de un cono El área total de un cono es la suma del área lateral y el área de la base. La fórmula del área total de un cono es A.T. = A.L. + B.

Surface area of a cube The surface area of a cube is the sum of the areas of the faces of the cube. The formula for the surface area, S.A., of a cube is S.A. $= 6s^2$, where s represents the length of an edge of the cube.

Área total de un cubo El área total de un cubo es la suma de las áreas de las caras del cubo. La fórmula del área total, A.T., de un cubo es A.T. $= 6s^2$, donde s representa la longitud de una arista del cubo.

Surface area of a cylinder The surface area of a cylinder is the sum of the lateral area and the areas of the two circular bases. The formula for the surface area of a cylinder is S.A. = L.A. + $2B$, where L.A. represents the lateral area of the cylinder and B represents the area of a base of the cylinder.

Área total de un cilindro El área total de un cilindro es la suma del área lateral y las áreas de las dos bases circulares. La fórmula del área total de un cilindro es A.T. = A.L. + $2B$, donde A.L. representa el área lateral del cilindro y B representa el área de una base del cilindro.

Surface area of a pyramid The surface area of a pyramid is the sum of the areas of the faces of the pyramid. The formula for the surface area, S.A., of a pyramid is S.A. = L.A. + B, where L.A. represents the lateral area of the pyramid and B represents the area of the base of the pyramid.

Área total de una pirámide El área total de una pirámide es la suma de las áreas de las caras de la pirámide. La fórmula del área total, A.T., de una pirámide es A.T. = A.L. + B, donde A.L. representa el área lateral de la pirámide y B representa el área de la base de la pirámide.

Surface area of a sphere The surface area of a sphere is equal to the lateral area of a cylinder that has the same radius, r, and height $2r$. The formula for the surface area of a sphere is S.A. $= 4\pi r^2$, where r represents the radius of the sphere.

Área total de una esfera El área total de una esfera es igual al área lateral de un cilindro que tiene el mismo radio, r, y una altura de $2r$. La fórmula del área total de una esfera es A.T. $= 4\pi r^2$, donde r representa el radio de la esfera.

Surface area of a three-dimensional figure The surface area of a three-dimensional figure is the sum of the areas of its faces. You can find the surface area by finding the area of the net of the three-dimensional figure.

Área total de una figura tridimensional El área total de una figura tridimensional es la suma de las áreas de sus caras. Puedes hallar el área total si hallas el área del modelo plano de la figura tridimensional.

System of linear equations A system of linear equations is formed by two or more linear equations that use the same variables.

Sistema de ecuaciones lineales Un sistema de ecuaciones lineales está formado por dos o más ecuaciones lineales que usan las mismas variables.

Systematic sampling Systematic sampling is a sampling method in which you choose every nth member of the population, where *n* is a predetermined number. A systematic sample is useful when the researcher is able to approach the population in a systematic, or methodical, way.

Muestreo sistemático El muestreo sistemático es un método de muestreo en el que se escoge cada enésimo miembro de la población, donde *n* es un número predeterminado. Una muestra sistemática es útil cuando el investigador puede enfocarse en la población de manera sistemática o metódica.

T

Taxable wages For federal income tax purposes, your taxable wages are the difference between your earned wages and your withholding allowance. Your employer divides your withholding allowance equally among the pay periods of one year.

Sueldos imponibles Para propósitos federales de impuesto de renta, sus sueldos imponibles son la diferencia entre sus sueldos ganados y su concesión que retienen. Su empleador divide su concesión que retiene igualmente entre los períodos de paga de un año.

Tenths One tenth is one out of ten equal parts of a whole.

Décimas Una décima es 1 de 10 partes iguales de un todo.

Term A term is a number, a variable, or the product of a number and one or more variables.

Término Un término es un número, una variable o el producto de un número y una o más variables.

Terminating decimal A terminating decimal has a decimal expansion that terminates in 0.

Decimal finito Un decimal finito tiene una expansión decimal que termina en 0.

English/Spanish Glossary

Terms of a ratio The terms of a ratio are the quantities x and y in the ratio.

Términos de una razón Los términos de una razón son la cantidad x y la cantidad y de la razón.

Theorem A theorem is a conjecture that is proven.

Teorema Un teorema es una conjetura que se ha comprobado.

Theoretical probability When all outcomes of an action are equally likely, $P(\text{event}) = \frac{\text{number of favourable outcomes}}{\text{number of possible outcomes}}$.

Probabilidad teórica Cuando todos los resultados de una acción son igualmente probables, $P(\text{evento}) = \frac{\text{número de resultados favorables}}{\text{número de resultados posibles}}$.

Third quartile For an ordered set of data, the third quartile is the median of the upper half of the data set.

Tercer cuartil Para un conjunto de datos ordenados, el tercer cuartil es la mediana de la mitad superior del conjunto de datos.

Thousandths One thousandth is one part of 1,000 equal parts of a whole.

Milésimas Una milésima es 1 de 1,000 partes iguales de un todo.

Three-dimensional figure A three-dimensional (3-D) figure is a figure that does not lie in a plane.

Figura tridimensional Una figura tridimensional es una figura que no está en un plano.

Total cost of a loan The total cost of a loan is the total amount spent to repay the loan. Total cost includes the principal and all interest paid over the length of the loan. Total cost also includes any fees charged.

El coste total de un préstamo El coste total de un préstamo es el cantidad total que es gastado para devolver el préstamo. El coste total incluye al director y todo el interés pagó sobre la longitud del préstamo. El coste total también incluye cualquier honorario cargado.

Transaction A banking transaction moves money into or out of a bank account.

Transacción Una transacción bancaria mueve dinero en o fuera de una cuenta bancaria.

English/Spanish Glossary

Transfer A transaction that moves money from one bank account to another is a transfer. The balance of one account increases by the same amount the other account decreases.

Transferencia Una transacción que mueve dinero de una cuenta bancaria a otro es una transferencia. El equilibrio de un aumentos de cuenta por la misma cantidad que la otra cuenta disminuye.

Transformation A transformation is a change in position, shape, or size of a figure. Three types of transformations that change position only are translations, reflections, and rotations.

Transformación Una transformación es un cambio en la posición, la forma o el tamaño de una figura. Tres tipos de transformaciones que cambian sólo la posición son las traslaciones, las reflexiones y las rotaciones.

Translation A translation, or slide, is a rigid motion that moves every point of a figure the same distance and in the same direction.

Traslación Una traslación, o deslizamiento, es un movimiento rígido que mueve cada punto de una figura a la misma distancia y en la misma dirección.

Transversal A transversal is a line that intersects two or more lines at different points.

Transversal o secante Una transversal o secante es una línea que interseca dos o más líneas en distintos puntos.

Trapezoid A trapezoid is a quadrilateral with exactly one pair of parallel sides.

Trapecio Un trapecio es un cuadrilátero que tiene exactamente un par de lados paralelos.

Trend line A trend line is a line on a scatter plot, drawn near the points, that approximates the association between the data sets.

Línea de tendencia Una línea de tendencia es una línea en un diagrama de dispersión, trazada cerca de los puntos, que se aproxima a la relación entre los conjuntos de datos.

Trial In a probability experiment, you carry out or observe an action repeatedly. Each observation of the action is a trial.

Prueba En un experimento de probabilidad, realizas u observas una acción varias veces. Cada observación de la acción es una prueba.

Triangle A triangle is a polygon with three sides.

Triángulo Un triángulo es un polígono de tres lados.

English/Spanish Glossary

Triangular prism A triangular prism is a prism with bases in the shape of a triangle.

Prisma triangular Un prisma triangular es un prisma cuyas bases tienen la forma de un triángulo.

True equation A true equation has equal values on each side of the equals sign.

Ecuación verdadera En una ecuación verdadera, los valores a ambos lados del signo igual son iguales.

Two-way frequency table A two-way frequency table displays the counts of the data in each group.

Tabla de frecuencia con dos variables Una tabla de frecuencia con dos variables muestra el conteo de los datos de cada grupo.

Two-way relative frequency table A two-way relative frequency table shows the ratio of the number of data in each group to the size of the population. The relative frequencies can be calculated with respect to the entire population, the row populations, or the column populations. The relative frequencies can be expressed as fractions, decimals, or percents.

Tabla de frecuencias relativas con dos variables Una tabla de frecuencias relativas con dos variables muestra la razón del número de datos de cada grupo al tamaño de la población. Las frecuencias relativas se pueden calcular respecto de la población entera, las poblaciones de las filas o las poblaciones de las columnas. Las frecuencias relativas se pueden expresar como fracciones, decimales o porcentajes.

Two-way table A two-way table shows bivariate categorical data for a population.

Tabla con dos variables Una tabla con dos variables muestra datos bivariados por categorías de una población.

Uniform probability model A uniform probability model is a probability model based on using the theoretical probability of equally likely outcomes.

Modelo de probabilidad uniforme Un modelo de probabilidad uniforme es un modelo de probabilidad que se basa en el uso de la probabilidad teórica de resultados igualmente probables.

English/Spanish Glossary

Unit fraction A unit fraction is a fraction with a numerator of 1 and a denominator that is a whole number greater than 1.

Fracción unitaria Una fracción unitaria es una fracción con un numerador 1 y un denominador que es un número entero mayor que 1.

Unit price A unit price is a unit rate that gives the price of one item.

Precio por unidad El precio por unidad es una tasa por unidad que muestra el precio de un artículo.

Unit rate The rate for one unit of a given quantity is called the unit rate.

Tasa por unidad Se llama tasa por unidad a la tasa que corresponde a 1 unidad de una cantidad dada.

Use To use given information, draw on it to help you determine something else.

Usar Para usar una información dada, apóyate en ella para determinar otra cosa.

V

Valid inference A valid inference is an inference that is true about the population. Valid inferences can be made when they are based on data from a representative sample.

Inferencia válida Una inferencia válida es una inferencia verdadera acerca de una población. Se pueden hacer inferencias válidas si están basadas en los datos de una muestra representativa.

Variability Variability describes how much the items in a data set differ (or vary) from each other. On a data display, variability is shown by how much the data on the horizontal scale are spread out.

Variabilidad La variabilidad describe qué diferencia (o variación) existe entre los elementos de un conjunto de datos. Al exhibir datos, la variabilidad queda representada por la distancia que separa los datos en la escala horizontal.

Variable A variable is a letter that represents an unknown value.

Variable Una variable es una letra que representa un valor desconocido.

Variable expenses Variable expenses are expenses that change from one budget period to the next.

Gastos variables Los gastos variables son los gastos que cambian de un período económico al próximo.

Vertex of a cone The vertex of a cone is the point farthest from the base.

Vértice de un cono El vértice de un cono es el punto más alejado de la base.

Vertex of a polygon The vertex of a polygon is any point where two sides of a polygon meet.

Vértice de un polígono El vértice de un polígono es cualquier punto donde se encuentran dos lados de un polígono.

Vertex of a three-dimensional figure A vertex of a three-dimensional figure is a point where three or more edges meet.

Vértice de una figura tridimensional El vértice de una figura tridimensional es un punto donde se unen tres o más aristas.

Vertex of an angle The vertex of an angle is the point of intersection of the rays that make up the sides of the angle.

Vértice de un ángulo El vértice de un ángulo es el punto de intersección de las semirrectas que forman los lados del ángulo.

Vertical angles Vertical angles are formed by two intersecting lines and are opposite each other. Vertical angles have equal measures.

Ángulos opuestos por el vértice Los ángulos opuestos por el vértice están formados por dos rectas secantes y están uno frente a otro. Los ángulos opuestos por el vértice tienen la misma medida.

Vertical-line test The vertical-line test is a method used to determine if a relation is a function or not. If a vertical line passes through a graph more than once, the graph is not the graph of a function.

Prueba de recta vertical La prueba de recta vertical es un método que se usa para determinar si una relación es una función o no. Si una recta vertical atraviesa la gráfica más de una vez, la gráfica no es la gráfica de una función.

Volume Volume is the number of cubic units needed to fill a solid figure.

Volumen El volumen es el número de unidades cúbicas que se necesitan para llenar un cuerpo geométrico.

Volume of a cone The volume of a cone is the number of unit cubes, or cubic units, needed to fill the cone. The formula for the volume of a cone is $V = \frac{1}{3}Bh$, where B represents the area of the base and h represents the height of the cone.

Volumen de un cono El volumen de un cono es el número de bloques de unidades, o unidades cúbicas, que se necesitan para llenar el cono. La fórmula del volumen de un cono $V = \frac{1}{3}Bh$, donde B representa el área de la base y h representa la altura del cono.

Volume of a cube The volume of a cube is the number of unit cubes, or cubic units, needed to fill the cube. The formula for the volume V of a cube is $V = s^3$, where s represents the length of an edge of the cube.

Volumen de un cubo El volumen de un cubo es el número de bloques de unidades, o unidades cúbicas, que se necesitan para llenar el cubo. La fórmula del volumen, V, de un cubo es $V = s^3$, donde s representa la longitud de una arista del cubo.

Volume of a cylinder The volume of a cylinder is the number of unit cubes, or cubic units, needed to fill the cylinder. The formula for the volume of a cylinder is $V = \pi r^2 h$, where r represents the radius of a base and h represents the height of the cylinder.

Volumen de un cilindro El volumen de un cilindro es el número de bloques de unidades, o unidades cúbicas, que se necesitan para llenar el cilindro. La fórmula del volumen de un cilindro es $V = \pi r^2 h$, donde r representa el radio de una base y h representa la altura del cilindro.

Volume of a prism The volume of a prism is the number of unit cubes, or cubic units, needed to fill the prism. The formula for the volume V of a prism is $V = Bh$, where B represents the area of a base and h represents the height of the prism.

Volumen de un prisma El volumen de un prisma es el número de bloques de unidades, o unidades cúbicas, que se necesitan para llenar el prisma. La fórmula del volumen, V, de un prisma $V = Bh$, donde B representa el área de una base y h representa la altura del prisma.

Volume of a pyramid The volume of a pyramid is the number of unit cubes needed to fill the pyramid. The formula for the volume V of a pyramid is $V = \frac{1}{3}Bh$, where B represents the area of the base and h represents the height of the pyramid.

Volumen de una pirámide El volumen de una pirámide es el número de bloques de unidades, o unidades cúbicas, que se necesitan para llenar la pirámide. La fórmula del volumen, V, de una pirámide es $V = \frac{1}{3}Bh$, donde B representa el área de la base y h representa la altura de la pirámide.

Volume of a sphere The volume of a sphere is the number of unit cubes, or cubic units, needed to fill the sphere. The formula for the volume of a sphere is $V = \frac{4}{3}\pi r^3$.

Volumen de una esfera El volumen de una esfera es el número de bloques de unidades, o unidades cúbicas, que se necesitan para llenar la esfera. La fórmula del volumen de una esfera es $V = \frac{4}{3}\pi r^3$.

W

Whole numbers The whole numbers consist of the number 0 and all of the natural numbers.

Números enteros no negativos Los números enteros no negativos son el número 0 y todos los números naturales.

Withdrawal A transaction that takes money out of a bank account is a withdrawal.

Retirada Una transacción que toma dinero fuera de una cuenta bancaria es una retirada.

Withholding allowance You can exclude a portion of your earned wages, called a withholding allowance, from federal income tax. You can claim one withholding allowance for yourself and one for each person dependent upon your income.

Retener concesión Puede excluir una porción de sus sueldos ganados, llamó una concesión que retiene, del impuesto de renta federal. Puede reclamar una concesión que retiene para usted mismo y para uno para cada dependiente de persona sobre sus ingresos.

Word form of a number The word form of a number is the number written in words.

Número en palabras Un número en palabras es un número escrito con palabras en lugar de dígitos.

Work-Study Work-study is a type of need-based aid that schools might offer to a student. A student must earn work-study money by working certain jobs.

Práctica estudiantil La práctica estudiantil es un tipo de ayuda necesidad-basado que escuelas quizás ofrezcan a un estudiante. Un estudiante debe ganar dinero de práctica estudiantil por ciertos trabajos de trabajo.

X

x-axis The x-axis is the horizontal number line that, together with the y-axis, forms the coordinate plane.

Eje de las x El eje de las x es la recta numérica horizontal que, junto con el eje de las y, forma el plano de coordenadas.

x-coordinate The x-coordinate is the first number in an ordered pair. It tells the number of horizontal units a point is from 0.

Coordenada x La coordenada x (abscisa) es el primer número de un par ordenado. Indica cuántas unidades horizontales hay entre un punto y 0.

Y

y-axis The y-axis is the vertical number line that, together with the x-axis, forms the coordinate plane.

Eje de las y El eje de las y es la recta numérica vertical que, junto con el eje de las x, forma el plano de coordenadas.

y-coordinate The y-coordinate is the second number in an ordered pair. It tells the number of vertical units a point is from 0.

Coordenada y La coordenada y (ordenada) es el segundo número de un par ordenado. Indica cuántas unidades verticales hay entre un punto y 0.

y-intercept The y-intercept of a line is the y-coordinate of the point where the line crosses the y-axis.

Intercepto en y El intercepto en y de una recta es la coordenada y del punto por donde la recta cruza el eje de las y.

Z

Zero exponent property For any nonzero number a, $a^0 = 1$.

Propiedad del exponente cero Para cualquier número distinto de cero a, $a^0 = 1$.

Zero Property of Multiplication The product of 0 and any number is 0. For any number n, $n \cdot 0 = 0$ and $0 \cdot n = 0$.

Propiedad del cero en la multiplicación El producto de 0 y cualquier número es 0. Para cualquier número n, $n \cdot 0 = 0$ and $0 \cdot n = 0$.

Formulas

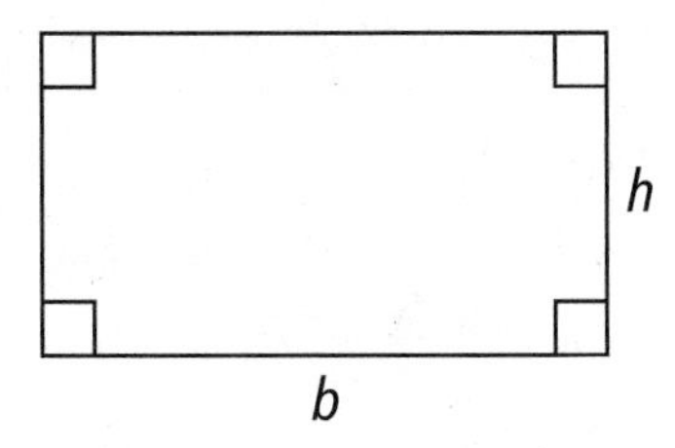

$P = 2b + 2h$

$A = bh$

Rectangle

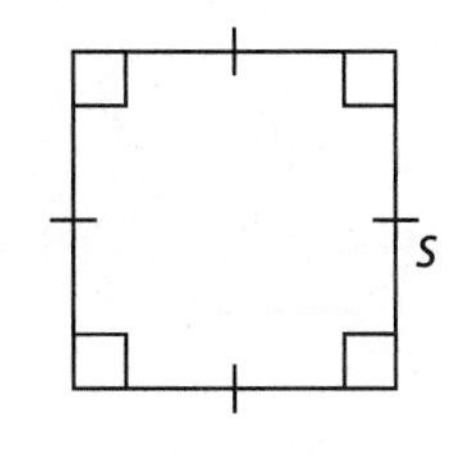

$P = 4s$

$A = s^2$

Square

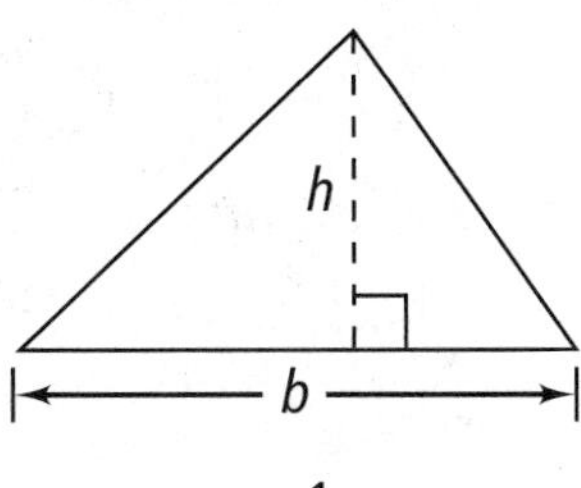

$A = \frac{1}{2}bh$

Triangle

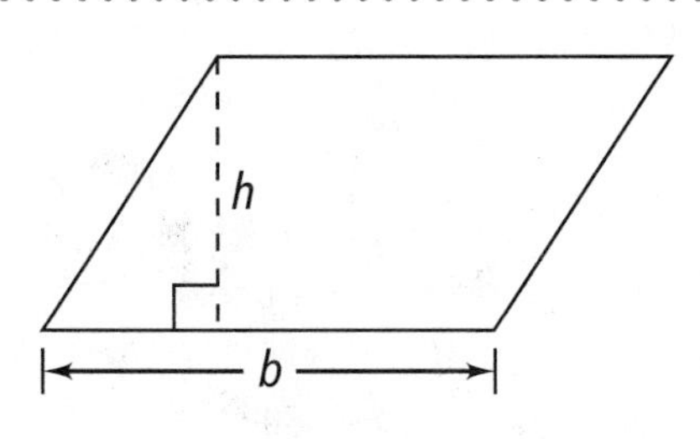

$A = bh$

Parallelogram

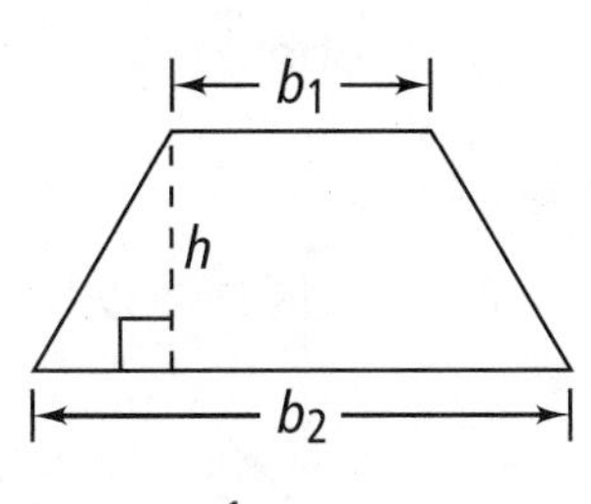

$A = \frac{1}{2}h(b_1 + b_2)$

Trapezoid

$C = 2\pi r$ or $C = \pi d$

$A = \pi r^2$

Circle

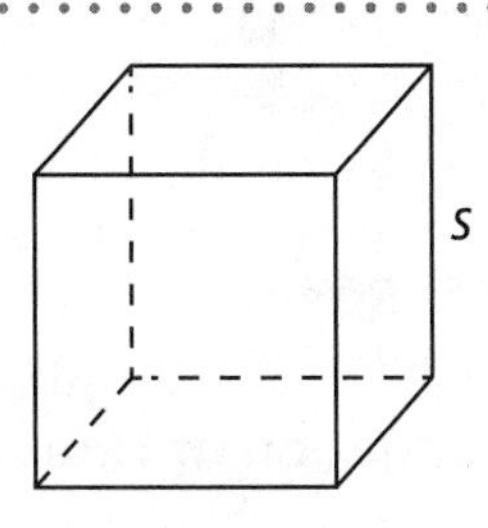

$S.A. = 6s^2$

$V = s^3$

Cube

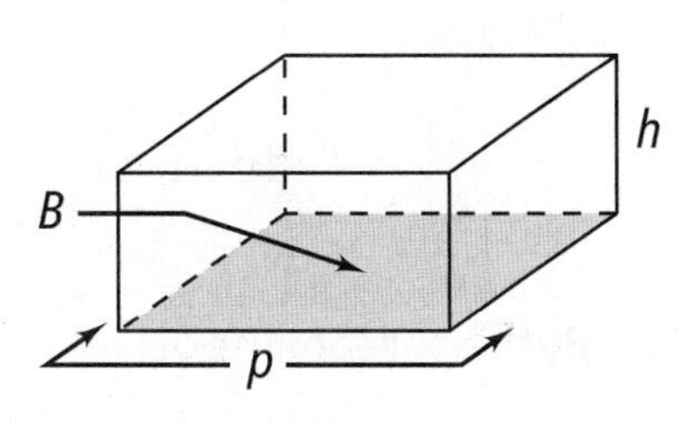

$V = Bh$

$L.A. = ph$

$S.A. = L.A. + 2B$

Rectangular Prism

Formulas

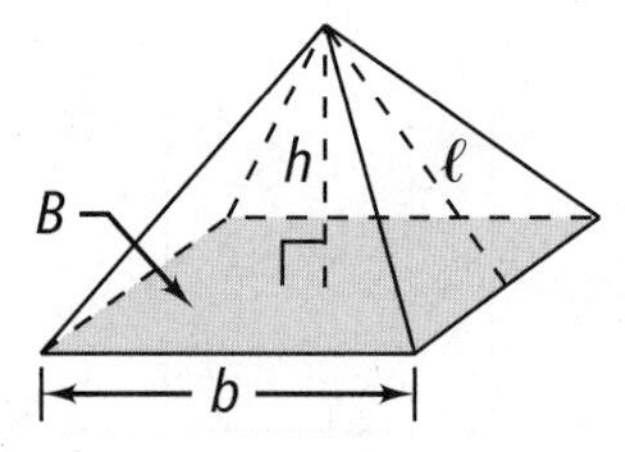

$V = \frac{1}{3}Bh$

L.A. $= 2b\ell$

S.A. $=$ L.A. $+ B$

Square Pyramid

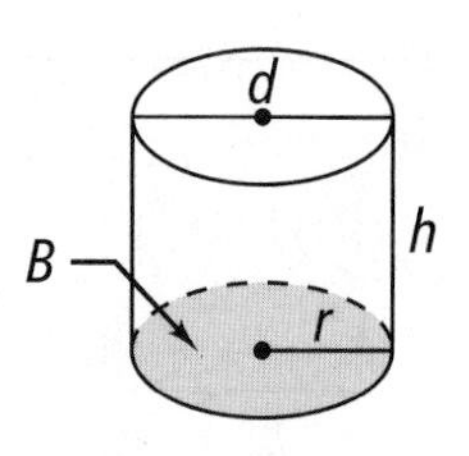

$V = Bh$

L.A. $= 2\pi rh$

S.A. $=$ L.A. $+ 2B$

Cylinder

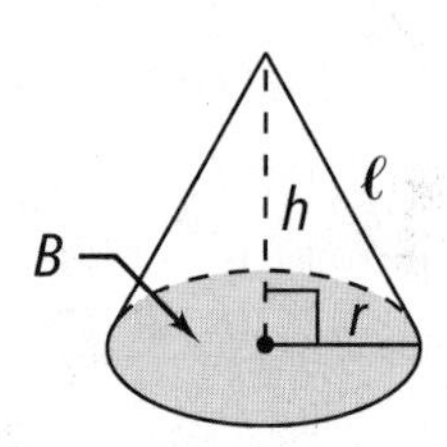

$V = \frac{1}{3}Bh$

L.A. $= \pi r\ell$

S.A. $=$ L.A. $+ B$

Cone

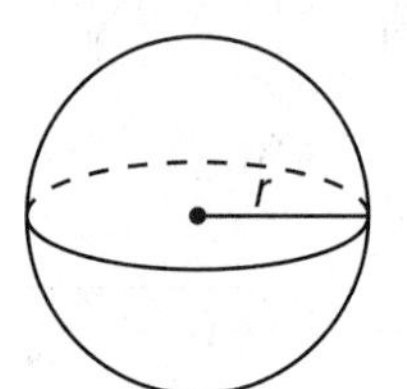

$V = \frac{4}{3}\pi r^3$

S.A. $= 4\pi r^2$

Sphere

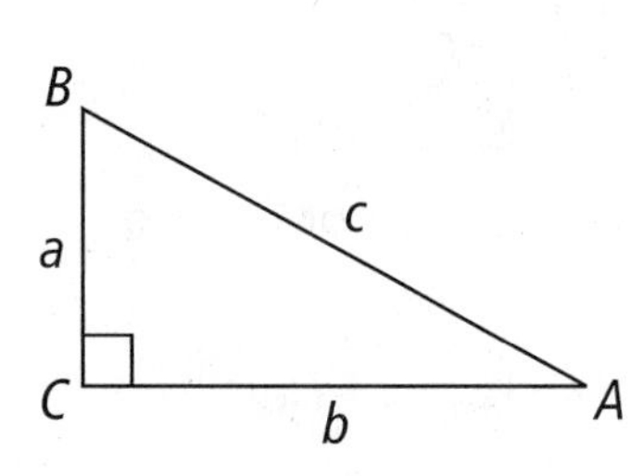

$a^2 + b^2 = c^2$

Pythagorean Theorem

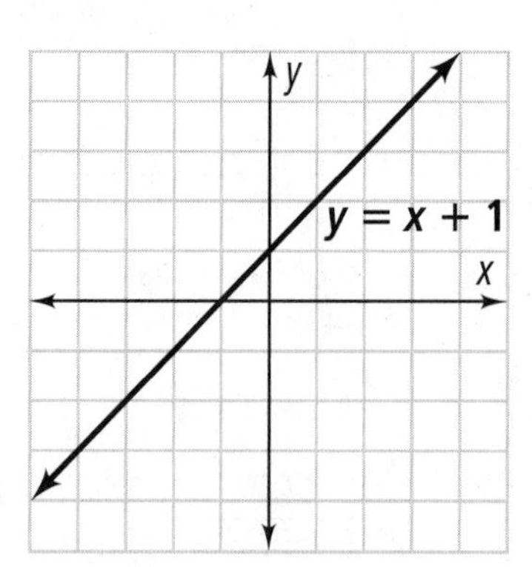

$y = mx + b$, where

$m =$ slope and

$b = y$-intercept

Equation of Line

Math Symbols

Symbol	Meaning
$+$	plus (addition)
$-$	minus (subtraction)
$\times$, $\cdot$	times (multiplication)
$\div$, $\overline{)\ }$, $\frac{a}{b}$	divide (division)
$=$	is equal to
$<$	is less than
$>$	is greater than
$\leq$	is less than or equal to
$\geq$	is greater than or equal to
$\neq$	is not equal to
$(\ )$	parentheses for grouping
[ ]	brackets for grouping
$-a$	opposite of a
. . .	and so on
$^\circ$	degrees
$\lvert a \rvert$	absolute value of a
$\stackrel{?}{=}$, $\stackrel{?}{<}$, $\stackrel{?}{>}$	Is the statement true?
$\approx$	is approximately equal to
$\frac{b}{a}$	reciprocal of $\frac{a}{b}$
A	area
ℓ	length
w	width
h	height
d	distance
r	rate
t	time
P	perimeter
b	base length
C	circumference
d	diameter

Symbol	Meaning
r	radius
S.A.	surface area
B	area of base
L.A.	lateral area
ℓ	slant height
V	volume
a^n	nth power of a
$\sqrt{x}$	nonnegative square root of x
π	pi, an irrational number approximately equal to 3.14
(a, b)	ordered pair with x-coordinate a and y-coordinate b
$\overline{AB}$	segment AB
A'	image of A, A prime
$\triangle ABC$	triangle with vertices A, B, and C
$\rightarrow$	arrow notation
$a : b$, $\frac{a}{b}$	ratio of a to b
$\cong$	is congruent to
$\sim$	is similar to
$\angle A$	angle with vertex A
AB	length of segment $\overline{AB}$
$\overrightarrow{AB}$	ray AB
$\angle ABC$	angle formed by $\overrightarrow{BA}$ and $\overrightarrow{BC}$
$m\angle ABC$	measure of angle ABC
$\perp$	is perpendicular to
$\overleftrightarrow{AB}$	line AB
$\parallel$	is parallel to
%	percent
P (event)	probability of an event

Measures

Customary	Metric
Length	**Length**
1 foot (ft) = 12 inches (in.) 1 yard (yd) = 36 in. 1 yd = 3 ft 1 mile (mi) = 5,280 ft 1 mi = 1,760 yd	1 centimeter (cm) = 10 millimeters (mm) 1 meter (m) = 100 cm 1 kilometer (km) = 1,000 m 1 mm = 0.001 m
Area	**Area**
1 square foot (ft^2) = 144 square inches ($in.^2$) 1 square yard (yd^2) = 9 ft^2 1 square mile (mi^2) = 640 acres	1 square centimeter (cm^2) = 100 square millimeters (mm^2) 1 square meter (m^2) = 10,000 cm^2
Volume	**Volume**
1 cubic foot (ft^3) = 1,728 cubic inches ($in.^3$) 1 cubic yard (yd^3) = 27 ft^3	1 cubic centimeter (cm^3) = 1,000 cubic millimeters (mm^3) 1 cubic meter (m^3) = 1,000,000 cm^3
Mass	**Mass**
1 pound (lb) = 16 ounces (oz) 1 ton (t) = 2,000 lb	1 gram (g) = 1,000 milligrams (mg) 1 kilogram (kg) = 1,000 g
Capacity	**Capacity**
1 cup (c) = 8 fluid ounces (fl oz) 1 pint (pt) = 2 c 1 quart (qt) = 2 pt 1 gallon (gal) = 4 qt	1 liter (L) = 1,000 milliliters (mL) 1000 liters = 1 kiloliter (kL)

Customary Units and Metric Units	
Length	1 in. = 2.54 cm 1 mi ≈ 1.61 km 1 ft ≈ 0.3 m
Capacity	1 qt ≈ 0.94 L
Weight and Mass	1 oz ≈ 28.3 g 1 lb ≈ 0.45 kg

Properties

Unless otherwise stated, the variables a, b, c, m, and n used in these properties can be replaced with any number represented on a number line.

Identity Properties

Addition $n + 0 = n$ and $0 + n = n$

Multiplication $n \cdot 1 = n$ and $1 \cdot n = n$

Commutative Properties

Addition $a + b = b + a$

Multiplication $a \cdot b = b \cdot a$

Associative Properties

Addition $(a + b) + c = a + (b + c)$

Multiplication $(a \cdot b) \cdot c = a \cdot (b \cdot c)$

Inverse Properties

Addition

$a + (-a) = 0$ and $-a + a = 0$

Multiplication

$a \cdot \frac{1}{a} = 1$ and $\frac{1}{a} \cdot a = 1$, $(a \neq 0)$

Distributive Properties

$a(b + c) = ab + ac$ $\quad (b + c)a = ba + ca$

$a(b - c) = ab - ac$ $\quad (b - c)a = ba - ca$

Properties of Equality

Addition If $a = b$, then $a + c = b + c$.

Subtraction If $a = b$, then $a - c = b - c$.

Multiplication If $a = b$, then $a \cdot c = b \cdot c$.

Division If $a = b$, and $c \neq 0$, then $\frac{a}{c} = \frac{b}{c}$.

Substitution If $a = b$, then b can replace a in any expression.

Zero Property

$a \cdot 0 = 0$ and $0 \cdot a = 0$.

Properties of Inequality

Addition If $a > b$, then $a + c > b + c$. If $a < b$, then $a + c < b + c$.

Subtraction If $a > b$, then $a - c > b - c$. If $a < b$, then $a - c < b - c$.

Multiplication

If $a > b$ and $c > 0$, then $ac > bc$.

If $a < b$ and $c > 0$, then $ac < bc$.

If $a > b$ and $c < 0$, then $ac < bc$.

If $a < b$ and $c < 0$, then $ac > bc$.

Division

If $a > b$ and $c > 0$, then $\frac{a}{c} > \frac{b}{c}$.

If $a < b$ and $c > 0$, then $\frac{a}{c} < \frac{b}{c}$.

If $a > b$ and $c < 0$, then $\frac{a}{c} < \frac{b}{c}$.

If $a < b$ and $c < 0$, then $\frac{a}{c} > \frac{b}{c}$.

Properties of Exponents

For any nonzero number n and any integers m and n:

Zero Exponent $a^0 = 1$

Negative Exponent $a^{-n} = \frac{1}{a^n}$

Product of Powers $a^m \cdot a^n = a^{m+n}$

Power of a Product $(ab)^n = a^n b^n$

Quotient of Powers $\frac{a^m}{a^n} = a^{m-n}$

Power of a Quotient $\left(\frac{a}{b}\right)^n = \frac{a^n}{b^n}$

Power of a Power $(a^m)^n = a^{mn}$